VARIORUM COLLECTED STUDIES SERIES

The Ottoman Economy and Its Institutions

Şevket Pamuk

Şevket Pamuk

The Ottoman Economy and Its Institutions

Routledge
Taylor & Francis Group
LONDON AND NEW YORK

First published 2009 by Ashgate Publishing

Published 2016 by Routledge
2 Park Square, Milton Park, Abingdon, Oxon OX14 4RN
52 Vanderbilt Avenue, New York, NY 10017

Routledge is an imprint of the Taylor & Francis Group, an informa business

British Library Cataloguing in Publication Data
Pamuk, Şevket
The Ottoman economy and its institutions.
– (Variorum collected studies series)
1. Turkey – Economic conditions – 1288–1918 2. Turkey – History – Ottoman Empire, 1288–1918
I. Title
330.9'56015
ISBN 9780754659815 (hbk)

Library of Congress Cataloging-in-Publication Data
Pamuk, Şevket.
The Ottoman economy and its institutions / Şevket Pamuk.
p. cm. – (Variorum collected studies series)
Includes index.
ISBN 978–0–7546–5981–5 (alk. paper)
1. Turkey – History – Ottoman Empire, 1288–1918 2. Turkey – Economic conditions – 1288–1918. 3. Turkey – Commerce – History. 4. Monetary policy – Turkey – History. 5. Turkey – Economic policy.
I. Title.

DR485.P35 2008
330.956'015–dc22

2008040981

ISBN 13: 978-0-7546-5981-5 (hbk)

VARIORUM COLLECTED STUDIES SERIES CS917

CONTENTS

This volume contains xii + 290 pages

INTRODUCTION

The Ottoman Empire stood at the crossroads of intercontinental trade, stretching from the Balkans and the Black Sea region through Anatolia, Syria, Mesopotamia and the Gulf to Egypt and most of the North African coast for six centuries until World War I. For most of the seventeenth and eighteenth centuries, its population exceeded 30 million (of which the European provinces accounted for half or more; Anatolia and Istanbul for 7 to 8 million, other Asian and North African provinces for another 7 to 8 million) but declined thereafter due to territorial losses.

Historians of the Ottoman Empire have made considerable progress in recent decades towards better understanding its trajectory. One might have expected this literature and the economic institutions that have sustained this large, multi-ethnic entity for so long would be of interest to economic historians. Unfortunately, most volumes offering surveys of non-European empires as well as explanations for the rise of the West have shown little interest for the Ottoman land regime, manufactures and state economic policies or the daily existence of ordinary men and women. The empire is depicted in these accounts as a centralized, monolithic entity lacking in internal dynamism and differentiation. With this perspective, however, the longevity of the Ottoman Empire becomes an anomaly and even a mystery.

The articles brought together in this volume examine the economic institutions of this empire, the long term performance of the Ottoman economy, and explore the reasons for the longevity of this large entity. Until recently, Ottoman historiography had depicted an empire in decline after the sixteenth century. Articles I through IV emphasize that the Ottoman empire did not simply and irreversibly decline after the sixteenth century. They argue that Ottoman state and society showed considerable ability to reorganize and adapt to changing circumstances in the early modern era, well before the nineteenth century reforms known as *Tanzimat* or 're-ordering'. The central bureaucracy managed to contain the many challenges it faced with its pragmatism, flexibility and habit of negotiation.

While pragmatism, flexibility, willingness to negotiate, and ability to adapt some of their institutions to changing circumstances were traits that enabled the Ottomans to retain power until the modern era, their limitations need to be equally emphasized. Because the central bureaucracy was able to retain its leading position in Ottoman society and politics, the influence of various social groups, not only of landowners but also of merchants, manufacturers and moneychangers, over economic matters, and more generally over the policies of the central government, remained limited until the end of the empire. As a result, most of the pragmatism and flexibility was utilized by the central bureaucracy for the defense of the existing order and of its own position. In contrast, institutional changes that may threaten the leading position of the central bureaucracy position were resisted more forcefully than others.

Despite the considerable expansion of research in Ottoman economic and social history in recent decades, our knowledge of the long term trends in prices has been rather limited until recently. Economic and social historians of the Balkans and the Middle East in the late medieval and early modern eras were unable to make sense of the most basic of monetary magnitudes involving prices, wages and wealth even though inter-temporal comparisons of these magnitudes are the most basic prerequisites for studying the *long durée*.

Articles V through IX establish the long term trends in prices and explore their causes. One of the reasons why the debate on the Price Revolution in Europe originally attracted so much attention was the rash claim made by Hamilton and his followers that by redistributing income into the hands of new groups, the price increases paved the way for the rise of capitalism. It is interesting that Ottoman historians have similarly interpreted the price increases as a turning point and a leading cause of the 'Ottoman decline' at the end of the sixteenth century. With the help of new evidence about Ottoman prices, articles V and VI show that the impact of silver inflation on the Ottoman economy and finances was actually less than it was believed until recently. The Ottoman system undoubtedly faced severe fiscal and economic difficulties at the end of the sixteenth and during the first half of the seventeenth century. However, these difficulties related more to other causes than to the impact of silver inflation *per se*. In light of these findings, those claims and the attempt to single out the Price Revolution as a key event in Ottoman history appear exaggerated if not unfounded.

There were many causes of inflation during the early modern period as evidenced by the large literature and the extensive debates on the subject. From a long-term perspective, however, debasements or the reduction of the specie content of the currency by the monetary authority emerge as the most important cause of Ottoman price increases. Articles VII, VIII and IX examine the causes and consequences of Ottoman debasements and more generally of monetary instability. They argue that debasements were utilized, especially during wars, as an alternative to additional taxation. Far from being an exercise in futility, these studies view debasements as a potentially effective instrument of fiscal policy, especially in the short term. Debasements created a good deal of political opposition especially in the capital city, however. This opposition acted as a major deterrent against the more frequent use of debasements by the government.

From the perspective of Ottoman history, the nineteenth century was a period quite different from the earlier era. On the one hand, it was characterized by major efforts at Western style reform aimed at the centralization of the empire, in administration, education, law and justice as well as economic, fiscal and monetary affairs. On the other hand, it was a period of integration into the world markets and rapid expansion in foreign trade, particularly with Europe. This process was facilitated by the construction of ports and railroads and the establishment of modern banking institutions, mostly by European capital. By the beginning of the twentieth century, patterns of production in the Ottoman empire had shifted considerably. Agriculture had become more market oriented and a substantially larger part of the agricultural production was being directed towards the export markets. On the other hand, the traditional crafts had resisted but in many instances they were forced to retreat in the face of the competition from the imported manufactures.

Articles X, XI and XII attempt to compare the experience of the Ottoman Empire and more generally of the Middle East during the nineteenth century with other less developed regions of the world. The transformation of the economies of the Middle East during the century before World War I had many aspects common with other less developed regions. At the same time, however, there were many dimensions in which this region differed considerably from others. These studies argue that Ottoman economic history during this century is best understood in terms of the complex interaction between the domestic forces, on the one hand, and those of the world economy, on the other. They emphasize that geography, agronomical conditions and political factors all need to be taken into account in placing this experience into a comparative framework.

In terms of long term economic change, one major question concerns the changes in the levels of income and standards of living and how the Ottoman Empire compared with other countries. From the recent work of economic historians we have learned that the gap between industrializing countries and the rest of the world widened considerably from the era of the Industrial Revolution until 1950. There is little information, however, about the period before 1820. How large was this gap in 1750, and was there a gap in 1600 or in 1500?

With the exception perhaps of a handful of countries, estimates for per capita GDP for the period before 1820 are difficult to construct and not sufficiently reliable. An alternative approach for studying the gap in levels of per capita income has been to compare real wages of specific occupations, most often of skilled and unskilled construction workers in urban areas. Real wage data are of far better quality than per capita GDP estimates especially for the early modern era and available for a wider sample. They also provide the most convenient vehicle for international comparisons of standards of living for this earlier era.

Utilizing a large volume of archival documents, article XIV established for the first time the long-term trends in wages of skilled and unskilled construction workers in Istanbul and other Ottoman cities in southeastern Europe and the Middle East from the second half of the fifteenth century until World War I. Comparisons between Ottoman real wage series and those for European cities indicate that Ottoman real wage levels were lower by about one third than those in northwestern Europe in the sixteenth century. This wage gap continued until the Industrial Revolution. At the same time, however, real wage levels in the Ottoman Empire were not very different from those in most parts of Europe until the nineteenth century. Ottoman standards of living did not decline but actually improved after the sixteenth century. These findings are consistent with recent arguments that the empire did not simply and irreversibly decline after 1600, but that Ottoman state and society was able to adapt to changing circumstances from the seventeenth through the nineteenth centuries. This economic record may also help explain the durability and longevity of the Ottomans.

Finally, article XV brings together data from a variety of sources to provide, for the first time, an overview of the growth record since 1820 of the Middle East, large parts of which, along with the Balkans, remained part of the Ottoman Empire until World War I. These estimates indicate that the cumulative growth experience of the Middle East during the last two centuries was not very different from other developing regions. The Middle East began to participate in modern economic growth during the nineteenth century. Yet, differences in per capita incomes between it and the high income regions of the world (United States and western Europe) widened considerably until World War I. In the twentieth century, the most important single factor contributing to increases in per capita incomes in the region was oil. Despite the sharp rise in oil production and revenues, however, the gap between the Middle East and the high income regions of the world is roughly the same in 2000 as it was in 1913. The sharp escalation of oil prices since 2005 would require an update of that conclusion, however.

It has been a pleasure to prepare this volume for publication. I am grateful to all of the publishers for providing permission to reprint these articles here. I would like to thank Variorum publisher John Smedley for expert guidance during all stages of this process, to Derya Göçer for editorial assistance and to Bahar Bilgen for the meticulous preparation of the index.

ŞEVKET PAMUK

Istanbul
August 2008

ACKNOWLEDGEMENTS

Grateful acknowledgement is made to the following institutions and publishers for their kind permission to reproduce the articles included in this volume: MIT Press, Cambridge, MA (article I); the Fondation Temini pour la Recherche Scientifique et l'Information, Zaghouan, Tunisia (II); University of Wisconsin, Madison, WI (III); Cambridge University Press, Cambridge (IV, V, VI, VII, XII, XIII, XIV, XV); Lynne Reinner Publishers (VIII); the Bulgarian National Bank, Sofia (IX); The Darwin Press, Princeton, NJ (X); Vassar College, Poughkeepsie, NY, and the editorial board of *New Perspectives on Turkey*, Istanbul (XI).

PUBLISHER'S NOTE

The articles in this volume, as in all others in the Variorum Collected Studies Series, have not been given a new, continuous pagination. In order to avoid confusion, and to facilitate their use where these same studies have been referred to elsewhere, the original pagination has been maintained wherever possible.

Each article has been given a Roman number in order of appearance, as listed in the Contents. This number is repeated on each page and is quoted in the index entries.

I

Institutional Change and the Longevity of the Ottoman Empire, 1500–1800

Institutional Change and the Longevity of the Ottoman Empire, 1500–1800 In recent decades, economists and economic historians have identified institutions and institutional change as key variables that help explain the widely disparate economic performance of different societies during the last 500 years. Based on the successful experience of Western Europe and European offshoots, new institutional economics has argued that long-run economic change is the cumulative consequence of innumerable short-run decisions about political and economic factors that both directly and indirectly shape performance. Economic growth occurs because the underlying framework persistently reinforces incentives for organizations to engage in productive activity. The state is seen as a major player in this context. In the Western European case, as the result of political struggles and alliances, the state and associated institutions moved to provide the legal framework that reinforced incentives for economic growth.

Institutional change, however, does not usually favor the most efficient outcomes; societies rarely arrive at, or create, institutions that are conducive to economic growth. In most cases, institutions promote redistributive rather than productive activity, restricting opportunities rather than expanding them. Similarly, rather than reinforcing incentives toward productive activity, states generally act as instruments to transfer resources from one group to another or to ensure their own survival. Politics and political struggles can be detrimental to economic growth.[1]

Earlier versions of this paper were presented at the Annual Meeting of the Middle East Studies Association of North America, Orlando, Florida, November 2000, and at the Annual Meeting of the American Economic Association ("The Economic Performance of Civilizations"), Atlanta, Georgia, January 2002. The author would like to thank the organizers and participants, as well as Timur Kuran and Nadir Özbek, for many helpful comments and suggestions.

1 Douglass C. North and Robert P. Thomas, *The Rise of the Western World: A New Economic History* (New York, 1973); North, *Institutions, Institutional Change and Economic Performance*

Focusing on the "rise of the West," institutional economics and economic historians have paid little attention to unsuccessful or less successful cases of institutional change, especially those outside Western Europe. This study examines institutional change of a different type outside the Western European context. Ottoman institutions did not come to resemble those that gave rise to capitalism. Ottoman society and Ottoman bureaucracy brought about institutional change in selective areas—for example, military technology and organization and public and private finance—thus enabling the Ottomans to continue their rule.

The Ottoman Empire stood at the crossroads of intercontinental trade, stretching from the Balkans and the Black Sea region through Anatolia, Syria, Mesopotamia, the gulf to Egypt, and most of the North African coast for six centuries until World War I. During the seventeenth and eighteenth centuries, its population exceeded 30 million (of which the European provinces accounted for half or more, Anatolia and Istanbul for 7 to 8 million, and other Asian and North African provinces for another 7 to 8 million) but declined thereafter due to territorial losses.

A comparison with the other two Muslim empires of Eurasia, the Safavids and the Mughals, brings the Ottoman trajectory into sharper focus. The political economy of these three empires showed similar patterns of evolution during the sixteenth and seventeenth centuries. They all enjoyed a long period of stability, agricultural expansion, and growing prosperity during the sixteenth century, followed by severe fiscal and military difficulties and rising internal conflicts during the seventeenth century. The decline of central political institutions in all three of the empires accompanied the rise of provincial elites, who began to make a greater impact on the evolution of regional economies. During the eighteenth century, both the Mughals and Safavids disintegrated under the pressure of tribal invasions. The Mughals eventually succumbed to the British, whereas the Safavids were replaced by a regional dynasty, the Qajars. In contrast, the Ottoman Empire enjoyed a period of recovery, stability, and economic expansion

(New York, 1990); Thrain Eggertsson, *Economic Behavior and Institutions* (New York, 1990); more recently, Daron Acemoglu, Simon Johnson, and James Robinson, "The Rise of Europe: Atlantic Trade, Institutional Change and Economic Growth," unpub. ms. (Berkeley, 2002).

from the beginning of the eighteenth century until the 1770s. Despite wars and internal conflicts from the 1770s through the 1830s, the Ottomans managed to regroup and survive into the modern era with a strong central state and many of their central institutions intact.[2]

In recent decades, historians of the Ottoman Empire have made considerable progress in understanding the trajectory of these institutions. Oddly, economic historians have not paid sufficient attention to either this literature or the economic institutions that sustained the large, multi-ethnic Ottoman Empire for so long. Recent studies by Jones, Cameron, and Landes, like many of their mainstream predecessors, provide surveys of non-European empires as well as explanations for the rise of the West but do faint justice to Ottoman land regimes, manufacturing interests, and state economic policies, not to mention the daily existence of ordinary men and women. The empire cursorily depicted in these accounts is a centralized, monolithic entity lacking in internal dynamism and differentiation. Landes virtually reduces the Ottoman Empire to a caricature of nomads and raiders, despotism, military conquest, corruption, and looting: "The Ottoman empire was a typical despotism, only more warlike." From this perspective, however, the longevity of the Ottoman Empire becomes an anomaly and even a mystery. In Landes' own words, "The empire of the Ottoman Turks proved more durable (than the Moghul Empire of India). That in itself is a mystery, because after some two hundred and fifty years of expansion (1300–1550), its downhill course should have brought about fragmentation and liquidation in a matter of decades."[3]

Pomeranz recently argued that core regions of China and Western Europe did not differ from each other significantly during the eighteenth century in their technology, their level of economic development, their land and labor markets, their degree of commercialization, and even their legal and social manner of handling large accumulations of commercial and financial capital.

2 Christopher A. Bayly, *Imperial Meridian, The British Empire and the World, 1780–1830* (Reading, Mass., 1989).

3 Eric L. Jones, *The European Miracle: Environments, Economies and Geopolitics in the History of Europe and Asia* (New York, 1987; 2d ed.), 175–191; Rondo Cameron, *A Concise Economic History of the World, from Paleolithic Times to the Present* (New York, 1993), 81–83; David Landes, *The Wealth and Poverty of Nations: Why Some Are So Rich and Some So Poor* (New York, 1998), 398, 396.

According to Pomeranz, were it not for the large amounts of energy and land resources provided by the New World, Western Europe may not have experienced the industrial breakthrough that began in the second half of the eighteenth century. Whatever resemblance parts of China might have had with parts of Western Europe, eighteenth-century Ottoman social, economic, legal, and financial institutions definitely did not share them.[4]

For most of its six-century existence, Ottoman economic institutions and policies were shaped, to a large degree, by the priorities of a central bureaucracy. Until recently, Ottoman historiography viewed the empire as in decline after the sixteenth century. On the contrary, Ottoman state and society were able to adapt to changing circumstances during the early modern era, well before the nineteenth-century reforms known as *Tanzimat* or "reordering." Pragmatism, flexibility, and negotiation enabled the central bureaucracy to co-opt and incorporate into the state the social groups that rebelled against it.

The Ottomans were flexible and pragmatic from the start. Emerging in a highly heterogeneous region populated by Christians and Muslims, Turkish and Greek speakers, the Ottomans' success in western Anatolia and later in the Balkans during the fourteenth and fifteenth centuries owed much to their willingness and ability to adapt, to utilize talent and accept allegiance from many sources, and to make multiple appeals for support. Thus were they able to attract not only warriors to fight Christians when necessary but also Muslims and Christians to fight together for riches and power when available. The Ottomans also displayed remarkable openness to technological innovation, as evident in their early and effective use of firearms. When expanding their territory, they did not hesitate to negotiate for the loyalty of local elites if the imposition of full control by conquest seemed impossible. They also proved willing and able to borrow institutions. The early Ottoman enterprise was not a religious state in the making; it was primarily a pragmatic one. On that basis, the Ottomans were able to retain power until the modern era while many of their contemporaries in both Europe and Asia were unable to do so, al-

4 Kenneth Pomeranz, *The Great Divergence, China, Europe and the Making of the Modern World Economy* (Princeton, 2000).

though the points at which their flexibility and pragmatism were liable to break down will become obvious as well.[5]

Institutional change did not apply equally to all areas of Ottoman economic life. Nor did it affect all types of institutions to the same degree. Because the central bureaucracy was able to retain its leading position in Ottoman society and politics, landowners, merchants, manufacturers, and moneychangers exerted little influence on economic matters and, more generally, on the policies of the central government, until the end of the empire. As a result, the central bureaucracy directed most of its ingenuity toward the defense of the traditional order and its own position within it, sometimes acting to stifle institutional changes that appeared threatening. Institutional change thus remaining selective, many of the pillars of the traditional order—such as state ownership of land, urban guilds, and restrictions on private capital accumulation—remained intact until the second half of the nineteenth century. These important limitations of Ottoman flexibility, pragmatism, and adaptivity should help provide a more balanced account of the empire's strengths, which helped it to survive through the early modern era, and its weaknesses, which contributed to its disintegration during the nineteenth century, despite the acceleration of institutional changes after 1839.

ECONOMIC INSTITUTIONS Until the end of the sixteenth century, the rise of the Ottoman Empire was closely associated with military conquest. Military success, in turn, depended closely on the land-tenure regime that supported a large, cavalry-based army. The Ottoman bureaucracy always took detailed censuses of new territories to assess their fiscal potential. Even after territorial expansion slowed during the second half of the sixteenth century, agriculture continued to provide the economic livelihood for

5 Cemal Kafadar, *Between Two Worlds: The Construction of the Ottoman State* (Berkeley, 1995); Heath W. Lowry, *The Nature of the Early Ottoman State* (Albany, 2003); Donald Quataert, *The Ottoman Empire, 1700–1922* (New York, 2000), 13–36. For the Ottoman propensity to adopt new military technologies, see Jonathan Grant, "Rethinking the Ottoman 'Decline': Military Technology Diffusion in the Ottoman Empire, Fifteenth to Eighteenth Centuries," *Journal of World History*, X (1999), 179–201. There is a good deal of evidence that the Ottoman state's pragmatism in noneconomic matters continued into later periods, permitting it to co-opt social groups that rebelled against it. See Karen Barkey, *Bandits and Bureaucrats, The Ottoman Route to State Centralization* (Ithaca, 1994).

I

close to 90 percent of the population, as well as key fiscal support for the Ottoman state. Neither the durability nor the eventual demise of the empire can be understood without attention to its agrarian institutions.

The peasant family farm was the basic economic and fiscal unit in most of the countryside of Anatolia and the Balkans, the core areas of the empire where the relatively high land/labor ratios favored smallholdings. The state quickly established extensive ownership of these lands—bestowing hereditary usufruct on peasant families, which typically cultivated individual plots with a pair of oxen—and did not relinquish it until the second half of the nineteenth century.[6]

Under the *timar* system, the *sipahis,* state employees often chosen for their wartime valor, who lived in the rural areas, collected mostly in-kind taxes from these peasant farmers and spent the revenues locally to train and equip a predetermined number of soldiers, as well as to subsidize themselves, creating a large provincial army. The Ottoman central administration did not attempt to impose the timar regime in all of its conquered territories. In many remote areas, such as Eastern Anatolia, Iraq, Egypt, Yemen, Wallachia (Romania), Moldavia, and the Maghrib, the Ottomans collected taxes but left the existing land regimes largely or completely unaltered to avoid economic disruption and popular unrest. The central government might not have had the fiscal, administrative, and economic resources to establish a new system in these areas, anyway.

This pragmatic approach was similar to Ottoman practices in other areas. As a result, the empire was comprised of zones with varying degrees of administrative control. The areas most closely administered by the capital had institutions nearly identical to those in the Istanbul region. As distance from the capital increased, institutions and administrative practices reflected the power balances between the capital and the local structures and forces. For example, land allocation and fiscal practice in Ottoman Egypt remained closely linked to the demands of irrigated agriculture along the Nile valley.[7]

6 Halil Inalcik, "The Ottoman State: Economy and Society, 1300–1600," in *idem* and Quataert (eds.), *An Economic and Social History of the Ottoman Empire, 1300–1914* (New York, 1994), 103–179.

7 For Ottoman pragmatism and flexibility in the administration of the frontier provinces,

In the urban economy, manufacturing and local trade remained under the control of the guilds. The mostly autonomous guilds sought and obtained the support of the government whenever merchants tried to organize alternative forms of production. Partly because of this support, commercial initiative remained weak in Ottoman lands. Moreover, even though the government had a reciprocal need of the independent guilds to preserve the traditional order, it was often wary of those, both Muslim and non-Muslim, that held heterodox religious beliefs.[8]

A long-standing assumption is that the use of markets and money in the Balkans and Anatolia was confined to long-distance trade and a fraction of the urban sector. Recent research has shown, however, that the urban population and some segments of the countryside were already a part of the monetary economy by the end of the fifteenth century. Even more significant was the substantial increase in the use of money during the sixteenth century, both because of the unprecedented availability of specie and the escalating commercialization of the rural economy. The upshot in the Balkans and Anatolia was an intensive pattern of periodic markets and market fairs in which peasants and larger landholders sold some of their produce to urban residents. These markets also provided an important opportunity for nomads to come into contact with both peasants and city dwellers. Nor were the Balkans and Anatolia unique in this respect. As Braudel pointed out, the same trend toward more frequent use of markets and money by large segments of the population also prevailed in the western Mediterranean region.[9]

The prohibition of interest in Islam supposedly prevented the development of credit, or at best, imposed rigid obstacles in its way. Similarly, the apparent absence of deposit banking and lending by banks has led many observers to conclude that financial institutions and instruments were, by and large, absent from Islamic

see Gabor Agoston, "A Flexible Empire: Authority and Its Limits on the Ottoman Frontiers," *International Journal of Turkish Studies,* IX (2003), 15–31.

8 Suraiya Faroqhi, *Towns and Townsmen of Ottoman Anatolia: Trade, Crafts and Food Production in an Urban Setting, 1520–1650* (New York, 1984).

9 Fernand Braudel, *Civilization and Capitalism, 15th-18th Century* (New York, 1982–1984), III, 471–473; I, 365–461; Faroqhi, "The Early History of Balkan Fairs," *Südost-Forshungen,* XXXVII (1978), 50–68; *idem,* "Sixteenth Century Periodic Markets in Various Anatolian Sancaks," *Journal of the Economic and Social History of the Orient,* XXII (1979), 32–80; Pamuk, *A Monetary History of the Ottoman Empire* (New York, 2000), 74–76.

societies. Yet, even though a religiously inspired (both Islamic and Christian) prohibition against usury was common to the Mediterranean world during the Middle Ages, by the classical era, Islamic law had already devised several ways to circumvent the anti-usury prohibition, as had European law during the late medieval period. Various legal fictions, based primarily on the model of the "double-sale," were, if not enthusiastically endorsed by jurists, at least not declared invalid. There was no insurmountable barrier against the use of interest-bearing loans for commercial credit.[10]

Neither the Islamic prohibitions against interest and usury nor the absence of formal banking institutions prevented the expansion of credit in Ottoman society. Utilizing the Islamic court records, Jennings showed that dense networks of lenders and borrowers flourished in and around the Anatolian cities of Kayseri, Karaman, Amasya, and Trabzon during the sixteenth century. Throughout the twenty-year period of his study, he found literally thousands of court cases involving debts. Many family members, including women, borrowed from, and lent to, other family members as well as to outsiders. These records leave no doubt that the use of credit was widespread among all segments of urban and even rural society. Most lending and borrowing was on a small scale, and interest was regularly charged on credit, in accordance with both Islamic and Ottoman law, with the consent and approval of the court and the *ulema* (learned men of Islam). In their dealings with the court, the participants apparently felt no need to conceal interest on loans or resort to legal tricks. Annual interest rates ranged from 10 to 20 percent.[11]

Cash vakifs—pious foundations established with the explicit purpose of lending cash and using the interest income to fulfill their goals—constituted an important source of loans in Istanbul, the Balkans, and the Anatolian urban centers. These endowments began to win approval in Ottoman courts by the early part of the fifteenth century and had become popular all over Anatolia and the Balkan provinces by the end of the sixteenth century. An in-

10 The practice of *riba*, the Arabic term for usury and interest, is sharply denounced in a number of passages in the Qur'an and in all subsequent Islamic religious writings. For a recent discussion of the classical Islamic views on interest, see Nabil A. Saleh, *Unlawful Gain and Legitimate Profit in Islamic Law: Riba, Gharar and Islamic Banking* (New York, 1988), 9–32.

11 Ronald C. Jennings, "Loans and Credit in Early 17th Century Ottoman Judicial Records," *Journal of the Economic and Social History of the Orient*, XVI (1973), 168–216.

teresting development especially evident during the eighteenth century was the allocation of the funds to trustees who used the borrowed funds to lend at higher rates of interest to large-scale moneylenders (*sarraf*) in Istanbul. The sarraf pooled these funds to finance such larger ventures as long-distance trade and tax farming.[12]

Not surprisingly, a lively debate developed during the sixteenth century within the Ottoman ulema regarding whether the cash vakif should be considered illegitimate. Those who believed that only goods with permanent value, such as real estate, should constitute the assets of a pious foundation argued that the cash vakifs contravened the Islamic prohibition of interest. Because the majority of the ulema remained pragmatic on the matter, the view that anything useful for the community was useful for Islam ultimately prevailed. Ebusuud Efendi, the prominent, state-appointed religious leader (*seyhulislam*) of the period, argued that the abolition of the income from interest would lead to the collapse of many pious foundations, a situation that would harm the Muslim community. Ottoman institutions of credit and finance retained their Islamic lineage and remained mostly uninfluenced by the developments in Europe until the end of the seventeenth century.[13]

ECONOMIC PRIORITIES AND POLICIES Late medieval and early modern states had to address a common range of economic problems, the most basic of which were related directly to the maintenance of the states themselves. Provisioning the capital city (and, to a lesser extent, other urban areas) and the armed forces, collecting taxes, regulating long-distance trade, and maintaining a steady supply of money were the leading concerns of economic policy.[14]

States did not pursue public interest in some abstract sense. Instead, both the goals and design of economic policies, as well as institutions related to their implementation, were shaped by the

12 Murat Çizakça, *A Comparative Evolution of Business Partnerships: The Islamic World and Europe with Specific Reference to the Ottoman Archives* (Leiden, 1996), 131–134.

13 Jon E. Mandaville, "Usurious Piety: The Cash Waqf Controversy in the Ottoman Empire," *International Journal of Middle East Studies*, X (1979), 289–308. Çizakça, *Comparative Evolution*.

14 Most societies in the late medieval and early modern periods did not have an economic sphere separate from the political, administrative, and fiscal one. Edward Miller, "France and England," in Michael M. Postan, Edwin E. Rich, and *idem* (eds.), *The Cambridge Economic History of Europe* (1963), III, 282–291.

social structure, the relationship between state and society, the needs of different social groups aligned with or represented by the state, and, more generally, social and political influences. Until late in the fifteenth century, relations between the Turkish landed aristocracy of the provinces, which was deeply involved in the territorial conquests, and the central bureaucracy, which was made up mostly of converted slaves (*devshirme*), were considerably strained; the balance of power often shifted between the two until the second half of the fifteenth century, when Mehmed II finally defeated the landed aristocracy, established state ownership over privately held lands, and concentrated power in the hands of the central bureaucracy. After this shift, the policies of the government in Istanbul began to reflect the priorities of this bureaucracy much more strongly. The influence of landowners, merchants, and moneychangers on the policies of the central government remained scant.

The Ottomans conceived an ideal order that included balances between such social groups as the peasantry, the guilds, and the commercial sector. The sultan and the central bureaucracy were at the top of this order. This ideal changed as the economy and society did, but the government took pains to preserve as much of the traditional structure of employment and production as possible. It tended to regard any rapid accumulation of capital by merchants, guild members, or any other interests as a potential disruption of the existing order.

The government's attitude toward independent merchants was profoundly ambiguous. On the one hand, merchants, large and small, were considered indispensable for the functioning of the urban economy. On the other hand, their activities occasionally led to higher prices of raw materials, bringing pressure on the guild system and the urban economy in general. Hence, the central administration often felt more compelled to restrain the merchants than to protect them. Yet, controlling the merchants was much more difficult than controlling the guilds. The guilds were fixed in location; the merchants were mobile. The official attitude toward financiers and moneychangers was similar. The state tolerated, and even encouraged, the activities of entrepreneurs who were independent of the guilds only so long as they helped to reproduce the traditional order.[15]

15 Huri Islamoğlu and Çağlar Keyder, "Agenda for Ottoman History," *Review, Fernand Braudel Center,* I (1977), 31–55. Cipolla noted a virtual identity between the merchants and

In the interest of social stability, the Ottomans were intent on keeping urban areas—especially the capital city, including the army—well supplied, making them dependent on merchants. Territorial expansion and the incorporation of Syria and Egypt during the sixteenth century made long-distance trade and the control of the intercontinental trade routes critical for meeting the need for provisions. Foreign merchants were particularly welcome because they brought goods not available in Ottoman lands. The various privileges, concessions, and capitulations that the Ottomans offered them, as early as the sixteenth century, should be understood in this context. The Ottomans, however, were more favorably disposed toward imports than exports. Occasionally, foreign merchants contributed to domestic shortages by exporting scarce goods—mainly foodstuffs and raw materials—forcing the Ottomans to impose temporary prohibitions on exports.[16]

These priorities and policies contrast sharply with European mercantilist practices. It would be a mistake, however, to consider this concern with provisioning urban areas unique to the Islamic world. Frequent crop failures, famines, and epidemics, combined with primitive modes of transportation, led most, if not all, medieval governments to focus on the urban food supply and provisioning in general. These Ottoman priorities had strong parallels in the governments of western and southern Europe during the late Middle Ages, from the twelfth through the fifteenth centuries. Ottoman and European economic policies did not diverge until the era of mercantilism in Europe. One important reason why mercantilist ideas never took root in Ottoman lands was that the merchants and domestic producers whose ideas were so influential in Europe did not have much impact on Ottoman economic thought, despite the general trend toward decentralization of the empire during the seventeenth and eighteenth centuries. Only in

the state in the trading towns of medieval Italy. "More than once the action of the guild of merchants seemed to imply the affirmation, *L'etat c'est moi.*" Ottoman merchants during the early modern era could not possibly have made a similar claim. Instead, as Udovitch has concluded for the merchants of eleventh-century Egypt, Ottoman merchants could at best proclaim, "*L'etat n'est pas contre moi.*" Carlo M. Cipolla, "Currency Depreciation in Medieval Europe," *Economic History Review,* XV (1963), 397; Abraham L. Udovitch, "Merchants and *Amirs:* Government and Trade in Eleventh Century Egypt," *Asian and African Studies,* XXII (1988), 53–72.

16 Mehmet Genç,"Osmanli Iktisadi Dünya Görüşünün Ilkeleri," *Istanbul Üniversitesi Edebiyat Fakültesi Sosyoloji Dergisi,* III (1989), 175–185; Inalcik, " Ottoman State," 44–54, 179–379.

the provinces, did groups become powerful enough to exert pressure on administrators.[17]

SELECTIVE INTERVENTIONISM Economic historians of the Ottoman Empire have long held that interventionism was a permanent feature of Ottoman economic policies. The early Ottoman government was definitely more interventionist than either Islamic law or general practice in medieval Islamic states would seem to warrant, not hesitating to intervene in local and long-distance trade to regulate markets and ensure the availability of goods. In economic and fiscal, as well as many administrative, contexts, it often issued laws (*kanun*) even if those came into conflict with the *shariat* (Islamic law). The enforcement of regulations (*hisba*) in urban markets and price ceilings (*narh*) had their origins in Islamic tradition, but the Ottomans relied more frequently on them. Furthermore, so far as provisioning the army and the urban economy was concerned, the state often required merchants to deliver some of the more important goods at fixed prices.[18]

Nonetheless, priorities and intentions do not always result in implementation. Mixed success in the area of intervention inevitably led Ottoman authorities to recognize the limitations of their power. As a result, Ottoman governments moved away from the extreme position of interventionism espoused during the reign of Mehmed II (1444 and 1451–1481) toward more selective interventionism during the sixteenth century.

Unfortunately, this development has gone largely unnoticed

17 Miller, "France and England," 290–340; Cipolla, "The Italian and Iberian Peninsulas," in Postan, Rich, and Miller (eds.), *Cambridge Economic History of Europe,* III, 397–429. The Ottomans were not unaware of mercantilist thought. Naima, an early eighteenth-century historian, for example, defended mercantilist ideas and practices, arguing that if the Islamic population purchased local products instead of imports, coinage would stay in Ottoman lands (Naima [ed.] Zuhuri Danismanand Danisman Yayinevi], *Tarih-i Naima* [Istanbul, 1968], IV, 1826–1827; VI, 2520–2525). For mercantilism in Europe, compare F. Eli Heckscher, *Mercantilism* (London, 1955; rev. 2d ed.); Donald C. Coleman, *Revisions in Mercantilism* (London, 1969); Robert B. Ekelund, Jr., and Robert F. Hebert, *A History of Economic Theory and Method* (New York, 1990), 42–72.

18 Genç,"Osmanlı Iktisadi Dünya Görüşü"; Sabri Ülgener, "İslam Hukuk ve Ahlak Kaynaklarinda Iktisat Siyaseti Meseleleri," in Kenan Matbaasis (ed.), *Ebulula Mardin'e Armagan* (Istanbul, 1949), 1151–1189; Mübahat S. Kütükoglu, *Osmanlilarda Narh Müessesesi ve 1640 Tarihli Narh Defteri* (İstanbul, 1983), 3–38. For the texts of late fifteenth- and early sixteenth-century laws regulating the markets in large Ottoman cities, see Ömer Lütfi Barkan, "Bazi Büyük Şehirlerde Eşya ve Yiyecek Fiyatlarinin Tesbit ve Teftişi Hususlarini Tanzim Eden Kanunlar," *Tarih Vesikalari,* I/II (1942/1943).

by scholars who continue to refer to laws issued by Mehmed II and his immediate successors as examples of a chronic governmental intervention in the economy. The inability of many historians to note the policy shift is due primarily to a state-centered perspective. But archival evidence has also misled historians to exaggerate both the frequency and the extent of state intervention in the economy. Not all of the available material is truly representative. Every government intervention was typically recorded as an order to a local judge (*kadi*) or some other authority. However, no documents exist for the countless occasions when the government let the markets function on their own. Faced with this one-sided evidence, many historians have concluded that state intervention and regulation were permanent fixtures of most markets at most locations across the empire.

The official price-ceiling (narh) lists are a perfect case in point. Despite their apparent ubiquity in the court archives, they were hardly as common as most historians have assumed them to be. Recent searches through all of the more than 1,000 registers of three Istanbul courts—those of the Old City, Galata, and Üskudar from the fifteenth through mid-nineteenth century—indicate that narh lists were not prepared regularly. They were issued primarily during periods of extraordinary instability and distress—wars, crop failures, and other detriments to the food supply, as well as such monetary crises as the debasement or reform of coinage—when prices, especially food prices, tended to show sharp fluctuations or upward movements. In the absence of such problems, however, local administrators did not issue narh lists for long intervals, sometimes decades.[19]

Another bias is related to the fact that a large part of the available evidence pertains to state intervention in the economy of the capital city, which should not be construed as evidence of conditions elsewhere in the empire. Istanbul was unique both in size and political importance. With its population approaching 500,000, it was the largest city in Europe and West Asia during the sixteenth century. Like other extraordinarily large cities, it tended to receive far more economic attention from the government than less-populated and less-important urban centers, where the state's

19 Narh lists were issued most frequently during from 1585 to 1640 and from 1785 to 1840—both periods of monetary instability. Pamuk, *Five Hundred Years of Prices and Wages in Istanbul and Other Cities, 1469–1998* (Ankara, 2000).

presence was not as strong, and authorities, who were appointed by the center, were more willing to cooperate with powerful local groups.[20]

Examples from Ottoman monetary practices confirm the Ottoman tendency to rely on markets and local practices in most economic matters. Until the sixteenth century, Ottoman territories in Anatolia and the Balkans had a unified monetary system based on the gold *sultani* and the silver *akçe;* on the lowest rung were copper coins used for small transactions. When the Ottoman state expanded into a full-fledged empire in the sixteenth century, however, this simple system could not continue. The newly conquered territories, each of which was subject to different economic forces and different patterns of trade, already had well-established currency systems of their own. In these areas, the Ottomans pursued a two-tiered approach to money and currency. For both symbolic and economic reasons, the *sultani* became the only gold coin in the empire in the sixteenth century. As the ultimate symbol of sovereignty, it helped to unify the empire from the Balkans to Egypt and the Maghrib. Ever the pragmatists, the Ottomans kept the *sultani*'s weight and fineness identical to those of the Venetian ducat, which had become the accepted standard of payment in long-distance trade across the Mediterranean and beyond.

The central government allowed existing silver coinage in newly conquered territories to be used, with modification, as the leading means of payment in daily transactions and, to some extent, in long-distance trade—mainly to avoid economic disruption and popular discontent. But the central government may not have had the fiscal, administrative, and economic resources to consolidate silver coinage thoughout the empire. Hence, the silver coinage minted in the new territories from Mesopotamia to Egypt and Tunis began to bear the name of the sultan, though its designs and standards, as well as its respective names, adhered to the pre-Ottoman precedents. Earlier styles and types of copper coinage persisted in a similar manner.

20 Istanbul was a large consuming city, dependent on its vast hinterland. The classic work on the economy of the capital city and the nature of state intervention in it remains Robert Mantran, *Istanbul dans la seconde Moitie du XVIIe Siecle* (Paris, 1962), 233–286. See also Inalcik, " Ottoman State," 179–87; *idem,* "Bursa and the Commerce of the Levant," *Journal of the Economic and Social History of the Levant,* III (1960), 131–147; Masters, *Origins of Western Economic Dominance;* Daniel Goffman, *Izmir and the Levantine World, 1550–1650* (Seattle, 1990).

The exchange rates of the Ottoman and foreign gold coins, expressed in terms of the local silver unit, was determined by the markets, subject to changes in silver content of the currency, fluctuations in the gold–silver ratio, and a host of other factors. The state encouraged the circulation of all types of foreign coin to facilitate payment in local markets. The government did not legally establish a fixed rate of exchange between the gold and silver coins or a fixed gold–silver ratio around which the face value or the standards of both type of coins would be determined, leaving them for local markets to determine. The virtue of this system was its flexibility. As long as the markets set these exchange rates, and the government could accommodate them quickly enough, none of the coins in use was likely to be over- or undervalued and thus to disappear. In this context, as well as in the general economy, when the biases of archival evidence and the limitations of state power are taken into account, Ottoman policy toward commercial activity looks less like permanent, comprehensive interventionism and more like selective interventionism.[21]

EVOLUTION OF FISCAL INSTITUTIONS The evolution of Ottoman fiscal institutions during the seventeenth and eighteenth centuries provides a good example of the Ottoman state's ability to face social and political challenges pragmatically and flexibly. Although European banking houses regularly made loans to kings, princes, and governments during the late medieval and early modern periods, such transactions transpired differently in the Islamic world because of restrictions on interest. Ottoman loans took the form of tax-farming arrangements; individuals possessing liquid capital assets lent to the government in return for the right to farm the taxes of a given region or fiscal unit for a certain amount of time. Tax-farming dominated the Islamic world from the Mediterranean to the Indian Ocean, from the earliest days through the early modern period.

From the outset, the Ottomans relied on tax farming for the collection of urban taxes. Until the late sixteenth century, however, agricultural taxes—the largest share of tax revenues—were collected locally and mostly in kind within the timar system. Thanks to the considerable revenue obtained through rapid terri-

21 Pamuk, *Monetary History,* 66–76, 88–111.

torial expansion, the state did not feel the need to increase collection at the center. Documents show evidence of the state taking out short-term loans during the sixteenth century, mostly from Greek and Jewish financiers, who, by virtue of these services, gained the inside track on some of the most lucrative tax-farming contracts.[22]

Changes in military technology during the sixteenth century and the need to maintain larger, permanent armies at the center, however, increased pressure on the state to collect a larger part of the rural surplus at the empire's center. As a result, the timar system gradually subsided in favor of tax farming; tax units were auctioned in Istanbul. During the seventeenth century, bureaucrats in the capital and provincial groups began to share tax-farming revenues with the central government. Although this shift had been designed to increase cash receipts at the empire's core, the decline of state power vis-à-vis the provinces reduced the expected benefits.[23]

Further deterioration of state finances during the seventeenth century forced the central government to take greater advantage of the tax-farming system for the purposes of domestic borrowing. The central government began to increase the length of tax-farming contracts from one to five years, and even longer, especially during war when the fiscal pressures were greatest. It also demanded an increasingly higher fraction of the contract's auction price in advance. Tax farming thus converted to a form of domestic borrowing, for which tax revenues served as the central government's collateral.

With the introduction of the *malikane* system in 1695, revenue sources began to be farmed out on a lifetime basis in return for a large initial payment and regular annual payments thereafter. One rationale frequently offered for this contract extension was the state's hope that tax contractors would take better care of the peasant producers, the primary tax source, and try to achieve long-term increases in production. In fact, the malikane system allowed the state to use tax revenues as collateral and to borrow on a longer term.[24]

22 Inalcik, " Ottoman State," 212–214.

23 Linda T. Darling, *Revenue-Raising and Legitimacy: Tax Collection and Finance Administration in the Ottoman Empire, 1560–1660* (Leiden, 1996); Inalcik, "Military and Fiscal Transformation in the Ottoman Empire, 1600–1700," *Archivum Ottomanicum,* VI (1980), 283–337.

24 Erol Özvar, *Osmanli Maliyesinde Malikane Uygulamasi* (Istanbul, 2003); Genç, "A Study of

These innovations conferred even greater importance on the financing of contracts. Private financiers began to play an increasingly important role in the tax-collection process. Behind many of the individuals, often Muslim, who joined the bidding at tax-farming auctions, was a partnership that included financiers and agents whose intention was often to divide the large initial contract into smaller pieces for sub-contracting. Non-Muslims were prohibited from directly holding most malikane contracts, but Greeks, Jews, and eventually Armenians served eminently as financiers, brokers, and accountants for them. These arrangements were mostly in the form of Islamic business partnerships involving both Muslims and non-Muslims.[25]

During the eighteenth century, 1,000 to 2,000 individuals based in Istanbul, together with 5,000 to 10,000 others in the provinces, and innumerable contractors, agents, financiers, accountants, and managers, controlled the lion's share of the state's revenues. This grand coalition constituted a semi-privatized but interdependent component of the regime. Many provincials were able to acquire, and transfer to the next generation, small- and medium-sized malikane shares on villages so long as they remained in the good graces of local administrators or their Istanbul sponsors. For both well-connected individuals in the capital city and those in the provinces, obtaining government tax revenues was more lucrative than investing in agriculture, trade, or manufacturing. This mutually profitable relationship between the central and the provincial elites is crucial for understanding how the central state maintained some control in the provinces long after its military power there had faded.[26]

Significantly, these changes in the tax-collection and revenue-sharing system did not alter the legal basis of land ownership until the nineteenth century. Despite the rise of provincial elites, most agricultural lands remained *miri,* or state-owned; peasant households held the usufruct while the sipahis gave way first to tax farmers and then malikane owners.

The malikane system led to a decline in state revenues be-

the Feasibility of Using Eighteenth Century Ottoman Financial Records as an Indicator of Economic Activity," in Huri İslamoğlu-İnan (ed.), *The Ottoman Empire and the World Economy* (New York, 1987), 345–373.

25 Çizakça, *Comparative Evolution.*

26 Ariel Salzman, "An Ancien Regime Revisited: 'Privatization' and Political Economy in the Eighteenth Century Ottoman Empire," *Politics and Society,* XXI (1993), 393–423.

cause of the inability of the state to regain control of the revenue sources after the death of the individuals who had purchased them. From the 1770s onward, the central government began to experiment with other methods of tax collection and domestic borrowing. Rising military expenditures and increasing fiscal constraints during wartime were once again responsible for institutional changes. The war with Russia in 1768 to 1774 exposed Ottoman military and financial weaknesses dramatically. In its wake, the financial bureaucracy started a new but related initiative of long-term domestic borrowing called *esham*. In this system, the annual net revenues of a tax source were specified nominally and divided into a large number of shares to be sold publicly for the lifetime of the buyers. Tax farmers continued to collect the annual revenues of the source. The esham generally sold for six to seven times the annual net payments, which remained fixed. As the linkage between the annual government payments to esham holders and the underlying revenues of the tax source weakened, the esham increasingly resembled a life-term annuity, which was also popular in many European countries of the period.[27]

One motivation for the new system was to create a larger pool of smaller-scale lenders beyond the limited number of large financiers who tended to dominate the malikane auctions. However, the state's inability to control or limit the sales of the esham between individuals and to prevent the heirs of the deceased from continuing to receive payments seriously limited the fiscal benefits of this system. During the next half century, the state vacillated between abolishing the esham during periods of fiscal stability and expanding it during fiscal crises when additional funds had to be secured with little regard for their long-term costs.[28]

The evolution of Ottoman fiscal institutions through the malikane and esham systems of the seventeenth and eighteenth centuries illustrates the state's ability to mitigate its own administrative limitations by entering into a pragmatic alliance with elites and financiers in the capital city and in the provinces. In the early part of the nineteenth century, however, the central government, supported by new technologies and a better military, was able to re-assert its power over the provinces. In the 1830s, it pulled many of the malikane contracts back to the center, assigning collection

27 Yavuz Cezar, *Osmanli Maliyesinde Bunalim ve Değişim Dönemi: XVIII. yy.dan Tanzimat'a Mali Tarih* (Istanbul, 1986), 81–83; Genç, "Esham," *İslam Ansiklopedisi*, XI (1995), 376–380.
28 Cezar, *Osmanli Maliyesinde Bunalim*, 128–134, 198–200.

of their revenues once again to tax farmers, only to phase out the system completely during the 1840s with a larger package of administrative and economic reforms. Its attempt to eliminate tax farming and collect rural taxes directly, however, failed because of its own administrative limitations. Yearly tax farming continued until World War I. Nonetheless, the power of the provincial partners steadily declined. The centralization of the nineteenth century helped to raise the central government's share of the tax revenues from about 2 to 3 percent of the underlying economy (GDP) during the late eighteenth century to 10 to 12 percent on the eve of World War I.[29]

Despite growing research, the causal connections between the evolution of Ottoman public finance, as outlined herein, and that of its European counterparts during the eighteenth century have not yet received due regard. The parallels between the two are striking. Increasing economic and financial integration with Europe during the eighteenth century appears to have brought about significant changes in Ottoman institutions of public finance. By contrast, changes in the institutions of private finance during this period were limited to those employed by Europeans and non-Muslim subjects of the empire.

LONG-TERM TRENDS IN STANDARDS OF LIVING Evidence about the long-term performance of the Ottoman economy is by no means inconsistent with the argument that selective institutional change enabled the Ottomans to maintain their empire far longer than should have been expected. A basic indicator of Ottoman economic performance during the early modern era is the empire's long-term trend in per capita income relative to that in Western Europe. With the exception of a handful of countries, however, estimates for per capita GDP for the period before 1820 are difficult to construct and not sufficiently reliable. In the absence of per capita GDP series, many economic historians have used urban wages, more specifically, real wages of skilled and unskilled construction workers, as a proxy. Despite many valid objections, real wage series offer the only solid information about living standards in many parts of the world before 1800.[30]

29 Estimates are based on a series of central government budget documents and our estimates of per capita income in the Ottoman Empire.

30 Even if the representative wage is accepted as an adequate proxy for the annual per capita earnings of labor, it would not be a good proxy for income per capita without the further as-

It is currently impossible to comment about changes in the empire's rural population's standards of living, but evidence about long-term urban trends in real wages during these centuries is beginning to emerge from the Ottoman archives. A recent study of the real wages of construction workers in Istanbul and other cities indicates that Ottoman real wages were comparable to those in most parts of Europe, though about one-third lower than those in northwestern Europe during the sixteenth century. This pattern prevailed until after the Industrial Revolution. After declining by 30 to 40 percent during the sixteenth century, probably due to population growth, urban real wages in the Ottoman Empire remained roughly unchanged until the second half of the eighteenth century, when they began to rise. Around 1800, urban wages in the Ottoman Empire were 10 to 20 percent lower than their levels around 1500.[31]

Per capita incomes began to rise after the Industrial Revolution, first in northwestern Europe and then in other parts of Europe. As a result, the gap in levels of per capita GDP between the Ottoman Empire and many parts of Europe began to widen after 1820. Institutional changes and integration into world markets, however, combined to create a slow but significant trend of economic growth in the Ottoman Empire during the decades leading up to World War I. Per capita incomes probably rose at an average of less than 1 percent per annum after 1880. Export-oriented agriculture, which mainly involved commercial coastal regions and port cities, was the leading sector. Estimates place per capita incomes for 1913 in the range of 12 to 14 then current pounds sterling, or more than $1,000 in parity-adjusted 1990 U.S. currency, leaving average incomes in the Ottoman Empire below those of most countries in southeastern Europe, but above those of Egypt

---

sumption that factor shares across countries were similar. In many parts of Europe and Asia during the early modern era, incomes of households were often determined by changes in employment levels; participation ratios of men, women, and children; and, above all, nonmarket incomes. Despite these qualifications, the link between wages and the living standards remains. A decline in real wages resulted in a decline in living standards or household welfare because more labor had to be supplied to buy the same amount of goods. Jan Luiten Van Zanden, "Wages and the Standards of Living in Europe, 1500–1800," *European Review of Economic History,* III (1999), 175–198; Jan de Vries, "The Industrial Revolution and the Industrious Revolution," *Journal of Economic History,* LIV (1994), 249–270.

31 Suleyman Ozmucur and Pamuk, "Urban Wages and the Standards of Living in the Ottoman Empire, 1469–1914," *Journal of Economic History,* LXII (2002), 293–321.

and Iran. Ottoman urban wages reflected these upward trends, increasing by two-thirds from the late eighteenth century until World War I, even as the real-wage gap with northwestern Europe began to widen after the Industrial Revolution. On the eve of World War I, the real wages of urban construction workers in the Ottoman Empire were about 40 percent above their levels in 1500, but the purchasing power of urban wages in northwestern Europe was two to three times higher than its Ottoman counterpart.

The real-wage series also point to a modest but statistically significant upward trend in Ottoman urban wages dating back to the sixteenth century, which suggests a modest but steady rise in demand for labor. It is not easy to draw conclusions from this finding because the existing literature does not point to a long-term growth trend, especially for the period before 1850. This new evidence, however, raises the possibility of a slow and modest rise in productivity around the eastern Mediterranean before the Industrial Revolution. Increased efficiency and/or the diffusion of new technology from Western Europe may help explain this trend. These indications that Ottoman standards of living improved after the sixteenth century are consistent with recent arguments in Ottoman historiography that the Ottoman Empire did not simply and irreversibly decline after 1600. Rather, as recent literature emphasizes, the Ottoman state, from the seventeenth through the nineteenth century, evinced an uncanny ability to reinvent itself and reorganize society in the face of changing circumstances.[32]

Economists and economic historians have recently identified institutions and institutional change as key variables that help to explain the widely disparate economic performances of different societies during the past 500 years. Based on the successful experience of Western Europe and European offshoots, the new institutional economics shows that long-run economic growth requires an underlying framework that constantly reinforces incentives for organizations to engage in productive activity. But a society rarely arrives at, or creates, institutions that are conducive to economic growth out of thin air. While fixating on the "rise of the West,"

32 *Ibid.*, 317.

institutional economics and economic historians have not paid sufficient attention to other examples of institutional change, especially those outside Western Europe—the Ottoman Empire being a case in point. This study of long-term changes in the Ottoman Empire's economic institutions, as well as its economic performance, reveals that the state's pragmatism, flexibility, and willingness to compromise, even before the nineteenth-century Tanzimat reforms, enabled the empire not just to persist but also to grow—despite its many challenges, both internal and external—while many of its contemporaries in Europe and Asia were unable to do so.

Resourceful as the Ottomans were, however, the dominance of the central bureaucracy in society and politics had a detrimental effect on many areas of Ottoman economic life. The influence of landowners, merchants, manufacturers, and moneychangers on the government remained limited. Despite the general trend toward decentralization of the empire during the seventeenth and eighteenth centuries, merchants and domestic producers—the leading proponents and developers of mercantilist policies in Europe—never became powerful enough in the empire to sway the Ottoman government to deviate from its traditional ways.

Before the Industrial Revolution and the European expansion of the nineteenth century, the Ottoman central bureaucracy engaged in a power struggle with the notables of the provinces for almost two centuries. Yet, the *ayan* (provincial notables) did not establish alternative institutions and mechanisms of capital accumulation. Despite their interests in trade, agriculture, and manufacturing, tax farming remained the most lucrative enterprise for them. In the early part of the nineteenth century, the center was able to re-assert its power over the provinces. The well-known reforms of the nineteenth century are best understood as attempts to maintain the privileged position of the center, as well as the territorial integrity of the empire.

The central bureaucracy reserved most of its pragmatism and flexibility, first, for defense of the traditional order and, second, for its own survival. Many of the traditional institutions, such as state ownership of land, the urban guilds, subsidy of the army and urban economy, selective interventionism, and, most important, restrictions on private capital, remained intact until the nineteenth century. Selective institutional change may have enabled the

Ottomans to survive into the modern era, but it did not further capitalist economic development or new forms of economic organization. These significant limitations of Ottoman pragmatism and flexibility help to explain the disintegration of the empire despite the many timely and extensive institutional changes that took place during the nineteenth century.

II

OTTOMAN INTERVENTIONISM IN ECONOMIC AND MONETARY AFFAIRS

In Honor of Professor Halil Sahillioğlu

Professor Halil Sahillioğlu devoted a significant part of his distinguished research and writing career to Ottoman monetary history (1). My own work on the same subject owes a good deal to his path breaking work (2).. In this essay, I examine the approach of the Ottoman central government to economic and monetary affairs. I question the prevailing interpretation in Ottoman historiography which assumes that government interventionism in economic and monetary affairs was the rule and, by implication, that these efforts were generally successful.

Ottoman Economic Priorities and Policies :

To understand the nature of Ottoman economic policies or practices, it is essential to examine the nature of the Ottoman state and its relations with different social groups. Until late in the fifteenth century, there existed considerable amount of tension in Ottoman society between the Turkish landed aristocracy of the provinces, who were deeply involved in the territorial conquests, and a bureaucracy at the center made up mostly of converted slaves (**devshirme**), with the balance of power often shifting between the two. The successful centralization drive of Mehmed II in the second half of the fifteenth century moved the pendulum again, this time decisively. The landed aristocracy was defeated, state ownership was established over privately held lands, and power concentrated in the hands of the central bureaucracy. After this shift, the policies of the government in Istanbul began to reflect much more strongly the priorities of this bureaucracy. The influence of various social groups, not only of landowners but also of merchants and moneychangers, over the policies of the central government remained limited.

The central bureaucracy tried, above all, to create and reproduce a traditional order with the bureaucracy at the top. The provisioning of the urban areas, long distance trade and imports were all necessary for the stability of that social order. The state tolerated and even encouraged the activities of merchants, domestic manufacturers more or less independent of the guilds and moneychangers as long as they helped reproduce that traditional order. Despite the general trend towards decentralization of the empire during the seventeenth and eighteenth centuries, merchants and

---

(1) For his seminal article in English, see Halil Sahillioğlu, "The Role of International Monetary and Metal Movements in Ottoman Monetary History" in J. F. Richards (ed.), **Precious Metals in the Later Medieval and early Modern Worlds**, Durham, North Carolina: Carolina Academic Press, 1983, pp. 269-304.

(2) Şevket Pamuk, "Money in the Ottoman Empire, 1326-1914" in Halil İnalcık with Donald Quataert (eds.), **The Ottoman Empire: Its Economy and Society, 1300-1914**, Cambridge University Press, 1994, pp. 947-980 and Şevket Pamuk, **A Monetary History of the Ottoman Empire, 1300-1918**, Cambridge University Press, 1999 (forthcoming).

domestic producers who were the leading proponents and actual developers of mercantilist policies in Europe, never became powerful enough to exert sufficient pressure on the Ottoman government to change or even modify these traditional policies. Only in the provinces, locally powerful groups were able to exert increasing degrees of influence over the provincial administrators.

In a recent essay, Mehmet Genç examines the economic functions and priorities of the central bureaucracy based on years of research on the archives of the central government (3). After cautioning that these never appeared in purely economic form but always together with political, religious, military, administrative or fiscal concerns and pronouncements, he argues that it is, nonetheless, possible to reduce the Ottoman priorities in economic matters to three basic principles. The first priority was the provisioning of the urban economy including the army, the palace and the state officials. The government wanted to assure a steady supply of goods for the urban economy and especially for the capital city. The bureaucracy was very much aware of the critical role played by merchants in this respect. With the territorial expansion of the empire and the incorporation of Syria and Egypt during the sixteenth century, long distance trade and control of the intercontinental trade routes became increasingly important and even critical for these needs.

Foreign merchants were especially welcome because they brought goods not available in Ottoman lands. Ottoman encouragement of European merchants and the granting of various privileges, concessions and capitulations as early as the sixteenth century can be best understood in this context. Occasionally, however, foreign merchants also contributed to domestic shortages by exporting scarce goods and the Ottomans had to impose temporary prohibitions on exports.

The emphasis on provisioning necessitated an important distinction between imports and exports. Imports were encouraged as they added to the availability of goods in the urban markets. In contrast, exports were tolerated only after the requirements of the domestic economy were met. As soon as the possibility of shortages emerged, however, the government did not hesitate to prohibit the exportation of basic necessities, especially foodstuffs and raw materials.

Genç emphasizes that a second priority of the center was fiscal revenue. The government intervened frequently to collect taxes from a broad range of economic activities and came to recognize, in the process, that at least in the longer term, economic prosperity was essential for the fiscal strength of the state. In the shorter term and especially during periods of crises, however, it did not hesitate to increase tax collections at the expense of producers.

A third priority, which was closely tied to the other two, was the preservation of the traditional order. For the Ottomans, there existed an ideal social order and balances between social groups such as the peasantry, guilds and the merchants. The sultan and the bureaucracy were placed at

(3) Mehmet Genç, "Osmanli Iktisadi Dünya Görüşünün Ilkeleri", **Istanbul Üniversitesi Edebiyat Fakültesi Sosyoloji Dergisi**, 3. Dizi, No. 1, 1989; for a similar argument see Halil Inalcik, "The Ottoman State : Economy and Society" in Halil İnalcık and Donald Quataert, (eds.), **An Economic and Social History of the Ottoman Empire, 1300-1914** Cambridge University Press, pp. 44-54.

the top of this social order. There was some flexibility in this view. The ideal of what constituted this traditional order and the social balances may have changed over time with changes in the economy and society. The government took care to preserve as much as possible the prevailing order and the social balances including the structure of employment and production. From this perspective, for example, rapid accumulation of capital by merchants, guild members or any other group was not considered favorably since it would lead to the rapid disintegration of the existing order.

As a result, the governments' attitude towards merchants was profoundly ambiguous. On one hand, merchants, large and small, were considered indispensable for the functioning of the urban economy. Yet, at the same time, their profiteering often led to shortages of basic goods bringing pressure on the guild system and, more generally, on the urban economy. Thus the central administration often considered, as its main task, the control of the merchants, not their protection. At the same time, however, the control of merchants was much more difficult than the control of guilds. While the guilds were fixed in location, the merchants were mobile. Needless to say, the official attitude towards financiers and moneychangers (**sarraf**) was similarly ambiguous.

In pursuit of these priorities, Genç argues, the Ottoman government did not hesitate to intervene in local and long distance trade to regulate the markets and ensure the availability of goods for the military, palace and, more generally, the urban economy. In comparison to both Islamic law and the general practice in medieval Islamic states, the Ottomans thus appear more interventionist in their approach. In economic and fiscal affairs as well as in many administrative practices, they often issued their own state laws (**kanun**) even if those came into conflict with the **shariat.** The practices they used such as the enforcement of regulations (**hisba**) in urban markets and price ceilings (**narh**) had their origins in Islamic tradition but the Ottomans relied more frequently on them. In addition, in the provisioning of the army and the urban economy, deliveries at fixed prices were required from merchants for some of the more important goods.

Based on extensive research on documents prepared by the bureaucracy, Genç's scheme is very useful in analyzing the priorities and intentions of the Ottoman bureaucracy. As Genç himself emphasizes, however, priorities and intentions need to be distinguished from the actual policies. Whether the governments succeeded in bringing about the desired outcomes through their interventions depended on their capabilities. It has already been argued that there existed serious limitations on the administrative resources, organization and capacity of the central governments. States in the late medieval and early modern periods did not have the capacity to intervene in markets comprehensively and effectively. The mixed success of government actions inevitably led the Ottoman authorities to recognize the limitations of their power. As a result, Ottoman governments moved away from a position of comprehensive interventionism as practiced during the reign of Mehmed II in the second half of the fifteenth century (1444 and 1451-1481) towards more selective interventionism in the sixteenth, seventeenth and eighteenth centuries.

Unfortunately, this evolution and the more selective nature of government interventionism after the fifteenth century has not been recognized by historians (4). In addition to the biases arising from state-centered perspectives shared by many, there are a number of practical reasons why archival evidence has misled historians to exaggerate both the frequency and the extent of state intervention in the economy. One basic source of error has been the unrepresentative nature of the available material. Each government intervention is typically recorded by a document in the form of an order to the local judge (**kadi**) or some other authority. In contrast, there are no records for the countless numbers of occasions when the government let the markets function on their own. Faced with this one sided evidence, historians have concluded that state intervention and regulation was a permanent fixture of most markets at most locations across the empire.

The case of the official price ceiling (**narh**) lists provides an excellent example in this respect. Historians who have run into individual documents with **narh** lists or those who obtained a few of these from the archives of the Islamic court records, have assumed that these lists were issued regularly and that **narh** was a permanent fixture of urban economic life. In fact, my recent searches through all of the more than one thousand registers of three of Istanbul's courts, those of the Old City, Galata and Üskudar from the fifteenth through the mid-nineteenth century indicate that **narh** lists were prepared and issued primarily during extraordinary periods of instability and distress in the commodity and or money markets when prices, especially food prices, tended to show sharp fluctuations or upward movements. Wars, crop failures and / other difficulties in provisioning the city and monetary instabilities such as debasements or reforms of coinage were examples of these extraordinary periods. In the absence of such problems, however, there were long intervals, sometimes lasting for decades, when the local administrators did not issue **narh** lists (5).

Another bias is related to the fact that a large part of the available documents provide evidence of state intervention directly related to the economy of the capital city (6). This evidence has led many historians to assume that the same pattern applied to the rest of the empire. In fact, Istanbul was unique both in terms of size and political importance. With its population approaching half a million, it was the largest city in Europe and West Asia during the sixteenth century. As was the case with monster cities elsewhere, government economic policy often revolved around it. In contrast, the central government was much less concerned about the provisioning of other urban centers. The state organization was not as strong there and the local authorities, who were appointed by the center, were more willing to cooperate with the locally powerful groups, the guild hierarchy, merchants, tax collectors and moneychangers.

In short, it is now time to make a more realistic assessment of the nature of Ottoman state interventionism in the economy. When the biases

(4) One notable exception is Ahmed Güner Sayar who points to a change in Ottoman attitudes towards **narh** after 1650. Sayar, **Osmanlı Iktisat Düşüncesinin Çagdaşlaşması**, Istanbul, 1986, pp. 73-74.

(5) This search was undertaken as part of ongoing work on the history of prices and wages in Istanbul.

(6) The classic work on the economy of the capital city and the nature of state intervention in that economy remains Robert Mantran, **Istanbul dans la seconde moitié du XVIIe siècle**, Paris, 1962, pp. 233-286. Also Halil Inalcik, "Trade", in Inalcik and Quataert, (eds.) **An Economic and Social History of the Ottoman Empire, 1300-1914**, pp. 179-87.

of archival evidence and the limitations of the power of states are taken into account, Ottoman policy towards trade and the markets is best characterized not as permanent and comprehensive interventionism, but as selective interventionism. In the later periods, interventions were used primarily for the provisioning of selected goods for the capital city and the army and during extraordinary periods when shortages reached crisis conditions.

The limitations of the central government was even more apparent in the case of money markets. In comparison to goods markets and long distance trade, it was more difficult for governments to control physical supplies of specie or coinage and regulate prices, that is, exchange rates and interest rates. The Ottoman administrators were well aware that participants in the money markets, merchants, moneychangers and financiers were able to evade state rules and regulations more easily than those in the commodity markets (7). Observing the mixed success of government actions, they learned that interventionism in money markets did not always produce the desired results. For this reason, government interventions in money markets remained selective and occurred mostly during extraordinary periods such as extreme monetary turbulence or wars. In fact, Ottoman monetary practices during this period exhibited a remarkable degree of flexibility and pragmatism.

One of the most telling examples of Ottoman flexibility concerned the determination of exchange rates between different kinds of coinage. In an environment of frequently recurring shortages of specie, the Ottoman administrators knew that it was essential to attract into the Ottoman lands and maintain in circulation as much coinage and bullion as possible. Their monetary practices were guided more by this concern than any other. They were also aware that the ratio between gold and silver as well as the value of different types of coins was subject to fluctuations. Under these conditions, a policy of fixed exchange rates between different coins would have driven the good or undervalued coins out of circulation through the workings of Gresham's Law. Instead, the authorities typically allowed local markets to determine the exchange rates, thereby reducing if not eliminating the distinction between good and bad coins and encouraging the circulation of all coins. Local court records show that the **kadis** relied on these market rates to settle disputes between individuals. In addition, the government announced the official rates at which different coins, gold and silver, would be accepted as payment. Usually, these rates, expressed in Ottoman units, did not diverge greatly from the prevailing market rates for the same coins. Large differences between official and market rates tended to be short in duration and took place mostly under crisis conditions such as wars or severe financial difficulties (8).

---

(7) Gilles P. Hennequin, "Points de vue sur l'Histoire Monétaire de l'Egypte Musulmane au Moyen Age", **Annales Islamologiques**, Le Caire, Institut Français d'Archéologie Orientale du Caire, vol. 12, 1974, pp. 3-44, "Nouveaux Aperçus sur l'Histoire Monétaire de l'Egypte au Moyen Age", **Annales Islamologiques**, Le Caire, Institut Français d'Archéologie Orientale du Caire, vol. 12, 1974, pp. 179-215 ; S.D. Goitein, **A Mediterranean Society, The Jewish Communities of the Arab World as Portrayed in the Documents of the Cairo Geniza, Vol. I : Economic Foundations,** University of California Press, 1967, pp. 209-272 ; Peter Spufford, **Money and Its Use in Medieval Europe**, Cambridge University Press, 1988.

(8) See, for example, Halil Sahillioğlu, "XVII. Asrın ilk Yarısında İstanbul'da Tedavüldeki Sikkelerin Raici", **Türk Tarih Kurumu, Belgeler**, Vol. 1, No. 2, Ankara, 1965, pp. 227-34.

The Ottoman attitude towards foreign coinage provides another example of Ottoman flexibility. From the earliest days, Ottoman authorities encouraged the circulation of foreign coinage. The government and courts accepted foreign coinage as payment. Official lists indicating the exchange rates between different types of coinage always included the European pieces. The primary reason for embracing foreign coinage, of course, was to add to the amount of specie in circulation. The Ottoman government exempted precious metals and foreign currency from import dues. In capitulations or privileges given to merchants of certain European states, the Ottoman government exempted them from all customs duties for the foreign coinage they brought. In addition, customs and mints officials were told not to demand that these coinage be surrendered to the authorities for the minting of Ottoman coinage. These privileges were eventually extended to the merchants of most European states.

Flexibility in Monetary Affairs :

Yet another example of Ottoman pragmatism in monetary affairs is the emergence of separate monetary zones within the empire during the sixteenth and seventeenth centuries. The newly conquered territories, each of which was subject to different economic forces, already had well established currency systems of their own. In most cases, the Ottoman governments did not attempt to change them as they wished to avoid economic disruption and possibly popular unrest. On the one hand, the central government insisted on the unification of all gold coinage, the ultimate symbol of sovereignty, around the sultani which began to be issued in 1477. At the same time, the government allowed the continuation of the local silver currencies in many regions of the empire. Although the silver coinage minted in these territories began to bear the name of the Sultan, they remained distinct from the Istanbul based akçe.

During the sixteenth and seventeenth centuries, the Balkans together with western and central Anatolia remained as the core regions of the akçe/sultani system described earlier. In outlying Wallachia, Moldavia and Hungary, on the other hand, Austrian, Poland, Hungarian and German coins were used more widely than Ottoman coins. In Crimea, coins were minted in the name of the local Khans even though Istanbul exerted some influence in monetary affairs especially since the prices of agricultural imports from Crimea played an important role in the economic life of Istanbul.

When the Ottomans conquered Egypt, they retained the standard small silver coin called **meidin, nisf** or **nisf fidda** which dated back to the early fifteenth century. Over time, this unit began to be called **para** and remained the basic silver standard in Egypt until the end of the eighteenth century. During the sixteenth century, the **meidin** also circulated in Arabia and Yemen. Other Ottoman coins were also minted in Yemen from the 1520s to the middle of the seventeenth century, but they do not appear to be significant economically. Syria, which remained as a transitional monetary zone between Egypt and Anatolia, akçes circulated together with **meidins.**

The areas neighboring Iran, from Eastern Anatolia to Iraq, were especially sensitive for the Ottoman government. In this region, the Ottoman mints produced a coin called **dirham** by the numismatists and **shahi** by the Ottoman documents and the local population. Its weight and silver content was similar to the **shahis** of Persia. Political factors may have contributed to this strategy of having a separate monetary zone next to Safavid Empire. Finally, in the Maghreb, political and economic ties to

Istanbul remained rather weak. Even though local coins carried the name of the Ottoman ruler, Istanbul exerted little influence over the evolution of the monetary system in Algeria, Tunisia and around Tripoli (9).

In conclusion, I would like to suggest that we need to revise our current views about the interventionism of the Ottoman governments especially in view of the serious limitations of the capabilities of pre-modern governments. The Ottoman governments were certainly well aware of these limitations and, for this reason, they chose to pursue a selective rather than comprehensive interventionism in economic and monetary affairs.

(9) For further details, see Pamuk, **A Monetary History of the Ottoman Empire**, chapters 6 and 11.

III

THE OTTOMAN MONETARY SYSTEM AND FRONTIER TERRITORIES IN EUROPE, 1500-1700

This short essay will examine the evolution of gold, silver and copper coinage and of currencies and monetary practices in general in the European frontier regions of the Ottoman Empire during the sixteenth and seventeenth centuries. As was emphasized in my recent book, the Ottomans were very careful about the political symbolism as well as the fiscal and economic consequences of their monetary practices.[1] They followed certain rules regarding the types of Ottoman coins that could be minted in territories with different political and administrative status. In the present study, I will review the details of Ottoman monetary practices in both the core regions and the frontier territories of the empire in Europe in order to bring into sharper focus the overall logic of the monetary system. Such a "big picture" perspective should also offer important insights into the history and evolution of Ottoman institutions and into the very concept of empire, the nature of the entity and how the Ottomans themselves viewed it.

Monetary Zones within the Empire

For a long time it has been assumed that the use of money in the Balkans and Anatolia was limited to long-distance trade and parts of the urban sector. Recent research has shown, however, that the urban population and some segments of the countryside were already part of the monetary economy by the end of the fifteenth century. Even more significant was a substantial increase in the use of money during the sixteenth century because of the greater availability of specie and the growing commercialization of the rural economy. The evidence for this important development comes from a number of sources. First, recent research has indicated that population growth and urbanization during the sixteenth century were accompanied by the growth of economic linkages between the urban and rural areas. As a result, there emerged in the Balkans and Anatolia an intensive pattern of periodic markets and market fairs where peasants and larger landholders sold parts of their produce to urban residents. These markets also provided an important opportunity for the nomads to come into contact with both peasants and the urban population. Large sectors of the rural population came to use coinage, especially the small denominations of silver *akçe* and copper *mangır*, through their participation in these markets.

[1] Şevket Pamuk, *A Monetary History of the Ottoman Empire* (Cambridge, 2000), chapters 4 and 6.

Until the sixteenth century, Ottoman territories in Anatolia and the Balkans had a unified monetary system based on the gold *sultani* and the silver *akçe*. Beneath them, was the copper *mangır*, or *pul*, used for small transactions. As the Ottoman state territorially expanded to become a full-fledged empire, however, this simple system could not be continued. The newly conquered territories, each of which was subject to different economic forces and very different patterns of trade, already had well-established currency systems of their own. The Ottomans pursued a two-tiered approach to money and currency in these areas. They unified the gold coinage at the existing international standards but allowed the creation of multiple currency zones in silver according to the sharply different commercial relations and needs of the new provinces.

By the first quarter of the sixteenth century three distinct levels had emerged in the Ottoman monetary system, each characterized by a different economic function and a different type of coin. At the top were the gold coins used by merchants for making large payments, both internally and in international trade. Financiers, money changers, high-level government officials, and to some extent, owners of medium and large-scale manufacturing establishments also used gold coins. In addition, larger landholders in the more commercialized villages as well as the *sipahi*s, who collected a variety of taxes both in money and in kind from the rural population, were well acquainted with gold coinage.

In gold, the *sultani* became the only Ottoman coin across the empire during the sixteenth century, for both symbolic and economic reasons. With a single gold coin, the ultimate symbol of sovereignty, the Ottomans thus unified the empire from the Balkans to Egypt and the Maghrib. The standards of the *sultani*, its weight and fineness, were kept identical to those of the Venetian *ducat* that had become the accepted standard of payment in long-distance trade across the Mediterranean and beyond. The gold *sultani* was issued regularly in Egypt, Algiers and Tunis as well as in the core regions of the Balkans and Anatolia.

In silver, the coinage used in daily transactions and to some extent in long-distance trade, the central government chose to maintain the existing monetary units in the newly conquered territories, with or without modifications. The most important reason was to avoid economic disruption and possible popular unrest, but it was also not clear that the central government had the fiscal, administrative and economic resources to unify the silver coinage of the empire. In any case, while the silver coinage minted in the new territories began to bear the name of the sultan, their designs and standards as well as their names often adhered to the pre-Ottoman forms and usages. Just as the *akçe* was the silver coin and unit of account in Anatolia and the Balkans, the *medin* or *para* became the silver coin and unit of account in Ottoman Egypt and the surrounding areas. The *shahi*, a larger silver coin, served the same purpose in Ottoman Iraq and the square-shaped *nasri* in Tunis.

At the bottom of the Ottoman monetary hierarchy were the copper coins which did not exchange at or near their intrinsic values, but at nominal values fixed by the state in fractions of the local silver coinage. The copper coinage was widely used for small daily transactions. In the Balkans and Anatolia, it was referred to as *mangır* or *pul*.

As was the case with most other contemporary states, Ottoman governments allowed and even encouraged the circulation of foreign coinage. Welcoming foreign coinage added to the amount of specie in circulation in local markets. In addition, foreign coinage helped support long-distance trade, which was important for the Ottoman government both for fiscal and provisioning reasons. Until the rise of the *sultani* in the sixteenth century, foreign coins were the leading means of payment in long-distance trade throughout Ottoman lands.

The central government handled the task of establishing a monetary system for the expanding empire with a large degree of pragmatism and flexibility. This approach was quite similar to Ottoman administrative practices in other areas. With respect to land tenure systems, for example, the Ottoman central administration did not attempt to impose the *timar* regime in all of the conquered territories. In many of the more distant areas administered more loosely from the capital, such as Eastern Anatolia, Baghdad, Basra, Egypt, Yemen, Moldavia, Wallachia, Georgia or the Maghrib, the Ottomans were eager to collect taxes but altered the existing land regimes either to a limited extent or not at all. Similarly the legal codes (*kanunname*) the Ottomans issued in these provinces combined to varying degrees pre-Ottoman practices with the Ottoman.[2] As a result, in monetary as well as other matters, there emerged inside the empire different zones with different degrees of administrative control. At the core were the areas most closely administered by the capital with institutions most closely resembling those in the Istanbul region, but at increasing distance from the capital, the institutions and administrative practices reflected the power balances between the capital and the local structures and forces in the provinces.

Core and Frontier in Europe

The Balkans, together with western and central Anatolia including the capital city and its environs, constituted the core region of the Ottoman monetary system. The silver *akçe* was both the leading unit of account and the leading means of exchange there. For large transactions and hoarding purposes, the *sultani* was used together with European gold pieces. The mint at the capital city, or "Kostantaniyye" as it was called on Ottoman coinage until the eighteenth century, was the leading mint of the region for both the *akçe* and the *sultani*.

The number of mints producing silver *akçe*s was limited until the end of the fifteenth century. Of the fourteen mints producing *akçe*s during the thirty-one-year reign of Bayezid II (1481-1512), six were located in the Balkans, one in the capital and the rest in Anatolia. In addition, two mints, Kostantaniyye and Serez in Macedonia, produced gold *sultani*s. The number of active mints in the Balkans as well as other regions across the empire increased substantially during the sixteenth century, especially during the reign of Süleyman the Magnificent (1520-1566).

[2] Ö. L. Barkan, *Zirai Ekonominin Mali ve Hukuki Temelleri, Kanunnameler*, Cilt 1 (Istanbul, 1942); and A. Akgündüz, *Osmanlı Kanunnameleri ve Hukuki Tahlilleri*, 8 vols. (Istanbul, 1990-94).

During the reign of Murad III (1574-1595) as many as thirty mints are known to have produced *akçe*s including fifteen in the Balkans and the Aegean islands. At the same time, nine mints in the Balkans and Anatolia produced gold *sultanis*.[3]

With a minor exception, all of the Balkan mints were located south of the Danube and as far west as Banja Luka in Bosnia. The most active mints in the Balkans were close to the mines in Macedonia and Serbia. The only mint in Anatolia located near a silver mine was that of Canca near Gümüşhane in northeastern Anatolia. The bulk of silver coinage was thus produced in the Balkans and transported to Anatolia in one way or another. In contrast, copper coinage was produced mostly in Anatolia and the capital city and transported to the Balkans. The Venetian gold *ducat* remained the most important foreign coin circulating in the Balkans and Anatolia during the sixteenth century. In the second half of the century, large European silver coins called *groschen*, most importantly the Spanish eight-*real* piece and the Dutch lion *thaler*, also began to circulate in the Balkans and Anatolia.

Hungary

The Ottomans governed Hungary directly during the sixteenth and seventeenth centuries, but they did not mint *akçe*s or *sultani*s in Hungary as they did in territories south of the Danube. There were no silver or gold deposits in the Ottoman regions of Hungary although major gold mines in other parts of Hungary had supplied large areas of Europe since the late medieval period. Evidence from coin hoards indicates that *akçe*s and *sultani*s produced in the Balkans circulated in Hungary in limited volume. Payments by the Ottoman state to troops or suppliers were an important source of the *akçe*s in Hungary. Circulating more widely was the silver coinage of neighboring states, chiefly the silver and gold coins of the independent Hungarian principalities; the small silver *groat*s, *zweir*s, and *pfenning*s from the Habsburg domains; small silver coins from Poland such as the half-*groat*s, and increasingly from the second half of the sixteenth through the seventeenth century, the large *thaler*s. Nonetheless, all taxes in Ottoman Hungary continued to be specified in *akçe*s. In other words, while the *akçe* served as the unit of account, at least in governmental transactions, the coinage of the neighboring states served as the leading means of exchange and payments, including taxes.[4]

---

[3] M. Erüreten, "Osmanlı Akçeleri Darp Yerleri," *The Turkish Numismatic Society Bülten* 17 (1985): 14-5; A. Schaendlinger, *Osmanische Numismatik* (Braunschweig, 1973), pp. 93-106 and S. Sreckovic, *Osmanlijski Novac Kovan na tlu Jugoslavije* (Ottoman Coins from Mints in Yugoslavia), (Belgrade, 1987), pp. 5-92.

[4] I. Gedai, "Turkish Coins in Hungary in the 16th and 17th Centuries," in *Turkish Numismatic Society, A Festschrift Presented to Ibrahim Artuk on the Occasion of the 20th Anniversary of the Turkish Numismatic Society* (Istanbul), pp. 102-19; P. Elemer, *Török Penzek a Hodoltsag Kori* (Turkish Coins Circulating in Hungary), (Budapest, 1986); and V. Zimanyi, *Economy and Society in Sixteenth and Seventeenth Century Hungary (1526-1650)* (Budapest, 1987), pp. 17-27.

The Danubian Principalities

Unlike the rest of the Balkans, the Danubian Principalities were never fully incorporated into the Ottoman Empire. Instead, in the late fifteenth century, Wallachia and, in the early sixteenth century, Moldavia became vassal states paying regular tribute. These principalities were mostly independent in their internal affairs and did not adopt Ottoman institutions such as the *timar* system of land tenure. The fact that neither the Ottomans nor the local governments minted any coins – gold, silver or copper – in Wallachia or Moldavia suggests both the extent and limits of their autonomy.

During the sixteenth century, the *akçe* was the leading unit of account in Wallachia but not in Moldavia. Evidence from coin hoards indicates that *akçe*s minted in the Balkans and Istanbul circulated widely in both principalities during the sixteenth century, much more so than in the Ottoman provinces of Hungary. *Akçe*s and *sultani*s accounted for more than 86 percent of the value of all coins found in Wallachia until the 1580s, but only for 38 percent during the remaining two decades of the sixteenth century. The corresponding percentages for Moldavia were 26 percent and 7 percent, respectively. In both cases, the balance was made up primarily by Hungarian coins in the earlier period and increasingly by the large silver coins from Central and Western Europe. In addition, Polish silver coins, especially the half-*groat*s, were significant in Moldavia by the end of the century. Circulation of gold coins remained limited.[5]

A short-lived episode towards the end of the sixteenth century provides important insights into the nature of payment flows across the empire, but particularly between the Danubian principalities and Istanbul. Large volumes of Ottoman *shahi*s minted in eastern Anatolia and Iraq during the war of 1578-90 with Iran were sent to the capital city as some form of payment. These *shahi*s then ended up in the principalities during the 1580s as payments for the exports of Wallachia and Moldavia. Because the official exchange rates overvalued the *shahi*s, however, they were promptly returned to Istanbul as part of the tribute payment. Istanbul returned the favor once again, and the flows of *shahi*s between the principalities and the capital continued until they were stopped by the central government.[6]

Crimea

It has long been debated to what extent the Crimean khan was a sovereign and heir to the political traditions of the steppe and to what extent he was a vassal of the

---

[5] B. Murgescu, *Circulatia Monetara in Tarile Romane in Secolul al XVI-lea* (Bucharest, 1996), pp. 69-201; M. Maxim, "Considerations sur la Circulation Monetaire dans les pays Roumains et l'Empire Ottoman dans le seconde moitie du XVIe Siecle," *Revue des Etudes Sud-est Europeennes* 13 (1975): 407-15.

[6] M. Maxim, "O Lupta Monetara In Sec. Al XVI-Lea: Padişahi Contra Aspru," *Cercetari Numismatice* 5 (1983): 129-52; B. Murgescu, "The Shahis in Wallachia," *Revue des Etudes du Sud-est Europeennes* 32 (1994): 1-8.

Ottoman sultan. But clearly the Khanate enjoyed a unique status among the territories considered part of the Ottoman Empire. After the incorporation of Crimea into the Ottoman lands in 1478, Caffa and part of the Crimean shore simply became another Ottoman province. The rest of the peninsula, however, continued to be ruled by a hereditary family of khans who joined the Ottoman army as tributary, providing manpower during military campaigns. Although the Ottomans played a role in the choice of the khans, they usually accepted the selection made by the Crimean aristocracy.[7]

The Crimean khans continued to display one of the most important symbols of steppe sovereignty, the Cengiz seal (*tamga*). They also retained the right to maintain diplomatic relations with Muscovy and Poland, and until the end of the seventeenth century, the Khanate received tributes of varying amounts directly from Muscovy, Poland and the Danubian Principalities. The relationship between the Crimean coinage and the Ottoman monetary system was thus unique.

The Crimean khans minted their own silver coins bearing the seal of the Giray dynasty without the name of the Ottoman sultan. Yet, they were not sufficiently independent to mint their own gold coins, the ultimate symbol of sovereignty. The Ottoman gold *sultani* was never minted in Crimea either.[8] During the century following the Ottoman conquest, the khans discontinued the use of terms such as "sultan" and various earlier expressions of sovereignty and displayed only their names on coins, but they resumed the use of "sultan" and "khan" in the second half of the sixteenth century.[9] The Crimean coinage remained only loosely related to the Ottoman monetary system even though Crimea was considered part of the Ottoman Empire in some senses of the term. Like the Crimean Khanate, the principalities of Wallachia and Moldavia were also autonomous in their internal affairs, and they, too, did not issue gold coins, Ottoman or otherwise. Crimean autonomy in monetary affairs was greater, however, as the khans issued silver and copper coinage with their own name but the principalities did not.

The first known silver coin minted by the Crimean khans as far back as 1441-42, the basic coin and the leading unit of account in Crimea during the Ottoman period was still the small silver *akçe*. Ottoman sources called it *Kefevi akçe* (the *akçe* of Caffa) although *akçe*s were also minted elsewhere in Crimea, most notably in Eski Kırım, Kırım (Solgat) and Kırk Yer. The *Kefevi akçe* was widely used in commercial transactions. Court documents from Bursa in the 1480s, for example, cite commercial transactions and debt in *Kefevi akçe*s, two of which equaled one Ottoman *akçe*.[10] During the sixteenth century, the *Kefevi akçe* was smaller in

---

[7] A.W. Fisher, *The Crimean Tatars* (Stanford, 1978), pp. 1-36; and H. İnalcık, "Yeni vesikalara göre Kırım Hanlığı'nın Osmanlı tabiliğine girmesi ve ahidname meselesi," *Belleten* 31 (1944): 185-229.

[8] Fisher, pp. 8-19.

[9] N. Agat, "Kırım hanlarının paralarının nitelikleri ve ışık tuttukları bazı tarihi gerçekler," reprints of three earlier articles, *The Turkish Numismatic Society Bülten* 7 (1982); 14-5.

[10] H. İnalcık, *The History of The Black Sea Trade: The Register of Customs of Caffa* (Cambridge, 1993), p. 151.

weight than the Ottoman *akçe*. Its official exchange rate against the *akçe* varied considerably, from two to five and as low as eleven for one, indicating increasing alloy and declining silver content. During the seventeenth century, however, the Crimean silver coinage fared better than the Ottoman *akçe* and its exchange rate against the *osmani* rose.

The small *akçe* remained the basic coin of the Khanate until 1774, bearing the name of the Crimean khan. Copper coins, in denominations of one *akçe* and its fractions, were also minted for daily use. Larger coins such as the six-*akçe* piece were minted in later periods but could not meet the demands of trade and the economy. The fact that the Khanate did not issue gold coinage is fully consistent with its less-than-independent status during the Ottoman period. In the absence of gold, however, domestic silver and copper coinage could not meet the demands of the economy and trade. As a result, large European silver coins such as the Polish *zloty*, the internationally more prominent Spanish eight-*real* piece and the Dutch *thaler*, circulated widely there during the seventeenth century.[11]

While the politically unique status and autonomy of the Crimean Khanate continued until the 1770s, Russian pressure on it grew steadily with the Ottoman military defeats of the eighteenth century.[12] The status of the Khanate changed in 1774 from autonomy within the empire to full independence, and it was annexed by Russia nine years later.[13] The special status of Crimea vis-à-vis the Ottoman monetary system, autonomous but not free of influence from Istanbul, also ended in 1774. The change in Crimean coinage and monetary practices during the nine-year period of independence consequently reveal much about the nature and symbolism of practices during the period of autonomy. In the early 1780s, Şahin Giray, the last of the Crimean khans, began to mint in Caffa large gold coins bearing his name, the first for any Crimean ruler.[14]

Conclusion

During the sixteenth century there emerged inside the Ottoman Empire different zones with varying degrees of administrative control. At the core were the areas most closely administered by the capital with institutions most closely resembling those in the Istanbul region. With increasing distance from the capital, institutions and administrative practices reflected the power balances between the capital and the local structures and forces in the provinces. In this context, the Ottomans approached the task of establishing and operating a monetary system across the large empire with a large degree of pragmatism and flexibility. They unified gold coinage at the existing international standards but allowed the creation of multiple currency zones in silver according to the sharply different commercial relations and needs of the different provinces. By the first quarter of the sixteenth

[11] Agat, pp. 18-28.
[12] For the status of the Khanate vis-à-vis Istanbul, see Fisher, pp. 1-36.
[13] Ibid., pp. 58-69.
[14] Agat, p. 36.

century, there had resulted three distinct levels – gold, silver and copper – in the Ottoman monetary system, each characterized by a different economic function and a different type of coin.

In the European territories of the empire the Ottomans issued both the gold *sultani* and the silver *akçe* in the large numbers of mints they operated in the core areas of the Balkans. On the other hand, even though Hungary was governed directly by the Ottoman authorities, neither gold nor silver coins were minted there during the Ottoman period. Ottoman gold and silver coins were also not minted in the autonomous Danubian principalities of Wallachia and Moldavia. The Danubian Principalities did not issue their own coinage either. In contrast, the Crimean Khanate was able to issue its own silver coinage, but no gold coinage was minted there for either the khans or the Ottoman sultans, suggesting that Crimean autonomy in monetary affairs was greater than that experienced by the Danubian Principalities.

This survey of Ottoman monetary practices in both the core and frontier regions of Europe further indicates that while the Ottomans paid attention to the fiscal and economic needs of each territory, they were quite careful about the political symbolism of their actions. They followed specific rules regarding the types of Ottoman coins that could be minted in territories with certain administrative and political status. The issue of Ottoman gold or silver coinage in a given territory depended upon whether the territory was part of the empire proper or was considered a province with some degree of autonomy. One can only hope that scholars will continue to approach this problem from a comparative framework and establish with greater certainty the economic and administrative, as well as symbolic, reasons behind the differences in Ottoman monetary practices in these territories.

IV

The evolution of financial institutions in the Ottoman Empire, 1600–1914

In recent decades institutions and institutional change have been identified by economists and economic historians as key variables that help explain the widely disparate economic performance of different societies over the last five hundred years. Based on the successful experience of Western Europe and European offshoots, new institutional economics has argued that long-run economic change is the cumulative consequence of innumerable short-run decisions by political and economic agents that both directly and indirectly shape performance. Economic growth is attained because the underlying framework persistently reinforced incentives for organisations to engage in productive activity. The state is seen as a major player in this context. In the Western European case, as the result of political struggles and alliances, the state and associated institutions moved to provide the appropriate legal framework and incentives.

Institutional economics and economic historians have come to recognise, however, that a society rarely arrives at or creates institutions that are wholly conducive to economic growth. In many cases, institutions have favoured activities that promote redistributive rather than productive activity, that restrict opportunities rather than expand them. Similarly, rather than reinforcing incentives towards productive activity, in most cases states acted as instruments for transferring resources from one group to another, or promoting their own survival at the expense of others. In short, the process of institutional change has not always been favourable to economic growth. Politics and political struggles have played an important role in these unfavourable or less successful outcomes as well.[2]

[1] Earlier versions of this paper were presented at the University of Venice Summer School in Financial History and the Research Division of the Bank of Italy at Rome. I would like to thank Patrick O'Brien, the participants of those meetings, and an anonymous referee of this journal for many helpful comments.

[2] Douglass C. North and Robert P. Thomas, *The Rise of the Western World: a New Economic History* (Cambridge, 1973); Douglass C. North, *Institutions, Institutional Change and Economic Performance* (Cambridge, 1990); Thrain Eggertsson, *Economic Behavior and Institutions* (Cambridge, 1990); more recently, Daron Acemoglu, Simon Johnson and James Robinson, 'The rise of Europe: Atlantic trade, institutional change and economic growth', unpublished manuscript, 2002.

Focusing on the 'rise of the West', institutional economics and economic historians have paid less attention to studying these unsuccessful or less successful cases of institutional change, especially those outside the Western European context. In this study we are interested in examining institutional change of a different type. We will not argue that Ottoman institutions changed before the nineteenth century and came to resemble those that gave rise to capitalism. We will argue, instead, that Ottoman society and Ottoman bureaucracy brought about institutional change in selective areas, in monetary institutions and in public finance, for example, and that such selective institutional change enabled the Ottomans to maintain their rule and the empire over a very considerable period.

The Ottoman Empire stood at the crossroads of intercontinental trade, stretching from the Balkans and the Black Sea region through Anatolia, Syria, Mesopotamia and the Gulf to Egypt and most of the North African coast, for six centuries until World War I. For most of the seventeenth and eighteenth centuries, its population exceeded 30 million (of which the European provinces accounted for half or more; Anatolia and Istanbul for 7 to 8 million, other Asian and North African provinces for another 7 to 8 million) but declined thereafter due to territorial losses.

For most of its six-century existence, the Ottoman Empire is best characterised as a bureaucratic and agrarian empire. The economic institutions and policies of this entity were shaped to a large degree by the priorities and interests of a central bureaucracy. Until recently, Ottoman historiography had depicted an empire in decline after the sixteenth century. In contrast, we will argue that the Ottoman state and society showed considerable ability to reorganise as a way of adapting to changing circumstances in Eurasia from the seventeenth century to the nineteenth century. The central bureaucracy managed to contain the many challenges it faced with its pragmatism and habit of negotiation to co-opt and incorporate into the state the social groups that rebelled against it. These traits enabled the Ottomans to retain power and survive until the modern era, while many of their contemporaries in both Europe and Asia were unable to do so.

The Ottoman state also showed considerable flexibility to adapt not only its military technology but also its fiscal, financial and monetary institutions in response to the changing circumstances. By pragmatism and flexibility we refer here to the willingness of the Ottoman bureaucracy not to be bound in its actions and in the institutions it adopted by specific and rigid rules based on custom, traditions, religion, past behaviour or past enmities.

The Ottomans showed traits of pragmatism and flexibility from the earliest period. Emerging in a highly heterogeneous region populated by Christians and Muslims, Turkish and Greek speakers, the Ottomans' success in western Anatolia and later in the Balkans during the fourteenth and fifteenth centuries owed much to their willingness and ability to adapt to changing conditions, to utilise talent and accept allegiance from many sources, and to make many-sided appeals for support. They were thus able to attract many followers, not only as warriors fighting against the Christians, but also Muslims and Christians fighting for the riches to be gained, the positions and power to be won. The Ottomans also displayed remarkable openness to technological innovation in adapting firearms on a greater scale, more effectively and earlier than the neighbouring states. Similarly, they exhibited a considerable degree of flexibility and pragmatism while expanding the territories under their control. They were prepared to negotiate for the loyalty of local elites whenever the new state was unable to impose full control. They also proved to be quite adept at learning about and borrowing institutions from others. In short, the early Ottoman enterprise was not a religious state in the making, but rather a pragmatic one.[3]

In this article, we will examine the long-term changes in Ottoman fiscal, monetary and financial institutions from this perspective of pragmatism, flexibility and adaptiveness. While such a perspective may provide key insights towards understanding the longevity of the empire, the limitations of this pragmatism need to be equally emphasised. Institutional change did not apply equally to all areas of Ottoman economic life. Moreover, not all types of institutions were affected to the same degree by those changes. Because the central bureaucracy was able to retain its leading position in Ottoman society and politics, the influence of various social groups, not only of landowners but also of merchants, manufacturers and money-changers, over economic matters, and more generally over the policies of the central government, remained limited until the end of the empire. As a result, most of the pragmatism and flexibility were utilised for the defence of the traditional order and its own position in that order. In contrast, institutional changes that threatened the leading position of the central bureaucracy were resisted more forcefully than others. Institutional change thus remained selective and many of the key institutions of the traditional order such as state ownership of land, urban guilds and restrictions on private capital accumulation remained intact until the nineteenth century. These important limitations of Ottoman flexibility, pragmatism and adaptiveness should help provide a more balanced picture regarding not only the ability of the empire to survive through the early modern era but also its disintegration during the nineteenth century, despite the acceleration of institutional changes.

II

For a long time it has been assumed that the use of money in the Balkans and Anatolia was limited to long-distance trade and parts of the urban sector.[4] Recent research has shown, however, that the urban population and some segments of the countryside were already part of the monetary economy by the end of the fifteenth

[3] C. Kafadar, *Between Two Worlds: the Construction of the Ottoman State* (Berkeley, 1995); H. W. Lowry, *The Nature of the Early Ottoman State* (Albany, 2003); and D. Quatert, *The Ottoman Empire, 1700–1922* (Cambridge, 2000), pp. 13–36.

[4] F. Braudel, *Civilization and Capitalism, 15th–18th Century*, vol. III: *The Perspective of the World* (New York, 1984), pp. 471–3.

century. Even more significantly, there occurred a substantial increase in the use of money during the sixteenth century, both because of the increased availability of specie and increasing commercialisation of the rural economy. The evidence for this important development comes from a number of sources. First, recent research has suggested that population growth and urbanisation during the sixteenth century were accompanied by the growth of economic linkages between the urban and rural areas. As a result, there emerged in the Balkans and Anatolia an intensive pattern of periodic markets and market fairs where peasants and larger landholders sold parts of their produce to urban residents. These markets also provided an important opportunity for the nomads to come into contact with both peasants and the urban population. Large sectors of the rural population came to use coinage, especially the small denominations of silver *akçe* and the copper of pilgrims through their participation in these markets.[5]

The annual pilgrimage to Mecca also gave rise to monetisation. A good deal has been written about the importance of Champagne fairs for European economic history. Available evidence indicates that these fairs were dwarfed by the numerous fairs along the pilgrimage routes and particularly by those around Mecca. The Ottoman government ensured the safety of these routes and tried to facilitate the monetary transactions of pilgrim merchants from different corners of Eurasia. The pilgrimage to Mecca also gave rise every year to one of the largest payments and specie flows within the Ottoman Empire. The financing of the caravans including provisioning, payments to tribal leaders *en route* for security and funds carried by tens of thousands of pilgrims – in some years close to 100,000 pilgrims – gave rise to large flows of gold and silver from Egypt, Syria and Anatolia to the Hijaz every year. Even more importantly, the governments in Istanbul and Egypt and the various official, semi-official and private foundations sent large sums every year to support the Holy Cities. In addition, the annual revenues of many small and large pious foundations in Anatolia and some of the largest foundations in Egypt were set aside for the Hijaz. Total remittances by the foundations roughly equalled the amounts sent by the governments in Istanbul and Cairo. From Egypt, some of these net revenues were sent in kind, as cereals. Faroqhi thus estimates that a total of 300,000 to 400,000 *sultanis* or ducats were sent to the Hijaz every year from Istanbul, Anatolia and Egypt combined, in addition to the payments and specie flows arising from the pilgrimage caravans themselves. The funds in cash were sent in gold whenever available, because gold was the preferred specie in the Hijaz.[6]

It has often been assumed that the prohibition of interest in Islam prevented the development of credit, or, at best, imposed rigid obstacles in its way. Similarly, the

[5] S. Faroqhi, 'The early history of Balkan fairs', *Südost-Forschungen*, 37 (1978); S. Faroqhi, 'Sixteenth century periodic markets in various Anatolian sancaks', *Journal of the Economic and Social History of the Orient*, 22 (1979).

[6] Suraiya Faroqhi, *Pilgrims and Sultans: the Hajj under the Ottomans 1517–1683* (London and New York, 1994), pp. 74–91, 158–68.

apparent absence of deposit banking and lending by banks has led many observers to conclude that financial institutions and instruments were, by and large, absent in Islamic societies. It is true that a religiously inspired prohibition against usurious transactions was a powerful feature shared around the Mediterranean during the Middle Ages, both by the Islamic world and the Christian West.[7] While the practice of *riba*, the Arabic term for usury and interest, is sharply denounced in a number of passages in the Qur'an and in all subsequent Islamic religious writings, already in the classical era, Islamic law had provided several means by which the anti-usury prohibition could be circumvented just as the same prohibitions were circumvented in Europe in the late medieval period. Various legal fictions, based primarily on the model of the 'double-sale' were, if not enthusiastically endorsed by jurists, at least not declared invalid. Thus, there did not exist an insurmountable barrier against the use of interest-bearing loans for commercial credit.

Neither the Islamic prohibitions against interest and usury nor the absence of formal banking institutions prevented the expansion of credit in Ottoman society. Utilising the Islamic court records, the late Ronald Jennings showed that dense networks of lenders and borrowers flourished in and around the Anatolian cities of Kayseri, Karaman, Amasya and Trabzon during the sixteenth century. Over a twenty-year period which his study covered, he found literally thousands of court cases involving debts. Many members of each family and many women are registered in these records as borrowing and lending to other members of the family as well as to outsiders. These records leave no doubt that the use of credit was widespread among all segments of the urban and even rural society. Most lending and borrowing was on a small scale and interest was regularly charged on credit, in accordance with both Islamic and Ottoman law, with the consent and approval of the court and the *ulema*. In their dealings with the court, the participants felt no need to conceal interest or resort to tricks in order to clear legal hurdles. Annual rates of interest ranged from 10 to 20 per cent.[8]

One important provider of loans in Istanbul, the Balkans and the Anatolian urban centres were the cash *vakifs*, pious foundations established with the explicit purpose of lending their cash assets and using the interest income to fulfill their goals. These endowments began to be approved by the Ottoman courts in the early part of the fifteenth century and had become popular all over Anatolia and the Balkan provinces by the end of the sixteenth century. An interesting development that became more pronounced during the eighteenth century was the increasing allocation of the funds to the trustees of these endowments. The trustees then used the borrowed funds to lend at higher rates of interest to large-scale moneylenders (*sarraf*) at

[7] For a recent discussion of the classical Islamic views on interest, see N. A. Saleh, *Unlawful Gain and Legitimate Profit in Islamic Law: Riba, Gharar and Islamic Banking* (Cambridge, 1988), pp. 9–32.

[8] R. C. Jennings, 'Loans and credit in early 17th century Ottoman judicial records', *Journal of the Economic and Social History of the Orient*, 16 (1973).

Istanbul, who pooled these funds to finance larger ventures, most importantly, long-distance trade and tax farming.[9]

Not surprisingly, a lively debate developed during the sixteenth century within the Ottoman *ulema* regarding whether the cash *vakif* should be considered illegitimate. The cash *vakifs* were opposed by those who believed that only goods with permanent value such as real estate should constitute the assets of a pious foundation and that the cash *vakifs* contravened the Islamic prohibition of interest. The majority of the *ulema*, however, remained eminently pragmatic and the view that anything useful for the community is useful for Islam ultimately prevailed. During the heated debate, Ebusuud Efendi, the prominent, state-appointed religious leader (*Seyhulislam*) of the period, defended the practice from a purely practical point of view, arguing that abolition of interest taking would lead to the collapse of many pious foundations, a situation that would harm the Muslim community.[10]

III

Even though there did not exist an insurmountable barrier to the use of interest-bearing loans for commercial credit, this alternative was not pursued in the medieval Islamic world. Instead, numerous other commercial techniques were developed which played the same role as interest-bearing loans and thus made the use of loans unnecessary. These included a variety of business partnership forms such as *mudaraba* or commenda, credit arrangements, transfers of debt and letters of credit, all of which were sanctioned by religious theory. Long-distance trade was thus financed not by simple credit relations involving interest, but by a variety of Islamic business partnerships, the specifics of which depended on the nature of the risks and the resources provided by the different partners.

Ottoman merchants widely used the varieties of Islamic business partnerships practised in the Islamic world from the classical era.[11] The most frequently used method in the financing of long-distance trade and certain other types of business ventures was the *mudaraba* partnership of classical Islam, in which an investor entrusted his capital or merchandise to an agent who was to trade with it and then return the original amount. The profits were then shared between the principal and the agent according to some pre-determined scheme. Any loss of the capital resulting from the exigencies of travel or the business venture itself were borne exclusively by the principal. The liability of the agent was limited to his time and

[9] M. Çizakça, *A Comparative Evolution of Business Partnerships: the Islamic World and Europe with Specific Reference to the Ottoman Archive* (Leiden, 1996), pp. 131–4.

[10] J. E. Mandaville, 'Usurious piety: the cash waqf controversy in the Ottoman Empire', *International Journal of Middle East Studies*, 10 (1979).

[11] A. L. Udovitch, *Partnership and Profit* (Princeton, 1970), pp. 170–217; and Çizakça, *A Comparative Evolution*, pp. 66–76.

efforts.[12] To a lesser extent the Ottomans also used *mufawada* partnership of the Hanefi school of Islam in which the partners were considered equals in terms of capital, effort, returns and liabilities. In the related *musharaka* or *inan* arrangement, the partners were free to invest different amounts and agree to share the returns and liabilities in unequal but prearranged amounts.

Evidence from Islamic court records on commercial disputes and their resolution until the middle of the nineteenth century indicates that in Anatolia and Istanbul, at least, the Ottoman jurists were well informed about the teachings of medieval Muslim jurists and, in general, adhered closely to the classical Islamic principles in disputes arising from these partnerships. There were some innovations over the centuries; for example, some interesting combinations of *mudaraba* and putting-out activities were developed. On the whole, however, evidence from hundreds of business partnerships indicates that classical Islamic partnership forms not only survived but were applied, with minor exceptions, true to their original forms until the nineteenth century. Çizakça suggests that the continued dominance of small-scale firms or partnerships was probably the most important reason for the limited changes in this area.[13]

One important instrument in the finance of long-distance trade was the *suftaja*, a bill of exchange or letter of credit. The basic purpose of the *suftajas* was to expedite long-distance payments or transfer of funds. In Europe the bill of exchange entailed the initial payment of one type of currency in return for the payment of another type of currency at a different location. In the Geniza documents of medieval Egypt the *suftajas* consistently appeared as involving the repayment of exactly the same type of money to the issuing banker. They were as good as money; the bearer could fully expect to redeem his *suftaja* for cash immediately upon arrival at his destination. The prompt payment was further assured by the government through the imposition of stiff penalties for any delays. *Suftajas* were used widely inside the Ottoman Empire between Anatolia, the Aegean islands, Crimea, Syria, Egypt and also with Iran. Ottoman court documents from fifteenth- and sixteenth-century Bursa, a major centre in long-distance trade, point to the high frequency of the use of *suftajas*. The local judges (*kadis*) were actively involved in the enforcement of the *suftajas* in their various forms.[14] Another type of letter of credit was the *hawala* which was the

[12] In essence, this was identical to the commenda of Europe. For discussions of the Islamic origins of European commenda, see A. L. Udovitch, 'At the origins of the Western commenda: Islam, Israel, Byzantium', *Speculum*, 37 (1962); and E. Ashtor, 'Banking instruments between the Muslim east and the Christian west', *Journal of European Economic History*, 1 (1972) and Çizakça, *A Comparative Evolution*, pp. 10–32.

[13] Çizakça, *A Comparative Evolution*, pp. 65–85 and 126–31; also M. Çizakça, 'Financing silk trade in the Ottoman Empire: 16th–18th centuries', in Simonett Cavaciocchi (ed.), *La seta in Europa secc. XIII–XX* (Prato, 1993), pp. 711–23.

[14] Udovitch, *Partnership and Profit*, pp. 268–9; Ashtor, 'Banking instruments', pp. 554–62; and H. Sahillioğlu, 'Bursa kadı sicillerinde iç ve dış ödemeler aracı olarak "Kitabü'l-Kadı" ve "Süftece"ler', in O. Okyar and H. Ü. Nalbandoğlu (eds.), *Türkiye İktisat Tarihi Semineri* (Ankara, 1975).

assignation of a fund from a distant source of revenue by a written order. It was used in both state and private transactions to avoid the dangers and delays involved in the transportation of cash.[15]

IV

In the Ottoman monetary system, there existed three levels of coinage: gold, silver and copper. The silver *akçe* until the middle of the seventeenth century and the silver *kurush* (from groschen/piaster) in the eighteenth century were the basic units of account and the leading means of payment in local transactions. The silver content of these units of account changed with the occasional debasements by the government. In contrast, the standards of the gold coins usually remained identical to those of the Venetian ducat and the gold coins of most other states around the Mediterranean. The exchange rate of gold coins, expressed in silver *kurush* and in terms of foreign coins, was determined by the markets, subject to the changes in the silver content of the *kurush*, fluctuations in the gold-silver ratio and a host of other factors. The state encouraged the circulation of gold and silver as well as foreign coinage. The government did not adhere to a legally fixed rate of exchange between the gold and silver coins or a fixed gold-silver ratio around which the face value or the standards of both types of coins would be determined.[16]

This monetary regime might loosely be called bimetallic, since both gold and silver coins were minted and circulated freely. One should be careful, however, about the use of this term and distinguish it from classical bimetallism as practised during the nineteenth century. Under the latter system, a country typically adopted both gold and silver as monetary standards. The relative amounts of the two metals necessary to create the same currency unit, known as the mint ratio or the legal ratio, was specified by the authorities. In other words, the face value of both gold and silver coins was fixed by the government.[17]

In searching for a label for the Ottoman monetary regime, it is more useful to adopt the strict definitions of monometallism and bimetallism used in the nineteenth century. According to these definitions, a monetary regime is characterised as monometallism if there is one standard commodity in terms of which the value of other commodities are measured, even if the circulation may include several metallic and paper elements. The Ottoman regime outlined above certainly fits this definition. The silver *kurush* was the basic unit of account in terms of which the value of all other commodities, including the gold and copper coins, was being measured.

The basic virtue of the Ottoman system was its flexibility. As long as the markets determined the exchange rate of the gold coins and if the official rates at which the

[15] İnalcık emphasizes the use of *hawala* in state transactions. H. İnalcık, 'Hawale', *Encyclopedia of Islam*, second edition, vol. III (Leiden and New York, 1969), pp. 283–5.

[16] S. Pamuk, *A Monetary History of the Ottoman Empire* (Cambridge, 2000), pp. 66–76.

[17] C. P. Kindleberger, *A Financial History of Western Europe*, second edition (Oxford, 1993), pp. 57–63.

government accepted these coins followed the markets closely, neither type of coin was likely to be over or undervalued. For this reason, they were not in danger of disappearing.

The Ottoman government adhered to this framework, with some exceptions, until the nineteenth century. While the practices of medieval and early modern states in Europe and the Near East varied in time and space, the majority pursued a flexible approach similar to that of the Ottomans. One of the most telling examples of Ottoman flexibility concerned the determination of exchange rates between different kinds of coinage. In an environment of frequently recurring shortages of specie, the Ottoman administrators knew that it was essential to attract into the Ottoman lands and maintain in circulation as much coinage and bullion as possible. Their monetary practices were guided more by this concern than any other. They were also aware that the ratio between gold and silver, as well as the value of different types of coins, was subject to fluctuations. Under these conditions, a policy of fixed exchange rates between different coins would have driven the good or undervalued coins out of circulation through the workings of Gresham's law. Instead, the government allowed the local markets to determine not only the exchange rates of the *sultani*, but those for all types of coins, Ottoman and foreign. Local court records show that the *kadıs* relied on these market rates to settle disputes between individuals. In addition, the government announced the official rates at which different coins, gold and silver, would be accepted as payment. Usually, these rates did not diverge significantly from the prevailing market rates for the same coins.

Government policies towards foreign coinage provides another example of flexibility. From the earliest days, the authorities encouraged the circulation of foreign coinage and accepted that as payment. The government also exempted precious metals and foreign currency from import dues. In capitulations or privileges given to merchants of certain European states, the central government exempted them from all customs duties for the foreign coinage they brought. In addition, customs and mint officials were told not to demand that these coins be surrendered to the authorities for the minting of Ottoman coinage. These privileges were eventually extended to the merchants of most European states during the sixteenth century.[18]

V

The evolution of Ottoman fiscal institutions during the eighteenth century provides another good example of the ability of the Ottoman state to contain the challenges it faced with pragmatism, flexibility and negotiation. It sought to co-opt and incorporate into a broad alliance the social groups that challenged its authority.

While loans to kings, princes and governments were part of the regular business of European banking houses in the late medieval and early modern periods, in the Islamic world advances of cash to the rulers and the public treasury were handled

[18] Pamuk, *A Monetary History of the Ottoman Empire*, pp. 63–6, 70–4.

differently. They took the form of tax-farming arrangements in which individuals possessing liquid capital assets advanced cash to the government in return for the right to farm the taxes of a given region or fiscal unit for a fixed period. Tax farming thus dominated the Islamic world from the Mediterranean to the Indian Ocean, from the earliest days through to the early modern period.

From the very beginning, the Ottomans relied on tax farming for the collection of urban taxes. Until late in the sixteenth century, however, the agricultural taxes which constituted the largest part of the tax revenues were collected locally and mostly in kind within the *timar* system. *Sipahis*, state employees who resided in rural areas, were expected to use these revenues to equip and prepare a given number of soldiers for the military campaigns. Until the second half of the sixteenth century, state finances were relatively strong, thanks to the revenues obtained through the rapid territorial expansion of the empire, and the state did not feel the need to increase the revenues collected at the centre. There are some examples, however, of the state engaging in short-term borrowing during the sixteenth century. These services earned the financiers, mostly Jews and Greeks, the inside track on some of the most lucrative tax-farming contracts.[19]

With the changes in military technology during the sixteenth century and the need to maintain larger, permanent armies at the centre, however, pressures increased to collect a larger part of the rural surplus. As a result, the *timar* system began to be abandoned in favour of tax farming and the tax units were auctioned off at Istanbul.[20] The shift away from the *timar* system had been designed to increase the cash receipts at the centre, but the decline of state power *vis-à-vis* the provinces reduced the expected benefits from this change. Bureaucrats in the capital and provincial groups began to share tax-farming revenues with the central government during the seventeenth century.

In the longer term, further deterioration of the state finances increased the pressures on the central government to take greater advantage of the tax-farming system for the purposes of domestic borrowing. The central government thus began to increase the length of the tax-farming contracts from one to three years to three to five years and even longer. In many instances, however, a tax farmer could lose his farm at any time, if a competitor offered to pay a higher amount. The government also demanded an increasingly higher fraction of the auction price of the contract in advance. Tax farming was thus converted to a form of domestic borrowing, with the actual tax revenues being used as collateral by the central government.

Further steps were taken in the same direction with the introduction, in 1695, of the *malikane* system in which the revenue source began to be farmed out on a

19 Halil Inalcik and Donald Quataert (eds.), *An Economic and Social History of the Ottoman Empire, 1300–1914* (Cambridge, 1994), pp. 212–14.

20 Linda T. Darling, *Revenue-Raising and Legitimacy: Tax Collection and Finance Administration in the Ottoman Empire, 1560–1660* (Leiden, 1996); H. İnalcık, 'Military and fiscal transformation in the Ottoman Empire, 1600–1700', *Archivum Ottomanicum*, 6 (1980).

life-time basis in return for a large initial fee to be followed by annual payments.[21] One rationale often offered for this system was that, by extending the term of the contract, the state hoped that the tax contractor would take better care of the tax source, most importantly the peasant producers, and try to achieve long-term increases in production. In fact, the *malikane* allowed the state to use tax revenues as collateral and borrow on a longer-term basis. In comparison to the straightforward tax-farming system, it represented an important shift towards longer-term borrowing by the state.

With the extension of their term and the introduction of larger advance payments, the long-term financing of these contracts assumed an even greater importance. The private financiers thus began to play an increasingly important role in the tax collection process. Behind the individual that joined the bidding in the tax-farming auctions, there often existed a partnership that included financiers as well as the agents who intended to organise the tax collection process itself, often by dividing the large initial contract into smaller pieces and finding sub-contractors. Non-Muslims were prohibited from holding most *malikane* contracts but Greeks, Armenians and Jews were very much part of this elite as financiers, brokers and accountants. These arrangements were mostly in the form of an Islamic business partnership involving both Muslims and non-Muslims.[22] Over the course of the eighteenth century, some 1,000 to 2,000 Istanbul-based individuals, together with some 5,000 to 10,000 individuals based in the provinces, as well as innumerable contractors, agents, financiers, accountants and managers controlled an important share of the state's revenues. This grand coalition of Istanbul-based elites and the rising elites in the provinces constituted a semi-privatised but interdependent component of the regime.[23] Many provincials were able to acquire and pass from one generation to the next small and medium-sized *malikane* shares on villages as long as they remained in favour with local administrators or their Istanbul sponsors. For both the well-connected individuals in the capital city and those in the provinces, getting a share of government tax revenues became an activity more lucrative than investing in agriculture, trade or manufacturing.

In the longer term, however, the *malikane* system did not fulfill the expectations of the central government. It actually led to a decline in state revenues because the state was unable to regain control of the revenue sources after the death of the individuals who had purchased them.[24] The central government thus began to experiment with other methods of tax collection and domestic borrowing as state finances came under increasing pressure from the 1770s onwards. After the end of

[21] M. Genç, 'A study of the feasibility of using eighteenth century Ottoman financial records as an indicator of economic activity', in Huri İslamoğlu-İnan (ed.), *The Ottoman Empire and the World Economy* (Cambridge, 1987).

[22] Çizakça, *A Comparative Evolution*, pp. 135–92.

[23] Ariel Salzman, 'An ancien régime revisited: "privatization" and political economy in the eighteenth century Ottoman Empire', *Politics and Society*, 21 (1993).

[24] Genç, 'A study of the feasibility', pp. 354–9.

the war of 1768–74, which had dramatically exposed the military as well as financial weaknesses of the Ottoman system, the financial bureaucracy introduced in 1774 a new and related system of long-term domestic borrowing called *esham*. In this system, the annual net revenues of a tax source were specified in nominal terms. This amount was divided into a large number of shares which were then sold to the public for the lifetime of the buyers. The annual revenues of the source continued to be collected by the tax farmers. The *esham* generally sold for six to seven times the annual net payments, which remained fixed.[25] As the linkage between the annual government payments to *esham* holders and the underlying revenues of the tax source weakened, the *esham* increasingly resembled a life-term annuity quite popular in many European countries of the period.

One motivation for the new system was to broaden the base of state borrowing and reach beyond the limited numbers of large financiers, who tended to dominate the *malikane* auctions, towards a larger pool of small and medium-sized lenders. However, the inability of the state to control or limit sales of the *esham* between individuals, and the difficulties in preventing the heirs of deceased holders from continuing to receive payments, seriously limited the fiscal benefits of this system. During the next half century, the state vacillated between abolishing the *esham* during periods of fiscal stability and expanding it when fiscal pressures mounted and additional funds had to be secured, with little regard for their long-term cost.[26]

In the early part of the nineteenth century, the centre, supported by the new technologies, was able to reassert its power over the provinces. After the central government began to undermine the power of the provincial notables in the 1820s and 1830s, many of the *malikane* contracts were pulled back to the centre and their revenues began to be collected once again by tax farmers. The *malikane* or the life-term tax-farming system was phased out in the 1840s as part of a larger package of administrative and economic reforms. With the same package of centralising reforms, the central government also attempted to eliminate short-term tax farmers. This last step failed, however, due to the administrative limitations of the central government. Short-term tax-farming continued until World War I. Nonetheless, the centralisation of the nineteenth century helped raise the central government's share of the tax revenues from about 2 to 3 per cent of the underlying economy (GDP) in the late eighteenth century to 5 to 6 per cent by the middle of the nineteenth century and to 10 to 12 per cent on the eve of World War I.[27]

The evolution of Ottoman tax collection institutions during the eighteenth century illustrates the state's ability and willingness to reorganise as a way of adapting to changing circumstances, albeit slowly and often with considerable time lags. This

[25] Yavuz Cezar, *Osmanlı Maliyesinde Bunalım ve Deiğişm Dönemi: XVIII. yy.dan Tanzimat'a Mali Tarih* (Istanbul, 1986), pp. 81–3; also M. Genç, 'Esham', *İslam Ansiklopedisi*, 11 (1995), pp. 376–80.

[26] Cezar, *Osmanlı Maliyesinde Bunalım*, pp. 128–34, 198–200.

[27] Based on series of central government budget documents and author's estimates of per capita income in the Ottoman Empire.

pragmatism and flexibility also provides important clues for understanding the longevity of the empire as well as the key position of the central bureaucracy until the end. In order to remain at the top, the central bureaucracy was thus willing to share the tax revenues with the provincial groups during the seventeenth and eighteenth centuries, until it was able to reassert itself in the nineteenth century.

This trajectory of Ottoman fiscal institutions also suggests that they were willing to borrow or adapt European customs and approaches prior to the nineteenth century. Despite growing research in this area, the causal connections between the evolution of Ottoman institutions of public finance as outlined here, and those in Europe, particularly in France during the seventeenth and eighteenth centuries, have not yet been investigated. The parallels between the two are quite striking, however. It appears that increasing economic and financial integration with Europe during the eighteenth century brought about significant changes in the institutions of public finance. In contrast, changes in the institutions of private finance during this period were limited to those employed by the Europeans and by non-Muslim subjects of the empire.

VI

From the 1770s until the 1840s the Ottoman state finances frequently experienced large budget deficits; these reached their peak during the 1820s and 1830s. In response, the state attempted to increase its control over revenue sources, made use of various forms of internal borrowing, and, when the short-term fiscal pressures mounted, resorted to debasements. The highest rates of debasement in Ottoman history took place during the reign of Sultan Mahmud II (1808–39). The timing and magnitude of these debasements suggest that the government was quite sensitive to the costs of debasements, especially the political opposition they generated amongst the janissaries and other urban groups.

Debasements had an impact on virtually all groups in Ottoman society and, in turn, each group took a position. Most men and women, both urban and rural, were clear about the consequences of different ways of dealing with the coinage, and who gained and who lost. The groups that stood to lose the most from debasements were those who were paid fixed amounts in terms of the unit of account. Most important groups in this category were the employees of the state, the bureaucracy, the *ulema* and especially the janissaries. There existed a large overlap between the guild members and the janissaries after the latter began to moonlight as artisans and shopkeepers in the seventeenth century.

Mahmud II was well aware of the constraints represented by the janissaries and related urban groups. From the very beginning of his reign, he wanted to replace the janissaries with a Western-style army. During the early years of his long reign, however, he did not have the political support to make this critical move. After the janissaries were finally defeated and the order was abolished in 1826, a major constraint in the way of debasements was lifted. Only two years later, the government began the largest debasement ever in Ottoman history, reducing the specie content of the *kurush* by 79 per cent within a period of four years.[28]

From the perspective of Ottoman economic and monetary history, the nineteenth century was a period quite different from the earlier era. On the one hand, it was characterised by major efforts at Western-style reform aimed at the centralisation of the empire, in administration, education, law and justice as well as economic, fiscal and monetary affairs. On the other hand, it was a period of integration into the world markets and rapid expansion in foreign trade, particularly with Europe. The Ottoman economy was increasingly transformed into an exporter of primary products and an importer of manufactures. The foreign trade of the areas within the 1911 borders of the empire, Macedonia, Anatolia and Syria, increased by about 15 fold between the 1820s and World War I.[29] This process was facilitated by the construction of ports and railroads and the establishment of modern banking institutions, mostly with European capital. As a result, the commercialisation of agriculture proceeded rapidly in Macedonia, western, northeastern and central Anatolia and along the Syrian coast. The rural population was drawn to markets, not only as producers of cash crops, but also as purchasers of imported goods, especially of cotton textiles. These developments substantially increased the demand for, and the use of, money, especially in these more commercialised regions.

For European governments, and especially the British who were concerned about Russian expansionism to the south, the success of Ottoman reforms was considered essential for the territorial integrity of the empire. European governments also believed that rapid expansion of commercial ties with Europe based on the principle of comparative advantage and European direct investment were essential for the development of the Ottoman economy. As a result, they began to exert considerable pressure on the Ottoman government to abandon debasements and establish a more stable monetary system. Bimetallism was proposed as a monetary regime that would bring the Ottoman Empire more in line with the prevailing international trends and help expand both trade and European investment. The European governments also linked Ottoman access to European financial markets to fiscal reform and monetary stability. They made clear that they were ready to provide the technical expertise necessary for this purpose.

Monetary conditions in the Ottoman Empire had assumed crisis proportions by the end of the 1830s. While the government had succeeded in raising short-term revenue from frequent debasements, the resulting inflation created political problems. The production of a large variety of coins since the beginning of the century and the inability of the government to retire the earlier series from circulation had added to the difficulties. These conditions created difficulties both for daily

[28] Pamuk, *A Monetary History of the Ottoman Empire*, pp. 193–200.

[29] C. Issawi, *The Economic History of Turkey, 1800–1914* (Chicago,1980), chapter 3; and S. Pamuk, *The Ottoman Empire and European Capitalism, 1820–1913: Trade, Investment and Production* (Cambridge, 1987), chapter 1.

transactions and international trade. At the same time, the appeal and use of European coinage had increased especially in international trade and for store of wealth purposes. Under domestic and international pressure, the Ottoman government thus abandoned debasements and embraced bimetallism and stable coinage in 1844. It was hoped that this move would achieve greater price stability and help expand both trade and capital flows between Europe and the Ottoman Empire. The adoption of bimetallism did not mean the end of Ottoman monetary difficulties, however. The expansion of the empire's internal tax base by the commercialisation of peasant agriculture, the extension of cultivation on to unused lands and the development of other forms of primary production such as mining, proceeded only slowly. Moreover, a large fraction of the revenues collected from peasant producers continued to remain in the hands of tax collectors. At the same time, military expenditures continued to mount. Ottoman governments had difficulties balancing the budget and resorted to a variety of methods, both short and long term, to deal with the fiscal problems.

VII

The *sarrafs* of Istanbul were active in the financing of trade and in the guilds during the seventeenth century. In general, they were free to lend with interest. In the closing years of the century, they organised around a guild and began to move their businesses to Galata, a suburb of Istanbul outside the old city walls and across the Golden Horn.[30] While the Jews were not as prominent in moneylending and trade as they had been in the sixteenth century, Greeks and especially the Armenians, often in partnerships of two, emerged as the leading *sarrafs* of the capital city. The Greek financiers often took advantage of the prominence of Greek merchants in maritime trade in the Black Sea and the Balkans to specialise in the financing of international trade.[31] Similarly, the links of the Armenian *sarrafs* to the European commercial and financial networks through the Armenian communities there played an important role in their rise. They also remained well connected to the Ottoman bureaucracy. After Greek independence, the Armenians began to assume even more prominent positions. The leading Armenian *sarrafs* also assumed leading positions within the Armenian community (*millet*) in the Ottoman Empire, often mediating between the community and Ottoman officialdom.[32] In addition, many

[30] The guild of *sarrafs* had a membership of 72 around 1750 and 89 in 1835; A. Şahiner, 'The sarrafs of Istanbul: financiers of the empire', MA dissertation, Boğaziçi University, Department of History (1995), pp. 78–83.

[31] T. Stoianovich, 'The conquering Balkan Orthodox merchant', *The Journal of Economic History*, 20 (1960).

[32] Şahiner, 'The sarrafs of Istanbul', pp. 87–99; O. Jamgocyan, 'Les finances de l'Empire Ottoman et les financiers de Constantinople, 1732–1853', unpublished PhD dissertation, Université de Paris I, Panthéon-Sorbonne (1988), traces the lives and financial affairs of the leading Ottoman *sarrafs* through their correspondence with their European associates, by utilising the European archives.

financiers operated in the provinces, financing trade and the tax collection process just like their counterparts in the capital city.[33]

The Ottoman state had relied on the financiers in the capital for short-term loans and the financing of the tax collection process ever since the sixteenth century. After the shift from short-term tax farming to the long-term *malikane* system, the financing of the large advance payments had assumed even greater importance. The rise of the moneychangers (*sarrafs*) to prominence during the eighteenth century, and their transformation into large financiers known as the Galata bankers during the first half of the nineteenth century, was thus closely related to the financial difficulties of the state and its needs for short- and long-term finance.

On the face of it, the *malikanes* remained almost exclusively in the hands of the Ottoman *askeri* or state class, including palace women. Other social groups were usually not allowed to participate in the auctions. In many instances, however, the *malikanecis* who won the auctions were not involved in the day-to-day operations of the *malikane* after the initial auction. Behind them were often the financiers who loaned the money for the advance payment, arranged the sub-contracting of the tax farm and made the annual payments (*mal*) to the treasury. The net proceeds were then divided between the state, the *malikaneci*, the sub-contractors and the *sarraf*. The original purchasers of the *malikanes* thus turned into absentee owners of the tax farms. Murat Çizakça estimates that the central government received only about one-third of the net or about a quarter of the gross tax receipts under this system.[34]

During the course of the eighteenth century, these absentee purchasers of the *malikanes* began to develop portfolios of *malikane* shares rather than investing their capital in a single tax farm. Investors maintaining shares in as many as 20 to 30 tax farms were frequently observed, although each of them possessed sufficient capital to buy one or more tax farms in their entirety. The motive for this behaviour was risk minimisation through portfolio diversification.[35]

The state needed and encouraged the activities of the *sarrafs*. The growing fiscal difficulties after the 1760s raised their importance as direct lenders. In addition, their connections with the European financial groups enabled them to begin organising in Europe short-term loans to the Ottoman state. Many *sarrafs* also acted as personal financiers to the sultans and many of the leading Ottoman bureaucrats. In the aftermath of the French Revolution, these financiers were also able to replace the European merchants in Istanbul and assume control of important parts of the trade in bills of exchange.[36] From traditional moneylenders and brokers, the sarrafs of Istanbul thus developed into large-scale financiers with well-established international

33 Genç, 'A study of the feasibility', pp. 347–54; and Çizakça, *A Comparative Evolution*, pp. 169–78.

34 Çizakça, *A Comparative Evolution*, pp. 165–6; also Salzman, 'An ancien régime revisited', pp. 393–423.

35 Çizakça, *A Comparative Evolution*, pp. 172–6.

36 E. Eldem, 'La circulation de la lettre de change entre la France et Constantinople au XVIIIe siècle', in H. Batu and J. L. Bacque-Gremmont (eds.), *L'Empire Ottoman, la république de Turquie et la France* (Istanbul, 1986), pp. 87–97.

connections, forming the embryo of a financial bourgeoisie in Istanbul. In the process they began to be referred to as the Galata bankers, although they did not establish banks until the 1840s.[37]

The leading Armenian members of the guild of *sarrafs* often rose to positions of prominence in the empire, such as master of the imperial mint, during this period. This was at once a powerful and a dangerous position, however. While they were able to assume positions of power and leadership in both the bureaucracy and the Armenian community, many of these *sarrafs* eventually lost their lives, their wealth was confiscated and their families sent into exile after being held responsible for financial or monetary problems such as debasements or the poor quality of coinage. Others lost their offices and even their lives after being accused of enrichment during their public careers.

The Armenian Düzoğlu family originally controlled some of the foreign trade and manufacturing related tax farms. The management of the imperial mint was given to a member of this family during the reign of Mustafa III (1757–74). Family members retained control of the day-to-day activities of the mint until the 1820s. Their ability to mobilise credit for the state both domestically and abroad was a key reason for the continuation of their appointments to the imperial mint during this difficult period. It is thus clear that thanks to the skills and connections of the Armenian *sarrafs*, the responsibilities of the head of the Istanbul mint went beyond the supply of coinage, to include critical areas of state finances.

Artin Kazaz, who was born into a modest family in eastern Anatolia, took over the imperial mint in the 1820s, upon the dismissal of the last member of the Düzoğlu family. He soon emerged as the key advisor to the sultan in economic affairs and was instrumental in eliminating food shortages in Istanbul during and after the Russian war of 1828–9, by advising the sultan to lift the price ceilings (*narh*). Kazaz also used his connections to obtain short- and medium-term loans for the Ottoman government from private financiers in Europe. At the end of the Russian war, the Ottoman government had agreed to pay the large sum of 400 million *kurush* as reparations.[38] Even though the original amount was subsequently reduced after territorial concessions by the Ottomans and the tsar had decided not to press for the first payment, the Ottoman government was experiencing difficulties in putting together the second instalment. It was at this critical juncture that Kazaz, along with other financiers, succeeded in obtaining short-term loans from Europe.[39] When he died in 1834,

[37] A. Udovitch has referred to the financiers in the medieval Islamic world as 'bankers without banks'. This apt term also characterises the position of the Galata bankers before the 1840s. A. Udovitch, 'Bankers without banks: commerce, banking and society in the Islamic world of the Middle Ages', *Princeton Near East Papers*, No. 30 (Princeton, 1981).

[38] Stanford J. Shaw and Ezel Kuran Shaw, *History of the Ottoman Empire and Modern Turkey*, vol. 11, *1808–1975* (Cambridge, 1977), p. 32. Annual revenues of the central government were close to 200 million *kurush* at that time.

[39] Haydar Kazgan, 'İkinci Sultan Mahmut Devrinde Enflasyon ve Darphane Amiri Kazaz Artin', *Toplum ve Bilim*, 11 (1980), pp. 122–5.

the sultan ordered a special funeral ceremony for the man who had provided indispensable services to the state at a very critical juncture.[40]

The growing influence of the *sarrafs* in trade and finance did not go unopposed, however. The growth of imports from Europe in the early part of the nineteenth century created enormous pressures for the declining guilds of the capital city. In addition, the debasements often associated with the Armenian masters of the imperial mint dealt serious blows to the guild membership and the janissaries. Since the seventeenth century, the overlap between the two groups had increased substantially as the soldiers began to rely increasingly on their second jobs to supplement their dwindling military pay. The rising tensions and occasional confrontations between these two groups and the financiers continued until the abolition of the janissaries in 1826.[41]

By the 1840s the ranks of the Galata bankers had expanded considerably to include more Jews and Levantines, Europeans who had settled in the eastern Mediterranean, as well as Greeks and Armenians. The abilities and connections of the Baltazzi, Camondo, Coronio, Eugenides, Mavrocordato, Mısırlıoğlu, Ralli, Zarifi and many other families to organise in Europe short-term loans for the Ottoman state had also grown substantially. In 1847, with the financial support of the government, Th. Baltazzi, from a prominent family of financiers, and J. Alleon, a member of a French banking family that had settled in Turkey during the French Revolution, finally founded Banque de Constantinople, the first bank of the Galata bankers.[42]

The financial power of the Galata bankers reached its peak around mid-century. In the meantime, however, the borrowing needs of the Ottoman state had expanded even faster. As a result, when the Ottoman government decided to turn directly to the European financial markets for its long-term borrowing needs, the Galata bankers began to feel the pressure of the more powerful European banks and bankers who began to open branches or establish banks of their own in the capital city as well as the provinces. The establishment, in 1863, by British and French capital of the Imperial Ottoman Bank, which would act a quasi-central bank for the empire in addition to its commercial operations, further consolidated the position of European capital in the Ottoman financial markets.

Even though they lost their unrivalled position, the Galata bankers were not easily pushed out of state lending or private finance. They entered alliances with European financial groups and opened new banks for lending to the Ottoman government, which continued to rely on them for short-term borrowing in between major bond

[40] Kazgan, 'İkinci Sultan Mahmut devrinde enflasyon', p. 119.

[41] H. Kazgan, *Osmanlıda Avrupa Finans Kapitali* (Istanbul, 1995), pp. 17–19.

[42] Hasan Ferid, *Nakid ve İtibar-ı Mali, 3. Kitab: Bankacılık* (Istanbul: Matbaa-i Amire, H.1334/1918), pp. 26–66; Kazgan, *Osmanlıda Avrupa Finans Kapitali*, p. 20; H. Kazgan, *Osmanlıdan Cumhuriyete Türk Bankacılık Tarihi* (Istanbul,1997), pp. 25–32; and İ. Tekeli and S. İlkin, *Türkiye Cumhuriyeti Merkez Bankası* (Ankara,1997), pp. 53–4.

issues in the European financial markets. During the crisis of 1875–81, when the Ottoman government declared a moratorium on debt payments and faced a costly war against Russia in both the Balkans and eastern Anatolia, the Ottoman Bank and the European financial markets refused to make new loans. The government then turned to the Galata bankers for the duration of the crisis. It is interesting that the Galata bankers, all of them Ottoman citizens, adopted a variety of patriotic Ottomanist themes to mobilise support for their centuries-old customer during this difficult period.[43]

VIII

One method of raising fiscal revenue which began to be used in 1840 was the printing and circulation in the Istanbul area of interest-bearing paper money called *kaime*. Since their volume remained limited, the *kaimes* performed reasonably well until 1852. A new phase in the history of the *kaime* began in 1852 when paper money that did not bear any interest was put into circulation for the first time. During the Crimean War large amounts of *kaimes* were printed and the market price expressed in gold liras declined to less than half the nominal value. One gold lira began to exchange for 200–220 *kurush* in *kaimes*. In 1861 a record volume of *kaimes* flooded the markets and the exchange rate against the gold lira plummeted to 400 paper *kurush*. The first experiment in paper money thus resulted, more than a decade after its initiation, in a major wave of inflation. With popular protests and general discontent, the government finally agreed to retire the *kaime* in 1862 with the help of short-term loans obtained from the Imperial Ottoman Bank.[44]

There was one other occasion prior to World War I in which the government resorted to non-convertible paper money. After the Ottoman government declared a moratorium on external debt payments in 1876, it became impossible to borrow from the European financial markets or the Imperial Ottoman Bank. With the Serbian uprising and the outbreak of war with Russia in 1877, the need to raise fiscal revenue became even more urgent. *Kaimes* were issued in both small and large denominations, and were proclaimed legal tender in all parts of the empire. Because of the large volume, however, the exchange rate of the *kaime* declined within two years to 450 *kurush* for the gold lira. They remained in circulation for almost three years and were retired at the end of the decade.[45]

In 1854, during the Crimean War, the Ottoman government began to sell long-term bonds in the European financial markets and this soon became the most

[43] Kazgan, *Osmanlıda Avrupa Finans Kapitali*, pp. 120–2; Tekeli and İlkin, *Merkez Bankası*, pp. 62–9.

[44] Ali Akyıldız, *Osmanlı Finans Sisteminde Dönüm Noktası: Kağıt Para ve Sosyo-Ekonomik Etkileri* (Istanbul, 1995), pp. 50–90; Roderic Davison, 'The first Ottoman experiment with paper money', in Osman Okyar and Halil İnalcık (eds.), *Social and Economic History of Turkey (1071–1920), Papers Presented to the First International Congress on the Social and Economic History of Turkey* (Ankara, 1980); M. Erol, *Osmanlı İmparatorluğu'nda Kağıt Para (Kaime)* (Ankara, 1970), pp. 5–7.

[45] Akyıldız, *Kağıt Para*, pp. 91–174; Erol, *Osmanlı İmparatorluğu'nda*, pp. 15–27.

important means of dealing with the recurring budgetary difficulties. In the early stages of this process, the Ottoman government was supported by its British counterpart and wartime ally, which guaranteed the first bond issue against the Ottoman annual receipts from the Egyptian tribute. In the following two decades, the Ottoman government borrowed large sums in London, Paris, Vienna and elsewhere under increasingly unfavourable terms. The net proceeds of these issues were directed almost entirely towards current expenditures, however. Only a small fraction was spent on infrastructure investment and on increasing the capacity to pay back. By the second half of the 1860s, Ottoman finances had deteriorated to the point where new bond issues had become necessary to maintain the debt payments. A moratorium was in sight but the financial markets kept the process going, lured by the unusually high rates of return.[46]

After the financial crises of 1873 led to the cessation of overseas lending by the European financial markets, the government was forced to declare in 1875–6 a moratorium on its outstanding debt, which stood at more than 200 million pounds sterling. After protracted negotiations, the Ottoman Public Debt Administration (OPDA) was established in 1881 to exercise European control over parts of Ottoman finances and ensure orderly payments on the outstanding debt, whose nominal value was reduced by approximately half during the negotiations.

In the same negotiations for debt resettlement, the nature of the new Ottoman monetary regime was also discussed. Following the lead of many European states during the 1870s, and under pressure from European interests, especially those of the creditors as represented by the OPDA and the Imperial Ottoman Bank, the Ottoman government moved away from the bimetallic system in 1881. The link between silver and gold was severed and gold was accepted as the standard for Ottoman currency. The government also decided to limit the supply of silver coinage. At the same time, however, the economy continued to rely heavily on silver for most daily transactions. The government did not have the reserves and financial strength to redeem the existing silver stock and move to a fully fledged gold standard. Receiving primary support from gold and partial support from silver, the Ottoman currency system thus became another example of the 'limping' standard (*topal mikyas*). Gold was at the centre of relations with the world economy, while silver fluctuated according to supply and demand in internal commerce. The *kurush* or piaster remained the basic unit of account for most daily transactions. In many ways, the emerging system was a compromise between the preferences of European interests and the realities of a low-income, agrarian country.

For the following three decades until the outbreak of World War I, a sizeable share of government revenues was controlled by the OPDA and applied to debt payments. This control and the regular payments on the debt were quite reassuring

[46] Christopher Clay, *Gold for the Sultan: Western Bankers and Ottoman Finance, 1856–1881* (London, 2000); for an earlier treatment, see D. C. Blaisdell, *European Financial Control in the Ottoman Empire* (New York, 1929).

for the European financial markets. As a result, the Ottoman government was able to resume borrowing towards the end of the century. With the rise in military spending, both external borrowing and the annual payments on the outstanding debt gained momentum after the turn of the century. The almost permanent search for new loans led, in turn, to new dependencies and complications in Ottoman foreign policy. On the eve of World War I, the volume of annual borrowing as well as the outstanding external debt had once again reached the unusually high proportions witnessed in the 1870s.

It may be useful to consider the long-term balance sheet for the mid-nineteenth-century regime change from debasements to stable currency and external borrowing. Relative monetary stability, rapid expansion of foreign trade and European direct investment should appear on the positive side. The annual rate of growth of Ottoman foreign trade averaged close to 5 per cent in real terms during the nineteenth century. There is also some evidence for economic growth in the period before World War I, which can be linked to the growing commercialisation of the Ottoman economy.[47] Monetary stability undoubtedly contributed to economic growth. At the same time, however, the default of 1875–6, the establishment of the Ottoman Public Debt Administration and the surrender of some of the leading sources of revenue to the European creditors in 1881 also suggest that the Ottomans paid a heavy price for borrowing large amounts from abroad before putting their fiscal house in order.

IX

Greater economic and financial integration with Europe meant that banks began to be established in the Ottoman Empire for the first time in the 1840s. Part of the demand for them came from the growth of trade with Europe and the financial needs of the merchants. In fact, the first bank to begin operations in the Ottoman Empire was the Commercial Bank of Smyrna which had been founded in London in 1844 by a group of English merchants to meet the growing needs of European and other merchants in the Izmir region. The bank was forced to close down during the financial crisis of 1847.[48]

For most of the banks established before the 1880s, however, lending to the state remained the more important part of their operations. The first bank to be established in the Ottoman Empire was Banque de Constantinople (Dersaadet Bankası), founded in 1847 with a capital of 200,000 pounds. The bank was to provide short-term loans to the government and stabilise the exchange rate of the Ottoman paper currency. The initiative and capital for the bank came from two of the leading

[47] Vedat Eldem, *Osmanlı Imparatorluğu'nun Iktisadi Şartları Hakkinda Bir Tetkik* (Istanbul, 1970), pp. 302–9; Osman Okyar, 'A new look at the problem of economic growth in the Ottoman Empire, 1800–1914', *The Journal of European Economic History*, 16 (1987).

[48] R. Kasaba, 'İzmir Ticaret Bankası', *Tarih ve Toplum*, 43 (1987), pp. 57–60.

Galata bankers. Because of the expansion in the volume of paper currency, however, the bank could not prevent the deterioration of the exchange rate for long. Due to the mounting losses and the inability of the state to continue to provide financial support for its activities, the bank was forced to close in 1852.[49]

Government efforts to establish another bank for its financial and monetary needs soon led to the formation of the Ottoman Bank by a British group in 1856, in the aftermath of the Crimean War. The bank obtained a royal charter in Britain and was founded in London with a capital of 500,000 pounds, but the centre of its operations was located in Istanbul. It was given permission to open branches in other cities of the empire, except in Egypt.

The continuing fiscal difficulties of the government soon forced it to seek a more powerful European institution. In 1863, the British owners of the Ottoman Bank were joined by a French financial group who took a 50 per cent share in the new Imperial Ottoman Bank. The new bank was managed by committees in London and Paris which directed the day-to-day administration in Istanbul. An important characteristic of the Imperial Ottoman Bank was its double nature, as a private Franco-British bank as well as a state bank at Istanbul. The bank was entrusted with most of the transactions of the state Treasury, in return for the obligation to provide certain short-term loans to the state. It agreed to help the state in withdrawing the existing paper currency and debased coinage from circulation. The Imperial Ottoman Bank also had a privileged position in the servicing of the external debt. Most payments of the Ottoman state on its outstanding external debt were handled by the Bank, which was to charge one per cent commission for this service. Finally, the Ottoman government promised not to issue any paper currency and the bank was granted the monopoly of issuing gold-backed banknotes. The Bank thus enjoyed unique financial and monetary privileges and was in a good position to derive maximum benefits from these circumstances.[50]

Until the middle of the 1870s, the continuing fiscal difficulties of the Ottoman government and the popularity of the high-interest Ottoman bond issues in the European financial markets made lending to the Ottoman state a very lucrative business. The Galata bankers tried to obtain a share of this market by forming alliances with British, French and Austrian financial groups and establishing a number of banks in the capital city. In addition to providing short-term loans of their own, these institutions played the role of intermediaries between the purchasers of Ottoman bonds and the Ottoman state, earning commission and interest from each

[49] Edhem Eldem, *A History of the Ottoman Bank* (Istanbul, 1999), pp. 29–126; A. du Velay, *Essai sur l'histoire financière de la Turquie* (Paris, 1903), pp. 126–9.

[50] A. Autheman, *La Banque Impériale Ottomane* (Paris, 1996), pp. 1–32; J. Thobie, 'European banks in the Middle East', in Rondo Cameron and V. I. Bovykin (eds.), *International Banking 1870–1914* (Oxford, 1991), p. 407; C. Clay, 'The bank notes of the Imperial Ottoman Bank, 1863–1867', *New Perspectives on Turkey*, 9 (1993); also A. Billiotti, *La Banque Impériale Ottomane* (Paris, 1909); and A. du Velay, *Essai sur l'histoire financière*.

transaction. Conditions were particularly favourable, the commissions amounting to between 10 and 12 per cent of the sums actually gathered.[51]

Although originally a Franco-British bank, the Imperial Ottoman Bank became more than 80 per cent French in the 1880s and the Paris Committee soon became the real decision-making body in its Ottoman affairs. The bank maintained its primacy in the market for Ottoman bonds until World War I. During this later period, however, its commercial and investment banking activities became increasingly more prominent. It developed an extensive network in the Ottoman Empire consisting of eighty establishments (branches and sub-branches) as well as others in Egypt and Cyprus. The Bank also supported and to some extent coordinated the activities of French capital groups, not only in the floatation of Ottoman bond issues but also in various direct investment projects, such as railways, ports, utilities, mining and insurance companies. In contrast, European direct investment in agriculture and manufacturing remained limited until World War I. As British capital and financial groups began to scale down their interests and investments in the Ottoman Empire after 1880, German groups, spearheaded by the Deutsche Bank, emerged as the main rival of French capital in these activities.[52]

After 1899 an intense competition developed between European commercial banks, both large and small, as many of them rushed to open branches in the Ottoman Empire. These banks aimed at drawing deposits from local customers to finance trade and agriculture. Most favourable conditions were offered to those possessing savings, to merchants, traders and local notables, as much to attract their deposits as to respond to their need for credit. While the Imperial Ottoman Bank was in a better position than any of its competitors, the new banks were also engaged in commercial operations, discounting commercial paper, offering terms of payment on bills of exchange.[53]

In addition to banks or branches of banks established by European capital, domestic groups founded a small number of regional banks in the 1880s. Numbers of Ottoman banks founded with domestic capital increased significantly after 1910 as a result of the policies of the Young Turk government that promoted the development of domestic capital and a Muslim-Turkish bourgeoisie. Four banks in Istanbul and two in Anatolia were established with the initiative and capital of domestic groups before World War I. These efforts reached a new stage with the establishment of the Osmanlı Itibar-ı Milli Bankası (Ottoman National Credit Bank) with a capital of 4 million lira in early 1917. It was hoped that this bank would play an important role in national economic development. There were also plans to convert

[51] Thobie, 'European banks', pp. 407–8, Tekeli and İlkin, *Merkez Bankası*, pp. 62–9.

[52] Eldem, *Ottoman Bank*, pp. 275–304; Thobie, 'European banks', pp. 413–37; Autheman, *La Banque*, chapters 6–11.

[53] Thobie, 'European banks', pp. 421–5; C. Clay, 'The origins of modern banking in the Levant: the development of a branch network by the Imperial Ottoman Bank, 1890–1914', *International Journal of Middle East Studies*, 26 (1994).

this institution into a state bank and let it assume the functions of the Imperial Ottoman Bank after the expiration of the latter's privileges in 1925.[54]

The most important domestic bank of the long nineteenth century, however, was the Agricultural Bank (Ziraat Bankası) established by the state in 1888 to support agricultural development through the extension of low-interest credit to cultivators. The origins of this institution went back to the Memleket Sandığı (regional fund) and the Menafi Sandığı (fund for public improvement) systems originated by the reformist governor Midhat Pasha in the Balkans during the 1860s and later duplicated throughout the empire. In an effort to make its facilities more widely available, the bank established more than 400 branches, more than any other financial institution. Although the bank as a credit institution could not meet the full needs of cultivators, it initiated an alternative to the high rates demanded by the traditional moneylenders. As one of the few indigenous banks in the empire, it was an important part of government organised efforts to finance economic development from domestic savings.[55]

X

Institutions and institutional change have been identified by economists and economic historians as key variables that help explain the widely disparate economic performance of different societies over the last five hundred years. Based on the successful experience of Western Europe and European off-shoots, new institutional economics has argued that long-run economic growth is attained because the underlying framework persistently reinforced incentives for organisations to engage in productive activity.

Institutional economics and economic historians recognise, however, that a society rarely arrives at or creates institutions that are wholly conducive to economic growth. While focusing on the 'rise of the West', institutional economics and economic historians have paid less attention to studying unsuccessful or less successful cases of institutional change, especially those outside the Western European context. This study offers an alternative perspective.

For most of its 600-year existence, the Ottoman Empire, its economic institutions and policies were shaped to a large degree by the priorities and interests of a central bureaucracy. The influence of various social groups, not only of landowners, but also of merchants and moneychangers, over the policies of the central government, remained limited. Despite the general trend towards decentralisation of the empire during the seventeenth and eighteenth centuries, merchants and domestic

[54] Z. Toprak, *Türkiye'de Milli İktisat 1908–1918* (Ankara,1982), pp. 137–49; Tekeli and İlkin, *Merkez Bankası*, pp. 136–61.

[55] Donald Quataert, 'Dilemma of development: the Agricultural Bank and agricultural reform in Ottoman Turkey, 1888–1908', *International Journal of Middle East Studies,* 6 (1975), pp. 210–27; Y. S. Atasagun, *Türkiye Cumhuriyeti Ziraat Bankası 1888–1939* (Istanbul, 1939).

producers, who were the leading proponents and actual developers of mercantilist policies in Europe, never became powerful enough to exert sufficient pressure on the Ottoman government to change or even modify these traditional policies.

Nonetheless, the Ottoman state and society showed considerable ability to reorganise as a way of adapting to changing circumstances from the seventeenth century to the nineteenth century. With its pragmatism, flexibility and habit of negotiation, the bureaucracy managed to contain many challenges, both internal and external, and succeeded in maintaining a traditional order. Pragmatism, flexibility, willingness to negotiate, and ability to adapt their institutions to changing circumstances, were traits that enabled the Ottomans to retain power while managing a transition to modern centralism in a period when many of their contemporaries in both Europe and Asia were unable to do so. Ultimately, however, pragmatism and flexibility characterised their response, and change was allowed only as far as necessary for the defence of the traditional order.

Institutional change did not apply equally to all areas of Ottoman economic life. Moreover, not all types of institutions were affected to the same degree by these changes. Because the central bureaucracy was able to retain its leading position in Ottoman society and politics, the influence of various social groups, not only of landowners but also of merchants, manufacturers and money changers over economic matters, and more generally over the policies of the central government, remained limited until the end of the empire. As a result, most of the pragmatism and flexibility was utilised by the central bureaucracy for the defence of the traditional order and its own position in that order. In contrast, institutional changes that threatened the leading position of the central bureaucracy were resisted more forcefully than others. Institutional change thus remained selective and many of the key institutions of the traditional order, such as state ownership of land, urban guilds and restrictions on private capital accumulations, remained intact until the nineteenth century.

This article has examined the long-term changes in the Ottoman financial, fiscal and monetary institutions from this perspective of pragmatism, flexibility and willingness to change in defence of a traditional order. Ottoman institutions of private and public finance retained their Islamic lineage and remained mostly uninfluenced by the developments in Europe until the end of the seventeenth century. Money was used widely both by the urban and rural population. Neither the Islamic prohibitions against interest and usury nor the absence of formal banking institutions prevented the expansion of credit in Ottoman society. The Ottoman government relied on tax farming during this period for both tax collection and short-term borrowing purposes, as had been the practice of most Islamic states.

European institutions of both private and public finance began to grow in influence during the eighteenth century. The evolution of Ottoman institutions of public finance during the period 1650 to 1840, from short-term tax farming to lifetime tax farms to government borrowing with tax revenues as collateral and finally to government bonds, was especially remarkable. The striking similarities between this trajectory of Ottoman institutions and the evolution of the European institutions of public finance, especially those of *ancien régime* France, need further scrutiny from historians.

With the onset of the Ottoman reform movement called *Tanzimat* and greater economic interaction with Europe during the nineteenth century, institutional change accelerated. Ottomans adopted a variety of modern fiscal, monetary and financial institutions up to the First World War. They struggled to centralise tax collection and increase revenue. The attempt, in the 1840s, to replace tax farming with direct state collection of agricultural and other taxes was not successful, however. Attempts were also made to move towards a more stable monetary regime. Debasements were abandoned in favour of bimetallism during the 1840s and the Gold Standard after 1880. The local financiers began to be replaced by modern banks, both European and Ottoman. The Ottoman economy also attracted substantial amounts of European direct investment until World War I, mostly in railroads, ports and other infrastructure. A stock exchange was opened in Istanbul in 1873.

Rising military expenditures and the mounting costs of centralising reform during the nineteenth century can all be viewed as the rising costs associated with keeping the disintegrating empire together. The budget deficits were financed mostly with debasements until the 1840s. After the Ottomans decided to embrace bimetallism and stable coinage, only one alternative remained for the finance of budget deficits: external borrowing. Ottoman borrowing in the European financial markets after 1854 led to a default in the 1870s and partial control of state finances by European creditors. Despite experimentation with different fiscal strategies, the inability to bring state finances under control during the nineteenth century thus proved to be the major, if not fatal, weakness of the Ottomans.

V

THE PRICE REVOLUTION IN THE OTTOMAN EMPIRE RECONSIDERED

The Price Revolution of the 16th century has been the subject of one of the most enduring debates in European historiography and, more recently, in the historiography of the world economy. That European prices, expressed in grams of silver, increased by more than 100 percent—and in some countries, by more than 200 percent—from the beginning of the 16th century to the middle of the 17th century has been well established and broadly accepted. In countries that experienced currency debasements, overall inflation was proportionately higher, reaching, in some cases, 600 percent or more for the entire period.[1]

Because these price increases may appear limited in comparison with the standards of the 20th century, some have questioned the term "Price Revolution."[2] Yet to the contemporaries, these price increases seemed harsh and unprecedented in their severity. They were certainly not insignificant in relation to the ability of those societies, economies, and institutions to withstand them. As a result, the causes and consequences of the price increases have been intensely debated ever since the 16th century. The empirical study and bold arguments put forth by Earl J. Hamilton in the 1920s generated a great deal of new interest in the topic. Hamilton linked the price increases to the arrival of massive amounts of silver from the New World. Equally important, he argued that by redistributing income into the hands of new groups, the Price Revolution played a key role in the rise of capitalism in Europe.[3]

After the publication in 1949 of Fernand Braudel's major study of the Mediterranean economy in the 16th century, historians of the Ottoman Empire also began to inquire about the impact of the Price Revolution. As early as 1951, Halil İnalcık took up and developed some of the themes that Braudel had suggested for the eastern Mediterranean.[4] It was, however, the late Ömer Lütfi Barkan who undertook the most important study on the subject.

In an article first published in Turkish in 1970 and later translated into English after some revisions and published in this journal in 1975, he argued that the Price Revolution of the 16th century played a key role in the economic decline of the Ottoman Empire and, more generally, the Near East.[5] After presenting evidence from the Ottoman archives indicating that the prices of food and raw materials increased more than fivefold, Barkan argued that these increases were imported into the Ottoman economy through trade with Europe across the Mediterranean. Even more important, he claimed that "the decline of the established Ottoman social and economic order began as a result of developments entirely outside the area dominated by the Porte, and in particular, and as a consequence of the establishment in western Europe of an Atlantic economy of tremendous vitality and force." He then concluded that "this grave inflationary current . . . together with other more internal factors disturbed the social and economic security of the Empire, and in the end, proved to be irreversible. . . . The sixteenth century came to an end with the countries of the Ottoman Middle East falling into a grave economic and social crisis which presaged a decisive turning point in their history."[6]

Even though Barkan's arguments were widely read and even cited, they have generated only a modest amount of debate, and his conclusions have remained mostly unchallenged.[7] It is true that most historians lacked the technical expertise to evaluate the validity of these arguments. It should also be mentioned, however, that for those adhering to the thesis of Ottoman decline and for those looking for an external cause for Ottoman difficulties, Barkan's arguments offered an appealing explanation.

The debate about the causes and consequences of the Price Revolution in Europe and in the world economy has taken new directions during the past quarter-century. In this article, I will reconsider Barkan's arguments and inferences about the Price Revolution both in light of the recent developments in the literature and new empirical evidence from the Ottoman archives.

COMPETING EXPLANATIONS

The debate about the Price Revolution in Europe has not been about whether the price increases took place. Rather, it has focused on their causes and consequences. With respect to the causes, one side has argued, since Bodin in 1568 and even earlier, that the price increases were caused by an expansion in the money supply arising from the inflow of New World treasure into Spain.[8] In the 20th century, this argument has been elaborated by Hamilton and adopted by the Annales School, and has more recently been reformulated by economic historians adhering to the quantity theory of money.[9]

Hamilton's research in the archives of Seville generated a large body of new evidence in support of this linkage. Assuming a stable function of demand for money or velocity of circulation, he argued that the increase in the money supply first led to a rise in Spanish prices and then, through trade and the balance-of-payments deficits of that country, began to spread to others in Europe and eventually to the Near East and Asia.[10] Braudel gave the idea his blessing in his book on the Mediterranean: "there is no possible doubt about the effect of the influx of gold and silver from the New World . . . the coincidence of the curve of influx of precious metals from the Americas and the curve of prices throughout the sixteenth century is so clear that there seems to be a physical, mechanical link between the two. Everything is governed by the increase in stocks of precious metals."[11]

Dennis Flynn reformulated the quantity-theory explanation by adopting a theoretical framework known as the monetary approach to balance of payments. Emphasizing that a single price should prevail for each of the internationally traded goods, he argued that price increases in Spain caused by the specie inflows then raised prices and increased demand for money in other countries through the balance-of-payments effects, even without the outflows of specie from Spain. Spanish inflation was thus transmitted to its trading partners whether or not bullion was actually exchanged. There was no need, therefore, to trace the volume and timing of the flows of silver from Spain and link those to the actual occurrence of inflation elsewhere.[12] Flynn used the same argument to explain why Potosi silver is not observed in the coinage of many states in the Old World.[13]

Recently, however, this long line of reasoning, based on various versions of the quantity theory of money, has been seriously damaged. New evidence recently compiled by Michel Morineau about the arrival of specie to the Old World from newspaper accounts in the Low Countries show that European receipts of New World treasure continued to increase during the 17th century, even after prices had started to decline. His detailed reconstruction indicates that European silver imports rose from 200 to 250 metric tons per year during the first half of the 17th century to more than 300 tons per year during the second half of the century. These data directly contradict Hamilton's estimates primarily because he grossly underestimated the extent of smuggling. Because prices in Europe actually declined during the 17th century, these findings cast serious doubt on the orthodox monetarist position linking bullion inflows or bullion stock directly to the price level. At the very least, they show that the same quantity-theory framework cannot be applied to the 17th century.[14]

In their recent work, Dennis Flynn, Arturo Giraldez, and Richard Von Glahn have introduced a new and more global dimension to the monetarist approach to the Price Revolution and flows of specie. They argue that precious-metal flows from Europe to Asia have long been attributed to Europe's trade deficits vis-à-vis Asia. In this framework, European demand for Asian products was dynamic while Asian demand for European products was weak or passive. Precious metals had to flow east as a result of the European trade deficit. In fact, they argue, it was not all precious metals, but only silver, that flowed consistently, not to Asia but specifically to China through both Europe and the Pacific and also from Japan. Gold flowed in the opposite direction during the same period. Such high volumes of silver flowed to China because its value was highest there. The high price of silver in China, by far the world's most populous country at the time, was due in turn to the conversion of the monetary and fiscal (taxation) systems in that country to silver during the 16th century.[15]

On the other side of the argument are those who have attempted to explain the price increases in terms of real factors—most notably, population growth and urbanization. From the very early stages of the debate, population growth has been proposed as one of the alternative explanations of the Price Revolution. It has been singled out primarily because agricultural prices rose much faster than the prices of manufactures during this period. The proponents of this explanation have then argued that as agricultural production failed to match the increase in population, the result was sharply higher food prices.[16]

There was a serious flaw with this argument, however. As Donald McCloskey has pointed out, all other things being equal, an increase in population should increase the volume of transactions and the volume of economic activity. Without a change in the velocity of circulation, this should lead to a decline, not an increase, in prices, as can be followed from the basic quantity identity as developed by Fisher: $M \times V = P \times T$, where M stands for the money supply, V for the velocity of circulation, P for prices, and T for the volume of transactions. Even if relative prices should move in favor of agriculture because of the inelastic supplies in that sector, the general price level must fall while the volume of transactions rises together with population. While pointing out the basic flaw in this argument, McCloskey suggested that some other chain of reasoning could still be found to link population growth to rising prices in the 16th century.[17] Both sides thus agree that American silver supported the price increases during the 16th century, but disagree on whether it caused them. It makes a good deal of difference for monetary history and theory, of course, whether money caused or simply sustained the price increases.

More recently, the debate has shifted from increases in the money supply to changes in the demand for money and an increase in the velocity of circulation during the 16th century. One of the more important and insightful contributions came from H. A. Miskimin, who inquired as to whether there may be a more indirect causal connection between population growth and rising prices. Miskimin reasoned that an increase in population would put greater numbers of persons in closer contact with one another and may have enhanced trading opportunities and thus led to increased velocity of circulation.[18]

Jack Goldstone pursued this idea and developed a simple model of exchange to show how urbanization and increasingly more dense urban networks of exchange might permit small amounts of silver to sustain a growing number of transactions. He argued that a larger volume of monetary transactions triggered by rising population density and household specialization should bring about smaller cash balances, thanks to more frequent and smaller individual transactions, thereby increasing the velocity of circulation. In response, governments might have sought to catch up with rising prices by increased minting and currency debasement. Money supplies would thus be expected to lag behind rising prices. Bullion imports would help sustain this spiral but would not drive this demand. Once population growth ceased and urbanization slowed, however, velocity of circulation would fall.[19] Also pursuing the trail opened by Miskimin, Peter Lindert provided evidence that the velocity of circulation in England was not in fact constant, as the quantity-theory explanation insisted or assumed, but fluctuated broadly during the early modern era.[20] However, in a recent study on England until 1700, N. J. Mayhew has argued that while the velocity of circulation did show long-term fluctuations and while it increased during the 16th century, it did not rise with increasing urbanization and monetization.[21]

These efforts have shifted the focus from the supply of money to the demand for money, the inverse of the velocity of circulation. While earlier literature based on orthodox interpretations of the quantity theory of money assumed that demand for money or the velocity of circulation was constant or stable and that it could safely be ignored, it is thus becoming evident that the determinants of the demand for money need to be examined in a more general framework. This new framework needs to include not only the more obvious factors such as commercialization and monetization but also demographic changes and, more broadly yet, social and cultural factors. For this reason, it is simplistic to assume that demand for money would remain stable.

Even though we lack the quantitative data for money supply and the volume of production or transactions that would be necessary for estimating the demand for holding money (or the velocity of circulation) for most societies, European and non-European, powerful arguments have been made as to why many of the variables cited earlier tend to vary temporally and from one society to another. As a result, it would be reasonable to expect wide inter-temporal and cross-societal variations in the demand for holding money.[22] Consequently, it is necessary to abandon the Eurocentric position with respect to the determinants of the demand for money and insert into this general framework the varying experiences of different areas of the Old World, from Western and Central Europe to India and China, as well as the Ottoman Empire.

Another aspect of the debate concerns the long-term consequences of the Price Revolution. Hamilton argued that by facilitating accumulation in the hands of those who were building a new order—or, at least, undermining the old—the price increases contributed to the transition to capitalism in Europe and were thus revolutionary in their impact.[23] It has since been shown, however, that agricultural prices and rents rose much faster than prices of manufactures and wages during this episode. The major beneficiaries of the price movements were, in fact, the landowners—hardly a revolutionary class. The manufacturers certainly did not benefit from the rising prices of raw materials and the lagging prices of their output. The real victims were the urban laborers, who witnessed a sharp reduction in their standards of living. At least in the European case, then, it would be difficult to show how the Price Revolution accelerated the decline of the old order and the transition to industrial capitalism. More generally, in comparison with the grand visions and bold claims of the earlier generation about the long-term consequences of the Price Revolution, contemporary historians of Europe have been downplaying such long-term consequences.[24]

NEW EVIDENCE AND A REVIEW OF THE OLD

For a long time, it had been assumed that markets and the use of money in the Ottoman Empire was limited to long-distance trade and parts of the urban sector.[25] Recent research has shown, however, that the urban population and segments of the countryside were already part of the monetary economy by the end of the 15th century. Even more significant, a substantial increase in the use of money occurred during the 16th century, because of both the increased availability of specie and increasing commercialization of the rural economy. An intensive pattern of periodic markets and market fairs also emerged where peasants and larger landholders sold parts of their produce to urban residents. These markets also provided an important opportunity for the nomads to come into contact with both peasants and the urban population. Large sectors of the rural population came to use coinage, especially the small denominations of silver *akçe* and the copper *mangır*, through their participation in these markets.[26]

Second, small-scale but intensive networks of credit relations developed in and around the urban centers. Evidence from thousands of court cases in these towns and cities involving lenders and borrowers leave no doubt that the use of credit, small and large, was widespread among all segments of the urban society and parts of rural society. It is clear that neither the Islamic prohibitions against interest and usury nor the absence of formal banking institutions prevented the expansion of credit in Ottoman society.[27] Thanks to these recent studies, we are more aware today than we were a quarter-century ago that prices and inflation had an impact on virtually all groups in Ottoman society, and in turn, each group took a position. Most men and women, both urban and rural, were clear about the consequences of different ways of dealing with prices and money, and about who gained and who lost.

It is against this background that Barkan's empirical study of the Price Revolution needs to be situated. Barkan attempted to measure both the rate of overall inflation and its timing by making use of the account books of several leading hospices (*imarets*) in Istanbul from 1489–90 to 1655–56. He constructed weighted price indexes based on purchases of firewood and sixteen standard items of food in twenty-four different years during this interval. However, Barkan could locate in the Ottoman archives only one such account book for the period before 1585–86, when the government undertook a major debasement that had a great impact on prices. That single account book belonged to the year 1489, the base year for his study. To make up for this deficiency, he included in his series account books from the palace kitchen for the years 1555–56 and 1573. He also examined the account books of hospices in the cities of Edirne and Bursa for the same period.[28] Thanks to the large volume of material available from the Ottoman archives in Istanbul, the price data utilized by Barkan were much more detailed than those available for any part of Asia and many of the European countries for this period. Nevertheless, questions were raised about his study regarding the limited nature of his price observations and whether prices paid by the hospices closely tended by the government could be considered representative.

I have recently completed a large study of prices and wages in Istanbul—and, to a lesser extent, in other leading cities of the Ottoman Empire—from the 15th to the 20th centuries.[29] This study used data on the prices of standard commodities collected from more than 6,000 account books and price lists located in the Ottoman archives in Istanbul. In the first stage of the study, three separate food-price indexes were constructed. One of these was based on the account books and prices paid by the many pious foundations (*vakıf*), both large and small, and their soup kitchens. Another index was based on the account books of the Topkapi palace kitchen, and the third used the officially established price ceilings (*narh*) for the basic items of consumption in the capital city.[30]

To the extent possible, standard commodities were used in these indexes to minimize the effects of quality changes. Each of the three indexes included the prices of eight to ten leading items of consumption, such as flour, rice, cooking oil, honey, mutton, chick peas, milk, eggs, and olive oil for burning. The weights of each of these items in the overall index were based on the average shares of each in total expenditures of the respective institutions. These weights were kept constant for each year. In cases where the prices of one or more of these items were not available for a given year, the missing values were estimated by an algorithm that applied regression techniques to the available values.

The annual values of these three food-price indexes were quite close to one another. Nevertheless, because the prices paid by the palace kitchen and the official price ceilings might reflect official or state-controlled prices, for the final index I used the prices obtained from the account books of the pious foundations. Only for those years of the 16th century before 1585, for which price data from this source were not available, I inserted into the index, like Barkan, food prices paid by the palace kitchen.

Based on the available evidence regarding the budget of an average urban consumer, the weight of food items in the overall index was fixed between 75 and 80 percent. The weight of each commodity in the overall index was then fixed according to its share in total food expenditures. For example, in the absence of a long series on bread prices, the weight of flour—mostly wheat flour—varies mostly between 32 and 40 percent of food expenditures and 24 to 32 percent of overall expenditures, depending on the fluctuations in prices. Similarly, the weight of meat (mutton) varies between 5 and 8 percent of the overall budget. It is likely that the diets of private households in the capital city differed from those offered by the soup kitchens. At this stage, however, it is not possible to approximate the private diets more closely.

In the second stage, prices of non-food items obtained from a variety of sources—most important, the palace account books—were added to the indexes. These commodities are soap, wood, coal, and nails by weight (used in construction and repairs). A cost-of-living index should also have included cloth prices and rental cost of housing, but adequate series for these are not available at this stage.[31]

As a result, detailed and reliable price series for these four-and-a-half centuries were obtained for the first time for the Middle East—in fact, for the first time for anywhere in the non-European world. These indexes now make it possible to compare Barkan's results with a much larger body of evidence also drawn from archival sources. The consumer price index I have calculated for the period 1469 to 1700, as well as the index originally calculated by Barkan for the period 1489 to 1655, are shown in Figure 1 and Table 1. These two series are broadly similar. As a whole, they

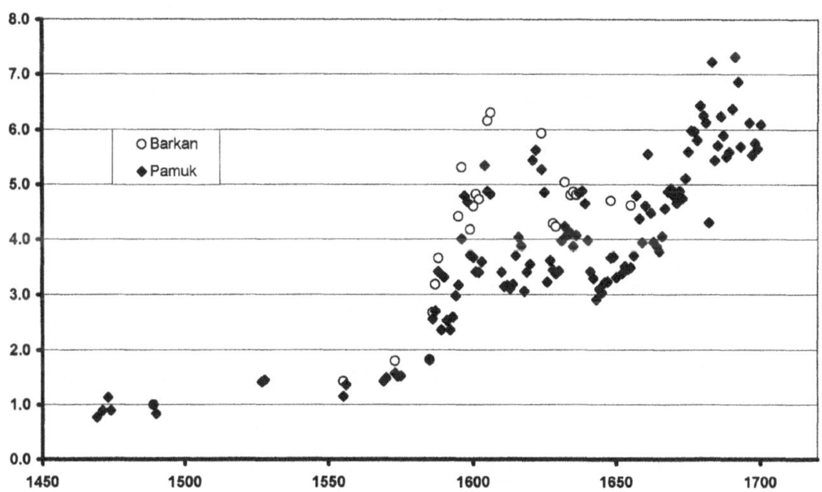

FIGURE 1. Consumer prices in Istanbul, in *akçes*, 1469–1700 (1489 = 1.0)

TABLE 1 *Consumer price indexes for Istanbul, 1469–1700*

	Prices in *akçes*[a]		Silver Content of *akçe* in Grams	Prices in Grams of Silver[a]	
	Barkan	Pamuk		Barkan	Pamuk
Year	1a	1b	2	3a	3b
1469		0.77	0.86		0.98
1471		0.89	0.84		1.10
1473		1.14	0.84		1.41
1474		0.89	0.84		1.11
1489	1.00	1.00	0.68	1.00	1.00
1490		0.84	0.68		0.84
1527		1.41	0.66		1.38
1528		1.45	0.66		1.41
1555	1.42	1.15	0.66	1.35	1.12
1556		1.36	0.66		1.33
1569		1.43	0.61		1.29
1570		1.48	0.61		1.35
1573	1.80	1.58	0.61	1.60	1.43
1574		1.52	0.61		1.38
1575		1.53	0.61		1.39
1585	1.82	1.81	0.61	1.62	1.64
1586	2.68	2.56	0.34	1.34	1.30
1587	3.19	2.70	0.34	1.59	1.37
1588	3.65	3.42	0.34	1.83	1.73
1589		2.37	0.34		1.20
1590		3.31	0.34		1.68
1591		2.54	0.34		1.29
1592		2.37	0.34		1.20
1593		2.60	0.34		1.32
1594		2.98	0.34		1.51
1595	4.42	3.18	0.34	2.21	1.61
1596	5.32	4.01	0.23	2.66	1.34
1597		4.79	0.23		1.60
1598		4.68	0.23		1.56
1599	4.18	3.72	0.23	2.09	1.24
1600	4.60	3.67	0.29	1.94	1.57
1601	4.82	3.42	0.29	2.03	1.46
1602	4.73	3.41	0.29	1.99	1.45
1603		3.60	0.29		1.53
1604		5.35	0.29		2.28
1605	6.16	4.87	0.29	2.59	2.08
1606	6.31	4.82	0.29	2.65	2.06
1610		3.41	0.29		1.46
1611		3.15	0.29		1.34
1612		3.16	0.29		1.35
1613		3.11	0.29		1.33
1614		3.19	0.29		1.36
1615		3.70	0.29		1.58
1616		4.04	0.29		1.72
1617		3.88	0.29		1.66
1618		3.06	0.28		1.27

(*continued*)

TABLE 1 *Continued*

Year	Prices in *akçes*[a]		Silver Content of *akçe* in Grams	Prices in Grams of Silver[a]	
	Barkan	Pamuk		Barkan	Pamuk
1619		3.41	0.28		1.41
1620		3.55	0.28		1.47
1621		5.45	0.28		2.25
1622		5.64	0.23		1.88
1624	5.93	5.28	0.12	2.50	0.92
1625		4.86	0.28		2.01
1626		3.23	0.28		1.33
1627		3.62	0.28		1.50
1628	4.28	3.44	0.23	1.71	1.15
1629	4.23	3.38	0.23	1.69	1.13
1630		3.43	0.23		1.14
1631		3.97	0.23		1.32
1632	5.05	4.23	0.23	2.01	1.41
1633		4.08	0.20		1.20
1634	4.81	4.11	0.20	1.92	1.21
1635	4.87	3.88	0.18	1.93	1.03
1636	4.81	4.07	0.18	1.92	1.09
1637		4.84	0.18		1.29
1638		4.88	0.18		1.30
1639		4.64	0.18		1.24
1640		3.99	0.16		0.96
1641		3.42	0.28		1.41
1642		3.29	0.28		1.36
1643		2.91	0.28		1.20
1644		3.10	0.28		1.28
1645		3.03	0.28		1.25
1646		3.22	0.28		1.33
1647		3.23	0.28		1.34
1648	4.70	3.67	0.28	1.87	1.52
1649		3.69	0.28		1.52
1650		3.31	0.28		1.37
1652		3.38	0.28		1.40
1653		3.51	0.28		1.45
1654		3.46	0.28		1.43
1655	4.62	3.49	0.28	1.84	1.44
1656		3.70	0.28		1.53
1657		4.80	0.28		1.98
1658		4.37	0.28		1.81
1659		3.94	0.23		1.37
1660		4.61	0.23		1.60
1661		5.55	0.23		1.92
1662		4.47	0.23		1.55
1663		3.95	0.23		1.37
1664		3.88	0.23		1.34
1665		3.78	0.23		1.31
1666		4.05	0.23		1.41
1667		4.56	0.23		1.58

(continued)

TABLE 1 *Continued*

Year	Prices in *akçes*[a]		Silver Content of *akçe* in Grams	Prices in Grams of Silver[a]	
	Barkan	Pamuk		Barkan	Pamuk
1668		4.87	0.23		1.69
1669		4.93	0.21		1.51
1670		4.79	0.21		1.47
1671		4.66	0.21		1.43
1672		4.88	0.21		1.50
1673		4.75	0.21		1.46
1674		5.11	0.21		1.57
1675		5.60	0.21		1.72
1676		5.98	0.21		1.83
1677		5.97	0.21		1.83
1678		5.81	0.21		1.78
1679		6.43	0.21		1.97
1680		6.26	0.21		1.92
1681		6.13	0.21		1.88
1682		4.31	0.21		1.32
1683		7.23	0.21		2.22
1684		5.44	0.21		1.67
1685		5.71	0.21		1.75
1686		6.24	0.21		1.91
1687		5.90	0.21		1.81
1688		5.51	0.21		1.69
1689		5.59	0.21		1.72
1690		6.37	0.13		1.23
1691		7.33	0.13		1.41
1692		6.87	0.13		1.32
1693		5.69	0.13		1.10
1696		6.13	0.13		1.19
1697		5.54	0.13		1.08
1698		5.76	0.13		1.12
1699		5.66	0.13		1.10
1700		6.09	0.13		1.19

Sources: Barkan, "The Price Revolution"; Pamuk, *Five Hundred Years of Price and Wages*; also see the text.
[a]1489 = 1.00.

indicate that prices in Istanbul increased by approximately 500 percent from the end of the 15th to the end of the 17th century. They also show that prices in the capital city need to be examined in two distinct periods: until the debasement of 1585–86, when the *akçe* was relatively stable, and after 1586, when monetary instability played havoc with prices. It is also worth noting that the debasement of 1585–86 led to a doubling of consumer prices within a period of three years, which is confirmed by both indexes.

Regarding the period before 1585, my comparison of the prices paid by the palace kitchen with the prices paid by the hospices indicates that they were quite similar. For this reason, Barkan's insertion of some prices from the palace kitchen into the series from the hospices did not cause serious problems. More serious in its implications is the apparent error in Barkan's calculation of his index for the years 1555 and 1573. The index values for these years are important because they give us the only measures of the extent of inflation prior to the debasements of 1585–86—hence, the only measure of silver inflation until that date. Because Barkan independently published the full texts of the account books he used for 1489, 1555, and 1573, I attempted to replicate his calculations for these years, especially because his index appeared unusually high, especially in 1555 and 1573, in relation to my palace-kitchen index using the same set of prices.[32] One problem arises from the fact that the palace kitchen's account books for these two years actually provide prices for no more than eleven of the seventeen items in Barkan's basket. Moreover, even though Barkan's calculations suggested that food prices paid by the palace kitchen in 1573 were 79.97 percent higher than the prices paid in 1489 by the hospice of the mosque built for Sultan Mehmed II, none of the items appearing in the original documents in fact showed price increases approaching this overall rate. My calculations based on the prices available from the documents used by Barkan indicate that his index in 1555 and 1573 should stand at approximately 125 and 150, respectively—not at 142.26 and 179.97. My own index provides slightly different values because additional data was used for these years (see Table 1).

Economic historians studying the Price Revolution have found it useful to make an analytical distinction between price increases in nominal terms and those expressed in grams of silver. The latter index is derived by multiplying the price indexes calculated in nominal *akçes* with the silver content of the *akçe* expressed in grams of silver for each year. It then becomes possible to break down the total increase in prices into its two components. The changes in the index measuring prices in grams of silver may be taken as an indicator for the price level in the absence of debasements. Because prices in grams of silver would tend to converge between countries under open-economy conditions—especially for the port city of Istanbul—the difference between the silver-price index and the other in nominal *akçes* would reflect the extent of price increases due to the debasement of the currency. This second component of price increases was not necessarily independent of the Price Revolution, however, because the latter created—or, at least, contributed to—the fiscal pressures leading to debasements. The price indexes for Istanbul, including that of Barkan, expressed in grams of silver are presented in Figure 2 and Table 1.

Between 1489 and 1585, the *akçe* was quite stable, losing 12 percent of its silver content in two minor debasements undertaken in 1491 and 1566. Because Barkan's calculations indicated a 79.97 percent increase in nominal food prices until 1573, his food-price index expressed in grams of silver rose by 60 percent during the interval from 1489 to 1573. On the basis of this result, Barkan argued that the impact of the Price Revolution was being felt strongly in the Ottoman economy before the past quarter of the 16th century. He then linked the Ottomans' fiscal difficulties and the debasement of 1585–86 to these price increases by arguing that the inflation-adjusted revenues of the treasury declined during this period because the government failed to adjust many of the fixed taxes upward. After my correction of Barkan's price index for the year 1573, however, the price increases between 1489 and 1573 expressed in

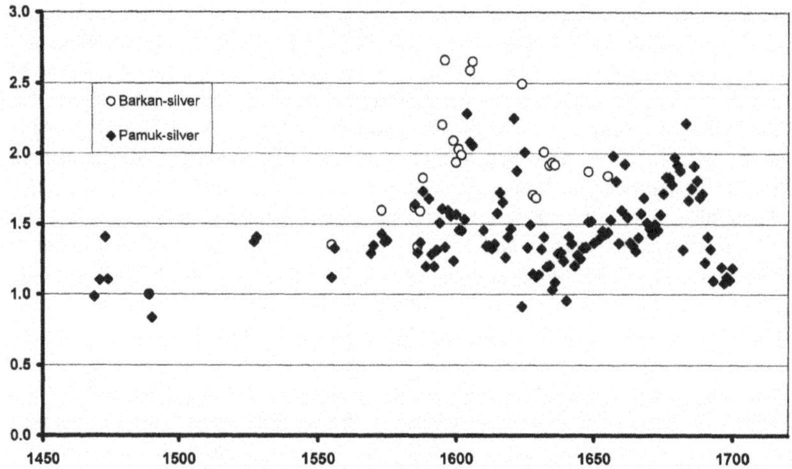

FIGURE 2. Consumer prices in Istanbul, in grams of silver, 1469–1700 (1489 = 1.0)

grams of silver is reduced to 43 percent, indicating a more modest rate of silver inflation. My calculations point to an even lower rate of silver inflation for the other years before 1585 for which data is available (see Figure 2 and Table 1). With this correction, it becomes more difficult to explain Ottoman fiscal difficulties primarily in terms of the Price Revolution, or imported inflation, as Barkan put it.

After the debasement of 1585–86, in which the *akçe* lost 44 percent of its silver content, the Ottoman currency entered a period of extreme instability.[33] Its silver content declined further while fluctuating sharply and frequently until the middle of the 17th century. Substandard *akçe*s circulated widely during this period. As a result, most of the increases in food prices after 1585 were due to the deterioration of the currency.[34] Unfortunately, we do not have the mint records or records of government orders to the mints to establish the precise standards of the *akçe* for each year of the period after 1585. Because the available series on the silver content of the *akçe* reflect only the official standards, and because substandard coinage often dominated the markets, we should recognize that Figure 2 probably overstates the extent of silver inflation for the period from 1586 to 1650 and again for 1670 to 1690.

After making some adjustments for the deficiency cited earlier, the indexes presented in Figure 2 suggest that prices expressed in grams of silver reached their peak in Istanbul during the first quarter of the 17th century, at approximately 80 to 100 percent above their levels in the base year of 1489. It is worth noting that food prices in Istanbul expressed in grams of silver declined during the last decades of the 17th century. By 1700, they were only 20 percent higher than their levels in 1489–90. This latter trend could not be observed in the indexes constructed by Barkan since his series ended in mid-century.

Overall, then, these findings agree with those of Barkan regarding the extent of nominal price increases in Istanbul from the end of the 15th to the end of the 17th century. As for the breakdown of this overall increase, however, my series, which is based on a greater variety of sources and more realistic estimates for the silver content of the *akçe*, diverge from those of Barkan. They show that silver inflation accounted for a smaller part, and Ottoman debasements for a larger part, of these increases than what Barkan suggested a quarter-century ago.

Istanbul was chosen primarily because the data were most detailed for the capital city. However, price data from the account books of the pious foundations is available for other cities of the empire, as well. In fact, Barkan provided some evidence from Edirne to suggest that prices in other Ottoman cities showed similar trends during this period.[35] As part of my price and wage study, I gathered price observations from a shorter list of commodities to construct separate food-price indexes for Edirne and Bursa, both in the Marmara basin, and Damascus for the interval from 1490 to 1700. These indexes are summarized in Figure 3. They indicate that changes in food prices in other Ottoman cities were broadly comparable to the price trends in the capital city from 1490 to 1700. The price data gathered by Ljuben Berov suggest that the Balkans experienced similar increases in nominal prices during this period.[36] The evidence thus points to similar price trends for the *akçe* region as a whole, stretching from the Balkans through Anatolia to Syria. For Egypt, where the local silver currency *para* or *medin* was not subjected to the same rates of debasements as the *akçe*, we can hypothesize that increases in nominal prices were more limited, but the rise in prices expressed in grams of silver must have been comparable to those in the *akçe* region. The well-developed maritime transportation and commercial networks around the eastern Mediterranean must have ensured the broad convergence of these price trends.

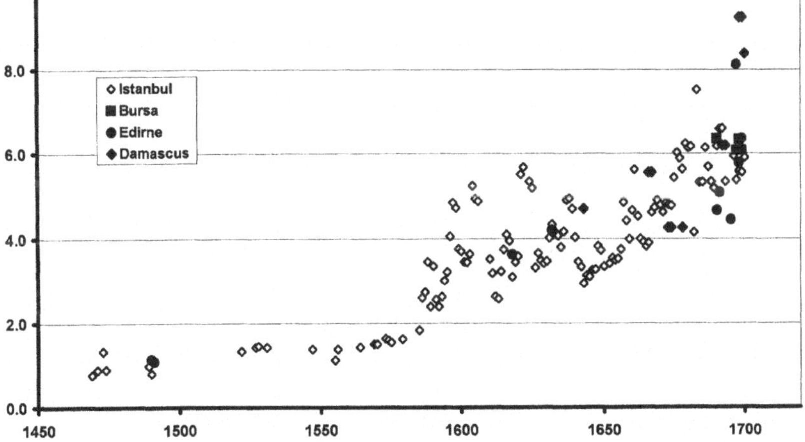

FIGURE 3. Food prices in Ottoman cities, in *akçes*, 1469–1700 (Istanbul, 1489 = 1.0)

In the English version of his article, Barkan is careful not to discuss directly the causes of the Price Revolution in Europe. In that version, he emphasizes that the Ottomans sought to establish a self-sufficient and tightly regulated economic system and argues that inflation, "the product of contact with the Atlantic economy," was an imported phenomenon for the Ottoman Empire. "The (inflation) in Europe gradually began a process by which those commodities were sucked out of Ottoman markets. Wheat, copper, wool, and the like, which had been the bases of the Ottoman economic strategy, now came in short supply and . . . here . . . developed a rapid inflation of prices which soon endangered the equilibrium and security of the closed (Ottoman) economic system."[37]

For Barkan's earlier ideas on the origins or causes of the Price Revolution, one has to go back to the Turkish version of his article, published five years earlier.[38] This piece presented the same empirical evidence, but also included a discussion on the origins of the Price Revolution. Presenting a graph borrowed from a text by Herbert Heaton, Barkan explicitly made the link between the arrival of specie from the New World and the price increases in Europe. He argued that the calculations by Hamilton show a "complete parallelism" between the volume of specie imports into Spain and the commodity-price level in that country.[39]

One section of that article, however, was titled "Other Causes of the Price Increases." There, Barkan showed that he was aware of the debates regarding the causes of the Price Revolution. Stating that "it would not be correct to link price increases solely to the accumulation of large stocks of gold and silver from Africa and America and to rely only on the quantity theory of money in the explanation of price formation and inflation," he went on to produce a long list of other possible causes, which included debasements, population growth, changes in the velocity of circulation of money, and the emergence of other forms of money such as letters of credit and bills of exchange. Aside from a detailed discussion of debasements, however, Barkan did not offer a critical examination of these explanations coming from very different theoretical origins.[40]

This is a good opportunity to take another look at the Ottoman case in light of the recent debates in the literature. Most important, recent debates confirm that explanations other than that based on the simple quantity-theory framework deserve greater consideration than has been given by Barkan or others since. In this respect, the arguments by Miskimin, P. H. Lindert, and J. A. Goldstone, which emphasize long-term changes in the velocity of circulation and the demand for money, appear quite plausible in the Ottoman context.[41] It has already been pointed out that the 16th century was a period of population growth, urbanization, growing economic linkages between rural and urban areas, commercialization, and monetization in the Ottoman Empire.[42] The spread of local and regional markets and fairs in the Balkans and Anatolia provide strong evidence for the spread of commercialization and the money economy during this period. During the 16th century, a significant increase occurred in the use of money, both because of the increased availability of specie and the growing economic linkages between the urban and rural areas. Large sectors of the rural population came to use coinage, especially the small denominations, through their participation in markets and because of state taxation of a wide range of economic activities. In addition, small-scale but intensive networks of credit relations developed in and around the urban centers in the Balkans and Anatolia. Ottoman price increases expressed in grams of silver may thus be due to the rise in the velocity of circulation arising from these changes, as Miskimin, Lindert, and Goldstone argued for other countries. Although increased availability of specie is not seen as the cause of price increases in this perspective, the former are seen as supporting and sustaining the latter. Moreover, this focus on the changing velocity of circulation during the 16th century does not necessarily imply that the price increases expressed in grams of silver were a local phenomenon. On the contrary, this perspective would imply that the long-term developments in the Ottoman Empire with respect to population growth, urbanization, and commercialization were part of a more general pattern in Europe and Asia during the 16th and early 17th centuries.

At the same time, increases in the velocity of circulation should not preclude the possibility that Ottoman price increases expressed in grams of silver were also due partly to the transmission of the European price increases through trade. The price rises in Europe and the ongoing trade with the West may have contributed to the ongoing inflation by creating strong demand for Ottoman agricultural products, as argued by Barkan. In other words, price increases in grams of silver may have been imported from Europe through trade and trade deficits and, at the same time, caused by changes in the velocity of circulation.

LONG-TERM CONSEQUENCES OF THE PRICE REVOLUTION

While the recent debates about the Price Revolution in Europe and the world economy have focused on the causes of the price increases, for historians of the Ottoman Empire the long-term consequences have attracted more attention. One important reason for this was Barkan's thesis that the price increases constituted a negative turning point and a leading cause of the "Ottoman decline" at the end of the 16th century. These arguments also deserve closer scrutiny.

Barkan identified three key areas in which the Price Revolution showed its adverse effects: state finances, agricultural organization, and industry. With respect to the first, he provided detailed evidence from his own research into Ottoman budgets to show that the revenues of the central government failed to keep pace with price increases and rising expenditures. The healthy surpluses of the earlier period had turned into deficits by the last decades of the 16th century.[43] Because some of the government revenues were fixed in nominal terms and the government failed adjust these upward, he argued, the Price Revolution did contribute to Ottoman fiscal woes. My price series showed that this effect was more modest than that suggested by Barkan. Further, there were other, more important causes of Ottoman fiscal difficulties. It was, above all, the growing need for maintaining larger central armies, as well as the increasing frequency of long and exhaustive wars in both the East and the West, that gave rise to the budget deficits and eventually led to the debasements.

During the earlier part of the 16th century, new territories, including Hungary, Syria, Mesopotamia, and Egypt, had been incorporated into the empire. State finances had benefited from these successful campaigns and the inflow of annual remittances from these provinces—most important, from Egypt. The territorial expansion of the empire reached its limits, however, after mid-century. At the same time, the changing technology of warfare began to raise military costs for the central government. Around the middle of the 16th century, when the *timar*-holding *sipahi*s formed the backbone of the Ottoman army, 30 to 40 percent of military expenses were met by revenues collected in rural areas by the *sipahi.* As the traditional cavalry, armed with conventional weapons of bow and arrow, lance, and sword, proved ineffective against the Austrian musketeers, however, the central government was forced to increase the number of janissaries, the standing infantry corps, from 13,000 in the 1550s to 38,000 in the 1600s. The additional costs of this shift fell upon the central treasury.[44]

The protracted and costly wars with the Safavids in the east and the Habsburgs in the west during the second half of the century thus began to drain the enormous financial reserves of the imperial treasury accumulated during the earlier period. With the outbreak of another war with Iran in 1578, the treasury began to experience shortages of silver for payments to the soldiers. In this respect, too, the Ottoman difficulties were part of a pattern that was repeated across Europe and parts of Asia during the 16th and 17th centuries.[45]

With respect to agriculture, Barkan argued that the Price Revolution and the debasement of 1585–86 played a key role in the disintegration of the *timar* system of land tenure.[46] The *timar* system had relied on the agricultural taxes collected from peasant producers to equip locally a cavalry-based force that joined the imperial army at wartime. Aside from the tithe, which was collected in kind, most of the other dues and taxes collected from the peasant households by the *sipahi* were fixed in terms of the *akçe.* Because the latter revenues failed to keep up with the increased cost of living and the necessary costs of armament, many *sipahi*s refused to join the army and began to leave their *timar*s after the debasement of 1585–86.[47]

The central government could have adjusted these dues upward, thereby increasing the incomes of the *sipahi*s. Instead, it left their nominal levels unchanged but chose to levy a series of extraordinary taxes, called *avarız-ı divaniyye* and *tekalif-i örfiyye*, on the rural population in order to bring cash directly into the treasury. This move further undermined the *sipahi* and the provincial army. The government soon abandoned the *timar* system and shifted to tax-farming, auctioning off the collection of rural taxes to the highest bidders.[48] This broad shift toward the collection of the agricultural taxes at the center was due to the changing techniques of warfare and the need to maintain larger permanent armies. The decline of the *timar* system, then, was due more to military considerations than the adverse consequences of the Price Revolution.[49]

One aspect of the Price Revolution in the Ottoman Empire that has not drawn any attention has been its distributional consequences. Because the prices of agricultural goods tended to rise faster than other prices during this period, the more market-oriented segments of the agricultural population—those in control of marketable surpluses such as medium-size landholders and estate owners—tended to benefit from the Price Revolution. On the other hand, it was the urban working groups—the artisans as well as the consumers—who carried the burden of the price increases. Because food prices rose in urban areas, detailed wage data recently collected from the Ottoman archives show that nominal wages failed to keep up with prices. The purchasing power of urban wages declined by 30 to 40 percent during the 16th century, and they remained roughly unchanged at those levels during the 17th century.[50]

Regarding the consequences on Ottoman industry, Barkan argued that the exportation to Europe of the basic raw materials arising from West–East price differentials created severe shortages for Ottoman guilds. When these price effects combined with the increasing competitiveness of European industry and the inability of Ottoman manufacturers to keep up with them, Barkan insisted, an irreversible crisis developed for Ottoman industry. He thus placed the decline of Ottoman guilds in the face of European competition firmly in the 16th century.[51]

It is true that Ottoman industry was adversely affected by the price movements. Ottoman guilds, especially those in coastal regions, were hurt by the shortages arising from the exportation of raw materials to Europe. In a similar vein, Murat Çizakça has argued that in the case of the silk industry from 1550 to 1650, even though wages lagged behind price increases, profit margins were squeezed between the stagnating prices of output and the rapidly rising prices of raw materials.[52] However, there is a good deal of evidence that these shortages were not permanent and that the guilds later recovered.[53] Moreover, this line of reasoning cannot explain why European manufacturers, which faced similar price movements, did much better than their Ottoman counterparts. If the 17th century, or most of it, was a period of stagnation for Ottoman guilds, the reasons must be sought elsewhere, not in the adverse price movements associated with the Price Revolution. In fact, the volume of trade with Europe remained limited, and Ottoman manufactures were not subjected to any serious competition from European industry, until the 19th century. The imports during this period were mostly luxury goods and items such as colonial wares. Recent research has also shown that the 18th century until the 1780s was a period of stability and expansion for the Ottoman economy, including manufacturing.[54]

One reason that the debate on the Price Revolution in Europe originally attracted so much attention had to do with the rash claims of Hamilton and his followers that by redistributing income into the hands of new groups, the price increases paved the way for the rise of capitalism. The international literature on the Price Revolution has since rejected this argument. It is interesting that Barkan similarly interpreted the price increases as a turning point and a leading cause of the "Ottoman decline" at the end of the 16th century. With the help of new evidence about Ottoman prices, we have shown in this study that the impact of the silver inflation on the Ottoman economy and finances was more limited than what Barkan suggested a quarter-century ago. The Ottoman system undoubtedly faced severe fiscal and economic difficulties at the end of the 16th and during the first half of the 17th centuries. However, these difficulties related more to other causes than to the impact of silver inflation per se. In retrospect, Barkan's as well as Hamilton's claims and the attempt to single out the Price Revolution as a key event appear exaggerated if not unfounded.

NOTES

Author's note: I thank three anonymous referees for useful comments; Bagış Erten and Nadir Özbek for assistance with the graphs; and the Bogaziçi University Research Fund for the support it provided through projects 97HZ101 and 99HZ02.

[1]See, for example, the collection of essays by P. H. Ramsey, ed., "Editor's Introduction," *The Price Revolution in Sixteenth Century England*, (London: Methuen and Company, 1971); F. Braudel and F. Spooner, "Prices in Europe from 1450 to 1750," in *The Cambridge Economic History of Europe*, ed. E. E. Rich and C. H. Wilson (1967), 4:374–486; and P. Vilar, *A History of Gold and Money, 1450–1920*, (London: New Left Books, 1976), chaps. 16–21. Much less is known, however, about trends in prices elsewhere in the Old World—most important, in India and China. For India, see I. Habib, "Monetary System and Prices," in *The Cambridge Economic History of India*, ed. I. Habib and T. Raychaudhuri (1982), 1:360–81; S. Moosvi, "The Silver Influx, Money Supply, Prices and Revenue Extraction in Mughal India," *Journal of the Economic and Social History of the Orient* 30 (1987): 47–94; and S. Subrahmanyam, "Precious Metal Flows and Prices in Western and Southern Asia, 1500–1750: Some Comparative and Conjunctural Aspects," *Studies in History* 7 (1991): 79–105. And for China, see W. S. Atwell, "International Bullion Flows and the Chinese Economy circa 1530–1650," *Past and Present* 95 (1982): 68–90.

[2]C. Cipolla, "La pretendue revolution des prix," *Annales, Economies, Societes, Civilisations* 10 (1955): 513–16.

[3]E. J. Hamilton, "American Treasure and the Rise of Capitalism (1500–1700)," *Economica* 9 (1929): 338–57; and idem, *American Treasure and the Price Revolution in Spain, 1501–1650* (Cambridge, Mass.: Harvard University Press, 1934).

[4]Fernand Braudel, *La Mediterranee et le Monde Mediterraneen a L'Epoque de Philippe II* (Paris, 1949); Halil İnalcık, "Osmanlı İmparatorlugu'nun kuruluş ve inkişafı devrinde Türkiye'nin iktisadi vaziyeti üzerine bir tetkik münasebetiyle," *Belleten* 15 (1951): 656–90. A decade later, Bernard Lewis also emphasized the contribution to the Ottoman decline of the developments unleashed by the arrival of American silver: B. Lewis, *The Emergence of Modern Turkey* (London and New York: Oxford University Press, 1961), 29–30.

[5]Ö. L. Barkan, "The Price Revolution of the Sixteenth Century: A Turning Point in the Economic History of the Near East," trans. Justin McCarthy, *International Journal of Middle East Studies* 6 (1975): 3–28; see also idem, "XVI. Asrın ikinci yarısında Türkiye'de fiyat hareketleri," *Belleten* 34 (1970): 557–607.

[6]Barkan, "The Price Revolution," 5–7.

[7]One important exception is H. Sundhaussen, "Die 'Preisrevolution' im Osmanischen Reich während der zweiten hälfte des 16. jahrhunderts," *Südost-Forschungen* 42 (1983): 169–81. See also the detailed empirical study by Ljuben Berov, *Prices in the Balkans during the 16th–19th Centuries and the European Revolution of Prices* (in Bulgarian), (Sofia: Publishing House of the Bulgarian Academy of Sciences, 1976); a summary is available in idem, "Changes in Price Conditions in Trade Between Turkey and Europe in the 16th–19th Century," *Etudes Balkaniques* 3 (1974): 168–78; M. Çizakça, "Osmanlı ekonomisinde akçe tagşişinin sebebleri üzerinde kısa bir inceleme," *Bogaziçi University Journal, Administrative Sciences and Economics* 4–5 (1976–77): 21–27; and idem, "Price History and the Bursa Silk Industry: A Study in Ottoman Industrial Decline, 1550–1650," *Journal of Economic History* 40 (1980): 533–49, which argued that the inter-sectoral price movements led to the decline of Ottoman silk industry during this period. C. Kafadar, "Les troubles monetaires de la fin du XVIe siecle et la prise de conscience Ottomane du declin," *Annales, Economies, Societes, Civilisations* 2 (1991): 381–400, returned to the subject from the perspective of the history of mentalities. Subrahmanyam, "Precious Metal Flows," 79–105, attempted a comparative perspective with South Asia, but his analysis of the Near Eastern or West Asian case remained thin.

[8]On the strength of his *Response* to the *Paradoxes sur le faict des Monnoyes* of M. de Malestroict, Bodin has been designated the "discoverer" of the Quantity Theory of Money; J. A. Schumpeter, *History of Economic Analysis* (Oxford University Press, 1954), 311–12.

[9]Hamilton, "American Treasure," and idem, *American Treasure and the Price Revolution*; Braudel, *La Mediterranee*, and idem, *The Mediterranean and the Mediterranean World in the Age of Philip II*, 2 vols. (London: William Collins Sons, 1972), 1:462–542; F. C. Spooner, *The International Economy and Monetary Movements in France*, (Cambridge, Mass.: Harvard University Press, 1972). For a recent restatement of the monetarist position, see D. O. Fisher, "The Price Revolution: A Monetary Interpretation," *Journal of Economic History* 49 (1989): 883–902; see also D. O. Flynn, "Use and Misuse of the Quantity Theory of Money in Early Modern Historiography," in *Minting, Monetary Circulation and Exchange Rates*, ed. E. van Cauwenberghe and F. Irsigler (Trier: Verlag Trier Historische Forschungen, 1984), 383–417; and idem, "The Microeconomics of Silver and East–West Trade in the Early Modern Period," in *The Emergence of a World Economy, 1500–1914*, ed. W. Fischer and R. M. McInnis (Wiesbaden: Franz Steiner Wiesbaden, 1986), 37–60.

[10]Hamilton, "American Treasure," 338–57, idem, *Price Revolution in Spain.*

[11]Braudel, *La Mediterranee*, 426.

[12]D. O. Flynn, "A New Perspective in the Spanish Price Revolution: The Monetary Approach to the Balance of Payments," *Explorations in Economic History* 15 (1978): 388–406; Carlo Cipolla had argued earlier that in Italy, the price increases came long before the arrival of Spanish silver. Therefore, he reasoned, Italian inflation was due to non-monetary, internal causes: Cipolla, "La pretendue," 513–16.

[13]Flynn, "Use and misuse," 401. It had been shown, on the basis of neutron-activity analysis, that Potosi silver was used in Spain's coinage but, surprisingly, not in the coinage of many other states in the Old World, including France, England, Persia, and the Ottoman Empire: A. A. Gordus, J. P. Gordus, E. Le Roy Ladurie, and D. Richet, "Le Potosi et la physique nucleaire," *Annales: E.S.C.* 27 (1972): 1–35; and A. A. Gordus and J. P. Gordus, "Potosi Silver and Coinage of Early Modern Europe," in *Precious Metals in the Age of Expansion*, ed. Hermann Kellenbenz (Stuttgart: Klett-Cotta, 1981), 225–41.

[14]M. Morineau, *Incroyables Gazettes et Fabuleux Metaux: Les retours des tresors Americains d'apres les gazettes Hollandaises (XVIe–XVIIIe siecles)* (New York: Cambridge University Press, and Paris: Editions de la Maison des Sciences de l'Homme, 1985), 564. Arthur Attman and Ward Barrett's recent surveys of the current research on the intercontinental flows of specie confirm that Morineau's argument is essentially correct: A. Attman, *American Bullion in the European World Trade, 1600–1800* (Goteborg: 1986); and W. Barrett, "World Bullion Flows, 1450–1800," in *The Rise of Merchant Empires*, ed. James D. Tracy (Cambridge University Press, 1990), 224–54.

[15]D. Flynn and A. Giraldez, "Born with a 'Silver Spoon': The Origin of World Trade in 1571," *Journal of World History* 6 (1995): 201–21; idem, "Arbitrage, China and World Trade in the Early Modern Period," *Journal of the Economic and Social History of the Orient* 38 (1995): 429–48; and R. von Glahn, *Fountain of Fortune, Money and Monetary Policy in China, 1000–1700* (Berkeley and Los Angeles: University of California Press, 1996), chaps. 1, 4, 7.

[16]Y. S. Brenner, "The Inflation of Prices in Early Sixteenth-Century England," *Economic History Review* 14 (1962): 225–39; and idem, "The Inflation of Prices in England, 1551–1650," *Economic History Review* 15 (1963): 266–84.

[17]Donald McCloskey, "Review of P. Ramsey, ed., *The Price Revolution in Sixteenth Century England*," *Journal of Political Economy* 80 (1972): 1333.

[18]H. A. Miskimin, "Population Growth and the Price Revolution in England," *Journal of European Economic History* 4 (1975): 179–86.

[19]J. A. Goldstone, "Urbanization and Inflation: Lessons from the English Price Revolution of the Sixteenth and Seventeenth Centuries," *American Journal of Sociology* 89 (1984): 1122–60. In a subsequent book, Goldstone went on to explain the pattern of social unrest, rebellion, and revolution in Europe and Asia—from England to China—during the early modern era in terms of population growth, rising prices, and fiscal crises: J. A. Goldstone, *Revolution and Rebellion in the Early Modern World* (Berkeley and Los Angeles: University of California Press, 1991). In a separate article, Goldstone then linked the long-term cycles in European and Asian population during the early modern era to climate, meteorological series, and solar activity: idem, "The Causes of Long Waves in Early Modern Economic History," in *Research in Economic History, Supplement 6*, ed. Joel Mokyr (Greenwich, Conn.: JAI Press, 1991), 64–68. Unfortunately, some of the evidence he employed to fit the Ottoman case to his framework simply does not exist. For example, contrary to his assertion, there is no reliable evidence at the moment suggesting that Ottoman population and real wages declined during the second half of the 17th century: idem, "Causes of Long Waves," 55.

[20]P. H. Lindert, "English Population, Wages and Prices, 1541–1913," *Journal of Interdisciplinary History*, 15 (1985): 609–34.

[21]N. J. Mayhew, "Population, Money Supply and the Velocity of Circulation in England, 1300–1700," *Economic History Review* 48 (1995): 238–57.

[22]F. Perlin, "Money-Use in Late Pre-Colonial India and the International Trade in Currency Media," in *Imperial Monetary Systems in Early Modern India*, ed. J. F. Richards (Delhi: Oxford University Press, 1987), 232–373; and Subrahmanyam, "Precious Metal Flows," 79–105.

[23]Hamilton, "American Treasure," 355–56; I. Wallerstein, *The Modern World System, Capitalist Agriculture and the Origins of the European World Economy in the Sixteenth Century* (New York: Academic Press, 1984), 70–85.

[24]See the introductory essay in Ramsey, *The Price Revolution.*

[25]F. Braudel, *Civilization and Capitalism, 15th–18th Century, Vol. III: The Perspective of the World* (New York: Harper & Row, 1984), 471–73.

[26]Soraiya Faroqhi, "The Early History of Balkan Fairs," *Südost-Forshungen* 37 (1978): 50–68; idem, "Sixteenth Century Periodic Markets in Various Anatolian *Sancaks*," *Journal of the Economic and Social History of the Orient* 22 (1979): 32–80; and idem, "Rural Society in Anatolia and the Balkans During the Sixteenth Century," *Turcica* 9 (1977): 161–96, and ibid. 11 (1979): 103–53. See also the studies on the rural economy that appeared in two collections: H. İnalcık, *The Middle East and the Balkans under the Ottoman Empire, Essays on Economy and Society,* Indiana University Turkish Studies and Turkish Ministry of Culture Joint Series (Bloomington, Ind., 1993); and S. Faroqhi, *Coping with the State, Political Conflict and Crime in the Ottoman Economy, 1550–1720* (Istanbul: ISIS Press, 1995).

[27]R. C. Jennings, "Loans and Credit in Early 17th Century Ottoman Judicial Records," *Journal of the Economic and Social History of the Orient* 16 (1973): 168–216; also H. İnalcık, "Osmanlı idare, sosyal ve ekonomik tarihiyle ilgili belgeler: Bursa kadı sicillerinden seçmeler," *Türk Tarih Kurumu, Belgeler* 14 (1981): 1–91.

[28]Barkan, "The Price Revolution," 8–17.

[29]Detailed results, including appendixes with annual price and wage series and lists of all source documents, will be published in Ş. Pamuk, *Five Hundred Years of Prices and Wages in Istanbul and Other Cities, 1469–1998* (Ankara: State Institute of Statistics, forthcoming).

[30]The account books of the pious foundations were obtained mostly from the Ottoman Archives in Istanbul, Başbakanlık Osmanlı Arşivi (hereafter, BOA), Maliyeden Müdevver and Evkaf Nezareti, Haremeyn Muhasebeciliği collections. The account books of the palace kitchen are available mostly from the BOA, Devlet Başmuhasebe, Matbah Emini collection. The *narh* prices were approved by the local judges and are available from the records of the Islamic courts in Istanbul, including those of Galata and Üsküdar. Some of these *narh* lists have been published—for example, M. S. Kütükoglu, *Osmanlılarda Narh Müessesesi ve 1640 Tarihli Narh Defteri* (Istanbul: Enderun Kitabevi, 1983).

[31]From the imperial palace's various account books, it is possible to obtain long-term price series on two types of woolen cloth: the locally produced *çuha* and the *çuha Londrine* imported from England. Their prices suggest, however, that they were not the varieties worn by ordinary people but, rather, expensive types of cloth purchased by high-income groups: Halil Sahillioglu, "Yeniçeri çuhası ve II. Bayezid'in son yıllarında yeniçeri çuha muhasebesi," *Güney-Dogu Avrupa Araştırmaları Dergisi,* vol. 2–3 (1973–74), 415–65. For this reason, cloth prices were not included in the overall index.

[32]Ö. L. Barkan, "Fatih camii ve imareti tesislerinin 1489–1490 yıllarına ait muhasebe bilançoları," *Istanbul Üniversitesi Iktisat Fakültesi Mecmuası* 23 (1962–63): 297–341; and idem, "Istanbul saraylarına ait muhasebe defterleri," *Türk Tarih Kurumu, Belgeler* 13 (1981): 108–49 (1–71 for 1555–56).

[33]The government ordered the mints to strike 800 *akçes* from 100 *dirhams* of silver, whereas the earlier standard had been 450 *akçes* per 100 *dirhams* of 3.072 grams. For more details about the monetary history of this period, see Ş. Pamuk, "In the Absence of Domestic Currency: Debased European Coinage in the Seventeenth-Century Ottoman Empire," *Journal of Economic History* 57 (1997): 350–60.

[34]The deterioration of the *akçe* is clear from the market exchange rates of the Ottoman silver unit against both gold *sultani* and leading European coinage. For example, the exchange rate of the *akçe* declined from 120 in 1620 to as low as 400 per *sultani* in 1624 and then rebounded back to 120. This suggests that the silver content of the *akçe*s declined by as much as two-thirds or more during that interval: H. Sahillioglu, "XVII. asrın ilk yarısında Istanbul'da tedavüldeki sikkelerin raici," *Türk Tarih Kurumu, Belgeler* 1/2 (1965): 227–34. For the exchange rate of the *akçe* against the European currencies during this period, see Ş. Pamuk, "Money in the Ottoman Empire, 1326–1914," in *The Ottoman Empire: Its Economy and Society, 1300–1914,* ed. Halil İnalcık and Donald Quataert (Cambridge University Press, 1995), 963. Barkan was aware of the deterioration of the *akçe* and cites these exchange rates by referring to Sahillioglu's study, but he did not attempt to adjust his calculations accordingly: Barkan, "The Price Revolution," 14.

[35]Barkan, "The Price Revolution," 16; Ö. L. Barkan, "Edirne ve civarındaki bazı imaret tesislerinin yıllık muhasebe bilançoları," *Türk Tarih Kurumu, Belgeler* 2 (1964): 235–377.

[36]For detailed evidence of price increases in the Balkans during this period, see Ljuben Berov, "Changes in Price Conditions" in *Prices in the Balkans during the 16th–19th Centuries.*

[37]Barkan, "The Price Revolution," 3–6.

[38]Ö. L. Barkan, "Türkiye'de fiyat hareketleri."

[39]Ibid., 581–84.

[40]Ibid., 589–95.

[41]See pp. 71–73.

[42]For Ottoman population growth and urbanization in the 16th century, see Ö. L. Barkan, "Essai sur les donnees statistiques des registres de recensement dans l'Empire Ottoman aux XVe et XVI siecles," *Journal of the Economic and Social History of the Orient* 1 (1957): 9–36; M. A. Cook, *Population Pressure in Rural Anatolia, 1450–1600* (London, 1972); L. Erder, "The Measurement of Pre-Industrial Population Changes, the Ottoman Empire from the 15th to the 17th Century," *Middle Eastern Studies* 9 (1975): 284–301; L. Erder and S. Faroqhi, "Population Rise and Fall in Anatolia, 1550–1620," *Middle Eastern Studies* 15 (1979): 322–45; and R. C. Jennings, "Urban Population in Anatolia in the Sixteenth Century: A Study of Kayseri, Karaman, Amasya, Trabzon and Erzurum," *International Journal of Middle East Studies* 7 (1976): 21–57.

[43]Barkan, "The Price Revolution," 17–27.

[44]Halil İnalcık, "Military and Fiscal Transformation in the Ottoman Empire, 1600–1700," *Archivum Ottomanicum* 6 (1980): 289, 311.

[45]For the fiscal burden of the wars, see also Sundhaussen, "Die 'Preisrevolution,'" 179.

[46]İnalcık, "Military and Fiscal Transformation."

[47]Barkan, "Türkiye'de fiyat hareketleri," 23–24.

[48]İnalcık, "Military and Fiscal Transformation."

[49]Ibid.

[50]Pamuk, *Five Hundred Years of Prices and Wages*, chap. 4. Real wages also declined in Europe during the 16th century.

[51]"One can see clearly that the advent of the new European commerce began the stagnation of the Ottoman craft industry. . . . [F]aced with the continuously evolving European industry, Ottoman industry could not find the dynamism necessary to adapt to the new conditions of the world economy. As an ever wider gap between it and European industry opened, the Ottoman system was condemned to degeneration. . . . The new European commerce must be included as one of the main causes of the sixteenth century Ottoman economic stagnation": Barkan, "The Price Revolution," 7–8.

[52]Çizakça, "Price History and the Bursa Silk Industry," 533–49.

[53]S. Faroqhi, "Crisis and change, 1590–1699," in *The Ottoman Empire*, 433–73.

[54]Mehmet Genç, "L'Economie Ottomane et la guerre au XVIIIe siecle," *Turcica* 27 (1995): 177–96; M. Genç, "Ottoman Industry in the Eighteenth Century: General Framework, Characteristics and Main Trends," in *Manufacturing in the Ottoman Empire and Turkey, 1500–1950*, ed. Donald Quataert (Albany: State University of New York Press, 1994), 59–86.

VI

PRICES IN THE OTTOMAN EMPIRE, 1469–1914

Despite the considerable expansion of research in Ottoman economic and social history in recent decades, our knowledge of the long-term trends in prices in the Ottoman Empire, and more generally in the Balkans and the Middle East, is very limited. Economic and social historians of these regions in the late medieval and early modern eras are still unable to make sense of the most basic of monetary magnitudes involving prices, wages, and wealth, even though inter-temporal comparisons of these magnitudes are the most basic prerequisites for studying the *long durée*.

The study of long-term price trends may also reveal new evidence regarding the long-term economic cycles and conjunctures in Ottoman history. There exists a strong, two-way interaction between monetary and economic conditions. Monetary stability often helps pave the way for the expansion of trade and production. Similarly, monetary instability or shortages of specie often have adverse effects on credit, production, and trade. Conversely, economic prosperity or expansion of economic activity often enables the state to raise additional fiscal revenue, which contributes to monetary stability. There may exist, therefore, a good deal of correlation in the long term between price trends and economic conditions.

The findings of this study indicate, for example, that the period of most rapid debasement and inflation in Ottoman history was not the late 16th and the early 17th centuries, the era of the so-called Price Revolution, as economic historians had come to believe, but the early decades of the 19th century before Tanzimat, a period of wars, internal rebellions, and reform. Establishing in more detail the causes, magnitudes, and consequences of this rapid wave of price increases could thus shed considerable light not only on economic and social history but also on the politics of that period.

A comparison of price trends in the Ottoman Empire with those of other areas around the Mediterranean and beyond for which similar series are available should also provide new insights into the degree of integration of markets and economies and how that degree of integration may have changed over time. Our results indicate that prices in other Ottoman cities moved together with those in the capital city in the medium and long term. There was also a correlation between the prices in Istanbul expressed in grams of silver and the prices in grams of silver around the Mediterranean in the medium and long term. These results confirm that, due to the strength of maritime trade, the empire remained reasonably well linked to markets and economies thousands of miles away.

Based on a large research project in the Ottoman archives in Istanbul, this paper establishes for the first time the long-term trends in consumer prices for Istanbul and other Ottoman cities from the second half of the 15th century until World War I. It also examines the leading causes of Ottoman price movements during these five centuries. A comparison with the price trends in leading European cities for which detailed data are available for the same period is undertaken in the last section of the paper.

CONSTRUCTION OF A CONSUMER PRICE INDEX

This study used data on the prices of standard commodities (food and non-food items) collected from more than 6,000 account books and price lists for Istanbul and, to a lesser extent, for other leading cities of the Ottoman Empire from the 15th to the 20th century. In the first stage of the study, three separate food price indexes were constructed for Istanbul with these annual observations. One of these is based on the account books and prices paid by the many pious foundations (*vakıf*), both large and small, and their soup kitchens (*imaret*). Another index is based on the account books of the Topkapi palace kitchen, and the third uses the officially established price ceilings (*narh*) for the basic items of consumption in the capital city.[1]

To the extent possible, standard commodities were used in the construction of these indexes to minimize the effects of quality changes. Each of the three food indexes includes the prices of eight to ten leading items of consumption—namely, flour, rice, honey, cooking oil, mutton, chickpeas, lentils, onions, eggs, and olive oil for burning. Among these, flour, rice, cooking oil, mutton, olive oil, and honey provided the most reliable long-term series and carried the highest weights in our food budget. In cases where the prices of one or more of these items were not available for a given year, the missing values were estimated using an algorithm that applied regression techniques to the available values.

The medium- and long-term trends shown by the three food price indexes are quite similar. In addition, account books found in the Ottoman archives showing the private purchases by the households of high-level bureaucrats also point to similar long-term trends in food prices at the retail level.[2] The fact that *narh* prices moved together with prices paid by the palace and the pious foundations, as well as by private individuals, suggests that government intervention did not alter prices especially in the medium and long terms. It also points to a good degree of government pragmatism in economic affairs. Historians have long argued that the permanent application and enforcement of *narh* in urban areas was a typical example of Ottoman interventionism and rigidity in defense of a traditional order. There is, in fact, a good deal of evidence that the Ottomans became increasingly more conscious, after the 16th century, about the limitations of interventionism in economic affairs. They learned that price ceilings that diverged substantially from the underlying market realities could not be enforced for long periods of time. For this reason, interventionism became increasingly selective. It was used primarily for the provisioning of the capital city and the army and for selected commodities. Perhaps more important, the *narh* came to be considered, after the first half of the 17th century, not permanent policy but an instrument reserved for extraordinary conditions such as wars, exceptional difficulties in the provisioning of the capital city, or periods of monetary instability. With increasing fiscal and monetary difficulties and growing price instability, however, the price ceilings once again became a regular part of Ottoman urban life from 1789 to 1850.[3]

Even though *narh* prices moved together with prices paid by the palace and the pious foundations, the study gives greater weight to the prices paid by the soup kitchens and the pious foundations because the palace and *narh* prices might be considered official or state-controlled prices. For the sake of consistency, the *narh* prices and the retail prices paid by the households of high-level bureaucrats were not included in the final index.

Since the availability and quality of price observations varied over time for most of the foodstuffs in our list, the 400-year period until 1860 was divided into five sub-periods, and indexes were calculated separately for each. In each sub-period, some commodities had to be excluded from the index because of the unavailability of price observations. The weights of the individual commodities were kept constant as long as they were included in the index.

Based on the available evidence regarding the budget of an average urban consumer, the weight of food items in the overall indices was fixed between 75 and 80 percent. The weight of each commodity in the overall index was then based on the shares of each in total expenditures of the pious foundations. To cite two prominent examples, in the absence of long series on bread prices, the weight of flour—mostly wheat flour—varies mostly between 32 and 40 percent of food expenditures and 24 to 32 percent of overall expenditures, depending on the fluctuations in prices. Similarly, the weight of meat (mutton) varies between 5 and 8 percent of the overall budget. It is likely that the diets of private households in the capital city differed from those offered by the soup kitchens. At this stage, however, it is not possible to approximate the private diets more closely.

What follow are the relative weights of commodities used most frequently in the food-price index:

11 *kile* of flour (1 *kile* in Istanbul equaled 37 liters; 1 *kile* of flour equaled 20.5 *okka*; 1 *okka* equaled 1,280 grams)
4 *kile* of rice (1 *kile* of rice in Istanbul equaled 10 *okka*)
9 *okka* of animal-based cooking oil
13 *okka* of honey
40 *okka* of mutton
0.2 *kile* of chickpeas (1 *kile* of chickpeas equaled 10 *okka*)
5 *okka* of olive oil

One important reason that the weights of the individual commodities were kept constant over time was the unavailability of consumer budgets for different points in time. It is likely that the changes in the commodity composition of the consumer budget were small since increases in average incomes were limited during these centuries. Nevertheless, some substitution must have occurred over time from commodities whose prices rose faster toward those whose prices declined in relative terms.

In the second stage of the study, prices of non-food items obtained from a variety of sources—most important, the palace account books—were added to the indexes. These commodities are soap, wood, coal, and nails by weight (used in construction and repairs). From the various account books of the imperial palace, it is possible to obtain long-term price series on two types of woolen cloth, the locally produced *çuha* and the *çuha Londrine* imported from England. Both the absolute level and long-term trends in the more reliable woolen-cloth prices suggest, however, that these were not the varieties worn by ordinary people but expensive types of cloth purchased by high-income groups.[4] For this reason, cloth prices were not included in the overall index until 1860. Price data for a large number of other types of cloth have also been collected, but none of these are available for long periods of time. A cost-of-living index should also include the rental cost of housing, but an adequate series for standard housing is not available at this stage.

It is well known that pre-modern prices showed large short-term fluctuations due to harvest conditions, difficulties in transportation, wars, and other causes. In the case of our indexes, however, a number of factors worked in the same direction to reduce year-to-year fluctuations. First, the capital city was subject to a higher degree of government involvement in price formation, which tended to reduce price volatility even if it did not have a medium- or long-term impact on the level of prices. Second, it is likely that soup kitchens and the imperial palace were subject to a smaller degree of price variation than the private households. Third, in the processing of price observations from the archival documents, we excluded prices more than 100 percent higher or more than 50 percent lower than the value of the previous year, unless the new price level was observed again in later years. Most of the excluded observations reflected errors in the original document, although some of them must have represented actual prices. As a result, we do not have a high degree of confidence in the year-to-year fluctuations of our indexes but are quite confident about the level of prices at the medium and long term.

For the period 1860–1914, data from the palace, pious, and *narh* sources are very limited. For this reason, the detailed quarterly wholesale prices of the Commodity Exchange of Istanbul covering about two dozen commodities were used. Indexes based on these prices were then linked to those for the earlier period with the help of detailed data for both retail prices of individual commodities and prices at the Commodity Exchange for 1860–62 and 1913–14.

OVERVIEW OF THE RESULTS

We have thus obtained for the first time for the Middle East—in fact, for the first time for anywhere in the non-European world—detailed price series for these four and a half centuries. For Istanbul, the results have been extended from 1914 to the present since published data on consumer prices is readily available for the recent period.[5] Figure 1 and Table 1 present the annual values of the overall price index that combines the food prices obtained from the account books of pious foundations with the prices of non-food items. The vertical axis in Figure 1 is given in log scale so that the slope of the line indicates the rate of change of nominal prices. These results indicate that prices increased by a total of about 300 times from 1469 until World War I. This overall increase corresponds to an average increase of 1.3 percent per year, end to end, and 1.1 percent per year for the fitted line.

The indexes show that Istanbul experienced a significant wave of inflation from the late 16th to the middle of the 17th century, when prices increased about fivefold. This is the period usually associated with the Price Revolution of the 16th century. The indexes also show, however, that a much stronger wave of inflation occurred beginning in the late 18th century and lasting into the 1850s, when the prices increased 12–15 times.

TABLE 1. *Summary of price indexes (decennial averages)*

Years	CPI, 1469 = 1.0	Silver Content of the *akçe*, in grams	CPI in Grams of Silver, 1469 = 1.0	Years	CPI, 1469 = 1.0	Silver Content of the *akçe*, in grams	CPI in Grams of Silver, 1469 = 1.0
1469–79	1.20	0.85	1.17	1720–29	6.98	0.13	1.06
1480–89	1.30	0.68	1.02	1730–39	7.62	0.12	1.10
1490–99	1.09	0.68	0.85	1740–49	9.93	0.12	1.39
1520–29	1.87	0.66	1.42	1750–59	10.1	0.11	1.30
1550–59	1.64	0.66	1.25	1760–69	11.1	0.10	1.23
1560–69	1.86	0.61	1.32	1770–79	17.8	0.093	1.93
1570–79	1.99	0.61	1.41	1780–89	17.2	0.080	1.58
1580–89	3.35	0.39	1.47	1790–99	24.5	0.053	1.50
1590–99	4.45	0.30	1.46	1800–09	34.7	0.048	1.91
1600–09	5.43	0.29	1.81	1810–19	49.5	0.032	1.86
1610–19	4.44	0.29	1.47	1820–29	62.8	0.018	1.26
1620–29	5.56	0.25	1.54	1830–39	130.1	0.0073	1.12
1630–39	5.49	0.20	1.24	1840–49	181.0	0.0081	1.70
1640–49	4.37	0.27	1.34	1850–59	240.5	0.0083	2.32
1650–59	4.92	0.27	1.56	1860–69	285.7	0.0083	2.76
1660–69	5.82	0.23	1.56	1870–79	265.6	0.0083	2.56
1670–79	7.06	0.21	1.69	1880–89	238.1	0.0083	2.30
1680–89	7.46	0.21	1.79	1890–99	235.6	0.0083	2.27
1690–99	7.96	0.13	1.21	1900–09	220.9	0.0083	2.13
1700–09	6.05	0.13	0.92	1910–14	294.2	0.0083	2.84
1710–19	6.87	0.13	1.03				

Note: CPI, consumer price index.

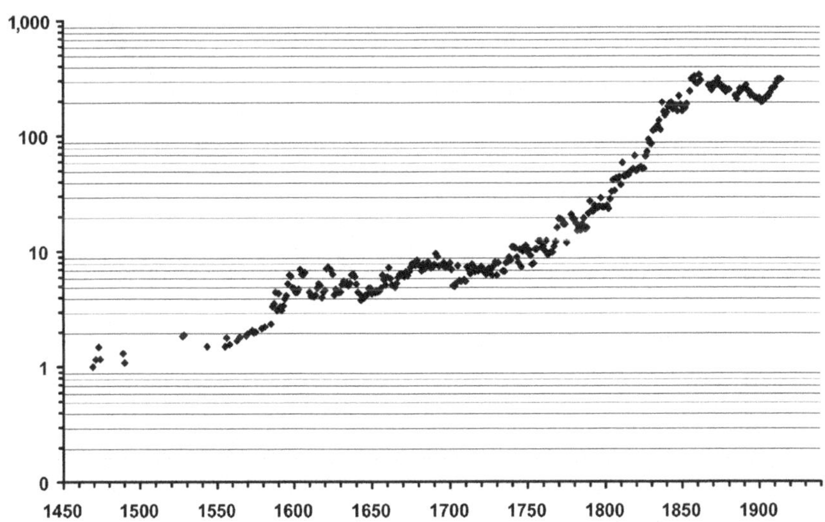

FIGURE 1. Consumer price index for Istanbul, 1469–1914 (1469 = 1.0).

Most of these increases were associated with the debasements that began in the 1780s and accelerated during the reign of Mahmud II (1808–39). In contrast, the overall price level was relatively stable from 1650 to 1780 and from 1860 until World War I. (For a period-by-period review of the price trends, see the Appendix.)

Istanbul was chosen primarily because the data were most detailed for the capital city.[6] However, price data from the account books of the pious foundations is available for other cities of the empire, as well. Price observations from a shorter list of commodities were used to construct separate indexes for the cities of Edirne, Bursa, Konya, Trabzon, Damascus, and Jerusalem. In these Ottoman cities, both the overall change in the price level from 1490 to 1860 and the two major jumps in the price level that occurred in the late 16th and early 19th centuries were comparable to the price trends in Istanbul (Figure 2). Price data gathered by Ljuben Berov suggest that the Balkans experienced similar increases in prices during the 16th and 17th centuries.[7] The evidence thus points to similar price trends for the *akçe* region as a whole, stretching from the Balkans through Anatolia to Syria. In Egypt, the local currency was the *para* or *medin*, whose silver content and rate of debasement differed from those of the *akçe*. Nevertheless, it is possible to construct price indexes in grams of silver for Cairo on the bases of data supplied by Andre Raymond from the court records of that city.[8] These indexes indicate that from 1624 to 1800, the period for which comparable data is available, prices in Cairo expressed in grams of silver moved together with those in Istanbul and other Ottoman cities in the *akçe* region.[9] The well-developed maritime transportation and commerce networks around the eastern Mediterranean must have ensured the broad convergence of these price trends.

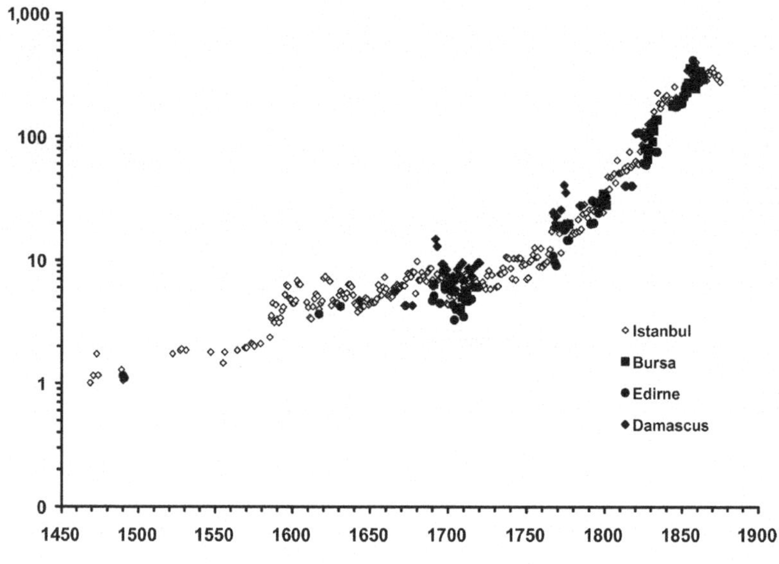

FIGURE 2. Food prices in Ottoman cities, 1469–1865 (Istanbul, 1469 = 1.0).

A MORE DETAILED LOOK AT THE INDEX

As pointed out earlier, some commodities were excluded from our price indexes because of the unavailability or poor quality of data. It would be useful to see how sensitive the long-term results are to the insertion of these commodities into our consumer price index. Cloth prices had been excluded from the index for the period before 1860 because they belonged to expensive types of cloth worn by high-income groups. Nevertheless, since long-term trends in the available Istanbul cloth-price series broadly paralleled those in Western Europe, they can be used in the index. Prices of woolen cloth decreased by about 80 percent in relation to our overall consumer price index from 1700 to 1860. Given a 7 percent share in the initial consumer budget, the inclusion of cloth prices would decrease the overall consumer index by a total of approximately 5 percent between these two dates.[10]

Another relatively important item excluded from our index is rents on residential housing. In view of the importance of this item in urban consumer budgets, some allowance can perhaps be made for this item by studying long-term trends in rental prices of residential housing elsewhere in European cities for which data are available. In view of the growth of Istanbul as an urban center, one should expect rents on residential housing to rise over time. Taking into account patterns in housing ownership, we estimated, as a first-round approximation, that rent payments on urban housing doubled in relation to the overall index, and the share of rents in the average urban budget rose from about 5 percent to about 10 percent from the 16th to the early 20th century. The inclusion of rents in our index would thus increase the overall index by 5 percent and match in the opposite direction the impact of the inclusion of cloth prices.

Finally, we consider the inclusion of sugar and coffee in the price index. Istanbul sugar prices declined by about 50 percent relative to the overall index during the 16th century and by an additional 50 percent during 1820–60. The available price series for coffee in Istanbul moved together with the overall index until the 19th century but declined by about 60 percent in relation to the index during 1820–60.[11] Since the share of these two items in the average consumer budget was limited until 1860, however, our overall results will not change significantly. We estimate that the inclusion of these two items in the consumer budget would reduce the overall price index by no more than 1 percent until 1914.[12] It is thus remarkable that the cumulative impact of the inclusion of cloth, sugar, coffee, and rents in the consumer budget is quite small because individual effects tend to work in opposite directions.

The inclusion of these items in the consumer budgets would change much more significantly the relative prices faced by lower- and higher-income groups, however. Since cloth, sugar, and coffee had larger shares in the budgets of higher-income groups, the decline in their prices should reduce prices faced by these groups more than others. However, the inclusion of rent payments in the budgets would tend to raise prices faced by lower-income groups more than those faced by higher-income groups, since the latter are likely to own their dwellings. We thus expect that the inclusion of these four items in the consumer budgets would shift relative prices in favor of higher-income groups. For example, we estimate that the inclusion of these items in the consumer budgets would widen the difference between the purchasing power of skilled and unskilled workers by approximately 10 percent for the entire period. At least until the late 19th century, the incomes of skilled construction workers must have been above the average for the urban population as a whole.

Another important characteristic of the Istanbul price series is the important divergences in relative prices over the course of these four and a half centuries. Prices of some foodstuffs (meat, flour, milk, eggs) and wood for burning rose 400- to 700-fold during this entire period, while prices of other foodstuffs—olive oil, honey, coffee, onions, and all manufactured items for which price series are available—rose less than 200-fold. To the extent the commodities with higher rates of price increases were essentials and had a higher share in the budgets of lower-income consumers, the overall rate of inflation faced by the lower-income groups must have been higher.[13]

When we combine the differential impact of the more rapid rise in the prices of essentials with differential impact on the lower- and higher-income groups of the items excluded from our indexes, we arrive at a cumulative difference of about 20 percent between the prices faced by unskilled and skilled workers during these four and a half centuries. In other words, we estimate that the cumulative rate of inflation faced by unskilled workers from 1469 to 1914 was 10 percent higher and the overall inflation faced by skilled construction workers was 10 percent lower than the averages provided by our consumer price index. The divergence between cumulative prices faced by unskilled workers and higher-income groups was probably even wider.[14]

CAUSES AND CONSEQUENCES OF PRICE CHANGES

There were many causes of inflation during the early modern period, as shown in the large literature and extensive debates on the subject. In the short term, harvest conditions and wars were the two most important causes of price fluctuations. From the long-term perspective offered by these price indexes and our study of the Ottoman currency, however, debasements or the reduction of the specie content of the currency by the monetary authority emerge as the most important cause of Ottoman price increases.

The relationship between debasements and the price level can be established more closely by following the silver content of the Ottoman currency after 1450. Figure 3 presents the annual silver content of the *akçe* and the *kuruş* after 1720, with 1 *kuruş* equal to 120 *akçes*. The vertical axis is again in log scale so that the slope of the curve indicates the rate of debasement. Figure 3 shows that the silver content of the Ottoman currency declined most rapidly during the late 16th and early 17th centuries and also during the late 18th and early 19th centuries. In contrast, prices were relatively stable after 1860, when the silver content of the Ottoman currency remained unchanged. The correlation between Figure 1 and Figure 3 is quite clear.

An alternative way to examine the relationship between debasements and the price level would be to construct price indexes expressed in grams of silver, which is obtained by multiplying the value of the price index by the silver content of the Ottoman currency for the same year. Figure 4 and the third column of Table 1 combine the evidence in Figures 1 and 3 and present the overall price index for Istanbul in grams of silver. The series was extended beyond 1870 even though world silver prices declined sharply after that date, because the nominal value of silver coinage was not changed under the Ottoman monetary system until World War I.

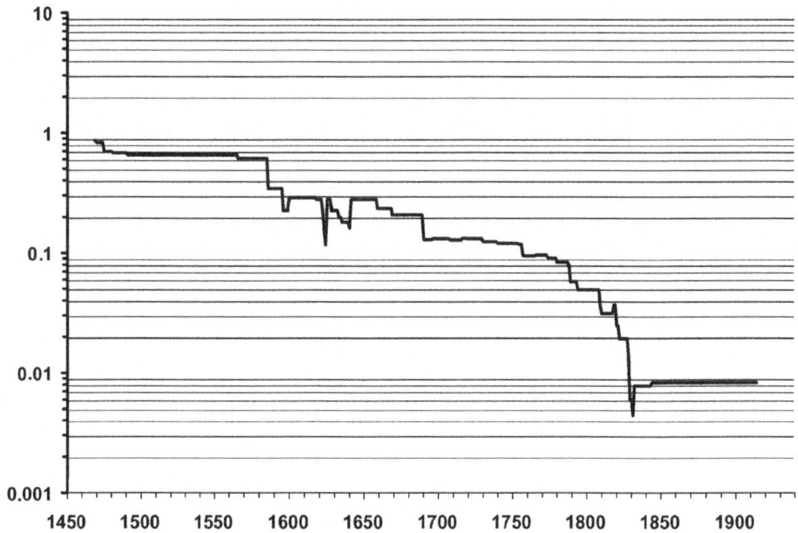

FIGURE 3. Silver content of the Ottoman monetary unit (*akçe*), 1469–1914 (in grams).

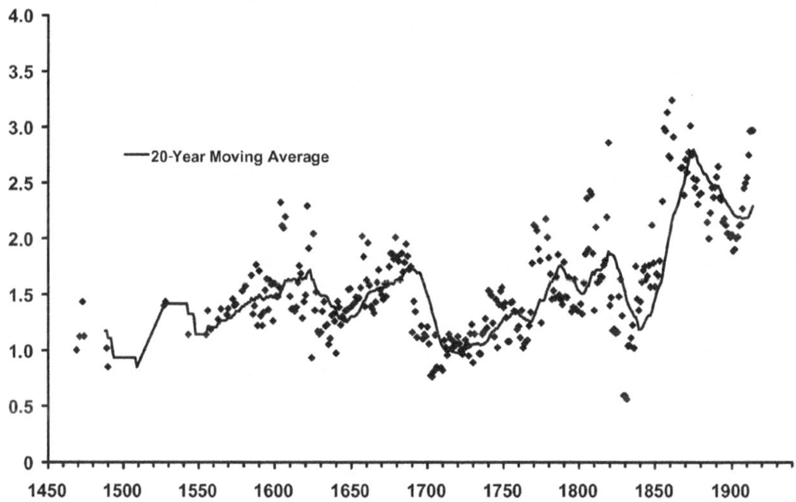

FIGURE 4. Consumer prices in Istanbul, 1469–1914 (in grams of silver; 1469 = 1.0).

It is remarkable that even though nominal prices in Istanbul increased about 300 times, prices expressed in grams of silver stayed within the relatively narrow range of 1.0 to 3.0 during these four and a half centuries. There were medium-term movements in prices expressed in grams of silver. Prices expressed in grams of silver increased by as much as 60 percent from 1500 until the second half of the 17th century, during the period of the

Price Revolution; declined during the first half of the 18th century; and then more than doubled until the second half of the 19th century.[15] All this, however, occurred around a long-term trend that was rising only modestly. In other words, debasements were the most important determinant of Ottoman prices in the long term. In the longer term, the so-called silver inflation also contributed to the changes in the overall price level, but its impact paled in relation to that of debasements. Needless to say, prices of individual commodities expressed in grams of silver also fluctuated within a narrower range during these centuries.[16]

The causes and consequences of pre-modern debasements have been the focus of much debate.[17] Some of the causes, such as the wear on the existing stock of coins in circulation and the mismanagement of the mints, appear to be technical or administrative in nature. Another possible cause was the increase in the economy's demand for money and the need to increase the money stock in circulation. In the short term, debasements provided relief from shortages of specie and coinage in circulation by increasing the nominal value of the coinage in circulation. However, the alteration and expansion of the money supply through debasements could provide only temporary relief, because prices tended to adjust upward sooner or later, and the volume of coinage in circulation adjusted for the price level tended to return to its earlier levels. For this reason, the efforts of pre-modern states to offset the detrimental effects of bullion shortage by means of debasement were doomed to frustration.

The persistence of debasements throughout the medieval and early modern periods suggests that these interventions could not simply be futile efforts. Although they did not solve the problems of specie shortages, debasements did provide fiscal relief for the states, and there lay their appeal. Since the obligations of the state to the soldiers, bureaucrats, and suppliers are expressed in terms of the monetary unit of account, a reduction in the silver content of the currency enabled the state to increase the amount it could mint from, or the payments it could make with, a given amount of silver. As a result, debasements were frequently used as an alternative to additional taxation.

Prices almost always rose in the aftermath of debasements because a debasement typically increased the nominal value of coinage in circulation. Even if the prices did not rise quickly because of the shortages of specie or some other reason, long-distance trade acted as the ultimate equalizer in the longer term. If prices expressed in grams of silver in a given region became less expensive vis-à-vis the neighboring areas, increased demand for the lower-priced commodities attracted large quantities of silver, thus raising prices. Price adjustments after a debasement tended to be more rapid the more open the economy and the more frequently debasements were used.[18]

Another possible cause of debasements was the pressure from some social groups in favor of inflation. Even if a social group did not always benefit from debasements and inflation, it could still prefer debasements to additional taxation. For example, merchants sometimes preferred debasements to increased taxation when the government faced fiscal difficulties. This is because the prices of goods held by the merchants typically rose together with other prices after a debasement. On the other side were social groups who stood to lose from debasements and the accompanying inflation and therefore opposed them. Under these circumstances, the fate of the currency was not determined solely by the government. It often depended on the struggle between it and various social groups. Before we begin an examination of Ottoman debasements, therefore, it would be useful to examine how different groups in Ottoman society fared in the face of debasements.

For a long time it has been assumed that the use of money in the Ottoman Empire was limited to long-distance trade and parts of the urban sector.[19] Recent research has shown, however, that the urban population and some segments of the countryside were already part of the monetary economy by the end of the 15th century. Even more significant, a substantial increase occurred in the use of money during the 16th century because of the increased availability of specie and increasing commercialization of the rural economy. An intensive pattern of periodic markets and market fairs also emerged where peasants and large landholders sold parts of their produce to urban residents. These markets also provided an important opportunity for the nomads to come into contact with peasants and the urban population. Large sectors of the rural population came to use coinage, especially the small denominations of silver *akçe* and the copper *mangır*, through their participation in these markets.[20]

Second, small-scale but intensive networks of credit relations developed in and around the urban centers. Evidence from thousands of court cases in these towns and cities involving lenders and borrowers leave no doubt that the use of credit, small and large, was widespread among all segments of urban and parts of rural society. It is clear that neither the Islamic prohibitions against interest and usury nor the absence of formal banking institutions prevented the expansion of credit in Ottoman society.[21]

As a result, debasements had an impact on virtually all groups in Ottoman society, and in turn each group took a position. Most men and women, urban and rural, were clear about the consequences of different ways of dealing with the coinage and about who gained and who lost. In general, all those who had future obligations expressed in terms of the unit of account—most important, borrowers and tenants paying fixed rents in cash—stood to gain from debasements. Conversely, those who expected to be paid fixed amounts in terms of the unit of account stood to lose from debasements.

In the rural areas, taxes and rents on public and privately held lands were paid almost entirely in kind during the 18th and 19th centuries. Moreover, those producers who sold part of their crop in local markets received higher prices during periods of inflation. As a result, debasements and inflation did not have a major impact on rural producers. The significant exception, of course, were the lenders and borrowers in the countryside. Local court records indicate that numbers of court cases involving lending and borrowing by rural as well as urban residents typically showed sharp increases during periods of frequent debasement and rapid inflation.

In the urban areas, a dense network of credit relations existed, most of which was involved small-scale lenders and small cash *vakıfs* that lent on interest. The local moneychangers (*sarrafs*), with their expert knowledge of the markets, often benefited from the uncertainty and fluctuations in exchange rates as well as from the requirement to surrender old coins in the aftermath of debasements. Most of them were net lenders, however, and they stood to lose from the inflation that followed debasements. As the fiscal problems of the Ottoman state intensified in the second half of the 18th century, the *sarrafs* of Istanbul began to provide larger loans to the state, using their connections to the financial markets in Europe. This lucrative process soon transformed the traditional moneychangers into the so-called Galata bankers, named after the financial district in the capital city. The Galata bankers also held considerable amounts of *esham*, or long-term government bonds.[22]

Merchants and shopkeepers in the urban areas did not appear to lose from debasements, since the prices of goods they sold tended to rise during periods of inflation. There was always the risk, however, that the government would impose price ceilings on essential goods sold in the urban markets when prices rose too fast. As a result, merchants and shopkeepers were also wary of debasements.

The groups that stood to lose the most from debasements were those who were paid fixed amounts in terms of the unit of account. The most important groups in this category were the employees of the state, the bureaucracy, the ulama, and, especially, the janissaries. A large overlap existed between the guild members and the janissaries after the latter began to moonlight as artisans and shopkeepers in the 17th century.

Given this configuration of winners and mostly losers from debasements, Ottoman governments' attitudes toward debasements entailed the weighing their short-term fiscal benefits against their short- and long-term costs. If the government perceived these costs to be lower than the expected fiscal benefits, then a debasement or a series of debasements could be adopted. In other words, far from being an exercise in futility, the debasements were viewed by the Ottoman administrators as a potentially effective instrument of fiscal policy, especially in the short term. At the same time, however, there were significant economic and political constraints on the state's ability to take advantage of debasements.

The fiscal benefits of a debasement are not difficult to establish. The government was able to issue a larger amount of coinage in nominal terms with the same amount of specie and meet a larger fraction of its obligations.[23] One related measure often adopted by the government in the aftermath of a debasement was to prohibit the use and sale of gold and silver in local markets and order that these be surrendered to the imperial mint at below market prices. Finally, the state also obtained revenue from the old coins brought to the mint by the public.

On the other side there were a number of costs that might be borne by the state as a result of debasements. As prices rose, including those paid by the state in the aftermath of a debasement, many of the state revenues that were fixed in nominal terms declined in real terms. In other words, debasements generated an initial surge in revenues, followed by a decline in real terms due to the inflation they created. In the longer term, a debasement might even lead to a real decline in revenues if the government did not adjust upward the taxes and other revenues that had been fixed in nominal terms.

Second, if the public lost confidence in the currency and began to anticipate further debasements, it became increasingly difficult for the government to take advantage of further reductions in the specie content of coinage. In the open mint system, for example, the public might begin holding another currency and stay away from the mints. A large degree of currency substitution must have taken place during the period of high inflation from 1585 to 1650 and during the reign of Mahmud II (1808–39) as varieties of foreign coinage were free to circulate.[24]

A third cost of Ottoman debasements was the spread of counterfeiting. When the government issued new coins with lower specie content, counterfeiters immediately began to mint the new coins with the same or even higher silver content to share the fiscal revenues of the state. This opportunity declined, however, when precious-metal prices adjusted upward along with other prices. Price ceilings on the specie and government attempts to obtain the specie at those official prices also encouraged counterfeiting.

Yet another cost was the adverse implications of debasements for the ability of the state to borrow domestically. As the government began to make use of debasements, the public typically began to anticipate more, and it became increasingly difficult to borrow from the public at large. There is evidence that with the acceleration of debasements after 1808, rates of interest increased even further, and it became even more difficult for the government to sell the government paper called *esham*. For example, it appears that the ratio between the initial sale price of *esham* and the annual payments declined after 1808 when the government began to use debasements more frequently.[25]

The most important cost of Ottoman debasements, however, was the political opposition they generated among the urban groups, especially in the capital city. One group that disliked debasements included the guild members, shopkeepers, small merchants, and wage-earning artisans. Another group that stood to lose from debasements were those who were paid fixed salaries by the state: the bureaucracy, the ulama, and the janissaries stationed permanently in the capital. This broad opposition acted as a major deterrent to the more frequent use of debasements by the government not only in the capital but also in the provincial centers. It would be interesting to explore the causal linkages between the debasements and the urban rebellions of the late 18th and early 19th centuries in Syria, Iraq, and elsewhere in the empire.[26]

The effectiveness of this urban opposition should not be measured in terms of the frequency of rebellions, however. Just as E. P. Thompson argued in his study of the moral economy of the English crowd in the 18th century that the effectiveness of the bread riots should not be measured in terms of their frequency, the threat of rebellions proved just as effective in the longer term.[27] It ensured that the governments would refrain from debasements—at least, during periods of peace.

Into this framework of costs and benefits and interaction between the state and society wars enter as exogenous shocks—events that raised both the need for short-term revenues for the state and the willingness of the public to accept extraordinary measures such as debasements. As the urgency of generating revenues increased, the state often invoked references to holy wars and even linked the new coinage explicitly to the ongoing wars—for example, calling the new issues of coins and bonds *cihadiyye*, or of holy war.

Mahmud II was well aware of the limitations imposed by the janissaries and related urban groups. From the very beginning of his reign in 1808, he wanted to replace the janissaries with a Western-style army. During the early years of his long reign, however, he did not have the political support to make this critical move. After the janissaries were finally defeated and the order was abolished in 1826 (in what is usually considered one of the most important political events of this period, the *Vaka-i Hayriye*, or the "Auspicious Event") a major constraint in the way of debasements was lifted. Only two years later, the government began the largest debasement ever in Ottoman history, reducing the specie content of the *kuruş* by 79 percent within a period of four years.

COMPARISONS ACROSS EUROPE

In a recent study of prices and wages in European cities from the Middle Ages to World War I, Robert Allen uses a large body of data, most of which was compiled during the early part of the 20th century by studies commissioned by the International Scientific Committee on Price History, founded in 1929.[28] To facilitate comparisons, he has converted all price and wage series into grams of silver and chosen as a base the index of average consumer prices prevailing in Strasbourg in 1700–49.[29]

Allen argues that even though prices in a single city can be accepted as a barometer of prices and wages in the whole economy, international comparisons need to be made between cities at similar levels in the urban hierarchy. Since his study uses data from cities at the top of their respective urban hierarchies, such as London, Antwerp, Amsterdam, Milan, Vienna, Leipzig, and Warsaw, it would make sense to insert Istanbul, another city at the top of the urban hierarchy of its region, into this framework. This is not difficult to do, because prices are already expressed in grams of silver in the present study. However, it is still necessary to express Istanbul prices in terms of the Allen base of Strasbourg 1700–49 equalling 1.0. For this purpose, Ottoman commodity prices for the interval 1700–49 were applied to Allen's consumer basket with fixed weights. A second and equally useful method of linking Istanbul's price level to the price levels of other European cities in the Allen set was to employ the detailed annual commodity-price series gathered by Earl Hamilton for Valencia and Madrid for 1500 to 1800 and compare them with the Istanbul prices for the same commodities.[30] Since Valencia and Madrid prices were already calibrated into the Allen set, it was then possible to determine the Istanbul price level vis-à-vis European cities for each interval. The price series for flour, mutton, olive oil, cooking oil, onions, chickpeas, pepper, sugar, and wood were used in these calculations. The two procedures produced results that were quite similar (Figure 5).

One revision in the Allen series concerns price levels during the 1850–99 and 1900–13 intervals. To remain consistent throughout, Allen continued to express all prices

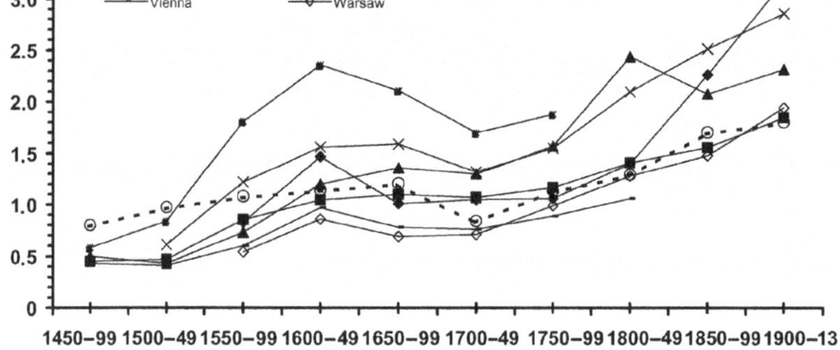

FIGURE 5. Consumer price indexes for European cities, 1450–1913 (prices in grams of silver; Strasbourg, 1700–49 = 1.0).

and wages in grams of silver, even after 1870, when silver prices declined sharply and most European countries abandoned the bimetallic system in favor of the gold standard. While technically correct, this procedure gives the impression that most European cities experienced a high rate of inflation during this period, while in fact nominal prices and wages remained quite stable. We chose to express all price and wage levels in gold after 1870 by deflating the Allen series by 1.3 and 2.1 for 1850–99 and 1900–13, respectively.

The insertion of Istanbul prices into this framework raises some questions and leads to a number of interesting observations. First, European price series indicate that during the first half of the 16th century, before the impact of the Price Revolution began to be felt, prices were higher in southern Europe than elsewhere in Europe. Similarly, my indexes show that in the early 16th century, prices in Istanbul were higher than prices in all of the sixteen cities covered by Allen (Figure 5). Second and relatedly, the rise in Istanbul prices expressed in grams of silver was slower than elsewhere in Europe until 1650. As a result, Istanbul prices expressed in grams of silver tended to converge with those in other Mediterranean and European cities during the era of the Price Revolution, with the exception of Spain, where prices rose fastest and remained higher than anywhere else in Europe.

Third, the European series indicate that, despite the huge growth in trade, the spread of European prices expressed in grams of silver was just as wide on the eve of World War I as it had been in 1500. European prices and price disparities began to increase after 1800, with London leading the way. Istanbul prices expressed in grams of silver began to rise in the second half of the 18th century but lagged behind other European cities during the 19th century. On the eve of World War I, Istanbul prices in grams of silver or gold were comparable to but lower than all of the other cities in the Allen set.

Istanbul and other Ottoman port cities remained linked to other European ports during these four centuries through the Black Sea and especially the Mediterranean. In the future, it would be useful to examine the issue of price integration more closely by applying statistical techniques to the annual Istanbul and other European price series. Even if prices on the eve of World War I do not show any greater degree of convergence than in 1500, it would be useful to identify more precisely the periods in which Istanbul prices tended to converge with those in other European cities and when they tended to move apart during these four centuries.

CONCLUSION

Based on a large research project in the Ottoman archives in Istanbul, this paper has established for the first time the long-term trends in consumer prices for Istanbul and other Ottoman cities from the second half of the 15th century until World War I. Our results indicate that prices increased about 300 times from 1469 until World War I. This overall increase corresponds to an average increase of 1.3 percent per year, end to end. Our price indexes also show that the Ottoman Empire experienced a significant wave of inflation from the late 16th to the middle of the 17th century, when prices increased about fivefold. This is the period usually associated with the Price Revolution of the 16th century. The indexes also show, however, that a much stronger wave of inflation occurred beginning in the late 18th century and lasting into the 1850s, when prices increased 12–15 times. Most of those increases were associated with currency debasements that began in the 1780s and accelerated during the reign of Mahmud II. In contrast, the overall price level was relatively stable from 1650 to 1780 and from 1860 until World War I.

Even though nominal prices in Istanbul increased about 300 times, prices expressed in grams of silver stayed within the relatively narrow range of 1.0 to 3.0 during these four and a half centuries. This result indicates that the so-called silver inflation contributed to the changes in the overall price level, but debasements were by far the most important determinant of Ottoman prices increases in the long term. Debasements were undertaken by the Ottoman government mostly for fiscal gain. Far from being an exercise in futility, the debasements were viewed by the Ottoman administrators as a potentially effective instrument of fiscal policy, especially in the short term. At the same time, however, there existed significant economic and political constraints on the state's ability to take advantage of debasements.

The last section of the article offered a comparison with the price trends in leading European cities for which detailed price data are available for the same period. Our comparisons indicate that in the early 16th century, prices in Istanbul expressed in grams of silver were higher than prices in most, if not all, of the leading urban centers of Europe. During the Price Revolution of the 16th and early 17th centuries, however, prices expressed in grams of silver rose much faster in Western Europe and exceeded Ottoman prices. By the 19th century, Istanbul prices expressed in grams of silver or gold were comparable to but lower than prices in most other cities in Europe.

NOTES

Author's note: This research project has been supported by the State Institute of Statistics of Turkey, Academy of Sciences of Turkey, and Boğaziçi University, Research Fund, through projects 99HZ02 and 01Z101. In addition to these institutions, the author thanks Figen Taşkın, Nadir Özbek, and Işık Özel for valuable research assistance. Thanks are also due to Robert Allen for sharing his data, insights, and experience.

[1]Most of the account books of the pious foundations used in this study are available from the Maliyeden Müdevver (MM); Bab-ı Defteri; Başmuhasebe Kalemi (BŞM); Evkaf Defterleri (EV); and Evkaf Nezareti, Haremeyn Muhasebeciliği (EV.HMH) Collections at the Prime Ministry, Ottoman Archives (Başbakanlık Osmanlı Arşivleri [BOA]) in Istanbul. The account books of the Topkapi palace kitchen are available from the Bab-ı Defteri, Matbah Emini (D.BŞM.MTE); Bab-ı Defteri, Başmuhasebe Kalemi (D.BŞM); MM; Kamil Kepeci (KK); Cevdet Saray (CS); Maliye Nezareti, Mesarifat Muhasebesi (ML.MSF); Bab-ı Defteri, Odun Emini (D.BŞM.ODE); and Bab-ı Defteri, İstanbul Ağası (D.BŞM.ISA) Collections, also at the BOA, and the Dosya (D) Collection, at the Topkapı Palace Archives. The *narh* lists were approved by the local judges (*kadi*) and were taken from the Istanbul, Üsküdar, and Galata Islamic court archives in Istanbul. Complete lists of all archival documents used in this price study are available on a year-to-year basis from the appendixes in Şevket Pamuk, *Istanbul ve Diger Kentlerde 500 Yıllık Fiyatlar ve Ucretler, 1469–1998* (Ankara: State Institute of Statistics, 2000).

[2]Annual values of these four food-price indexes are not provided here because of space limitations. For further details, see Pamuk, *500 Yıllık Fiyatlar*, Figs. 2.2, 2.3.

[3]Şevket Pamuk, *A Monetary History of the Ottoman Empire* (Cambridge: Cambridge University Press, 2000), 9–19.

[4]Halilsah Sahillioğlu, "Yeniçeri Çuhası ve II. Bayezid'in Son Yıllarında Yeniçeri Çuha Muhasebesi," *Güney-Doğu Avrupa Araştırmaları Dergisi* 2–3 (1973–74): 415–65.

[5]Pamuk, *500 Yıllık Fiyatlar*, chap. 1.

[6]Detailed indexes of the prices of basic foodstuffs expressed in grams of silver and the terms of trade between foodstuffs and manufactured goods have also been calculated from the Istanbul data: ibid., chap. 2.

[7]Ljuben L. Berov, *Prices in the Balkans During the 16th–19th Centuries and the European Revolution of Prices* (in Bulgarian) (Sofia: Publishing House of the Bulgarian Academy of Sciences, 1976). A summary is

available in L. Berov, "Changes in Price Conditions in Trade Between Turkey and Europe in the 16th–19th Century," *Etudes Balkaniques* 3 (1974): 168–78.

[8]Pamuk, *500 Yıllık Fiyatlar*, apps.; Andre Raymond, *Artisans et commerçants au Caire au XVIIIe siècle* (Damascus: Institut Français de Damas, 1973–74), 1:17–80. For these calculations, the silver content of the Cairo *para* is taken from Pamuk, *Monetary History*, 95–101, 172–78.

[9]Pamuk, *500 Yıllık Fiyatlar*, Fig. 3.2.

[10]As a measure of cloth prices in Western Europe in the early modern era we have used the textile-price index for the Netherlands constructed by Jan Luiten Van Zanden. This index is available in nominal and grams-of-silver terms from the International Institute of Social History's website at www.iisg.nl/hwp.

[11]Sugar and coffee were brought to Istanbul from Egypt in the earlier period. It was the arrival of imports from Atlantic sources that led to the sharp decline in the prices of both commodities during the 19th century.

[12]Our index includes prices of imported cotton cloth, sugar, and coffee after 1860: see Pamuk, *500 Yıllık Fiyatlar*, apps., for details.

[13]Prices of flour, meat, and wood increased faster than the overall index after 1750. This may be due—at least, in part—to a decrease in, if not the end of, government attempts to regulate the prices of essentials in the capital city. All annual price observations used in the study are presented in ibid.

[14]A recent study of prices and inequality in Europe since 1500 similarly argues that relative price movements favored higher-income groups and increased income inquality in Western Europe from 1500 to 1800: Philip Hoffman, David Jacks, Patricia A. Levin, and Peter H. Lindert, "Prices and Real Inequality in Europe Since 1500," Working Paper Series no. 102, Agricultural History Center, University of California, Davis, October 2000. For a study of urban real wages in the Ottoman Empire during these four centuries utilizing wage data from the same archival sources, see Süleyman Özmucur and Şevket Pamuk, "Real Wages and Standards of Living in the Ottoman Empire, 1489–1914," *Journal of Economic History* 62 (2002): 292–321.

[15]For differing views on the extent of silver inflation and its causes and consequences during the 16th and 17th centuries, see Ömer Lütfi Barkan, "The Price Revolution of the Sixteenth Century: A Turning Point in the Economic History of the Near East," trans. Justin McCarthy, *International Journal of Middle East Studies* 6 (1975): 3–28; and Şevket Pamuk, "The Price Revolution in the Ottoman Empire Reconsidered," *International Journal of Middle East Studies* 33 (2001): 69–89. The latter study shows that silver inflation accounted for a smaller part, and debasements accounted for a larger part, of Ottoman price increases during the period 1500–1650 than Barkan suggested a quarter-century ago.

[16]Pamuk, *500 Yıllık Fiyatlar*, chap. 2 (figs.).

[17]C. M. Cipolla,"Currency Depreciation in Medieval Europe," *Economic History Review* 15 (1963): 413–15, provides a useful list of the causes of debasements and a good starting point. See also Harry A. Miskimin, *Money and Power in Fifteenth Century France* (New Haven, Conn.: Yale University Press, 1984); Michael D. Bordo, "Money, Deflation and Seigniorage in the Fifteenth Century," *Journal of Monetary Economics* 18 (1986): 337–46; and Nathan Sussman, "Debasements, Royal Revenues and Inflation in France During the Hundred Years' War, 1415–1422," *Journal of Economic History* 53 (1993): 44–70.

[18]Bordo, "Money, Deflation and Seigniorage."

[19]F. Braudel, *Civilization and Capitalism, 15th–18th Century, Vol. III: The Perspective of the World* (New York: Harper and Row, 1984), 471–73.

[20]S. Faroqhi, "The Early History of Balkan Fairs, "*Südost-Forschungen* 37 (1978): 50–68; idem, "Sixteenth Century Periodic Markets in Various Anatolian Sancaks," *Journal of the Economic and Social History of the Orient* 22 (1979): 32–80; and idem, "Rural Society in Anatolia and the Balkans During the Sixteenth Century," *Turcica* 9 (1977): 161–96, and 11 (1979): 103–53; Pamuk, *Monetary History*, 74–76.

[21]Pamuk, *Monetary History*, 77–87.

[22]Araks Şahiner, "The Sarrafs of Istanbul: Financiers of the Empire" (unpublished M.A. diss., Department of History, Bogaziçi University, Istanbul, 1995); *Islam Ansiklopedisi*, vol. 11 (Istanbul, 1995), 376–80, s. v. "Esham" (Mehmet Genç). It would be interesting to explore the attitudes of the notables or *ayan* of the provinces toward money and inflation during the 18th and early 19th centuries. Many *ayan* were the holders of various types of tax farms, both short term and long term. To the extent that the tax farmers were expected to make fixed payments to the state each year, they tended to benefit from debasements and inflation. At the same time, however, many *ayan* were engaged in trade, especially long-distance trade. In their role as long-distance merchants, they must have favored monetary stability.

[23]Contemporary Ottoman commentators argued that debasements were not useful for the state because the prices rose and the state revenues, which were fixed in nominal terms, declined in real terms after each

debasement: Cezar, *Osmanlı Maliyesinde Bunalım* (Istanbul: Alan Yayincilik), 147. This argument, however, does not take into account the revenue obtained by the state during the first round by issuing additional coinage. With the time horizon severely shortened under the pressure of war and severe financial crises, it thus made sense to pursue debasements for short-term fiscal gains.

[24]For an episode of currency substitution arising from the instability of the *akçe* during the 17th century, see Şevket Pamuk, "In the Absence of Domestic Currency: Debased European Coinage in the Seventeenth-Century Ottoman Empire," *Journal of Economic History* 57 (1997): 345–66; and idem, *Monetary History*, 138–58.

[25]Cezar, *Osmanlı Maliyesinde Bunalım*, 79–89, 133–35, 239–41.

[26]I am indebted to Dina Rizk Khoury for information on the urban uprisings in Syria and Iraq during the period 1770–1830.

[27]E. P. Thompson, "The Moral Economy of the British Crowd in the Eighteenth Century," *Past and Present* 50 (1971): 76–135. See also Charles Tilly, "Food Supply and Public Order in Modern Europe," in *The Formation of Nation States in Western Europe*, ed. Charles Tilly (Princeton, N.J.: Princeton University Press, 1975), 35–151.

[28]Arthur Cole and Ruth Crandall, "The International Scientific Committee on Price History," *Journal of Economic History* 24 (1964): 381–88.

[29]Robert Allen, "The Great Divergence in European Wages and Prices from the Middle Ages to the First World War," *Explorations in Economic History* 38 (2001): 411–47.

[30]Earl J. Hamilton, *American Treasure and the Price Revolution in Spain, 1501–1650* (Cambridge, Mass.: Harvard University Press, 1934); and idem, *War and Prices in Spain, 1650–1800* (Cambridge, Mass.: 1947).

APPENDIX : LONG-TERM TRENDS OF THE INDEX

Based on trends in money and prices, it is best to examine these four and a half centuries in five distinct time periods. Piecewise regressions were used to estimate separate trend lines for each period. Data on the silver content of the Ottoman currency are taken from Pamuk's *A Monetary History of the Ottoman Empire*.

The first period, from 1469 until 1585, is characterized by stable money, rising population, and rising prices expressed in grams of silver (the era of the so-called Price Revolution). The trend lines indicate that the silver content of the currency declined at an annual rate of 0.52 percent, and prices rose at an annual rate of 1.13 percent during this period.

During the second period, from 1585 to 1690, there was a high degree of monetary and price instability, together with declining population. The silver content of the currency fluctuated wildly and declined at an annual rate of 1.05 percent. Prices rose at an annual rate of 0.67 percent during this period.

The third period, from 1690 to 1768, was once again a period of monetary and price stability. The silver content of the currency declined at an annual rate of 0.30 percent, and prices rose at an annual rate of 0.44 percent.

The fourth period, from 1769 to 1843, is characterized by the most rapid rates of debasement in Ottoman history, high inflation, and rising real wages. The silver content of the currency declined at an annual rate of 3.49 percent, and prices rose at an annual rate of 3.81 percent during this period.

The fifth period, from 1844 to 1914, witnessed stable money under bimetallism, rapidly expanding international trade, and stable prices. The silver content of the currency remained unchanged, and prices increased at an annual rate of 0.67 percent until World War I. Most of the price increases occurred early in the period and were the lagged result of the debasements of the previous period.

VII

In the Absence of Domestic Currency: Debased European Coinage in the Seventeenth-Century Ottoman Empire

The Near East was subject to many of the same fiscal and monetary forces that affected Europe and parts of Asia during the early modern era. For almost two decades during the seventeenth century, debased European coinage circulated widely in Ottoman markets at values far above their specie content. This article provides an explanation in terms of Ottoman fiscal deficits, currency instability, currency substitution, and decline in local silver mines all of which led to the closure of mints. The reasons behind the conspicuous absence of Ottoman copper coinage during this period are also explored.

For almost two decades during the middle of the seventeenth century, French, Italian, and Dutch merchants minted in southern France, northern Italy, and elsewhere in Europe large amounts of European coinage whose specie content had been reduced to mostly copper with a thin silver coating. These coins were then transported across the Mediterranean and used as payment for Ottoman goods or even sold wholesale to local merchants and moneychangers. Initially they fetched prices far above their metal content, but these premiums declined over time with the increasing volume of trade that eventually involved hundreds of ships and close to 200 million pieces of coin. The gross revenues of the European merchants have been estimated at more than ten million Spanish pieces of eight or somewhere between six to eight million Venetian gold ducats.

This episode has been described in detail by at least half a dozen European travelers including the authors of well-known volumes such as Chevalier Chardin, J. B. Tavernier, and Paul Rycaut.[1] Published documents from the archives of mints in northern Italy also confirm the production of these coins.[2] In addition, the numismatics literature provides a detailed inventory and description of these coins, including their inscriptions and dates of

I would like to thank Emre Alper, Cihan Bilginsoy, Murat Çizakça, Hasan Ersel, Mehmet Genç, Halil Sahillioğlu, Osman Sarı, two anonymous referees of this JOURNAL, and Joel Mokyr for valuable comments on earlier versions. I am also indebted to Reşat Kasaba for help with source materials and Türkan Rado for expert assistance with the Latin inscriptions on European coinage. Research support from the Academy of Sciences of Turkey is gratefully acknowledged.

[1]Chardin, *Voyages*, pp. 7–22; Rycaut, *History*, pp. 258–68; and Tavernier, *New Relation*, pp. 15–33.

[2]Hasluck, "Levantine Coinage", pp. 58–59.

production.[3] Many of these coins are now available in numismatics collections throughout Europe.

Contemporary European observers were incredulous that debased coins could be so popular in the markets of the Levant. Rycaut lamented that the Turks "had no wit enough to understand" what was happening.[4] In an article published in the early part of this century, F. W. Hasluck provided the most detailed treatment of the coins involved and insisted that "the Turkish public refused to be undeceived." He concluded that "in all times certain foreign currencies have had special vogue among alien, and especially illiterate nations. . . . The scandalous exploitation of the Turkish markets by the importers of *luigini* was neither the first attempt of its kind nor the last. It differed from others by the scale on which it was carried out, by the success that attended it, in spite of repeated protest and exposure, down to the final abolition of the traffic, and perhaps by the more than ordinary shamelessness of those engaged in it."[5] Writers in twentieth-century Turkey have accepted this interpretation and argued that in this "biggest counterfeiting scheme in history," the unscrupulous European merchants robbed the unsuspecting Ottomans.[6] It is also interesting that the Ottoman archives, which offer extensive records on a wide variety of phenomena around the empire, have so far revealed little about this episode.[7]

There are two related puzzles here. The first concerns the popularity of the European coins. Attempts at counterfeiting coins are not always successful and rarely at this scale. It was always easy for the local merchants and moneychangers who initially accepted these coins from the European merchants to assay them, a practice known in the Near East for almost two millennia. Even if the moneychangers were reluctant to divulge their trade secrets, the silver content of these coins could not possibly have remained hidden for so many years. Clearly, it remains to be explained why the Ottoman public was willing to accept them at rates far above their specie content at this particular time.

I will provide an explanation from the Ottoman side, in terms of the fiscal and monetary conditions prevailing in the Ottoman Empire at the time. I will show that at the eastern end of the Mediterranean, the period from the 1560s until late in the seventeenth century was at least as turbulent for state finances and money as it was at the western end. The Ottomans faced severe fiscal pressures and struggled with rising military expenditures and the adverse consequences of the silver inflation during this period. One response

[3]Ibid, pp. 68–76.

[4]Rycaut, *History*, p. 258.

[5]Hasluck, "Levantine Coinage," pp. 59, 63.

[6]Berkes, *Türkiye Iktisat Tarihi*, vol. 2, pp. 183–91.

[7]Robert Mantran is the first to draw attention to the silence of the Ottoman archives on this episode. Mantran, *Istanbul*, book 2, chap. 2 and "Politique, Economie et Monnaie."

was currency debasements that provided temporary fiscal relief but also added new momentum to price increases. The massive Ottoman debasement of 1585 to 1586 was followed by a period of wars, rebellions, fiscal crises, and extreme instability of the silver *akçe*, the leading Ottoman unit, lasting until the middle of the seventeenth century.[8]

One important question these debasements raise is whether the government employed them as a long-term strategy for generating revenue. This question has been debated in some detail in the recent literature on the monetary history of the late medieval and early modern periods. On the one side, Harry Miskimin has argued that in fourteenth- and fifteenth-century France debasements reflected, more than anything else, the despair of the rulers and did not help them fiscally. Michael D. Bordo has questioned this argument and in recent contributions published in this JOURNAL, Nathan Sussman and Akira Motomura have argued that debasements were employed as a rational and sometimes long-term strategy for raising fiscal revenue in fifteenth-century France and seventeenth-century Spain. In his detailed study of the monetary history of medieval Europe, Peter Spufford also argues that central governments benefited from debasements during the fourteenth and fifteenth centuries.[9] This article provides evidence from the Ottoman debasements that support the latter position.

I will also show that this extended period of monetary volatility resulted in considerable amount of currency substitution: loss of confidence in the Ottoman currency and a shift by the public towards European coinage that had always circulated in Ottoman lands. Not coincidentally, this was a period when many European states and economies also faced silver shortages. The flow of silver from America and Europe through the Near East towards Asia must have also contributed to this common pattern. When silver stopped coming to the mints and the Ottoman government was unable to acquire additional supplies most of the mints were closed down and the production of the silver *akçe* came to a virtual halt in the 1640s. It was in this context that the debased European coinage found widespread acceptance. This perspective is either missing altogether or not adequately

[8]Two decades ago, Ömer Lütfi Barkan linked these fiscal, economic, and monetary difficulties to the arrival of American silver and the Price Revolution of the sixteenth century. Labeling the Price Revolution "a turning point" in the history of the Near East, he argued that the price increases led to the decline of industry from which the empire never recovered. Barkan, "Price Revolution." Recent research has shown that Barkan's claims about the impact of inflation on the Ottoman economy were exaggerated. A reexamination of the causes and consequences of the Price Revolution in the Ottoman Empire falls outside the scope of the present article, however. A partial critique of Barkan was provided by Sundhaussen, "Die Preisrevolution."

[9]Miskimin, *Money*, p. 59; Bordo, "Money"; Sussman, "Debasements"; Motomura, "Best and Worst of Currencies"; and Spufford, *Money*, pp. 289–318. Carlo Cipolla has also underlined the fiscal motive in medieval and early modern debasements. Cipolla, *Money*, p. 28 and "Currency Depreciation."

considered in the writings of contemporary European observers as well as in more recent interpretations based on those accounts.

The second and related puzzle concerns the absence of Ottoman copper coinage under these circumstances. For most of the seventeenth century, fiscal pressures as well as the disappearance of silver forced the governments in Spain, France, Sweden, Poland, Russia, and elsewhere in Europe to place greater emphasis on copper coinage both in order to raise fiscal revenue and also provide a medium of exchange.[10] In contrast, the Ottoman government abandoned the production not only of silver but also copper coinage some time during the second quarter of the century. The absence of copper coinage in the Ottoman case certainly contributed to the sharp differences between the European and Ottoman experiences during this period despite the apparent similarity of fiscal and monetary conditions. I will argue that the government was aware of the opportunities provided by copper coinage, but due to a combination of technological and organizational limitations, it could not pursue this alternative.

DEBASED COINS IN OTTOMAN MARKETS

It is well known that Europe experienced large trade deficits towards Asia during the sixteenth and seventeenth centuries. Often unable to find a sufficient volume of goods to sell to the markets in the East, European merchants paid the difference with bullion and coinage imported from the Americas. There are many accounts of European ships leaving for the Near East and Asia loaded with cargoes of silver and silver coinage and, less frequently, with gold. As a result, large silver coins minted in America and Europe known as *grosso* or *groschen*, the most popular of which was the Spanish piece of eight, circulated extensively in Ottoman markets and Asia after 1550. A large part of these coins continued to move towards Iran and ports on the Indian Ocean, however, since the Ottoman economy experienced trade deficits towards the east while it enjoyed surpluses towards the west.[11]

The episode to be examined here also began with the efforts of European merchants trying to secure coinage before another trip to the Levant in 1653. From that point on, however, it unfolded in a new direction; the trade balances between the western and eastern ends of the Mediterranean ceased to be the driving force for the ensuing monetary flows. Instead, fiscal and monetary conditions in the Ottoman Empire emerged as the primary explanation for what happened, as I shall show.

[10]Spooner, *International Economy*, pp. 33–53, 171–96.

[11]Chaudhuri relates, for example, how the ships of the East India Company occasionally experienced difficulty in securing silver coinage before their departure for Asia. Chaudhuri, *Trading World of Asia*, p. 135; see also Attman, "Flow"; Barrett, "World Bullion Flows"; and Gaastra, "Exports."

When French merchants could not obtain the Spanish pieces of eight due to political tensions between Spain and France, they brought from Marseilles to the eastern Mediterranean a five-sols piece originally issued in 1641 for Louis XIII. This was an attractive coin, probably one of the earliest examples of milled coins to be seen in the Levant. In addition to serving as a medium of exchange, the coin was also used, at least initially, as ornamentation by peasant women who could not afford the more expensive silver and gold pieces.[12]

In France 12 of these five-sols pieces exchanged for one gold ecu or one Spanish piece of eight. Soon after their arrival in the Ottoman markets, eight of these coins began to exchange for one piece of eight.[13] At this rate, the purchasing power of the five-sols piece was not at all small. If an unskilled construction worker in Istanbul was paid with these coins, he would receive approximately two of them for one day's work.[14] Given the substantial difference in their exchange rates between the western and eastern ends of the Mediterranean, the French merchants soon began to import the five-sols pieces in bulk. After a number of years, they also began to manufacture on a large scale coins of identical weight and appearance but containing smaller amounts of silver and a larger percentage of alloy. The Italians and the Dutch soon joined the trade.

The method used was to approach a local potentate in southern France or northern Italy who possessed the right of coinage and contract him or her for the use of the seignorial mint in order to strike, with his knowledge, a large number of base coins bearing his name.[15] Very soon, debased coins minted with the names of the Princess of Trevoux, the princes of Dombes, Oranges, Monaco, Masse, Avignon, Genova, and others were circulating in the Ottoman markets.[16] In his examination of another episode of trade in debased coinage, Charles Kindleberger emphasizes that this was not an unusual practice in Europe. According to Kindleberger, "many states in Europe were interested in raising seigniorage within their boundaries, but it was soon discovered that debased money could be taken abroad and exchanged for

[12]Hasluck, "Levantine Coinage," p. 56.

[13]Chardin, *Voyages*, p. 7; and Hasluck "Levantine Coinage," p. 56. In the Ottoman markets these coins were called *sumun* (or *tumn*), which meant one-eighth in Arabic-Ottoman. The standard *akçe* exchanged at 80 to 90 for one piece of eight during this period (see Table 2 below). The physical appearance of these coins may have contributed to but can not entirely explain the higher rate they fetched in the Ottoman markets, as I will argue below. Similarly, the large differences in the exchange rates of the five-sols piece between western Europe and the eastern Mediterranean can not be explained away by the east-west differences in gold-silver ratios. Recent research has shown the differences in the gold-silver ratios between the two ends of the Mediterranean rarely exceeded 10 percent during the sixteenth and seventeenth centuries. Pamuk, "Money," tables A-2, A-5.

[14]This wage rate is taken from construction account books in the Ottoman archives as part of a long-term price and wage study being undertaken by the author.

[15]Tavernier, *New Relation*, pp.16–24.

[16]For a full list, see the catalogue provided by Hasluck,"Levantine Coinage," pp. 65–71.

good money, which could in turn be brought back and recoined with greater seigniorage."[17] This was not a simple propagation of a monetary crisis from one part of the Mediterranean to the other, however. As far as I can determine, this substandard coinage did not circulate in any significant amount in southern Europe at this time.

As the silver content of the coins began to fall, the inscriptions on the coins began to change. *Bonitatis unciarum sex* (six-twelfths) gave way to *bonitatis unciarum quinque* (five) and then to *bonitatis unciarum quatuor* (four) and even *trium*. In some cases, an Arabic numeral indicating the fineness was inserted at the end of the corresponding legend in Latin. There are also examples of coins on which the Arabic numerals are higher than the standard inscribed in Latin.[18] With the disappearance of the silver and the increasing volume of trade, the market rates of the coins sunk as low as 20 for one Spanish piece of eight, thus making them even more suitable for daily transactions. In the meantime, the mint authorities wanted to prevent the circulation of these coins in Europe. One method was to differentiate the coins from export from those circulating in Europe. Inscriptions like *per totam asiam cvrrens* (current in all of Asia) or *Voluit hanc Asia mercem De procul pretium eius* (payment for goods in distant Asia) were added to some of the coins to warn Europeans about the boundaries of their circulation.[19]

The peak in the traffic was reached between 1656 and 1669. J. B. Tavernier estimates the total volume of European coinage that went through the Ottoman customs at 180 million pieces, or at more than ten million Spanish pieces of eight. In gold, this corresponded to more than six million Venetian ducats. In addition, some unknown quantity was smuggled into Ottoman territory in part by bribing customs officials. According to another estimate, an average of 22 ships arrived at the port of Izmir every year during this period, all loaded with these debased pieces.[20] Such volumes suggest that the remaining good coins in the Ottoman markets were being taken back to southern Europe and reminted as base *luigini* and re-imported to the Ottoman markets.[21]

MONETARY AND FISCAL CONDITIONS IN THE OTTOMAN EMPIRE

To understand the willingness of the Ottoman public to accept the debased coins, it is essential to examine the fiscal and monetary conditions in the Ottoman empire during this period. More generally, this episode needs to be placed in the context of deteriorating economic, fiscal, and monetary

[17]Kindleberger, "Economic Crisis," p. 158.
[18]Hasluck, "Levantine Coinage," p. 59.
[19]Ibid., pp. 65–71, 86.
[20]Tavernier, *New Relation*.
[21]Hasluck, "Levantine Coinage," p. 59.

conditions in the core regions of the empire beginning in the last quarter of the sixteenth century. Many of these trends were quite similar to the difficulties experienced in many parts of Europe and Asia. Located between these two continents, the Near East was very much part of the fiscal and monetary processes that affected the Old World during the sixteenth and seventeenth centuries. It still needs to be explained, however, why Ottoman monetary difficulties unfolded so differently than those of European states during the same period.

Money

In and around the Mediterranean basin, the Ottomans were influenced by and became the carriers of the great monetary traditions of the Old World, from the Roman and Byzantine empires to the medieval Islamic states, to the Mongols of Persia and the Italian city states. The Ottoman state needed some form of money in order to collect taxes and make payments to the soldiers, bureaucrats, and suppliers of the army and the palace. More importantly, the bureaucracy was very much aware that there existed a strong link between the availability of money and the prosperity of trade and the economy especially since the Ottoman state had been located on long-distance trade routes ever since the earliest days in the fourteenth century.

Recent research has shown that the use of money in the Ottoman economy was not limited to narrow segments of the urban population. Through their participation in markets and because of state taxation of a wide range of economic activities, large segments of the rural population came to use coinage, especially the small denominations, during the sixteenth century.[22] A close examination of the provincial legal codes (*kanunname*) of this period point to an economy with strong urban and rural linkages, considerable market orientation and frequent collections of small amounts of taxes in money from the artisans and merchants as well as the nomads and sedentary peasants.[23] In addition, small-scale but intensive networks of credit relations developed in and around the urban centers. Peasants as well as urban residents took part in these monetary transactions.[24] A considerable part of the Ottoman economy as well as state finances thus depended on money and monetary stability, and the Ottoman administrators were well aware of that.

During the sixteenth century, the Ottoman monetary system in the Balkans, Anatolia and, parts of Syria was based on gold, silver, and copper coinage. The central piece was the silver *akçe*, the basic unit of account dating back to the fourteenth century. For most of the sixteenth century, this

[22]Faroqhi, "Early History" and "Sixteenth Century Periodic Markets"; Jennings, "Loans"; and Inalcık, "Osmanlı."

[23]A compilation of these provincial codes are available from Barkan, *Zirai Ekonomi*.

[24]Pamuk, "Money," pp. 950–61.

was a small coin weighing about 0.7 grams.[25] The official standards that were closely followed by the local mints until the 1570s, required that *akçes* be minted from "clean" silver without any alloy.[26] The gold *sultani* that began to be minted in the 1470s with standards identical to those of the Venetian ducat was used in large transactions, including international trade and also for storing wealth. The purchasing power of these two coins was determined by their specie content, which remained stable between the 1480s and the 1580s. At the bottom of the hierarchy were copper coinage called *mangır* or *pul* with nominal values and for small daily transactions. During the sixteenth century, eight of the large copper coins and 24 of the small copper coins equaled one *akçe* in value. The state did not accept copper coinage as payment, however. One shortcoming of the Ottoman coinage system was the absence of larger silver coins for medium-sized payments. Multiples of the *akçe* such as the ten-*akçe* piece were occasionally minted but these were discontinued. Thus, there existed a large gap in the hierarchy of coins between the gold *sultani*, whose exchange rate edged up from 55 to 65 *akçes* during the sixteenth century and the small *akçe* itself. As a result, the pressure on the *sultani* and the ducat persisted. Whenever gold coinage was not available in sufficient quantities, larger payments had to be made with piles of *akçes*.[27]

Foreign coins circulated extensively and without any form of government intervention. In local markets, Ottoman and foreign coins changed hands on the basis of their market rates of exchange, which closely reflected their specie content. For example, the Ottoman *sultani* and the Venetian ducat, with identical gold contents, exchanged at par until late in the sixteenth century. The government often announced the official rates at which gold and silver coins, Ottoman as well as foreign, would be accepted as payment. For the most part, the mints were kept open for the coinage of both silver and gold subject to seigniorage payments to the state.[28]

State Finances

Until the last quarter, the sixteenth century was a period of fiscal and monetary stability coupled with demographic and economic expansion in the Ottoman Empire. During the earlier part of the century new territories including Hungary, Syria, Mesopotamia, and Egypt had been incorporated into the empire. State finances benefited from these successful campaigns and the

[25]See Table 2 and Pamuk, "Money," for greater detail.

[26]It is not clear what "clean" meant in practice. The specie content of the available coins have not been studied in detail. Most specialists assume that standard *akçes* were minted from silver approximately 90 percent pure silver.

[27]This gap becomes more evident when compared with the coinage patterns of sixteenth-century Europe, for example. Grierson, "Monetary Pattern."

[28]Pamuk "Money," pp. 950–61; and Sahillioğlu, "Role."

inflows of annual remittances from these provinces, most importantly from Egypt. Along with increases in population and land under cultivation, internal and long-distance trade expanded. With growing commercialization, economic ties between the countryside and urban areas became stronger. The increasing monetary needs of this economy were met by the increased availability of gold, primarily from Egypt, and silver arriving from the Americas by way of Europe.

These favorable fiscal and economic trends were reversed, however, during the last quarter of the century. One important change was the deterioration of state finances. As military campaigns against Iran in the east and the Habsburgs in the west turned into long, protracted affairs, the budget surpluses enjoyed in the earlier part of the century began to disappear. Since some of the state revenues were fixed in nominal terms, the silver inflation of the sixteenth century also had adverse consequences for state finances.[29] A compilation of the available imperial budgets as summarized in Table 1 shows that deficits became more or less permanent by the end of the century. This new pattern lasted for most of the seventeenth century, eventually exhausting the reserves of the imperial treasury accumulated during earlier periods. The inflation-adjusted series presented in Table 1 indicates that revenues entering the imperial treasury failed to keep pace with inflation while nominal expenditures rose faster than inflation after the middle of the sixteenth century. At the very least, it is clear that expenditures rose faster than revenues during this period.[30]

Social and political upheavals known as the *Celali* rebellions that began late in the sixteenth and lasted well into the seventeenth century only exacerbated these fiscal difficulties. As the peasants took flight or returned to nomadism, agriculture, especially commercial agriculture, was adversely affected. Moreover, the discovery of the sea route to Asia finally began to show its effects on the intercontinental trade routes during the early decades of the seventeenth century. While the ocean triumphed over the mainland, after a lag of one century, many towns of the Levant as well as Ottoman state finances began to feel the decline in commercial activity.[31] As a result of these developments, it appears that in the Balkans and Anatolia and perhaps even in Syria, the demographic and economic expansion of the sixteenth century came to an end in the 1580s or soon thereafter. Population and economic activity stagnated and may have even declined in many parts of the empire during the seventeenth century.[32]

[29]Barkan, "Price Revolution"; and Inalcık, "Military and Fiscal Transformation."

[30]See Table 1, note 3.

[31]Steensgaard, *Asian Trade Revolution*, p. 9.

[32]Faroqhi and Erder, "Population"; Inalcık, "Military and Fiscal Transformation"; and, most recently, Faroqhi, "Crisis."

TABLE 1
A COMPILATION OF THE AVAILABLE BUDGETS OF THE OTTOMAN CENTRAL GOVERNMENT, 1523–1688

Year	Revenues: Current *Akçes* (millions)	Revenues: Index in Constant *Akçes*	Expenditures: Current *Akçes* (millions)	Expenditures: Index in Constant *Akçes*	Balance: Current *Akçes* (millions)
1523–1524	116.9 }		118.8 }		-1.9
1524–1525	141.3 }	100.0	126.6 }	100.0	+14.7
1527–1528	221.6 }		150.2 }		+71.4
1546–1547	241.7 }		171.9 }		+69.8
1547–1548	198.9 }	128.4	112.0 }	111.3	+86.9
1565–1566	183.1 }		189.7 }		-6.6
1567–1568	348.5 }		221.5 }		+127.0
1582–1583	313.7 }		277.6 }		+36.1
1592–1593	293.4 }	70.4	363.4 }	95.4	-70.0
1608	503.7 }		599.2 }		-95.5
1643–1644	514.5 }		513.8 }		+0.7
1650	532.9 }		687.2 }		-154.3
1652–1653	517.3 }		528.9 }		-11.6
1654	537.4 }	92.8	658.4 }	127.4	-21.0
1661–1662	581.3 }		593.6 }		-12.3
1666–1667	553.4 }		631.9 }		-78.5
1669–1670	612.5 }		637.2 }		-24.7
1687–1688	700.4 }		901.0 }		-200.6

Notes: These budget documents do not include all revenues and expenditures of the state. Most notably, they exclude revenues and expenditures collected and spent in the provinces including most of the taxes in kind collected from agricultural producers and spent to equip and train a cavalry-based provincial army. The provincial revenues that did not reach the capital were roughly equal in magnitude to the figures appearing in these budgets.

The revenue and expenditure figures given in current *akçes* are adjusted for inflation with the help of a food price index for the Istanbul region constructed by Barkan. His index, which begins with 100 for the base year 1489–1490, rose to 142 in 1555–1556, 180 in 1573, 182 in 1585–1586, 442 in 1595–1596, 630 in 1605–1606 and then declined to 504 in 1632–1633, 470 in 1648–1649, and 462 in 1655–1656. Since Barkan's price index is available for selected years only, I chose to provide, for the revenue and expenditure indices above, average values only for each of the subperiods.

It is well known that the terms of trade moved in favor of agriculture during the sixteenth-century Price Revolution in Europe. Available evidence suggests that this was the case in the eastern end of the Mediterranean as well. Barkan, "Price Revolution"; and Çizakça, "Price History." If so, then the food-price index above tends to overstate the extent of overall price increases.

Sources: The budgetary figures are taken from Tabakoğlu, *Gerileme Döneminde*, pp. 14–15. For a shorter list of budgets that point to the same pattern and a detailed discussion in English, see Barkan, "Price Revolution," pp. 17–21. The food-price index for Istanbul was taken from ibid, pp. 10–11.

Debasements

These adverse trends culminated in the debasement of 1585 or 1586, which reduced the silver content of the Ottoman unit by 44 percent after one century of stability.[33] This operation did not end the fiscal and monetary

[33]Whereas the mints used to strike 450 *akçes* from 100 *dirhams* of "clean" silver, they were now instructed to mint 850 *akçes* from the same amount. See Table 2 and also Kafadar, "Les Troubles Monetaires," pp. 381–89. The exact date of the debasement remains unclear.

TABLE 2
THE OTTOMAN *AKÇE* AND ITS EXCHANGE RATE AT ISTANBUL, 1500–1640

Years	Akçes minted from 100 dirhams of silver	Weight in Grams	Venetian Ducat	Spanish Piece of Eight
1500	420	0.73	54	—
1550	420	0.73	60	40
1584	450	0.68	65–70	40–42
1586	800	0.38	120	80
1596	—		220–230	
1600	950	0.32	125	78
1618	1,000	0.31	150	100
1620	—		160	100
1622	—		180–210	120–150
1623	—		210–280	120–170
1624	—		330–420	170–320
1624	1,000	0.31	130	
1628	—		190	100–110
1634	—		230	110–120
1640	—		270	125
1641	1,000	0.31	168	80
1650	—		175	90

Notes: The Ilkhanid dirham of Tabriz used by the Ottomans in monetary practices equaled 3.072 grams. Pamuk," Money," p. 954.

Until 1585 the standard *akçe* was minted from "clean" silver without any alloys. See note 26. For this early period, the standards of the *akçe* are available from mint records and imperial orders to the mints.

After the debasement of 1585–1586, however, unknown amounts of copper began to be added to the silver. For this latter period, the standards of the *akçe* are available from archival evidence for the years 1600, 1618, 1624, and 1640 since these were years of correction of coinage operations. For other years the silver content of the *akçe* can be approximated but not determined precisely from its exchange rates against the Spanish pieces of eight since European coins may have enjoyed a premium against the Ottoman unit based on respective specie contents.

Sources: Pamuk, "Money," tables A-2, A-3, A-5, and A-6 ; and Sahillioğlu,"XVII. Asrın," p. 233.

difficulties, however. The period until the 1640s was one of exceptional instability for the *akçe*; the fluctuations of the currency can be followed from a combination of sources. As shown in Table 2, the available mint records provide information about the weight and silver content of the standard *akçe* only for selected years of this period. For most years of this period, however, *akçes* produced by the mints fell below those standards. Although the silver content of the substandard or defective (*hurde*) coins can not be determined precisely, court records provide detailed information about their market exchange rates against the stable ducat and other leading European coins on a monthly basis. From these exchange rates, it is possible to approximate the sharp fluctuations in the silver content of the Ottoman unit. For example, from the last column of Table 2 it appears that during 1623 to 1624 the silver content of the *akçe* dropped to about one-third and during 1638 to 1640 to about half of its standard levels. Each time the deterioration of the *akçe* reached crisis proportions, the government attempted to return to the old standard or establish a new one. These operations, called *tashih-I sikke* (correction of coinage), were carried out in 1600, 1618, 1624, and 1640. Adding to the confusion were the clipped versions of the standard *akçes* that circulated together with the substandard versions.[34]

Two related questions that have been debated in the recent literature on the monetary history of the late medieval and early modern periods are whether governments benefited from debasements and whether debasements were used as a long-term strategy for generating revenue.[35] In the Ottoman case, there is overwhelming evidence that the debasements were the result of fiscal difficulties and that the state benefited in the short run from the production of substandard coinage. The available evidence also indicates that there did not exist such a long-term strategy during this particular period. The frequency of correction of coinage operations that increased the silver content of the *akçe* also suggests that the government tried to maintain the standards of coinage but was unable to do so.[36]

Perhaps the most important reason for the government's struggle for a stable currency and the major constraint against a more systematic use of debasement as a fiscal tool was the opposition of the janissaries in Istanbul, who were paid with this coinage. After the debasement of 1585–1586, they revolted, demanded, and obtained the execution of the vizier responsible for the currency.[37] The janissaries remained a force to be reckoned with in the turbulent politics of the capital city during this period. They were involved in the deposition of three sultans in 1618, 1622, and 1623.[38] There is detailed evidence, at least for later periods, that guild members joined the soldiers in opposition to debasements. Of the four correction-of-coinage operations undertaken during this period, the last three took place after the accession to the throne of new sultans. It is clear that these operations repre-

[34]Sahillioğlu, "Role"; and Gerber, "Monetary System," pp. 310–14.These operations were similar to the *reinforcements* of western Europe. Munro, "Deflation," pp. 392–93. After each of these operations, the state faced the task of forcing the prices down. For this purpose, local governments prepared very detailed lists of price ceilings (*narh*) for hundreds of goods. These lists now constitute useful sources not only for price history but also for studying the range of economic activity in the urban centers. Kütükoğlu, *Osmanlılarda Narh*. For an interesting account of the Ottoman perceptions of these monetary difficulties, see Kafadar, "Les Troubles Monetaires."

[35]See note 9.

[36]Since the relevant mint records are not available, the volume of coin production for each subperiod can not be established. It appears, however, that the mint volume remained sporadic and that coins were produced whenever the state was able to acquire specie. Years of maximum debasement often coincided with the lack of specie and low output and not vice versa.

[37]Known as the "*beylerbeyi* incident," this was only the second time in Ottoman history that the janissaries organized to protest a debasement. The first had occurred in 1444 and had led to a pay raise. The reason for the long interim was the stability of the Ottoman currency. The specie content of the akçe changed very little from the 1480s until the 1580s. See Table 2.

[38]Shaw, *History*, pp. 193–94.

sented attempts by the sultans to win the good will of the soldiers, and more generally, of the urban population.[39]

Currency Substitution

In addition to the instability, the debasements reduced the *akçe* into an exceptionally small and thin coin. Its weight and silver content declined from about 0.7 grams until the 1580s to 0.3 grams in 1640. It thus became very difficult to handle; large numbers of *akçes* were needed even for small, daily transactions. Larger silver coins such as ten-*akçe* pieces were minted only occasionally and these disappeared quickly when substandard *akçes* flooded the markets.[40] The government also began to mint a new coin called *para*, which was based on the monetary unit in circulation in Egypt and parts of Syria and carried three times as much silver as the *akçe*.[41] The volume of *para* production remained limited, however.

It appears that half a century of instability and the inconvenience of using *akçes* in daily transactions led to a considerable degree of currency substitution. The public became increasingly reluctant to hold the *akçe* or take bullion and foreign coins to local mints. Instead, there emerged greater demand for the more stable European coinage, especially the well-known and large silver pieces of the seventeenth century.[42] It is possible that during these extended periods of deterioration of the Ottoman unit, European coins began to circulate at a premium over their small Ottoman counterparts, measured in terms of their respective silver content. Since the precise mint records are not available, however, except for the years of correction of coinage operations, the existence and magnitude of these premiums can not be established from the available evidence summarized in Table 2.[43]

[39]Peter Spufford points out to similar struggles in many parts of western Europe during the fourteenth and fifteenth centuries between the monarchs who stood to gain and the landed aristocracy with fixed rent incomes who stood to lose from debasements. Spufford, *Money*, pp. 289–318.

[40]Schaendlinger, *Osmanische Numismatik*, pp. 100–12.

[41]It appears that the first minting of *para* in Istanbul was undertaken during the reign of Murad IV (1623–1640). Schaendlinger, *Osmanische Numismatik*, p. 110.

[42]There are a number of documented episodes of currency substitution in late medieval Europe. For a discussion of the consequences of the recurrent debasement-reinforcements cycles observed in fourteenth- and fifteenth-century France and Burgundy, see Bordo, "Money," pp. 344–45. Cipolla has examined another episode in the "Affair of the Quattrini," which occurred in fourteenth-century Florence. Cipolla, *Monetary Policy*, pp. 63–85.

[43]Until 1642 when its silver content was reduced by 20 percent, the Spanish real was minted at 67 per marc of 230.05 grams. The piece of eight thus contained 27.46 grams of silver. Motomura, "Best and Worst of Currencies," pp. 106–07; and Shaw, *History of Currency*, pp. 340–41. Considering that the *akçe* was minted from approximately 90 percent pure silver, the exchange rates given in Table 2 for the years of correction of coinage operations do not point to the existence of such premiums.

Intercontinental Monetary Flows

Another source of instability for the *akçe* was the decline of Ottoman silver mines. Until the sixteenth century the Ottoman mints had relied on the state-operated silver mines of Serbia and Bosnia as the principal source of specie.[44] The arrival of large amounts of silver from the New World, however, lowered the relative price of that metal, leading first to the decline of their output after the turn of the century and then to their closure during the 1640s.[45] When fiscal pressures began to intensify, therefore, the state could not fall back on the earlier sources to maintain steady supplies of coinage.

It is also possible that intercontinental monetary flows contributed to Ottoman monetary difficulties more directly. Despite the continued flows of silver from the Americas, Europe began to experience increasing scarcities of silver towards the end of the sixteenth century and this tendency lasted through most of the seventeenth century.[46] Recently, Dennis O. Flynn and Arturo Giraldez and Richard Von Glahn have put forward the thesis that a large part of the output of the American silver mines was absorbed by China, either by direct shipments to Asia or via Europe. The increased demand in China was due to the monetization of silver in the 1570s.[47] The Ottoman empire happened to be on the latter trade routes, and the growing monetary difficulties experienced in the Ottoman lands may have been due to these intercontinental flows as well as the fiscal deficits. At the moment, however, there is not sufficient evidence for or against this explanation. There is a good deal of evidence that the Ottoman government welcomed the arrival of silver and silver coinage from Europe, but it could not prevent their outflow towards Iran and India as the empire continued to run trade deficits towards the east. This overland transit trade of goods from Asia to Europe diminished after the turn of the century, however.[48] Although it is impossible to establish empirically the overall trade balance for the Ottoman Empire during the sixteenth and seventeenth centuries, the continued circulation of European groschen, especially the Spanish pieces of eight and the Dutch thaler, throughout the empire confirms that silver did not disappear from Ottoman markets.

[44] Sahillioğlu, "Role."

[45] Sahillioğlu, *Bir Asırlık*, p. 14; and Murphey, "Silver Production." Even though Rhoads Murphey argues that the output of silver mines did not decline until after the 1630s, the considerable drop in output after the turn of the century is in fact clear from the tables he provides. This is especially true of the mine in Üsküp (Skopje), which accounted for more than half of the total output of Ottoman silver mines in Serbia. Ibid., pp. 82–86. For the closure of European mines as a result of the arrival of American silver, see Spooner, *International Economy*, pp. 24–53.

[46] Ibid., pp. 33–53.

[47] Flynn and Giraldez, "Born with a Silver Spoon"; and Von Glahn, "Myth."

[48] Steensgaard, *Asian Trade Revolution*.

Closure of the Mints

In addition to the problems associated with attracting silver and foreign coinage to the mints, the continuing fiscal pressures and the decline in mine output made it increasingly difficult for the state to supply the mints itself, thus leading to a deterioration in the quality of coinage, especially in the provinces. As a result of these difficulties, the government began to close down the mints. In orders sent to provincial mints, the government expressed its reluctance to maintain their operations in view of the poor quality of coinage being produced.[49] Evidence from numismatic collections and catalogues also indicates that the numbers of provincial mints producing the silver *akçe* declined sharply during the second quarter of the century, especially in the 1640s.[50] The output of the mint in Istanbul also remained sharply lower until the mid-1680s. The limited volume of gold and silver coins produced in the capital city during this period were used primarily as payments to soldiers at war and by the sultan and his retinue in ceremonial occasions.[51] Both archival and numismatic evidence thus point to a decline in the production of silver and gold coinage for at least four decades.[52]

When the Ottoman government could not or did not meet the economy's demand for money, this need was met increasingly by European coins, initially silver and gold. Although foreign coins had always circulated in Ottoman lands, they played a qualitatively different role during the seventeenth century. As Ottoman coinage disappeared, the *akçe* was reduced to little more than a unit of account. Gold and especially silver European coins became the leading forms of actual money from the Balkans and Istanbul to Anatolia and Syria. Local court records and recent studies by economic and social historians on Ottoman provinces provide ample evidence in this respect.[53] The Ottoman government did not attempt to restrict the circulation

[49] Sahillioğlu, *Bir Asırlık*, pp. 18–37.

[50] Since most Ottoman coins carried the name of the sultan, the year of his accession, and the location of the mint, it is possible to follow from the available coins the decline in the numbers of provincial mints active during each reign. At the same time, since the coins of this period did not feature regnal years, it is not possible from this evidence to establish how many mints were active during any given year. Most of this numismatic evidence is summarized in Schaendlinger, *Osmanische Numismatik*, pp. 102–13; and Erüreten, "Osmanlı Akçeleri," pp. 18–19. Rhoads Murphey also considers the reign of Ibrahim I (1640–1648) the critical period for the cessation of activity in Ottoman silver mines. Murphey, "Silver Production," pp. 76, 82–86.

[51] Sahillioğlu, *Bir Asırlık*, pp. 18–36.

[52] For more detail, see Pamuk "Disintegration," pp. 74–75.

[53] Tavernier, *New Relation*; and Chardin, *Voyages*. Robert Mantran was one of the first to point out the decline of the *akçe* in local markets. His account is especially striking since it describes the conditions not in the distant provinces but in the capital city. Mantran, *Istanbul*, book 2, chap. 2. With the appearance during the last decade of new studies on the economic and social history of the provincial cities that make extensive use of local court records, it is now possible to get a geographically detailed account of the disappearance of the *akçe* and the spread of European coinage. See Masters, *Origins*; Establet and Pascual, "Damascene Probate Inventories"; and Ze'evi, *Ottoman Century*, pp. 143–45.

of these coins. In fact, it regularly accepted and sometimes even demanded payment in European coinage.[54]

WHY NOT COPPER COINAGE ?

The popularity of debased European coinage was, therefore, closely related to the inability of the Ottoman state to supply silver coinage after 1640. This raises a second puzzle, namely the cessation of the production of copper coinage in addition to silver. Just as it was the case with silver and gold coinage, the numismatic evidence points to an almost complete absence of Ottoman copper coinage for almost half a century, from the 1630s until the late 1680s.[55] This is quite intriguing since many states in Europe, from Spain and France to Germany, Sweden, Poland, and Russia relied on copper coinage during this period both as a medium of exchange and to raise seigniorage revenue.[56]

The absence of copper coinage is all the more puzzling because towards the end of the century, during another fiscal crunch from 1689 to 1691, the government did exactly what it had failed to do earlier. It issued, within a 30-month period, as many as 600 million pieces of copper *mangır* weighing half *dirhams* (1.6 grams) each.[57] Initially, these pieces were given the nominal value of one-half *akçe,* but the government quickly raised that to one *akçe*. Even though some merchants in the provinces refused to accept the new coins, on the whole, this was a reasonably successful operation for the short period it was employed. It also provided the state with much needed seigniorage revenue.[58]

It appears that the failure or inability of the central government to issue copper coinage during the midcentury was not due to one single reason but to a combination of factors. One possibility is that adequate supplies of

[54]One of the more prominent silver coins in circulation from the Balkans to Egypt was the Dutch thaler. Even more important was the Spanish piece of eight *(reales de a ocho)*. There were others such as the Austrian rix-thaler and the Polish isolette. Most of these European silver coins were called *gurush*, which was the local adaptation of groschen, a diminutive for gross or grosso, terms used for large silver coins in Europe since the thirteenth century. The Venetian ducat together with the Hungarian piece in the Balkans remained the most important gold coins. Fractions of these coins also circulated but in a more limited fashion. Pamuk, "Money", pp. 950–66.

[55]Tavernier, for example, is unequivocal: "In all the Ottoman Empire, there is not any money of copper to be seen." Tavernier, *New Relation*, p. 15. For a summary of the numismatic evidence on copper coinage in the seventeenth century, see Schaendlinger *Osmanische Numismatik,* pp. 106–14.

[56]Spooner, *International Economy*, pp. 10–86.

[57]About one-third of this amount was due to the reminting of the same coins with the accession of a new sultan, Ahmed II, in 1691.

[58]The detailed account books of the mint at Istanbul indicate that after all expenditures, including the share of the private entrepreneurs who managed the mint are subtracted, as much as 70 percent of the nominal value of the coins thus struck was left as net revenue for the state. Sahillioğlu,"Bakır Para," pp. 16–19. The seigniorage revenues obtained over this two-and-a-half-year period exceeded 10 percent of the total revenues of the imperial treasury during the same period. There is no doubt that this experiment provided a significant boost to the hard pressed treasury.

copper were simply not available. Of the two Anatolian mines in Gümüşhane and Küre, which were active during the 1690s and which supplied part of the copper for that experiment, the latter was not active in midcentury. The availability of copper was not a significant bottleneck, however, since the government could have acquired, at least in the short run, substantial volumes of used copper from the local markets as it did in the 1690s.

The organizational and technological reasons were probably much more important. The right to issue copper coinage in the provinces were typically auctioned off by the government to private entrepreneurs as was the case for some of the mints producing silver coinage. Since the nominal value of the *mangır* had always been in fractions of the *akçe*, such as one-eighth or one-fourth, the decline in the value and purchasing power of the *akçe* after the debasement of 1585–1586 brought the costs of production of copper coinage closer to their nominal values and reduced the margin for seigniorage. The private entrepreneurs were thus reluctant to purchase the regional *mangır* monopolies under those circumstances. This was probably the most important reason for the breakdown of the network of provincial mints producing copper coinage. One possible solution would have been to raise the nominal value of copper coins to at least one-half *akçe* or even to one *akçe*, which was done in the 1690s when the mint in Istanbul and not the regional mints issued the copper coinage. The provincial markets may not have accepted locally produced copper coinage with higher nominal values, however.

Another important shortcoming of the Ottoman mint system around midcentury was technological. Until the 1690s the Ottomans continued to use the traditional hammer and produced coins of inferior quality. Perhaps more importantly, this technology limited the volume of production and dictated a more decentralized approach to the coin supply. There existed a network of copper mints in the provinces and these were able to supply copper coinage in sufficient quantities until the seventeenth century. After the government decided at the end of the 1680s to adopt the mechanical technology and build new minting equipment with the help of a European convert, it was possible to issue a much larger volume of higher-quality coinage from the central mint in Istanbul. The government was able then to raise the nominal value of the copper coins and distribute them in the provinces as well as in the capital.[59]

Finally, the 1650s and 1660s, when this episode took place, was an especially difficult period for the Ottoman government because it was engaged in a long and protracted war with Venice over the island of Crete. It is clear that the Ottoman bureaucracy could not bring together the time, energy, and resources to devise a solution to their monetary problems during these years.

[59]Sahillioğlu, "Bakır Para."

The willingness of the Ottoman public to accept the debased European coinage, then, can not be understood without this context. The Ottoman markets were in need of money, especially the small denominations for daily use. They were willing to pay a premium for these coins. The Ottoman government had earlier supplied this subsidiary coinage and enjoyed the seigniorage. When it could not or did not fulfill this function, European entrepreneurs were only happy to serve as suppliers of money.

CONCLUSION

The arrival of enormous volumes of debased coinage eventually glutted the Ottoman markets and created adverse consequences for the economy and for European trade. European accounts emphasize that while merchants who brought debased coinage were willing to offer high prices for Ottoman goods, those that did not could not compete for Ottoman exports. The English merchants who were prohibited by the English consul in Izmir from participating in this trade were thus driven out of Ottoman markets. In turn, they and the English representatives began to pressure the Ottoman authorities to prohibit the circulation of base coinage. Other unfavorable consequences were being felt in those regions of southern Europe exporting the base coinage. Faced with a net outflow of silver, the parliament of Provence as well as the Chamber of Commerce of Marseilles attempted to ban this traffic in 1665.

The Ottoman authorities were not necessarily pleased with the outcome, but they were deeply involved in a long and protracted war with Venice over Crete. As long as the war continued, the government could not mobilize the necessary financial resources to stabilize or reform the currency. Until that time debased coinage was better than no coinage. The economy had come to depend on the debased coinage for its daily functioning. Similarly, the state continued to receive tax revenues and make payments with the debased coins. This pragmatism may help explain why so little material has so far been located in the Ottoman archives about the debased coins while European observers paid so much attention to the same phenomenon. Ottoman authorities did make several attempts to restrict the importation of these coins and seized some of the cargoes. As long as the war continued, however, these half-hearted attempts to ban base coinage proved unsuccessful.

As the war came to an end, the government moved to take more serious action. In 1669 it was announced that base coinage would no longer be accepted in tax payments. The government also demanded that all debased coinage be brought to the mints and reminted at the earlier standards. Later in the same year, riots broke out in Bursa and Ankara when defaulters who could not find "good" money to pay their taxes were imprisoned by the local authorities. "The torrent of the peoples' rage was not appeased without the blood and lives of some of their officers, alleging with good reason that their ministers and governors, having introduced or permitted this money amongst them, and allowed it as current in that manner, as they had for some years known no other for all the fruits of their labour and their possessions, they ought not now refuse to receive that which they themselves had made passable."[60]

The apparent reluctance of the Ottoman administration to prohibit the circulation of debased coinage need not imply that the decline and disappearance of the *akçe* did not pose serious challenges to them. Without control over the currency, their control over the economy diminished considerably. In addition, without its own currency the state could not use debasement as a means of obtaining fiscal revenue in times of difficulty. It is for these reasons as well as the more obvious reason of coinage as a symbol of sovereignty that the Ottoman government attempted to establish a new currency as the series of demanding wars began to wind down towards the end of the century. Not surprisingly, this new unit was called the Ottoman *gurush*, after the large European groschen in circulation. The first Ottoman *gurushes*, containing roughly the same amount of silver as their European counterparts, began to be minted after 1690. In financing this major effort, the government received considerable support from the large volume of copper coinage it issued during the years 1689 to 1691. In the early part of the seventeenth century a new standard in which 1 *gurush* equaled 120 *akçes* was adopted. Fractions of the new *gurush* were also issued to facilitate small transactions.[61] Because of fiscal and economic difficulties, however, it took a long time for the new coinage to be established in the provinces.

The study of this episode should serve as a reminder that the eastern end of the Mediterranean was subject to many of the same fiscal and monetary forces that affected Europe and Asia during the sixteenth and seventeenth centuries. Although the underlying forces were similar, however, the outcomes were very different in the Ottoman case. The invasion of the Ottoman markets by debased European coinage, their widespread acceptance and the premia they fetched over and above their specie content were due to the absence of subsidiary coinage for the daily functioning of the economy. If the government had been able to issue copper coinage in sufficient volumes as the silver *akçe* began to disappear in the 1640s, it would have met the economy's demand for a medium of exchange and, at the same time, raised substantial amounts of revenue for the much deprived imperial treasury, especially during the war. In the absence of copper coinage, however, those seigniorage revenues were captured by the mints and merchants from the other end of the Mediterranean.

[60]Hasluck, "Levantine Coinage," p. 61, citing Rycault, *History of the Turkish Empire*, App. VIII.
[61]Sahillioğlu, *Bir Asırlık*, pp. 90–122 and "Role"; and Pamuk, "Disintegration."

REFERENCES

Attman, Artur. "The Flow of Precious Metals along the Trade Routes between Europe and Asia up to 1800." In *Asian Trade Routes*, edited by Karl Reinhold Haellquist, 7–20. London: Scandinavian Institute of Asian Studies, 1991.

Barkan, Ömer Lütfi. *Zirai Ekonominin Mali ve Hukuki Temelleri, Kanunnameler, Cilt 1*. Istanbul, 1942.

Barkan, Ömer Lütfi. "The Price Revolution of the Sixteenth Century: A Turning Point in the Economic History of the Near East." *International Journal of Middle East Studies* 6 (1975): 3–28.

Barrett, Ward. "World Bullion Flows, 1450–1800." In *The Rise of Merchant Empires* , edited by James D. Tracy , 224–54. Cambridge: Cambridge University Press, 1990.

Berkes, Niyazi. *Türkiye Iktisat Tarihi, Cilt II*, Istanbul: Gerçek Yayınları, 1970.

Bordo, Michael D. "Money, Deflation and Seigniorage in the Fifteenth Century." *Journal of Monetary Economics* 18 (1986): 337–46.

Chardin, Chevalier. *Voyages du Chevalier Chardin en Perse et aux Indes Orientales*. London, 1686.

Chaudhuri, K. N. *The Trading World of Asia and the English East India Company 1660–1760*. Cambridge and New York: Cambridge University Press, 1978.

Cipolla Carlo M. *Money, Prices and Civilization in the Mediterranean World*. Princeton: Princeton University Press, 1956.

________. "Currency Depreciation in Medieval Europe." *Economic History Review* 15 (1963): 413–22.

________. *The Monetary Policy of Fourteenth-Century Florence*. Berkeley: University of California Press, 1982.

Çizakça, Murat. "Price History and the Bursa Silk Industry: A Study in Ottoman Industrial Decline, 1550–1650." this JOURNAL 40, (1980): 533–49.

Erüreten, Metin. "Osmanlı Akçeleri Darp Yerleri". *The Turkish Numismatic Society Bülten*, 17 (1985): 12–21.

Establet, Colette, and Jean-Paul Pascal. "Damascene Probate Inventories of the 17th and 18th Centuries : Some Preliminary Approaches and Results." *International Journal of Middle East Studies* 24 (1992): 373–93.

Flynn, Dennis O., and Giraldez Arturo. "Born with a 'Silver Spoon': The Origin of World Trade in 1571." *Journal of World History* 6 (1995): 201–21

Faroqhi, Suraiya. "The Early History of Balkan Fairs." *Südost-Forschungen* 37 (1978): 50–68.

______. "Sixteenth Century Periodic Markets in Various Anatolian Sancaks." *Journal of the Economic and Social History of the Orient* 22 (1979): 32–80.

______."Crisis and Change, 1590–1699", In The Ottoman Empire : Its Economy and Society : 1300–1914," edited by H. Inalcık and D. Quataert , 411–636. Cambridge: Cambridge University Press, 1994.

Faroqhi, Suraiya, and Leila Erder. "Population Rise and Fall in Anatolia, 1550–1620." *Middle Eastern Studies* 15 (1979): 322–45.

Gaastra, F. S. "The Exports of Precious Metals from Europe to Asia by the Dutch East India Company." In *Precious Metals in the Later Medieval and Early Modern Worlds*, edited by J. F. Richards, 447–76. Durham, North Carolina: Carolina Academic Press, 1983.

Gerber, Haim. "The Monetary System of the Ottoman Empire." *Journal of the Economic and Social History of the Orient* 25 (1982): 308–24.

Grierson, Philip. "The Monetary Pattern of Sixteenth Century Coinage". *Transactions of the Royal Historical Society, Fifth Series* 21 (1971): 45–60.

Hasluck, F. W. "The Levantine Coinage." *Numismatic Chronicle, Fifth Series* 1 (1921): 339–91.

Inalcık, Halil. "Military and Fiscal Transformation in the Ottoman Empire, 1600–1700." *Archivum Ottomanicum* 6 (1980): 283–337.

_________. "Osmanlı Idare, Sosyal ve Ekonomik Tarihiyle Ilgili Belgeler: Bursa Kadı Sicillerinden Seçmeler." *Türk Tarih Kurumu, Belgeler* 10, no. 14 (1981): 1–91.

Jennings, Ronald C. "Loans and Credit in Early 17th Century Ottoman Judicial Records." *Journal of the Economic and Social History of the Orient* 16 (1973): 168–216.

Kafadar, Cemal. "Les Troubles Monetaires de la Fin du XVIe Siecle et la Prise de Conscience Ottomane du Declin." *Annales, Economies, Societes, Civilisations* 46 (1991): 381–400.

Kindleberger, Charles P. "The Economic Crisis of 1619 to 1623." this JOURNAL 51, no. 1(1991): 149–175.

Kütükoğlu, Mübahat S. *Osmanlılarda Narh Müessesesi ve 1640 Tarihli Narh Defteri.* Istanbul: Enderun Yayınevi, 1983.

Mantran, Robert. *Istanbul dans la seconde Moitie du XVIIe Siecle* . Paris, 1962.

__________. "Politique, Economie et Monnaie dans l'Empire Ottoman au XVIIeme Siecle." In *Social and Economic History of Turkey (1071–1920), Papers Presented to the First International Congress* , edited by O.Okyar and H.Inalcık , 123–25. Ankara, 1980.

Masters, Bruce. *The Origins of Western Economic Dominance in the Middle East : Mercantilism and the Islamic Economy in Aleppo, 1600–1750.* New York: New York University Press, 1988.

Miskimin, Harry. *Money and Power in Fifteenth Century France.* New Haven: Yale University Press, 1984.

Motomura, Akira. "The Best and Worst of Currencies : Seigniorage and Currency Policy in Spain, 1597–1650." this JOURNAL 54, no. 1(1994), 104–27.

Munro, John H. "Deflation and the Petty Coinage Problem in the Late-Medieval Economy: The Case of Flanders, 1334–1484." *Explorations in Economic History* 25 (1988): 387–423.

Murphey, Rhoads. "Silver Production in Rumelia According to an Official Ottoman Report Circa 1600." *Südost-Forschungen* 39 (1980): 75–104.

Pamuk, Şevket. "The Disintegration of the Ottoman Monetary System during the Seventeenth Century." *Princeton Papers in Near Eastern Studies* 2 (1993): 67–81.

_________. "Money in the Ottoman Empire, 1326 to 1914." In *The Ottoman Empire : Its Economy and Society : 1300–1914,*" edited by H. Inalcık and D. Quataert , 947–85. Cambridge: Cambridge University Press, 1994.

Rycaut, Paul. *History of the Turkish Empire from the year 1623 to the year 1677.* London, 1680.

Sahillioğlu, Halil. "Bir Asırlık Osmanlı Para Tarihi." Diss. for docent. University of Istanbul, 1965.

_________. "XVII. Asrın ilk Yarısında Istanbul'da Tedavüldeki Sikkelerin Raici." *Türk Tarih Kurumu, Belgeler* 1, No. 2 (1965), Ankara, 227–34.

_________. "Bakır Para Üzerine bir Enflasyon Denemesi (H. 1099–1103/M. 1687–1691)." *The Turkish Numismatic Society Bülten* 10 (1982): 7–40.

__________. "The Role of International Monetary and Metal Movements in Ottoman Monetary History. In *Precious Metals in the Later Medieval and Early Modern Worlds*, edited by J. F. Richards, 269–304. Durham, North Carolina, 1983.

Schaendlinger, Anton C. *Osmanische Numismatik* . Braunschweig, 1973.

Shaw, Stanford J. *History of the Ottoman Empire and Modern Turkey*. Vol. 1. *1280–1808*. Cambridge and New York: Cambridge University Press, 1976.

Shaw, W. A. *The History of Currency, 1252 to 1894*. New York and London: G. P. Putnam's Sons and Clement Wilson, 1896.

Spooner, Frank C. *The International Economy and Monetary Movements in France*. Cambridge, MA: Harvard University Press, 1972.

Spufford, Peter. *Money and Its Use in Medieval Europe*. Cambridge: Cambridge University Press, 1988.

Steensgaard, Niels. *The Asian Trade Revolution of the Seventeenth Century: The East India Companies and the Decline of the Caravan Trade*. Chicago: The University of Chicago Press, 1974.

Sundhaussen, Holm. "Die 'Preisrevolution' im Osmanischen Reich wahrend der zweiten Halfte des 16. Jahrhundrets." *Südost-Forschungen* 42 (1983): 169–81.

Sussman, Nathan. "Debasements, Royal Revenues and Inflation in France during the Hundred Years' War, 1415–1422." this JOURNAL 53, no.1(1993): 44–70.

Tabakoğlu, Ahmet. *Gerileme Döneminde Osmanlı Maliyesi*. Istanbul: Dergah Yayınları, 1985.

Tavernier, J. B. *A New Relation of the Inner-Port of the Grand Seignor's Seraglio*. London, 1677.

Von Glahn, Richard. "Myth and Reality of China's Seventeenth Century Monetary Crisis." this JOURNAL 56, no. 2 (1996): 429–54.

Ze'evi, Dror. *An Ottoman Century, The District of Jerusalem in the 1600s* . Albany: State University of New York Press 1996.

VIII

The Great Ottoman Debasement, 1808–1844: A Political Economy Framework

At the threshold of the modern era, from the 1770s until the 1840s, Ottoman state finances frequently experienced large budget deficits arising mostly from wars and, to a lesser extent, from costs of military reform. These deficits reached their peak during the 1820s and 1830s. In response, the government attempted to increase its control over revenue sources and made use of various forms of internal borrowing. However, the state's demand for funds in relation to both the size of the economy and the ability of the fragile domestic institutions to handle them was too large.[1] As a result, when short-term fiscal pressures mounted, the government resorted to debasements. The highest rates of debasement in Ottoman history took place during the reign of the reformist and centralizing Sultan Mahmud II (1808–1839). This chapter will argue that debasements were not the result of a haphazard process but were undertaken or not undertaken by the government after the weighing of associated benefits and costs. In other words, far from being an exercise in futility, debasements are viewed here as a potentially effective instrument of fiscal policy, especially in the short term. In fact, one may even argue that debasements were used as an instrument of centralization by Mahmud II. The timing and magnitude of the debasements also suggest, however, that the government was quite sensitive to the political opposition they generated among the janissaries and other urban groups.

Toward a Political Economy Framework

The causes and consequences of premodern debasements, that is, the reduction of the specie content of the currency by the monetary authority, have been the focus of much debate.[2] Some of the causes, such as the wear on the existing stock of coins in circulation or the mismanagement of the mints, appear technical or administrative in nature. Another possible cause was the increase in the economy's demand for money and the need to increase the money stock in circulation. In the short term, debasements provided relief from shortages of specie and coinage in circulation by increasing the nominal value of coinage in circulation. However, the alteration and expansion of the money supply through debasements could provide only temporary relief because prices tended to adjust upward sooner or later, and the volume of coinage in circulation adjusted for the price level tended to return to its earlier level. For this reason, the efforts of premodern states to offset the detrimental effects of a bullion shortage by means of debasement were doomed to frustration.

The persistence of debasements throughout the medieval and early modern periods suggests that these interventions were not simply futile efforts. Although they did not solve the problems of specie shortages, debasements did provide fiscal relief for the states, and there lay their appeal. Because the obligations of the state to the soldiers, bureaucrats, and suppliers are expressed in terms of the monetary unit of account, a reduction in the silver content of the currency enabled the state to increase the amount it could mint from or the payments it could make with a given amount of silver. As a result, debasements were frequently utilized as an alternative to additional taxation.

Prices almost always rose in the aftermath of debasements because a debasement typically increased the nominal value of coinage in circulation. Even if the prices did not rise quickly because of the shortages of specie or for some other reason, long-distance trade acted as the ultimate equalizer in the long term. If prices expressed in grams of silver in a given region became less expensive vis-à-vis the neighboring areas, increased demand for the lower-priced commodities attracted large quantities of silver, thus raising prices. Price adjustments after a debasement tended to be more rapid, the more open the economy and the more frequently debasements were used.[3]

Another possible cause of debasements was the pressure from some social groups in favor of inflation. Even if a social group did not always benefit from debasements and inflation, it could still prefer debasements to additional taxation. For example, merchants sometimes preferred debasements to increased taxation whenever the government faced fiscal difficulties. This is because the prices of goods held by the merchants typically rose together with other prices after a debasement. On the other side of the coin were social groups who stood to lose from debasements and the accompanying inflation and therefore opposed them. Under these circumstances, the fate of the currency was not determined solely by the government but often depended upon the struggle between it and various social groups. Before we begin an examination of Ottoman debasements in the early decades of the nineteenth century, let us examine how different groups in Ottoman society fared in the face of such debasements.

For a long time it has been assumed that the use of money in the Ottoman Empire was limited to long-distance trade and parts of the urban sector.[4] Yet recent research has shown that the urban population and some segments of the countryside were already part of the monetary economy by the end of the fifteenth century. Even more significant, there occurred a substantial increase in the use of money during the sixteenth century, both because of the increased availability of specie and increasing commercialization of the rural economy. There also emerged an intensive pattern of periodic markets and market fairs where peasants and larger landholders sold parts of their produce to urban residents. These markets also provided an important opportunity for the nomads to come into contact with both peasants and the urban population. Large sectors of the rural population came to use coinage, especially the small denominations of silver akçe and the copper mangır, through their participation in these markets.[5]

Second, small-scale but intensive networks of credit relations developed in and around the urban centers. Evidence from thousands of court cases in these towns and cities involving lenders and borrowers leave no doubt that the use of credit, small and large, was widespread among all segments of urban as well as parts of rural society. It is clear that neither the Islamic prohibitions against interest and usury nor the absence of formal banking institutions prevented the expansion of credit in Ottoman society.[6] As a result, debasements had an impact on virtually all groups in Ottoman society, and in turn, each group took a position. Most men and women, both urban and rural, were clear about the consequences of different ways of dealing with the coinage, and who gained and who lost. In general, all those who had future obligations expressed in terms of the unit of account—mainly borrowers and tenants paying fixed rents in cash—stood to gain from debasements. Conversely, those who expected to be paid fixed amounts in terms of the unit of account stood to lose from debasements.[7]

In the rural areas, taxes and rents on both public and privately held lands were paid almost entirely in kind during the eighteenth and nineteenth centuries. Moreover, those producers who sold part of their crop in local markets received higher prices during periods of inflation. As a result, debasements and inflation did not have a major impact on rural producers. The significant exception, of course, were the lenders and borrowers in the countryside. Local court records indicate that numbers of court cases involving lending and borrowing by rural as well as urban residents typically showed sharp increases during periods of frequent debasement and rapid inflation.

In the urban areas there existed a dense network of credit relations, most of which involved small-scale lenders and small-cash *vakıf*s (pious foundations) that lent on interest. The local *sarraf*s (money changers), with their expert knowledge of the markets, often benefited from the uncertainty and fluctuations in exchange rates as well as the requirements to surrender old coins in the aftermath of debasements. Most of them were net lenders, though, and they stood to lose from the inflation that followed debasements.

As the fiscal problems of the Ottoman state intensified in the second half of the eighteenth century, the *sarraf*s of Istanbul began to provide increasingly larger loans to the state, utilizing their connections to the financial markets in Europe. This lucrative process soon transformed the traditional money changers into the so-called Galata bankers, named after the financial district in the capital city. The Galata bankers also held considerable amounts of *esham* (long-term government bonds). As a result, they were in favor of monetary stability.[8]

It would be interesting to explore the attitudes of the *ayan* (notables) of the provinces toward money and inflation during the eighteenth and early nineteenth centuries. Many *ayan* were the holders of various types of tax farms, both short-term and long-term. To the extent that the tax farmers were expected to make fixed payments to the state each year, they tended to benefit from debasements and inflation. At the same time, however, many *ayan* were engaged in trade, especially long-distance trade. In their role as long-distance merchants, they must have favored monetary stability.

Merchants and shopkeepers in the urban areas did not appear to lose from debasements, as the prices of goods they sold tended to rise during periods of inflation. There was always the risk, though, that the government would impose price ceilings on essential goods sold in the urban markets whenever prices rose too fast. As a result, they were also wary of debasements.

The groups that stood to lose the most from debasements were those who were paid fixed amounts in terms of the unit of account. The most important groups in this category were the employees of the state, the bureaucracy, the ulema, and especially the janissaries. There existed a large overlap between the guild members and the janissaries after the latter began to moonlight as artisans and shopkeepers in the seventeenth century.

The Great Debasement, 1808–1844

When Mahmud II ascended the throne in 1808, the standard kuruş or piaster contained 6.90 grams of silver, unchanged since the debasement of 1789. During the next three decades, the silver content of the Ottoman currency declined at times sharply, at times more slowly. The lowest point was reached in 1831–1832 at 0.5 grams of silver, although the kuruş subsequently rose to 0.9 grams in 1832 and then to 1.0 gram in 1844, where it stayed until World War I. All in all, the kuruş lost more than 83 percent of its silver content from 1808 to 1844.[9] (See Table 2.1.)

Table 2.1 The Silver Kuruş and Its Exchange Rate, 1780–1914

Year	Weight (grams)	Fineness (percent)	Pure Silver Content (grams)	Exchange Rate of the British Pound (in kuruş)
1780	18.50	54.0	10.00	11.0
1789	12.80	54.0	6.90	15.0
1800	12.60	54.0	6.90	15.0
1808	12.80	46.5	5.90	19.0
1809	9.60	46.5	4.42	20.5
1810	5.13	73.0	3.74	19.8
1818	9.60	46.5	4.42	29.0
1820	6.41	46.0	2.95	35.0
1822	4.28	54.0	2.32	37.0
1828	3.20	46.0	1.47	59.0
1829	3.10	22.0	0.72	69.0
1831	3.00	17.5	0.53	80.0
1832	2.14	44.0	0.94	88.0
1839	2.14	44.0	0.94	104.0
1844	1.20	83.3	1.00	110.0
1914	1.20	83.3	1.00	110.0

Sources: Chester L. Krause and Clifford Mishler, with Colin R. Bruce II, *Standard Catalog of World Coins,* 21st edition, (Iola, Wisc.: Krause Publications, 1994); Benjamin Sass, "The Silver and Billon Coins Minted at Constantinople Under Sultan Mahmud II (1223–1255 H ["Hegira/Hijra"])," *The American Numismatic Society Notes* 18 (1972): 167–175; Çüneyt Ölçer, *Sultan II. Mahmud Zamanında Darp Edilen Osmanlı Madeni Paraları,* (Istanbul: Yenilik Basımevi, 1970); Jem Sultan, *Coins of the Ottoman Empire and the Turkish Republic: A Detailed Catalogue of the Jem Sultan Collection,* 2 vols. (Thousand Oaks, Calif.: B&R Publishers, 1977), pp. 213–297; İsmail Galib, *Takvim-i Meskukat-ı Osmaniye* (Istanbul, H. 1307/1889–1890); Daniel Panzac, "La Piastre et le Cyclotron: Essai sur les Monnaies Ottomanes, 1687–1844," paper presented to the Conference on *Money and Currencies in the Ottoman Empire, 1690–1850* (Istanbul, November 1997); and Charles Issawi, *The Economic History of Turkey, 1800–1914* (Chicago: University of Chicago Press, 1980), pp. 327–331.

Note: The Tashih-i Sikke (correction of coinage) operation of 1844 introduced the new gold lira, which equaled 100 silver kuruş and fixed the gold-silver ratio at 15:09. The standards of Ottoman silver and gold coinage did not change after that date.

Closely paralleling the debasement of the currency was the sharp fall in its exchange rate and the rapid rise in the general price level, both of which were equally dramatic. In 1808, one Venetian gold ducat exchanged for 8 kuruş and one British pound sterling for 19 kuruş. By 1844 one ducat equaled 50 to 52 kuruş and the British pound exchanged for 110 kuruş. In other words, the Ottoman unit also lost about 83 percent of its value against the leading European currencies during these thirty-five years. Indices recently constructed from data obtained from the account books of *vakıfs*, their soup kitchens, and the account books of the imperial kitchen at Istanbul show that food prices increased by about fourfold between 1808 and 1844 and about tenfold between 1789 and 1844.[10] It is possible to follow the silver content of the kuruş on an annual basis from the available numismatic evidence. During his thirty-two-year reign, Mahmud II issued ten different series of silver coins each with different standards. Most of these series covered the full range of coins from the small one, or five para, to the two, five, and even six kuruş pieces. Each of these series remained in circulation anywhere from one to eight or more years. Mahmud II ended up issuing forty-seven different types of silver coins, more than any other Ottoman ruler. Detailed information is available about the standards of each coin for each of these series. In addition, a limited number of coins have been subjected to content analysis to establish their specie and alloy content (Table 2.1).

The government continued to issue varieties of gold coins such as zeri mahbub, rumi, adli, hayriye, and mahmudiye, each with different and changing standards during the reign of Mahmud II. These gold coins were not subjected to such rapid rates of debasement, however. The overall decline in the specie content of the gold coins during these three decades remained below 20 percent.[11] It is clear that the government did not view the gold coins with the same fiscal logic that was applied to the silver kuruş. This was because the obligations of the state were expressed in terms of the silver kuruş and not linked to any gold coin. As a result, the government did not stand to gain much from debasing the gold coins.[12]

An examination of the timing and magnitudes of the debasements provides important insights into the motives of the government. On the basis of the available evidence presented in Table 2.1, the debasements during the reign of Mahmud II can be divided into two subperiods. The first subperiod covers the early years of his reign, from 1808 until 1822. Six separate series, or sets, of silver coins were issued during this period. By the sixth series, the silver content of the kuruş had been reduced to 2.32 grams, by a total of 60 percent in comparison to 1808. The fiscal difficulties created by the wars against Russia, Iran, and the Greek revolution figured prominently in the decline of the currency during the first subperiod.[13] In fact, the third series of silver coins issued by Mahmud II in 1810 with lower silver were called cihadiyye, in reference to the ongoing war with Russia and the need to raise fiscal revenue for that effort. These coins remained in circulation for eight years.[14] The government also issued special cihadiyye eshamı during this period, which can be considered the first example of Ottoman war bonds.[15]

The second and even more rapid subperiod of debasement took place during and after the war of 1828–1829 with Russia. In addition to wartime expenditures, the large, 400-million kuruş indemnity the Ottomans agreed to pay at the end of the war weighed heavily on Ottoman finances and the currency for a number of years.[16] Between 1828 and 1831, the silver content of the kuruş was thus reduced sharply from 2.32 grams to 0.53 grams, a decline of 79 percent in four years. As financial conditions began to improve after 1832, the silver content of the currency was raised to 0.94 grams.[17]

We can now examine the attitudes and behavior of the Ottoman government toward debasement during the reign of Mahmud II. In this framework the government is viewed as weighing the short-term fiscal benefits accruing from debasements against both the short-term and long-term costs of such action. If the government perceives these costs to be less than the expected fiscal benefits, then a debasement or a series of debasements may be adopted. In other words, far from being an exercise in futility, the debasements are seen as a potentially effective instrument of fiscal policy, especially in the short term. At the same time, this framework will emphasize the economic and political constraints on the state's ability to take advantage of debasements.

The fiscal benefits of a debasement are not difficult to establish. The government was able to issue a larger amount of coinage in nominal terms with the same amount of specie and meet a larger fraction of its obligations.[18] One related measure often adopted by the government in the aftermath of a debasement was to prohibit the use and sale of gold and silver in local markets and order that these be surrendered to the imperial mint at below-market prices.[19] Finally, the state also obtained revenue from the old coins brought to the mint by the public.

On the other side, there are a number of costs that may be borne by the state as a result of debasements. As prices rose, including those paid by the state in the aftermath of a debasement, many of the state revenues, fixed in nominal terms, declined in real terms. In other words, debasements generated an initial surge in revenues followed by their decline in real terms due to the inflation they created. In the longer term, a debasement might even lead to a real decline in revenues if the government did not adjust upward the taxes and other revenues that had been fixed in nominal terms.[20]

Second, if the public loses confidence in the currency and begins to anticipate further debasements, it will become increasingly difficult for the government to take advantage of further reductions in the specie content of coinage. In the open-mint system, for example, the public may begin holding another currency and stay away from the mints. A large degree of currency substitution must have taken place during the reign of Mahmud II, as varieties of foreign coinage were free to circulate.[21]

A third cost of Ottoman debasements was the spread of counterfeiting.

When the government issued new coins with a lower specie content, counterfeiters immediately began to mint the new coins with the same or even higher silver content in order to share the seigniorage revenues of the state. This opportunity declined, however, when precious metal prices adjusted upward along with other prices. Price ceilings on the specie and government attempts to obtain the specie at those official prices also encouraged counterfeiting.[22]

Another cost was the adverse implications of debasements for the ability of the state to borrow domestically. As the government began to make use of debasements, the public began to anticipate more, and it became more difficult to borrow from the public at large. There is evidence that with the acceleration of debasements after 1808, rates of interest increased even further and it became even more difficult for the government to sell the esham. For example, it appears that the ratio between the initial sale price of esham and the annual payments declined after 1808 when the government began to use debasements more frequently.[23]

Yet the most important cost of Ottoman debasements was the political opposition they generated among the urban groups, especially in the capital city. One group that disliked debasements consisted of the guild members, shopkeepers, small merchants, and the wage-earning artisans. Another group that stood to lose from debasements were those who were paid fixed salaries by the state, the bureaucracy, the ulema, and especially the janissaries stationed permanently in the capital. There existed a large overlap between the guild members and the janissaries because the latter began to moonlight as artisans and shopkeepers. This broad opposition acted as a major deterrent against the more frequent use of debasements by the government not only in the capital but also in the provincial centers. It would be interesting to explore the causal linkages between the debasements and the urban rebellions of the late eighteenth and early nineteenth centuries in Syria, Iraq, and elsewhere in the empire.[24]

The effectiveness of this urban opposition against debasements should not be measured in terms of the frequency of their rebellions, however. Just as E. P. Thompson had argued in his study of the moral economy of the English crowd in the eighteenth century, that the effectiveness of the bread riots should not be measured in terms of their frequency, it was the threat of rebellions that proved just as effective in the longer term;[25] it ensured that the governments would refrain from debasements, at least during periods of peace.

Into this framework of costs and benefits and interaction between the state and society, wars enter as exogenous shocks, events that raised both the need for short-term revenues for the state and the willingness of the public to accept extraordinary measures such as debasements. As the urgency of generating revenues increased, the state often invoked references to holy wars and even linked the new coinage explicitly to the ongoing wars, calling the new issues of coins and bonds cihadiyye, for example.

During the reigns of both Selim III and Mahmud II, the governments were well aware of the limitations imposed by the janissaries and related urban groups. From the very beginning of his reign, Mahmud II wanted to replace the janissaries with a Western-style army. But during the early years of his long reign, he did not have the political support to make this critical move. After the janissaries were finally defeated and the order was abolished in 1826—in what is usually considered one of the most important political events of this period, known as Vaka-i Hayriye, or the Auspicious Event—a major constraint in the way of debasements was lifted. Only two years later, the government began the largest debasement of Ottoman history, reducing the specie content of the kuruş by 79 percent within a period of four years.

In terms of revenues for the state, the debasements of 1828–1831 were considered a major success by the contemporaries. The credit for this accomplishment was given to Artin Kazaz, an Armenian financier who had risen through the ranks of the *sarraf* guild to head the imperial mint in the 1820s. Kazaz was actually only one in a long chain of Armenian financiers to administer the imperial mint from the late eighteenth century until the 1840s. One of his biographies relates that during the war of 1828–1829 with Russia, the grand vizier considered issuing copper coinage. However, Kazaz convinced the sultan that there should be at least some silver in the new coinage. He then went on to produce a very large volume of five kuruş pieces.[26] His rationale was that the presence of some silver would help the state raise more revenue by making the coins more acceptable to the public and helping the state retain the opportunity to raise additional revenues by lowering the silver content in the future.[27]

One unique aspect of this debasement episode was that the contemporaries calculated the seigniorage revenues of the state from the mint records. According to these calculations, during the regnal years of 22 to 25 (approximately 1828–1831), the imperial mint produced 23 million units of the large five kuruş pieces as the eighth series of Mahmud II after lowering the silver content of the coins. The net seigniorage revenues of the state were estimated at 39.7 million kuruş. During the regnal years 25 and 26 (1831–1832), an additional 245 million kuruş worth of new coinage with even lower silver content was issued as the ninth series. This operation is estimated to have provided the state with net revenues of 119 million kuruş. After the end of the war, during the regnal years 26 through 32 (1832–1838), the mint issued a variety of new coins with a total value of 137.8 million kuruş as the tenth series. The silver content of these coins, however, was higher than both the eighth and the ninth series, and the state did not obtain any seigniorage revenue from them. The purpose of this last phase was to bring back price stability and renew confidence in the currency.[28]

These were large magnitudes in relation to the size of total state revenues and expenditures at the time. Since the various revenues and expenditures were not yet incorporated into a single budget, it is difficult to estimate total annual revenues, but the sum of 250 to 300 million kuruş appears as a reasonable figure for these years. Yavuz Cezar provides an estimate of 300 million kuruş for the budget of 1838.[29] In other words, the debasements of 1828–1832 provided the state with total revenues associated with the debasements amounting to more than one-half of one year's total revenues, or an average of more than 10 percent of annual revenues for these five troubled years.

The debasements provided another, and somewhat unexpected, benefit to the treasury by reducing the borrowing requirements of the state and bringing down interest rates. The decline in interest rates then provided fiscal relief through its impact on the tax-farming system as well. Tax farmers who entered state auctions for the right to collect specific tax revenues were required to make a certain fraction of these payments in advance for which they typically borrowed from private financiers. When the domestic interest rates declined, therefore, the auction prices of tax farms tended to rise.

Bimetallism and External Borrowing

Monetary conditions had assumed crisis proportions by the end of the 1830s. While the government had succeeded in raising short-term revenue from frequent debasements, the resulting inflation created serious political problems. In addition, the production of a large variety of coins since the beginning of the century and the inability of the government to retire the earlier series from circulation had added to the difficulties. These conditions created difficulties both for daily transactions and international trade. At the same time, the appeal and use of European coinage had increased, especially in international trade and for store-of-wealth purposes.[30]

For European governments and especially the British, who were concerned about Russian expansionism to the south, the success of Ottoman reforms was considered essential for the territorial integrity of the empire. European governments also believed that rapid expansion of commercial ties with Europe based on the principle of comparative advantage and European direct investment were essential for the development of the Ottoman economy. As a result, they began to exert considerable pressure on the Ottoman government to abandon debasements and establish a more stable monetary system. Bimetallism was proposed as a monetary regime that would bring the Ottoman Empire more in line with the prevailing international trends and help expand both trade and European investment. The

European governments also linked Ottoman access to European financial markets to fiscal reform and monetary stability. They made clear that they were ready to provide the technical expertise necessary for this purpose.

After the death of Sultan Mahmud II in 1839, the new government openly expressed the intention to carry out such an operation. New machines and technology were imported from England. Mint technicians and other specialists were invited from England and France to install the machines and advise the Ottoman government about the new standards of coinage.[31] After some delay, the government finally decided to adopt the bimetallic standard in which the silver kuruş and the new gold lira were both accepted as legal tender, freely convertible at the fixed rate of 100 kuruş for one gold lira and obtainable at the government mint. The new gold coins began to be produced in 1843, and the new silver coins were issued the following year along with an official declaration from the imperial mint, setting out the reasons for the reform. The gold-silver ratio was fixed at 15:9. The open mint system was to be continued. All silver and gold coinage minted until 1922 adhered to the standards established in 1844.

In the early part of the nineteenth century, governments in Cairo and Tunis, facing very similar constraints and pressures, also abandoned fiscally motivated debasements in favor of bimetallism and stable coinage.[32] It was not so much the interaction between these governments that brought about the monetary regime shift. In addition to the growing domestic costs of debasements, it was the rising forces of globalization, the rapid increase in trade with Europe, and the growing interaction with European merchants and governments as well as their advice and pressure that led these governments to embrace those monetary institutions that conformed to the requirements of international trade.

The decision to abandon debasements as a means of raising fiscal revenue without the elimination of the budget deficits proved very costly in the long term. All three governments began to borrow in the European financial markets during the 1850s in order to meet their short-term budgetary needs. By the middle of the 1870s, with their annual debt payments far in excess of their ability to pay, they were all forced to declare moratoriums on their outstanding debt. The establishment of the European Public Debt Administration in Istanbul (1881) and, even more dramatically, the occupation of Tunis (1881) and Egypt (1882) by the European powers were directly linked to these moratoriums.[33]

Notes

1. For state attempts to increase its control over revenue sources and the evolution of the domestic institutions for credit during the late eighteenth and early

nineteenth centuries, see Şevket Pamuk, *A Monetary History of the Ottoman Empire* (Cambridge, UK: Cambridge University Press, 1999), pp. 188–192.

2. Carlo. M. Cipolla, "Currency Depreciation in Medieval Europe," *Economic History Review* 15 (1963): 413–415, provides a useful list of the causes of debasements and a good starting point. Also see Harry A. Miskimin, *Money and Power in Fifteenth-Century France* (New Haven, Conn.: Yale University Press, 1984); Michael D. Bordo, "Money, Deflation, and Seigniorage in the Fifteenth Century," *Journal of Monetary Economics* 18 (1986): 337–346; and Nathan Sussman, "Debasements, Royal Revenues, and Inflation in France During the Hundred Years' War, 1415–1422," *The Journal of Economic History* 53 (1993): 44–70.

3. Bordo, "Money, Deflation, and Seigniorage."

4. F. Braudel, *Civilization and Capitalism, 15th–18th Century,* Vol. III: *The Perspective of the World* (New York: Harper and Row Publishers, 1984), pp. 471–473.

5. R. C. Jennings, "Loans and Credit in Early 17th-Century Ottoman Judicial Records," *Journal of the Economic and Social History of the Orient* 16 (1973): 168–216; Suraiya Faroqhi, "The Early History of Balkan Fairs," *Südost-Forschungen* 37 (1978): 50–68; Suraiya Faroqhi, "Sixteenth Century Periodic Markets in Various Anatolian Sancaks," *Journal of the Economic and Social History of the Orient* 22 (1979): 32–80; Suraiya Faroqhi, "Rural Society in Anatolia and the Balkans During the Sixteenth Century," *Turcica* 9 (1977):161–196, and vol. 11 (1979):103–153; and Halil İnalcık, "Osmanlı İdare, Sosyal ve Ekonomik Tarihiyle İlgili Belgeler: Bursa Kadı Sicillerinden Seçmeler," *Türk Tarih Kurumu, Belgeler* 14 (1981): 1–91. See also the studies on the rural economy by these authors that appeared in two collections: Halil İnalcık, *The Middle East and the Balkans Under the Ottoman Empire: Essays on Economy and Society* (Bloomington: Indiana University Turkish Studies and Turkish Ministry of Culture Joint Series, 1993); and Suraiya Faroqhi, *Coping with the State, Political Conflict, and Crime in the Ottoman Economy, 1550–1720* (Istanbul: ISIS Press, 1995).

6. Pamuk, *Monetary History*, pp. 77–87.

7. For greater detail on the responses of different social groups to Ottoman debasements during the fifteenth, sixteenth, and seventeenth centuries, see ibid., pp. 55–58, 138–142.

8. Araks Şahiner, "The Sarrafs of Istanbul: Financiers of the Empire" (M.A. thesis, Department of History, Boğaziçi University, 1995); Mehmet Genç, "Esham," in *Islam Ansiklopedisi*, Vol. XI (Istanbul: Diyanet Vakfı, 1995), pp. 376–380.

9. The overall rate of debasement is even higher if 1789 is taken as the beginning point. Until that year, the kuruş contained approximately 8.4 grams of silver. The Ottoman unit lost 88 percent of its silver content between 1789 and 1844. For both the 1808–1844 and 1789–1844 periods, these represent the highest rates of debasement in Ottoman history. There is no other period in which the Ottoman currency was subjected to such a high rate of debasement in such a short period of time.

10. Şevket Pamuk, *Five Hundred Years of Prices and Wages in Istanbul and Other Ottoman Cities, 1469–1998* (Ankara: Turkey State Institute of Statistics, Historical Statistics Series, forthcoming).

11. Chester L. Krause and Clifford Mishler, *Standard Catalog of World Coins,* 21st ed. (Iola, Wisc.: Krause Publications, 1994); also Remzi Kocaer, *Osmanlı Altın Paraları* (Istanbul: Güzel Sanatlar Matbaası, 1967).

12. In a different context Akira Motomura has argued that the Spanish government of the seventeenth century made a similar distinction between copper coinage on the one hand and silver and gold on the other. The government obtained large revenues from the minting and international circulation of silver coinage and, in order to maintain worldwide confidence in the currency, did not want to change the standards of these coins. However, the copper coinage used in the domestic economy was subjected to a policy of regular debasements. See Akira Motomura, "The Best and Worst of Currencies: Seigniorage and Currency Policy in Spain, 1597–1650," *The Journal of Economic History* 54 (1994):104–127.

13. Stanford J. Shaw and Ezel Kuran Shaw, *History of the Ottoman Empire and Modern Turkey*, Vol. II, *1809–1975* (London: Cambridge University Press, 1977), pp. 12–19.

14. BOA (Başbakanlık Osmanlı Arşivleri/ Prime Ministry, Ottoman Archives), Cevdet Darphane, 158, 3220, 1964, 1656, and 1632.

15. Çüneyt Ölçer, *Sultan II. Mahmud Zamanında Darp Edilen Osmanlı Madeni Paraları* (Istanbul: Yenilik Basımevi, 1970); Benjamin Sass, "The Silver and Billon Coins Minted at Constantinople Under Sultan Mahmud II (1223–1255 H.)," *American Numismatic Society Notes* 18 (1972): 167–175; Krause and Mishler, *Standard Catalog of World Coins*.

16. The Ottomans were expected to make this payment over a period of ten years. This sum amounted to approximately 150 percent of the annual revenues of the Ottoman state. It was subsequently reduced after territorial concessions by the Ottomans. Shaw and Shaw, *History of the Ottoman Empire*, Vol. II, p. 32; Yavuz Cezar, *Osmanlı Maliyesinde Bunalım ve Değişim Dönemi: XVIII. yy.dan Tanzimat'a Mali Tarih* (Istanbul: Alan Yayıncılık, 1986), pp. 244–301.

17. The exchange rate of the kuruş followed its silver content closely during these decades, with two exceptions. First, the decline in exchange rate of the kuruş slowed and even stopped during the Napoleonic wars as the European currencies also depreciated. Second, the link between the silver content of the Ottoman currency and its exchange rate was severed and the kuruş became a fiat currency during the rapid debasements of 1828–1833 (see Table 2.1).

18. Contemporary Ottoman commentators have argued that debasements were not useful for the state because the prices rose and the state revenues, which were fixed in nominal terms, declined in real terms after each debasement (Cezar, *Osmanlı Maliyesinde Bunalım*, p. 147). This argument, however, does not take into account the revenue obtained by the state during the first round by issuing additional coinage. With the time horizon shortened under the pressure of war and severe financial crises, it thus made sense to pursue debasements for short-term fiscal gains.

19. This measure was used during the debasement of 1789 and later during some of the debasements of Mahmud II (Cezar, *Osmanlı Maliyesinde Bunalım*, pp. 99, 139). For government attempts to bring in more silver to the Istanbul mint during this period, also see BOA, Cevdet Darphane 823, 13, and Hatt-ı Hümayun, 16505.

20. When the public can immediately observe or learn of the rate of debasement, prices adjust more quickly and the fiscal benefits of the debasement are exhausted sooner. If, on the other hand, both the size and the degree of fineness of the coins are constantly changed, as was the case during this period, the public might underestimate the extent of the debasement and adjust to the actual rate of debasement with a lag. In that case, the government's revenues will be higher. Sussman ("Debasements," pp. 44–70) argues that manipulating the monetary stan-

dard in this fashion offers the government the same kind of opportunity to raise revenues as with fiat money.

21. For an earlier episode of currency substitution in the Ottoman Empire arising from the instability of the akçe during the seventeenth century, see Şevket Pamuk, "In the Absence of Domestic Currency: Debased European Coinage in the Seventeenth-Century Ottoman Empire," *Journal of Economic History* 57 (1997): 345–366; and Pamuk, *Monetary History*, pp. 138–158.

22. For examples of counterfeiting and the circulation of counterfeit coinage during this period, see BOA, Hatt-ı Hümayun, 52541/A, 52563, 27644, 48486, 48487, 48488, 24243, and Cevdet Darphane, 1816, 1472, 1818.

23. Cezar, *Osmanlı Maliyesinde Bunalım*, pp. 79–89, 133–135, 239–241.

24. I am indebted to Dina Rizk Khoury for information on the urban uprisings in Syria and Iraq during the period 1770 to 1830.

25. E. P. Thompson, "The Moral Economy of the British Crowd in the Eighteenth Century," *Past and Present* 50 (1971): 76–135; also Charles Tilly, "Food Supply and Public Order in Modern Europe," in C. Tilly (ed.), *The Formation of Nation States in Western Europe* (Princeton, N.J.: Princeton University Press, 1975), pp. 35–151.

26. Haydar Kazgan, "İkinci Sultan Mahmut devrinde enflasyon ve darphane amiri Kazaz Artin," *Toplum ve Bilim* 11 (1980): 115–130; Diran Kelekyan, "Kazaz Artin," *Tarihi Osmani Encümeni Mecmuası*, 26 and 27 (June and August H.1330/1912).

27. According to a story still being told among the Armenian community of Istanbul, the Russian government demanded and obtained a large payment of indemnity after the war ended with the defeat of the Ottomans. Aware that the Ottoman government frequently debased the currency, however, the Russians demanded that the sum be paid in old kuruş, not new and debased currency. The Ottoman government produced new and debased coinage anyway but soon realized they had a problem on their hands. The coins were obviously new, very bright, and shiny. So, the story goes, they lined up the new reform soldiers on the Asian side of the Bosphorus for several miles and instructed them to hold out their hands. The new coinage was then passed on from hand to hand. By the time they reached the other end, they all looked just like the old kuruş. I am indebted to Dr. Nurhan Davutyan for this story. For the negotiations with the Russian government regarding the indemnity payment and the Ottoman request to pay the indemnity in silver kuruş rather than Hungarian gold coins, see BOA, Hatt-ı Hümayun, 42935, 46216, 20194.

28. A. du Velay, *Essai sur l'Histoire Financière de la Turquie* (Paris: Arthur Rousseau, 1903), pp. 28–32.

29. Cezar, *Osmanlı Maliyesinde Bunalım*, pp. 244–301.

30. For a detailed list of Ottoman and foreign coinage circulating in the Balkans, see David Cohen, "La circulation monétaire entre les Principautés Roumaines et les terres Bulgares (1840–1878)," *Bulgarian Historical Review* 4, no. 2 (1976): 55–71. For the different varieties of coinage in circulation in Baghdad in the 1830s and their exchange rates, see Hatt-ı Hümayun, 27815/D, 52490.

31. Ölçer, *Sultan II. Mahmud*, p. 17.

32. It is interesting that even during the 1820s and 1830s when Governor Muhammad Ali successfully fought and defeated the Ottoman armies for the independence of Egypt, he chose to keep the two currencies linked. The strength of commercial linkages between the two regions must have played an important role in the persistence of the monetary linkage. It is also likely that in the rapid deprecia-

tion of the kuruş in Istanbul, Muhammad Ali saw an opportunity for his own government to generate additional fiscal revenue and thus went along with the debasements. As a result, the timing of the overall decline of the para and kuruş of Egypt was remarkably similar to those in Istanbul. For the rapid decline in the exchange rate of the para of Egypt during this period, see Kenneth Cuno, *The Pasha's Peasants: Land, Society, and Economy in Lower Egypt, 1740–1858* (Cambridge, UK: Cambridge University Press, 1992), Appendix 2, pp. 211–215. Muhammad Ali was the first to invite European monetary specialists. With the monetary reforms of 1834, Egypt embraced the bimetallic system ten years ahead of the Ottomans in Istanbul. The standards adopted for gold and silver Egyptian coinage remained unchanged until World War I.

33. David Landes, *Bankers and Pashas: International Finance and Economic Imperialism in Egypt* (London: Heinemann, 1958); Roger Owen, *The Middle East in the World Economy, 1800–1914* (London: Methuen, 1981), pp. 122–135; and Abdelhamid Fenina, "Les Monnaies de la Régence de Tunis sous les Husaynides, Études de Numismatiques et d'Histoire Monétaire (1705–1891)" (Thèse de Doctorat, Nouveau Régime, Université de Paris-Sorbonne, 1993).

IX

From Debasement to External Borrowing: Changing Forms of Deficit Finance in the Ottoman Empire, 1750–1914

1. Introduction

Large fiscal deficits arising mostly from wars were a major problem for many of the European states during the early modern period but less so in the nineteenth century. The existing literature examines the strategies pursued and choices made by individual governments as they attempted to finance these deficits over the long term subject to the constraints and opportunities provided by the domestic and international financial markets. These public sector financial policies, of course, had far reaching implications not only for money and monetary policy but also for the economy at large.[1] During the eighteenth and nineteenth centuries the central budgets of the Ottoman empire also showed large deficits during periods of war. When the frequency of these extraordinary periods increased, the cumulative effects of the deficits tended to create major pressures on state finances and the economy.

This paper identifies and analyzes an important change in the way the budget deficits were financed before and after the 1850s. The Ottoman budget deficits tended to increase after the late 1760s and reached their peak during the 1820s and 1830s. In response, the state attempted to increase its control over revenue sources, relied on internal borrowing, and when the short term fiscal pressures mounted, resorted to debasements. The timing and magnitude of debasements during this period suggests that the governments were quite sensitive to the costs of debasements, especially the urban political opposition they generated.

Then, in the middle of the 19th century, bi-metallism was embraced, new standards were adopted for coinage and the government began to borrow in the European financial markets. From the 1850s to World War I, debasements were abandoned, relative monetary stability was maintained and external borrowing remained the most important mechanism for financing the budget deficits. The paper examines the reasons for as well as the consequences of this shift. It is argued that the shift was due to the combination of European

[1] For examples, see Weir (1989), Bordo and White (1991) and Velde and Weir (1992); also Parker (1974).

pressure and a desire on the part of the Ottoman government to maintain credibility in and access to the European financial markets. In the long term, however, the Ottomans paid a heavy price for borrowing abroad without establishing fiscal discipline since European creditors established financial control over Ottoman finances after the moratorium of 1875.

2. The Eighteenth Century: Relative Peace and Stability

The eighteenth century until the 1760s was a period of relative peace, stability and economic expansion for the Ottoman empire. While the available evidence on production is limited, it does point to an increasing trend for agriculture and artisanal activity as well as investment in manufacturing for many parts of the Balkans and Anatolia.[2] There also occurred a considerable expansion in the trade between the Ottoman empire and central and western Europe during this period especially through the Mediterranean, and to a lesser extent, across land in the Balkans. French merchants based in Marseille controlled the maritime trade until the French revolution.[3] This was also a period of stability for state finances. From the 1720s until the end of the 1760s, the evidence on Ottoman finances suggests that the overall trend was towards balanced budgets and surpluses were enjoyed in many years. The favorable financial conditions were especially apparent during the extended period of peace in mid-century, 1747 to 1768.[4]

The silver kurush (or gurush or piaster) was the leading unit of account as well as the leading means of exchange in the eighteenth century Ottoman monetary system. Virtually all prices and government obligations were expressed in terms of this unit. The state also minted a number of gold coins without face value. Their exchange rates against the kurush were determined by the markets although during extraordinary periods the goverment attempted control these rates. Gold coins including the Venetian ducat played a limited role in daily transactions. They were used in large payments and for store of value purposes. In addition, the European silver such as the Dutch thaler and Spanish eight real piece were used both in international trade and domestic payments. The exchange rates of these coins were also determined in the local markets.[5]

The Ottoman kurush was relatively stable during this period. In addition to the favorable state finances, the Ottoman currency was supported by the rising levels of output in the new silver mines of Anatolia, in Gumushane, Keban, Espiye and Ergani whose total output reached 35 to 40 tons per year in mid-century. The older silver mines in the Balkans, in Sidrekapsi and Kratova continued to contribute as well. Numismatic and archival evidence summarized Figure 1 shows that the silver content of the kurush declined at a moderate pace, by a total of 40 percent until the end of the 1760s.

---

[2] Genç (1984).

[3] Panzac (1992), Frangakis-Syrett (1992), Paris (1957).

[4] Tabakoglu (1985), pp. 74–113.

[5] Pamuk (2000), pp. 159–70.

From the 1760s until the end of the century, however, Ottoman state finances and money were jolted by two exhausting wars, 1768 to 1774 and 1787 to 1792, the first with Russia and the second with Russia and the Habsburgs. Although the first of these created financial difficulties, a major debasement was avoided by relying on the reserves accumulated in the earlier era of peace. During the second war, however, the government was forced to reduce the silver content of the piaster by about one third. The debasement was accompanied by a demand, which included a reference to the ongoing holy war, that the public surrender to the government all available silver at official, below market prices.

To keep prices from rising both as a result of this operation and in the face of wartime shortages, the government tried to enforce a system of price ceilings (*narh*) for most goods in urban areas, especially in the capital city. These price ceilings were extended to the exchange rates of other coins, both gold and foreign, against the silver piaster. The available evidence is too scanty to attempt an evaluation of this package of intervention. It appears, however, that the government was not particularly successful in achieving its ends. Even though mint records are not available, it appears that the government could not induce significant flows of silver to the mints. Mint output, therefore, remained limited until the government later raised the mint price of silver. At the same time, the price ceilings only exacerbated the shortages in urban areas, especially in the capital. Merchants in the provinces simply refused to send goods to the capital. This was in fact the first and the last time in the eighteenth century that the government attempted to use coercion to generate seigniorage revenue. It was also the most severe crisis of provisioning faced by the urban areas, especially the capital city.[6]

3. Financial Reform and Attempts at Internal Borrowing

The reign of sultan Mahmud II (1808–1839) was a very difficult period for the Ottoman empire and especially the central government. During these three decades the central government was forced to deal with a series of uprisings, nationalist revolutions and a series of wars abroad. While it was able to suppress the various uprisings of notables in both the Balkans and Anatolia, the Serbian and Greek revolutions led to the secessions of these territories from the empire. Much more costly to the state finances than any of these were a series of wars against Russia (1806–1812 and 1828–29), Iran (1820–28) and Egypt (1831–33 and 1838–39). This was also a critical period of Western style and centralizing reform for the Ottoman empire. The attempts to establish a western style army had started earlier, during the reign of Selim III (1789–1807) but progress had been limited due to the opposition of the janissaries. After the suppression of the janissary revolt and the abolition of the order in 1826, the efforts to establish a new army (*Nizam-i Cedid*) gained new momentum.[7] Another important and difficult task was the reorganization and modernization of the internal administration of the empire. In this respect, the strategy of

---

[6] Pamuk (2000), pp. 170–1.

[7] Shaw and Shaw (1977), pp. 1–54.

Mahmud II was the elimination of intermediate authorities both in the capital and the provinces and the centralization of power in his own hands. As the reform movement began to spread beyond the military field in the 1820s, to administration, justice, and education, the demands for resources increased as well. While precise budget figures do not exist, recent estimates suggest that after adjusting for inflation, the expenditures of the central government increased by 250 to 300 percent from the end of the eighteenth century until 1840. Roughly half of the budget expenditures were being allocated for military purposes and this share rose considerably during periods of war. To deal with changes of such magnitudes, of course, constituted a financial task of enormous proportions for the central government. As a result, one of the key goals of the reform process was the financial re-organization of the empire and greater centralization of the revenues.[8]

During the eighteenth and nineteenth centuries, the political and administrative capacities of the Ottoman government often determined the limits on fiscal revenue. Without an administrative network for tax collection, the government was forced to share tax collections with the powerful groups in the provinces. Beginning in the 1820s, the state was able to reduce the power of the alliance between high level bureaucrats and financiers at the capital and the locally powerful groups at the provinces. It thus became possible to exert greater control over the tax collection process. Through this centralization the state was able to increase, in real terms, the revenues collected at the center. However, the expenditures continued to rise at a faster pace throughout this period. For this reason, in addition to its efforts at financial re-organization and centralization, the government devoted a considerable part of its energies, from the late eighteenth century until the 1840s, to developing new methods of long term internal borrowing.

Ever since the sixteenth century, the state had relied on the financiers at the capital for short term loans. Even though these financiers, or bankers without banks, expanded their activities considerably in the second half of the eighteenth century, their lending capacity was still small in relation to the needs of the state. One obvious way for the government to borrow on a long term basis was to link the borrowed funds explicitly to the revenue sources of the state. In fact, the malikane or life-term tax-farm system which was initiated at the end of the seventeenth century, was based on this principle.

After the end of the war of 1768–1774 which had dramatically exposed the military as well as financial weaknesses of the Ottoman system, the financial bureaucracy started a system of long term domestic borrowing called esham. In this system which was based partly on the malikane system, the annual net revenues of a tax source were specified in nominal terms. This amount was divided into a large number of shares which were then sold to the public for the lifetime of the buyers. The annual revenues of the source continued to be collected by the tax farmers.[9]

---

[8] Cezar (1986), pp. 279–281.

[9] These arrangements were similar to those used by the European states in the early modern era, most notably in France. See Weir (1989) and Parker (1974).

Clearly, one motivation here was to broaden the base of state borrowing and enable the state go beyond the limited numbers of large financiers who tended to dominate the malikane auctions and to reach a larger pool of small and medium sized lenders. However, the inability of the state to control or limit the sales of the esham between individuals and the difficulties in preventing the heirs of the deceased from continuing to receive payments seriously limited the fiscal benefits of this system. As a result, it proved to be a rather costly system of long term internal borrowing. Many Ottoman thinkers argued in favor of abolishing it especially when the fiscal pressures subsided. During the next half century the state vascillated between abolishing the esham during periods of fiscal stability and continuing and even expanding it when fiscal pressures mounted and additional funds had to be secured with little regard for their longer term cost. [10]

During the war of 1787–92 the Ottoman government also considered the possibility of borrowing from abroad, which would have been a a first for the Ottoman state, from France, Spain or Netherlands. In response, the Dutch government indicated in 1789 that it was not in a position to lend and referred the Ottoman government to the private sector. However, due to difficulties both in Europe arising from the French revolution and the Ottoman side, this possibility could not be pursued any further. Another proposal was to borrow from Morrocco because it was a friendly Muslim country, but it was obvious that the ability of Morrocco was quite limited. From the late eighteenth century until the 1840s, extraordinary wartime taxes and the expropriation of the wealth of prominent individuals especially of those who accumulated their wealth as a public servant or in their financial dealings with the state continued to serve as other means of raising fiscal revenue during troubled times.[11]

4. The Great Ottoman Debasement (1809–1839)

In addition to these long and short term measures, the Ottoman government made extensive use of currency debasements during this extraordinary period. When the centralizing and reformist sultan Mahmud II ascended the throne in 1808, the standard kurush still contained 5.90 grams of silver, unchanged since the debasement of 1789. During the next three decades, the silver content of the Ottoman currency declined at times sharply, at times more slowly. The lowest point for the kurush was reached in 1831–32 at 0.5 grams of silver although it subsequently rose to 0.9 grams in 1832 and then to 1.0 gram in 1844 where it stayed until World War I. In other words, the kurush lost more than 90 percent of its silver content until 1832 and then recovered somewhat. All in all, from 1808 to 1844 it lost 83 percent of its silver content. (Figure 1)

[10] Cezar (1986), pp. 128–34, 198–200.

[11] Cezar (1986), pp. 89–92, 137–38.

Figure 1

Silver Content of the Ottoman Monetary Unit. Akçe. 1469–1914

in grams; 1 kurush = 120 akçe (source: Pamuk, 2000)

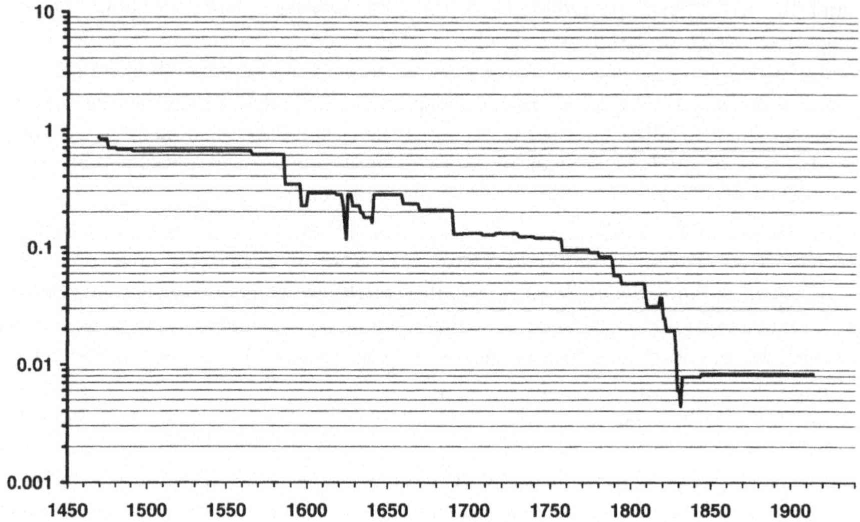

Closely following the debasement of the currency, of course, was the sharp fall in its exchange rate and the rapid rise in the general price level both of which were were equally dramatic. In 1788, 5 and a half kurush exchanged for one Venetian ducat and 11 kurush for one British pound sterling. In 1844 one ducat equalled 50–52 kurush and the British pound exchanged for 110 kurush. In other words, during these six decades the price of these leading currencies in terms of the kurush had increased 9 to 10 fold or the Ottoman unit had lost about 90 percent of its value against them and most other European currencies.[12] Consumer price indices for Istanbul constructed by the present author from the account books of the imperial kitchen at Istanbul indicate that food prices paid by the palace kitchen increased approximately 8 fold from between 1780 and 1845, reflecting closely the changes in the silver content of the currency and its exchange rate against the leading European units. (Figure 2).

[12] The slide of the kurush against the most European currencies slowed down during the Napoleonic Wars as the others also depreciated but resumed with the end of European hostilities. Issawi (1980), pp. 329–31, Pamuk (2000), pp. 191.

Figure 2

Consumer Price Index for Istanbul. 1469–1914

1469 = 1,0; (source Pamuk 2004)

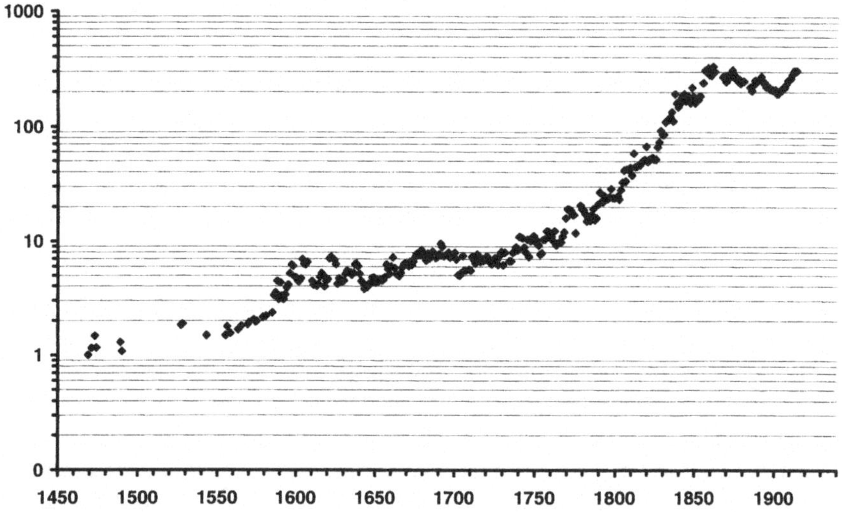

During the reign of Mahmud II the government continued to issue varieties of gold coins such as *zeri mahbub* , *rumi* , *adli* , *hayriye* , *mahmudiye* , each with different and changing standards. However, these gold coinage were not subjected to such rapid rates of debasement. The overall decline in the specie content of the gold coins remained below 20 percent. It is thus clear that the government did not view the gold coins with the same seigniorage logic that was applied to the silver kurush. This was because the unit of account for the economy and state finances was the kurush and not any of the gold coins. All obligations of the state were expressed in terms of the silver kurush and not linked to any gold coin. Under the circumstances, the expected seigniorage gains from debasing the gold coins was very limited.[13]

[13] In a different context Motomura has argued that the Spanish government of the seventeenth century made a similar distinction between copper coinage on the one hand, and silver and gold on the other. The government enjoyed substantial seigniorage revenues from the minting and international circulation of silver coinage and, in order to maintain worldwide confidence in the currency, did not want to change the standards of these coins. On the other hand, the copper coinage used in the domestic economy were subjected to a policy of regular debasements. Motomura (1994).

The debasement during the reign of Mahmud II unfolded in an uneven fashion, in fits and spurts. An examination of the timing and magnitudes of each debasement should provide important insights into the motives of the government as well as the fiscal consequences. There is no doubt that the fiscal difficulties and crises created by the wars figured prominently in the decline of the currency and its timing. For example, highest rates of debasement in Ottoman history took place during and after the war of 1828–29 with Russia. Between 1828 and 1831, the silver content of the kurush was reduced from 2.32 grams to 0.53 grams, a decline of 79 percent during 4 years. As the financial conditions began to improve after 1832, however, the silver content of the currency was raised to 0.94 grams. (Figure 1)

A simple model can be employed here to examine the attitudes and behavior of Ottoman governments towards debasement during these three decades, and more generally during the period 1789–1844. In this framework the government is viewed as weighing the short term seignorage revenues accruing from debasements against both the short term and long term costs of such action. If the state perceives these costs to be less than the expected seigniorage benefits, then, a debasement or a series of debasements may be adopted. In other words, far from being an exercise in futility, the debasements are viewed as a potentially effective instrument of fiscal policy, especially in the short term.

The fiscal benefits of a debasement are not difficult to establish. With the amount of specie at hand the state is able to issue a higher amount of money in nominal terms and thus meet a larger amount of its obligations. In addition, the state obtains additional seigniorage revenue from the old coins brought to the mint by the public. As prices and wages paid by the state rise, however, many of the state revenues which are fixed in nominal terms will decline in real terms. In other words, debasements generate an initial surge in revenues followed by their decline in real terms due to the high levels of inflation they create. In the longer term, a debasement may even lead to a real decline in state revenues if the state does not adjust upwards the taxes and other revenues which have been fixed in nominal terms.

There are a number other possible costs of debasements that may be borne by the state. If the public loses confidence in the currency and begins to anticipate further debasements, it will become increasingly difficult, for the state to take advantage of further reductions in the specie content of coinage. For example, in the open mint system, the public may begin holding another currency and stay away from the mints. Some degree of currency substitution did that place in this Ottoman episode as varieties of foreign coinage were always free to circulate.

Another cost of debasement in the Ottoman context was the emergence of widespread counterfeiting. When the state issued new coins with lower specie content, counterfeiters immediately began to mint the new coins with the same or even higher silver content in order to share the seigniorage revenues of the state. This opportunity declined, however, when the prices of metals adjust upwards along with other prices.

Yet another cost of was the adverse implications of debasements for the ability of the state to borrow domestically. One of the reasons why the state did not pursue further the option of long term internal borrowing was that, for a variety of reasons, this process was perceived to be too costly. When the state begins to resort to debasements, however, it loses whatever credibility it might have in these markets. There is evidence that with the acceleration of debasements after 1808, rates of interest increased even further and it became even more difficult for the state to sell the esham.

In the Ottoman case, probably the most important cost of debasements was the political opposition it generated amongst the urban groups, especially in the capital city. Since incomes of some groups were fixed in nominal terms, they stood to lose from debasements and the subsequent price increases unless their wages and salaries were also adjusted upwards. Best organized and most powerful amongst them were the janissaries stationed permanently in the capital. In Ottoman history, there are a number of successful revolts by the janissaries against the debasements of the state. Their opposition was a major constraint faced by the governments considering debasements. During the reign of Mahmud II, the janissaries were an especially important part of the political picture in the capital as they opposed his efforts of western style reform. Mahmud II wanted to replace the janissaries with a western style army. However, during the early years of his long reign, he did not have the political support to make this critical move.

Into this equation of costs and benefits, wars enter as exogeneous shocks, events which raise both the need for short term revenues for the state and the willingness of the public to accept or excuse extraordinary measures such as debasements. As the urgency of generating revenues increased, the state often invoked references to holy wars and even linked the new coinage explicitly to the ongoing wars, by calling the new issues of coins and bonds, cihadiyye, for example.

During the reigns of both Selim III and Mahmud II under examination here, the governments were well aware of the limitations imposed by the janissaries. Hence, debasements were used only in connection with wars. After the janissaries were finally defeated and the order was abolished in 1826, in what is usually considered as one of the most important political events of this period known as Vaka-i Hayriye or the Auspicious Event, a major constraint in the way of debasements was lifted. While the government did not embrace debasements as a peacetime policy, it is not a coincidence that during the first major war following this event, it undertook the largest debasement ever in Ottoman history, reducing the specie content of the kurush by 79 percent within a period of four years.

It is interesting that by reducing the borrowing requirements of the state, these seigniorage revenues also brought down the interest rates in domestic financial markets and provided indirect benefits for the state treasury. In addition to any amount the state may have borrowed in the domestic markets, the decline in interest rates provided fiscal relief through its impact on the tax farming system. The tax farmers who entered state auctions for the right to collect specific tax revenues of the state were required to make a certain fraction of these payments in advance for which they typically borrowed from the private financiers. When the domestic interest rates declined, therefore, the auction prices of tax farms tended to rise, thereby increasing the net tax revenues of the state.

This examination of the currency policy of the Ottoman government during these three turbulent decades shows both the benefits and limitations of debasements. While the Ottoman administrators were well aware of the seigniorage calculus and state did obtain obvious fiscal benefits, it is also clear that they were reluctant to view debasements as a permanent instrument for raising revenue, to be used during peace as well as wartime. The time series I have constructed for the silver content of the Ottoman currency also shows that twice during this period, in 1818 and 1832, the government raised the silver content of the kurush after the return of peace, confirming those limits of debasement as perceived by the government. (Figure 1)

5. A New Strategy: Stable Money and External Borrowing

From the perspective of Ottoman economic and monetary history, the nineteenth century, especially the period after 1840, constitutes a period quite different from the earlier era. On the one hand, it was characterized by major efforts at Western style reform, in administration, in economic, fiscal and monetary affairs as well as education, law and justice. This was also a period of integration into the world markets and rapid expansion in foreign trade particularly with Europe turning the Ottoman economy increasingly into an exporter of primary products and an importer of manufactures. It is estimated that the foreign trade of the areas within the 1911 borders of the empire, Macedonia, Anatolia and Syria, increased by more than 12 to 15 fold between 1820s and World War I.[14] This process was facilitated by the construction of ports and railroads and by the establishment of modern banking institutions by European capital. As a result, the commercialization of agriculture proceeded rapidly in Macedonia, western Anatolia and along the Syrian coast. The rural population was drawn to markets not only as producers of cash crops but also as purchasers of imported goods, especially of cotton textiles. These developments substantially increased the demand for and the use of money in these more commercialized regions of the Empire.

For the European governments and especially the British, the success of reforms was considered essential for maintaining the territorial integrity of the retreating empire. They also believed that rapid expansion of commercial ties with Europe based on the principle of comparative advantage and European direct investment in the Ottoman economy which would contribute to that end were essential for the economic development of the country. In this context, monetary stability was perceived as an important pre-requisite for both reform and the expansion of international trade. As a result, the Europeans and especially the British began to exert considerable pressure on the Ottoman government to establish a more stable monetary system. They also made clear that they were ready to provide the technical expertise necessary for this purpose. The Europeans also linked future

[14] Issawi (1980), Chapter 3 and Pamuk (1987), Chapter 1.

Ottoman access to European financial markets explicitly to fiscal reform and monetary stability.

As for the Ottoman government, the monetary conditions had reached chaotic proportions by the end of the 1830s. While the government had succeeded in raising short term revenue from frequent debasements, the resulting inflation had brought unfavorable political consequences. In addition, the production of large variety of coins each with different standards since the beginning of the century and the inability of the government to retire the earlier series from circulation had added to the difficulties. The earlier coins exchanged according to their silver content rather than the nominal value at which they had been issued. The quality of the many types of gold coinage that were produced during this turbulent period had also deteriorated although these were not debased as often or as extensively. While these conditions created difficulties for daily transactions, they made it even more difficult to carry out international trade. At the same time, the appeal and use of European coinage had increased especially in international trade and for store of wealth purposes.[15]

A reform in coinage was undoubtedly in order, and after the death of Sultan Mahmud II in 1839, the new government openly expressed that intention in 1840 as one of the first items in its agenda. Mint technicans and other specialists were invited from England and France to provide advise the ottoman government about the new standards of coinage. New machines and technology was imported from England. [16]

After some delay, the decision was made to adopt the bimetallic standard, a system in which the silver kurush and the new gold lira were both legal tender, freely convertible at the fixed rate of 100 kurush for one gold lira and obtainable at the government mint. The government began to produce the new gold coins in 1843 and the following year the new silver coins were issued along with an official declaration from the imperial mint, setting out the reasons for the reform. The gold-silver ratio was fixed at 15.09. [17] In practice, however, the government did not command sufficient resources to withdraw all the previous coinage from circulation by compulsory redemption. As a result, it was soon forced to recognize them as legal tender and even announce the official rates at which each of these, especially the large silver coins minted in the 1830s, would be accepted. Some of these coins remained in circulation until World War I.

The Ottoman governments abandoned debasements as a means of raising fiscal revenue after 1844. All silver and gold coinage minted until 1922 adhered to the standards established in 1844. (Figure 1) In addition, copper coinage of small denominations continued to be minted for daily transactions. Nickel coinage was introduced for the same purpose in 1910.

---

[15] For a detailed list of all coinage, both Ottoman and foreign, circulating in the Balkans, for example, see Cohen (1976).

[16] Olçer (1970), p. 17.

[17] Pamuk (2000), pp. 206–8.

The stability of coinage did not mean the end of fiscal difficulties and the need to raise additional revenue, however. Throughout the century, the Ottoman administrations had difficulties balancing the budget and resorted to a variety of methods to deal with its fiscal problems. One method of raising fiscal revenue which began to be used in 1840 was the printing and circulation in the Istanbul area of interest bearing paper money called kaime-i muteber-i nakdiyye or kaime for short. As their volume remained limited until 1852, the kaime performed reasonably well despite problems with counterfeiting. During the Crimean War, however, large amounts of kaime were printed and the market price expressed in gold Liras declined to less than half the nominal value. One gold Lira began to exchange for 200–220 kurush in kaime. As a result, this first experiment in paper money resulted in a major wave of inflation. The kaimes were finally retired in the early 1860s with the help of short term loans obtained from the Imperial Ottoman Bank. [18]

There were two other occasions, both of them during major wars, when the government resorted to non-covertible paper money as a fiscal measure. The second kaime episode took place during the war of 1877–78 with Russia and they circulated in most parts of the empire. Because of their large volume, however, they declined to one quarter of their nominal value within two years even though the government agreed to accept some payments in paper currency. Similarly, during World War I, non-convertible paper circulated regularly and was one of the leading sources of fiscal revenue. By 1917 one gold Lira equalled six paper Liras. Once again, the use of kaime resulted in considerable rise in prices expressed in paper currency. For the period 1844–1914 as a whole, then, non-convertible paper remained an exception used only under extraordinary circumstances.

The most important method adopted by the Ottoman government after mid-nineteenth century to deal with the recurring budget deficits was borrowing in the European financial markets. This process was initiated in 1854 during the Crimean War. In the early stages, the Ottomans were supported by their wartime allies, the British government, which fully guaranteed the first bond issue against the Ottoman annual receipts from the Egyptian tribute. In the following two decades, the Ottoman government borrowed very large sums in London, Paris, Vienna and elsewhere under increasingly unfavorable terms. The net proceeds of these issues were directed almost entirely towards current expenditures. Only a small fraction was spent on infrastructure investment and on increasing the capacity to pay back. By the second half of the 1860s, the Ottoman finances had deteriorated to the point where new bond issues had become necessary to maintain the debt payments. A moratorium was in sight but the financial markets kept up the process lured by the unusually high rates of return. [19]

---

[18] Davison (1980).

[19] Blaisdell (1929) remains the classic treatment of this topic. For the magnitudes of funds flows arising from external borrowing, see Pamuk (1987), Chapter 4 and Appendix III.

When the financial crises of 1873 led to the cessation of overseas lending by the European financial markets, the Ottoman government was forced to declare a moratorium on its outstanding debt which stood at more than 200 million pounds sterling in 1876. After a period of prolonged negotiations, the Ottoman Public Debt Administration was established in 1881 to exercise European control over parts of Ottoman finances and ensure orderly payments on the outstanding debt whose nominal value was reduced approximately by half during the negotiations. For the following three decades until the outbreak of World War I, a sizable share of Ottoman tax revenues were controlled by the OPDA and used for debt payments. This control and the regular payments on the debt was quite reassuring for the European financial markets. As a result, the Ottoman government was able to resume borrowing towards the end of the century. With the rise of military spending, Ottoman borrowing gained momentum after the turn of the century. On the eve of World War I, the volume of annual borrowing as well as the outstanding external debt had reached unusually high proportions reminiscent of the 1870s. [20]

6. Credibility in the International Markets

From the perspective of the present paper, the important question, then, is why the Ottoman government pushed aside alternative methods of financing its deficit such as internal borrowing, debasements and/or issueing inconvertible paper and continued almost exclusively with external borrowing during these seven decades. We might point out that internal borrowing, especially long term internal borrowing, was not a serious possibility because of the limited size of the domestic market for funds in relation to the borrowing needs of the state. In addition, it might be argued that debasements of coinage had become an impractical method of seigniorage in the nineteenth century. Inconvertible paper currency often served the same purpose without some of the limitations and disadvantages of debasements. Hence, the actual choices facing the Ottomans can be reduced to two : inconvertible paper currency and external borrowing. Why did the ottoman governments insist on the latter and used the former only during exceptional periods such as wars ?

Part of the answer lies with the fact that, until the moratorium of 1875, the Ottoman government was a novice in external borrowing. Selling bonds in the European markets with maturities of 20 years or longer and thereby postponing the short term fiscal problems to the future must have appeared as an easy solution for them at the beginning, especially in view of the political and economic costs associated with debasements and inconvertible paper which burdened the Ottoman governments without any respite from 1808 until the 1860s.

---

[20] Pamuk (1987), Chapter 4.

After the establishment of the OPDA and European control over Ottoman finances, however, inexperience can not be considered as an explanation. By that time the Ottomans had learned more about the costs and consequences of borrowing abroad without bringing the budget deficits under control. For this second period, we need to focus on a combination of pressure from the OPDA and more generally the European interests for maintainning monetary stability and the need for the Ottomans to maintain credibility in the European markets if they wanted to retain their option of external borrowing.

The reasons for European pressure on the Ottomans to maintain monetary stability were the same after 1880s as they were in the earlier part of the century. Monetary stability was considered as an important condition for the expansion of trade with Europe and for attracting direct European investment. The representatives of the OPDA also made clear that monetary stability was necessary if the Ottomans wanted to retain their access to the European financial markets. Even though the Ottoman government issued bonds in European currencies, the perception was that high seigniorage and high inflation would seriously hurt the chances for borrowing abroad both in the short and long term.

In fact, the financial control exercised by the OPDA enabled the Ottoman government to borrow long term in the European markets at 4 to 5 percent per annum, which was reasonably low at the time wheras the effective rates paid by the Ottoman government in the earlier period leading up to the moratorium had fluctuated between 10 to 12 percent at a time of roughly stable commodity prices world wide. The ability of the Ottomans to continue borrowing at these low rates, according to this argument, depended on maintaining their credibility in the European financial markets especially in view of its poor record before 1875. [21]

At that juncture it was clear that the Ottoman government had to be willing to burn all bridges with European commercial and financial interests in order to abandon monetary stability and return to debasements and/or inconvertible paper as the basic form of deficit finance. Instead, the government made great efforts to retire the inconvertible paper issued during the war of 1877–78, which took place after the moratorium was declared and before the negotiations with the creditors had ended. After these paper issues were retired, the government adhered to some form of the gold standard and the inconvertible paper experiment was not repeated until World War I.

[21] Bordo and White have contrasted the financial and currency policies of Britain and France during the Napoleonic Wars. They argued that the reason why France, the financially weaker country followed more "orthodox" policies during this period was its poor reputation and lack of credibility in the international financial markets. Bordo and White (1991).

7. Conclusion

After using debasements for deficit finance for many decades, the Ottoman government, along with many others around the world, embraced bi-metallism in mid–19th century and began to borrow in the European financial markets. From the 1850s to World War I, debasements were abandoned, relative monetary stability was maintained and external borrowing remained the most important mechanism for financing the budget deficits. The paper has examined the reasons for as well as the consequences of this shift. It has been argued that the shift was due to the combination of European pressure and a desire on the part of the Ottoman government to maintain credibility in and access to the European financial markets.

What was the long term balance sheet, then, for the mid-nineteenth century regime change ? Monetary stability, rapid expansion of foreign trade and European direct investment should appear on the positive side. Annual rate of growth of Ottoman foreign trade averaged close to 5 percent in real terms during the nineteenth century. There is also some evidence for economic growth from mid-century to World War I. If true, this economic growth was certainly related to the growing commercialization of the Ottoman economy. Monetary stability undoubtedly contributed to that process. However, the Ottoman default in 1875, the establishment of the Ottoman Public Debt Administration and the surrender of some of the leading sources of revenue to to the European creditors in 1881 suggest that the Ottomans paid a heavy price for borrowing large amounts from abroad before putting their fiscal house in order.

References

Blaisdell, Donald C. (1929), *European Financial Control in the Ottoman Empire* , New York, Columbia University Press.

Bordo, Michael D. (1986), "Money, Deflation and Seigniorage in the Fifteenth Century", *Journal of Monetary Economics* , Vol. 18, pp. 337–46.

Bordo, Michael D. and Eugene N. White (1991), "A Tale of Two Currencies : British and French Finance During the Napoleonic Wars", *The Journal of Economic History* , Vol. 51, pp. 303–16.

Cezar, Yavuz (1986), *Osmanli Maliyesinde Bunalim ve Degisim Donemi : XVIII. yy.dan Tanzimat'a Mali Tarih* , Istanbul : Alan Yayincilik.

Cohen, David (1976), "La Circulation Monetaire entre les Principautes Roumaines et les Terres Bulgares (1840–1878)", *Bulgarian Historical Review* , Vol. 4, No. 2, pp. 55–71.

Davison, Roderic (1980), "The First Ottoman Experiment with Paper Money", in Osman Okyar and Halil Inalcik (eds.), *Social and Economic History of Turkey (1071–1920)*, Papers Presented to the First International Congress on the Social and Economic History of Turkey , Ankara, pp. 243–51.

Frangakis-Syrett, Elena (1992), *The Commerce of Smyrna in the Eighteenth Century (1700–1820)* , Centre for Asia Minor Studies, Athens.

Genç, Mehmet (1984), "XVIII. Yuzyilda Osmanli Ekonomisi ve Savas", *Yapit* , Ankara, No. 4, pp. 52–61.

Issawi, Charles (1980), *The Economic History of Turkey, 1800–1914*, Chicago: University of Chicago Press.

Kiray, Emine (1993), *Osmanli'da Ekonomik Yapi ve Dis Borclar*, Istanbul.

Motomura, Akira (1994), "The best and Worst of Currencies: Seigniorage and Currency Policy in Spain, 1597–1650", *The Journal of Economic History*, Vol. 54, pp. 104–27.

Olçer, Cuneyt (1970), *Sultan II. Mahmud Zamaninda Darp Edilen Osmanli Madeni Paralari*, Istanbul.

Pamuk, Şefket (1987), *The Ottoman Empire and European Capitalism, 1820–1913: Trade, investment and production*, Cambridge: Cambridge University Press.

Pamuk, Şefket (2000), *A Monetary History of the Ottoman Empire*, Cambridge University Press, Cambridge and New York.

Pamuk, Şefket sw(2004), "Prices in the Ottoman Empire, 1469–1914", *International Journal of Middle East Studies*, Vol. 36, 2004, pp. 451–68.

Panzac, Daniel (1992), "International Trade and Domestic Maritime Trade in the Ottoman Empire during the 18th Century", *International Journal of Middle East Studies*, Vol. 24, pp. 189–206.

Robert Paris, *Histoire du Commerce de Marseille, Tome V : de 1660 a 1789, Le Levant*, Paris, Librairie Plon, 1957.

Parker, Geoffrey (1974), "The Emergence of Modern Finance in Europe, 1500–1730", Carlo Cipolla (ed.), *The Fontana Economic History of Europe*, Vol. 2, pp. 527–89.

Stanford J. Shaw and Ezel Kuran Shaw (1977), *History of the Ottoman Empire and Modern Turkey, Vol. II, 1808–1975*, Cambridge University Press, Cambridge and New York.

Nathan Sussman (1993), "Debasements, Royal Revenues and Inflation in France during the Hundred Years' War, 1415–1422", *The Journal of Economic History*, Vol. 53, pp. 44–70.

Tabakoğlu, Ahmet (1985), *Gerileme Donemine Girerken Osmanli Maliyesi* , Dergah Yayinlari, Istanbul.

Velde, François R. and David R. Weir (1992), "The Financial Market and Government Debt Policy in France, 1746–1793", *The Journal of Economic History*, Vol. 52, pp. 1–39.

Weir, David R. (1989), "Tontines, Public Finance and Revolution in France and England, 1688–1789", *The Journal of Economic History*, Vol. 49, pp. 95–124.

X

The Middle East in Nineteenth-Century World Trade

THE CENTURY BETWEEN the Napoleonic Wars and the First World War witnessed the impact of the Industrial Revolution around the globe. For the economies of the Middle East, this was a period of rapid integration into the world markets. Between 1820 and 1913 the foreign trade of the Middle East expanded more than fifteenfold. The expansion in foreign trade was accompanied by considerable shifts in the patterns of production. In many areas of the Middle East, agriculture became increasingly more commercialized, and increasingly larger shares of agricultural production were directed toward the export markets. These changes had significant repercussions on the systems of land tenure and property rights. Another important trend associated with the expansion of foreign trade was deindustrialization. Traditional handicrafts resisted but for the most part declined under the competition of imported manufactures. On the other hand, the beginnings of the factory system remained weak.

After midcentury, European commercial penetration began to be accompanied by financial penetration. European direct investment concentrated in railroads and other infrastructure. There was also a good deal of indiscriminate borrowing by the Middle Eastern governments in the European financial markets, which led to increasing European control over state finances. Standards of living remained low, particularly in comparison to Europe. There was, however, some economic growth, at least during the decades before World War I.

If we know much more today than we did three decades ago about these economic processes and their far-reaching ramifications, this is above all due to the pioneering work of Charles Issawi. His work not only established the contours of European economic penetration and the specific forms of local response in Egypt, Iran, Turkey, Syria, Iraq, and more generally in the Middle East, but it also set the agenda for further research in this field (Issawi 1961, 1966, 1971, 1981, 1988).

While the economic experience of the Middle East during the nineteenth century represented a dramatic break with its previous history, the Middle East was hardly alone in this respect. Virtually every region of the world was affected by the European expansion and each, in turn, developed its own response to the European challenge. A second and very important contribution of Charles Issawi's work has been his insistence on employing a comparative perspective in the economic historiography of the Middle East. He has emphasized that the economic experience of the Middle East shared many dimensions with other areas, particularly with those in the underdeveloped regions of the world during the nineteenth century. He has also argued that there were a number of special dimensions in the economic experience of the Middle East and that these special dimensions could be best understood by placing the Middle East in a comparative framework. Through intraregional and interregional comparisons, Charles Issawi has attempted to identify both the general and the specific in the economic history of the Middle East (e.g., Issawi 1968, 1970, 1981b).

This paper will adopt the same comparative perspective to reexamine a topic that has already received considerable attention from Professor Issawi: the expansion of the foreign trade of the Middle East during the nineteenth century. First, I will attempt to establish the basic trends both in absolute terms and in relation to worldwide trends during this period. In the second half of the paper I will discuss some of the reasons why the volume and the rate of expansion of the foreign trade of different countries in the Middle East diverged from long-term trends in other areas, particularly from those in the contemporary Third World.

Estimates for exports and per capita exports from the Middle East during different periods of the nineteenth century will be presented. Because of the poor quality of underlying data on trade and population, these figures are subject to a wide degree of potential error and must be treated with caution. For this reason the discussion in this paper will be concerned primarily with the broad, long-term trends, which these estimates can support and which are also supported by a larger body of secondary evidence.

The limitations of available data also determine the temporal and spatial dimensions of our inquiry. Since the reliability of the available estimates are particularly low for the earlier years, I have decided to focus on the period after 1840. Moreover, since the more reliable estimates on foreign trade are prepared in terms of the political boundaries that existed during the nineteenth century, I will define the nineteenth-century Middle East in terms of three political entities: Egypt, Iran, and the Asiatic provinces of the Ottoman Empire, including twentieth-century Turkey in Europe but excluding Arabia.

The century between the end of the Napoleonic Wars and World War I witnessed an unprecedented expansion in world trade. Although the available estimates differ somewhat regarding the extent and rhythms of this expansion, it appears that the rate of growth of world trade fluctuated from one period to another but averaged over 4 percent per year, leading to an approximately eighteenfold increase in volume terms for the period 1840 to 1913 (Rostow 1978, 67, 669; Hanson 1980, 14). A large part of this expansion involved the trade between the industrialized countries, particularly within Europe. However, exports from the underdeveloped areas expanded at approximately the same rates as total world exports during this period. The appropriate question concerning the Middle East, then, is not whether its commodity exports expanded during the nineteenth century but how their volume and rates of growth compared with the corresponding levels for world trade and for other underdeveloped regions of the world economy. Such a comparison will tell us more about the extent and the rate of integration of the Middle East into the world markets.

The estimates presented in Table 1 summarize the basic trends in the expansion of exports from the Middle East for the period after 1840. These figures also reflect broadly the expansion of the total trade of the region since for the Middle East as a whole, though not for the individual countries, the volume of imports followed closely the changes in the volume of exports. These estimates show that exports from the Middle East increased more than tenfold in constant priced and about sixteenfold in volume terms during the seven decades preceding World War I.

As shown in Table 2, this overall expansion is close to but somewhat lower than the growth of world trade during the same period;

that is, the share of Middle Eastern exports in world trade appears to have declined slowly but steadily until World War I. The divergence between the two rates of growth becomes more pronounced if levels of per capita exports are examined. As indicated in Table 3, although per capita exports from the Middle East exceeded per capita exports for the world by more than 20 percent in the early 1840s, they had

Table 1. Estimates for Commodity Exports from the Middle East During the Nineteenth Century[1]
(Annual Averages in Millions of Current British Pounds Sterling)

		1840–42	1860–62	1880–82	1900–2	1910–12
Ottoman	I	5.2	12.3	15.2	20.3	26.9
Empire[2]	II	2.4	8.6	12.0	16.4	22.0
Egypt		1.6	3.5	13.2	17.6	31.5
Iran		1.6	2.5	2.8	3.1	7.1
Total for Middle East[3]		5.6	14.6	28.0	37.1	60.6
Total in constant 1880 British Pounds Sterling[4]		4.6	12.9	28.3	49.9	73.2

Sources: For the Ottoman Empire: Pamuk 1987, chap. 2 and Appendix 1; Issawi 1981, 17–18, 82.

For Egypt: Issawi 1966, 373; Owen 1969, 168, 306; Great Britain, *Parliamentary Papers, Accounts and Papers,* "The Statistical Abstract of Foreign Countries," for 1904 and 1914.

For Iran: Issawi 1971, chap. 3; Issawi 1970, 1981; Great Britain, "The Statistical Abstract of Foreign Countries," for 1904 and 1914.

NOTES TO TABLE 1

1. Due to the quality of underlying data, all figures, particularly those for the earlier period, should be accepted as approximations.

2. For the Ottoman Empire, line I indicates total exports and line II shows exports from the area covered by twentieth-century Turkey in Europe and the Asiatic provinces of the Ottoman Empire, excluding Arabia. Total figures for the Middle East use line II.

3. The figure for the Middle East is the simple sum of the individual country exports. As a result, it includes intraregional trade, the relative importance of which declined steadily during the nineteenth century.

4. Imlah's price index for British imports was used in arriving at export figures in constant prices. See Imlah 1958, 94–99.

Table 2. Share of the Middle East and Other Selected Regions in World Exports (%)

Region	1840–42	1860–62	1880–82	1900–2	1910–12
Middle East	0.34	0.32	0.30	0.30	0.29
United Kingdom	22	21	17	14	n.a.
Other Western Europe	33	39	40	41	n.a.
Other Europe	9	9	8	7	n.a.
North America	12	11	14	16	n.a.
Central and South America	10	7	7	7	n.a.
Africa	1	<2	2	2	n.a.
Asia	12	10	10	9	n.a.
Oceania	<1	3	2	2	n.a.

Sources: Based on Table 1; Hanson 1980, 14, 21; Rostow 1978, 67, 669.

fallen behind per capita world exports by a similar margin by the turn of the century.

Table 3 also shows that per capita exports from the Middle East lagged far behind those of Western Europe and North America throughout the nineteenth century, although the rates of growth of per capita exports were higher for the Middle East. This is hardly surprising in view of the considerable differences in the per capita levels of production and income between the Middle East and the industrialized regions of the world. Higher rates of growth of per capita exports from the Middle East was in part due to the low levels of foreign trade of the Middle East in the earlier period.

As for comparisons with other areas of the world where levels of per capita income were closer to those prevailing in the Middle East, Tables 3 and 4 make it clear that in terms of the degree of integration into the world markets, the Middle East remained distinctly behind South America but ahead of Asia; and in terms of exports from the three countries in the Middle East, it was comparable to the average rates of growth of per capita exports from the medium-sized countries of Asia and South America. Table 4 does not attempt comparisons with smaller economies in the Third World since smaller economies were more easily integrated into the world markets and typically had higher levels of per capita exports during the nineteenth century.

The aggregate figures for the Middle East and these interregional comparisons can be quite misleading, however. What they do not reveal are the striking differences between the Mediterranean and Gulf areas of the Middle East and more specifically the differences between the three political entities of the region in terms of both the volume of foreign trade and its rate of growth during the nineteenth century.

As shown in Tables 1 and 3, on the one end of the spectrum lay Iran, whose links with the world markets remained relatively weak until early in the twentieth century. In contrast to worldwide trends, exports from Iran merely doubled in current prices or approximately tripled in volume terms between 1840 and 1900. Around the turn of the century, per capita exports from Iran stood at less than one-third of the levels for the Middle East and at less than one-sixth of their levels for Egypt. Despite a doubling of the volume of exports during the first decade of the twentieth century, per capita exports from Iran remained below one-half of the average for the region as a whole on the eve of World War I. Available evidence suggests that the differences between Iran and the rest of the Middle East with respect to levels of per capita production and income were certainly not that large. These differences in per capita exports, therefore, reflect differences in the degree of integration into the world markets.

In the early part of the nineteenth century levels of per capita foreign trade of the Asiatic provinces of the Ottoman Empire were comparable to those of Iran. However, exports from the Ottoman Empire are estimated to have increased twice as rapidly as those from Iran, by about eightfold in current prices or by more than twelvefold in volume terms between 1840 and World War I. The years of the Crimean War and more generally the 1850s was a critical time in the integration of the Asiatic provinces of the Ottoman Empire into the world trade network. Although Ottoman foreign trade continued to expand during the remainder of the century, the high rates of growth attained under the favorable world market conditions of the 1850s were not matched in later decades (Pamuk 1987, chap. 2).

Much more striking is the case of Egypt, which is often considered to be one of the most prominent examples of specialization in the exportation of primary commodities by an underdeveloped economy during the nineteenth century. Estimates presented in Table 1 indicate that exports from Egypt increased by about twentyfold in current prices and by about twenty-eightfold in constant prices between the early 1840s and the early 1910s. These rates were substantially higher

Table 3. Per Capita Exports from the Middle East and Other Selected Regions (In Constant 1880 British Pounds Sterling)

Region	1840–42	1880–82	1900–2	1910–12
World	0.16	0.91	1.55	n.a.
Middle East	0.20	0.85	1.28	1.65
Ottoman Empire*	0.20	0.78	1.17	1.25
Egypt	0.28	1.65	2.32	3.17
Iran	0.19	0.31	0.41	0.75
United Kingdom	1.49	6.38	7.46	n.a.
Other Western Europe	0.60	3.05	5.33	n.a.
Other Europe	0.26	0.88	1.22	n.a.
North America	1.06	3.90	5.51	n.a.
South America	0.41	1.87	3.10	n.a.
Asia	0.03	0.16	0.27	n.a.
Africa	0.02	0.32	0.49	n.a.
Oceania	0.51	n.a.	9.54	n.a.

Sources: Based on Table 1 and Hanson 1980, 21. The population of the areas covered in this study (twentieth-century Turkey in Europe, Anatolia, Greater Syria, Iraq, Iran, and Egypt) is estimated to have increased from approximately 23 million in 1840 to about 45 million on the eve of World War I. The population estimates for the Middle East are derived from the following: for the Ottoman Empire, Issawi 1981a, 17–18; Eldem 1970, 49–65; for Egypt, Issawi 1970, 1981b; for Iran, Issawi 1971, 20–34; Issawi 1981b; also McEvedy and Jones 1978.

* The figures for the Ottoman Empire are for the entire empire, whereas the figures for the Middle East exclude most of the European provinces as defined in the notes to Table 1. Per capita exports from the Asiatic provinces of the Ottoman Empire appear to be lower than those for the European provinces throughout the century.

than rates of growth of world trade and of total exports from the Third World during the same period. Similarly, Table 4 indicates that on the eve of World War I, per capita exports from Egypt were two and a half times as high as those from the Ottoman Empire and four times as high as per capita exports from Iran. It appears that early in the twentieth century per capita incomes in Egypt were higher than those in the Ottoman Empire and Iran. Nonetheless, these differences were not as large as the differences in per capita export levels.[1] It is clear that, in comparison with the other two countries, a larger share of the total production in Egypt was oriented toward exports.

Since cotton and cottonseed dominated Egypt's exports for most of the century, for better or worse, these high rates of export growth were due to the specialization in cotton. Egypt's emphasis on cotton started during the reign of Mohammad Ali, but it was the Cotton Famine during the American Civil War that catapulted the long staple varieties into worldwide prominence. The value of Egypt's exports tripled during the 1860s. Equally importantly, they did not decline

Table 4. Per Capita Exports from Medium-Sized Countries in the Third World, 1860–1910*

(In Constant 1880 British Pounds Sterling)

Country	Annual per Capita Exports 1860–62	Annual per Capita Exports 1910–12	Average Annual Rate of Growth of per Capita Exports 1860–1910 (%)
Ottoman Empire	0.66	1.25	1.3
Egypt	0.51	3.17	3.7
Iran	0.28	0.75	2.0
Weighted average for the Middle East	0.49	1.65	2.4
Algeria	0.49	4.96	4.7
Morocco	0.24	0.60	1.8
India	0.13	0.54	2.9
China	0.04	0.15	2.8
Ceylon	0.43	3.51	4.3
Dutch East Indies	0.37	1.26	2.5
French Indochina	n.a.	0.28	n.a.
Weighted average for Asia excluding India and China	0.36	1.14	2.3
Argentina	1.60	12.49	4.2
Mexico	n.a.	2.31	n.a.
Brazil	1.47	3.43	1.7
Peru	2.29	1.97	0.3
Colombia	0.51	0.87	1.1
Weighted average for Latin America	1.48	3.95	2.0
Overall average excluding India and China	0.62	2.15	2.5

after the American Civil War despite the fall in cotton prices. After the 1880s the economic policies of the British colonial administration further strengthened the specialization in and reliance on a single crop, as Egypt became one of the world's leading exporters of cotton, second only to the United States (Owen 1969).

What were the determinants of these long-term trends in exports from the Middle East as a whole and the substantial differences between the experiences of the individual countries in the Middle East? One can start with the external factors. A simple comparison of these trends with those of the eighteenth century makes it clear that the Industrial Revolution and the emergence in Europe of economies producing inexpensive manufactures and needing foodstuffs and raw materials was the primary reason for the unprecedented expansion of the foreign trade of the Middle East. This emphasis on external factors, however, can only be considered the beginning of an explanation, since the evidence summarized in Tables 2, 3, and 4 indicates that both within the Middle East and elsewhere the responses to the developments following the Industrial Revolution varied greatly. What needs to be explained, then, is not only the absolute rate of export expansion but the rate of export expansion in relation to trends elsewhere, for example, in relation to those of the medium-sized countries

NOTES TO TABLE 4

* For purposes of this table, medium-size countries were defined as those with populations between 4 and 50 million in 1913. China and India were the only Third World countries with populations exceeding 50 million on the eve of World War I.

Sources: See Table 1.

Population: Great Britain, *Parliamentary Papers, Accounts and Papers*, "The Statistical Abstract of Foreign Countries" (annual publication); idem, "The Statistical Abstract of the Colonies" (annual publication); McEvedy and Jones 1978.

Exports: Great Britain, *Parliamentary Papers, Accounts and Papers*, "Commercial Reports"; idem, "The Statistical Abstract of the Colonies"; United States, *Commercial Relations of the United States with Foreign Countries* (all annual publications); also Hanson 1980, appendixes A and B.

The export figures in current prices obtained from the above sources were deflated by Imlah's index for British import prices to arrive at values in constant 1880 prices. See Imlah 1958, 94–99.

in the Third World that can be meaningfully compared with Egypt, Iran, and the Ottoman Empire

The problem of evaluating the contributions of internal and external factors to long-term expansion of exports has been addressed in studies of international trade. One technique employed by Maizels, Kravis, and others analyzes the changes in the volume of exports of a country in terms of four factors: (1) a world market factor, (2) a competitiveness factor, (3) a diversification factor, and (4) an "own performance" variable (Maizels 1968; Kravis 1970a, 1970b).

The world market variable provides a comparison of the country's actual exports at the initial date with what exports would have been at the terminal date if the country had maintained its share in world trade for each of its traditional exports. This variable measures the rate of growth of world market demand for the country's traditional export commodities. The competitiveness factor is a comparison of the value of the country's exports in the initial period with the hypothetical value in the terminal period if the value of world trade in each of the country's traditional exports stayed constant and the country's share in trade in each commodity had been allowed to change as it in fact did. In other words, this variable measures the country's performance against its competitors in its traditional exports. The diversification factor is a ratio of the share of traditional commodities in exports at the initial date to the share of the same commodities at the terminal date. This variable measures the extent to which the exports of the country shifted away from the traditional commodity bundle. Finally, the "own performance" variable is computed by multiplying the second and third variables. It summarizes total change due to supply factors.

In view of the quality and detail of the available foreign trade data for the Middle East, it would be difficult to obtain precise estimates for each of these variables. However, it is still possible to develop more qualitative estimates for each of these variables based on the data for leading commodity exports from the three countries.

In Egypt cotton was by far the most important export commodity during the nineteenth century. Its share in Egypt's commodity exports averaged around 30 percent in the 1850s. This share increased steadily to exceed 90 percent by the first decade of the twentieth century (Owen 1969). By contrast, the exports from the Ottoman Empire and from Iran were quite diversified. For the Ottoman Empire, tobacco, figs, raisins, opium, raw silk, and mohair were the leading commodities throughout the nineteenth century, and the share of any single commodity rarely exceeded 12 percent of the total value of exports for any given year (Pamuk 1987, chap. 2 and appendix 1). For Iran, silk and silk products (close to 40 percent), cotton and woolen cloth, and tobacco were the leading export commodities around 1850. The composition of exports changed rapidly in the later period. While the shares of silk and cloth declined, opium, raw cotton, and carpets became increasingly more important toward World War I (Issawi 1970, chap. 3).

How rapidly did world market demand for these commodities expand? Data for the earlier period is incomplete and ambiguous. For the half century between 1860 and World War I, however, simple calculations based on the foreign trade statistics of major European countries and on estimates of total exports from the Third World countries suggest that world market demand for the leading export commodities of the Middle East expanded more slowly than demand for all primary commodities and world trade as a whole. There is considerable evidence that after 1860 demand in the industrialized countries, while continuing to grow in absolute terms, was shifting in relative terms away from the traditional export commodities of the Ottoman Empire, Iran, and Egypt, as will be discussed below in the country by country review. These world market trends, then, can provide a partial explanation for the export performance of the Middle East. They cannot, however, account for the striking differences within the Middle East. For that we have to turn to internal factors and examine each case separately.

In the case of the Ottoman Empire, the relative decline in world market demand for its leading export commodities appears to have started after the 1870s. This relative decline in world market demand was compounded by a decline in the Ottoman share of world trade in these traditional export commodities. In other words, in the markets of industrialized countries the Ottoman Empire began to lose ground to other exporters of the same commodities, particularly after the 1870s. The composition of Ottoman exports remained unchanged, however. Until World War I there was little shift toward other commodities whose demand might be growing more rapidly (Pamuk 1987, 36–40).

In contrast to the Ottoman case, the commodity composition of Iran's exports changed substantially between the 1850s and World War I. But it also appears that world market demand in relative terms was shifting away from the leading commodity exports of Iran, with the exceptions of silk, cotton, and woolen manufactures. Moreover, in the world markets of its leading export commodities, Iran like the Ottoman Empire steadily lost ground to other exporters. In fact, the "own performance" variable, or factors specific to Iran, appear to be more important than changes in world market demand in explaining the relatively slow growth of Iran's exports until World War I (Issawi 1970, chap. 3; Hanson 1980, appendixes).

Nineteenth-century Egypt provides one of the most extreme examples of an underdeveloped country that did not diversify its exports in the face of slower rates of growth of world market demand for its export commodity yet still managed to maintain high rates of export growth by steadily increasing its share in the world markets at the expense of other exporters of the same commodity (Owen 1969; Hanson 1980; appendixes). In other words, in contrast to the cases of Iran and the Ottoman Empire, the rate of growth of Egypt's exports was above the rate of growth of world market demand for its traditional exports. Clearly, factors specific to Egypt were behind this trend, and in this respect Egypt differs sharply from the nineteenth-century export experiences of Iran and the Ottoman Empire.

Why did Egypt differ so sharply from Iran and the Ottoman Empire with respect to the "own performance" variable? An explanation cannot be attempted here. At the expense of a major generalization, however, one might point to the considerable differences between the Ottoman Empire and Iran on the one hand and Egypt on the other with respect to the political environment that accompanied the expansion of foreign trade.

During the nineteenth century the Ottoman Empire and Iran shared three interrelated characteristics:

1. Their governments did not place high priority on export expansion or greater integration with world markets. Exports were encouraged only to the extent that the recurring fiscal, political, and military crises pressured the governments to accept this alternative.
2. Formal poliltical independence was not completely lost; these countries did not become colonies.
3. The environment of Great Power rivalry between Great Britain and Russia in the case of Iran and between Great Britain, France, and later Germany in the case of the Ottoman Empire

> continued until World War I. Despite the changing balances between these powers throughout the century, none of them was able to eliminate its rivals. This environment allowed the local governments greater room to maneuver and they often resisted greater European penetration. Under these circumstances, commercial and financial penetration by the European powers proceeded more slowly.

In contrast, after the failure of Mohammad Ali's industrialization drive and even before his death, Egypt was already on the road to an export-oriented economy. Following the occupation of 1882, the colonial administration proceeded farther down the same road, as evidenced by its emphasis on irrigation projects aimed at expanding cotton production. In comparison with the environment of Great Power rivalry, the conditions of a formal colony enabled the British to bring about greater integration with the world markets.

These considerations inevitably lead to the link between the expansion of exports of primary commodities and economic growth. Does the experience of these three countries during the nineteenth century lend support to Nurkse's view (1961) of exports as an engine of growth? The examples in the Middle East do not add up to a strong case for this argument. First, it needs to be emphasized that the foreign trade sector remained too small for high rates of exports to translate into appreciable rates of increase in the aggregate levels of production and income. In the cases of Iran before World War I and of the Ottoman Empire until the turn of the twentieth century the share of exports in total production remained below 10 percent. If these economies experienced increases in per capita levels of production, as was probably the case at least for the Ottoman Empire in the decades preceding World War I, the primary explanation needs to be sought elsewhere. At best, export growth was only one of a number of factors contributing to economic growth.

In the case of Egypt the export sector was clearly larger in relation to the rest of the economy. Exports did expand more rapidly and levels of per capita income were rising in the decades preceding World War I. On the eve of World War I per capita income in Egypt was probably higher than in Iran and the Asiatic provinces of the Ottoman Empire. However, there is also considerable evidence that by the first decade of the twentieth century the cotton boom in Egypt had indeed reached its peak. The large irrigation projects favored by the colonial administration were beginning to face major problems, the area under cultivation reached its limits, and cotton yields were beginning to decline. In the longer term Egypt paid a heavy price for its inability to develop its industry, for its exclusive reliance on the world market, and for its specialization in one crop. Levels of per capita income declined considerably until the 1950s. In retrospect, it is clear that the economic growth that took place in Egypt until the First World War had indeed been brought about by a pattern of "lopsided development"—and hence the title of Charles Issawi's 1961 article on Egypt.

NOTE

1. Issawi 1968 provides estimates for per capita income levels in Egypt and the Ottoman Empire on the eve of World War I. For the Ottoman Empire, see also Eldem 1970, chap. 13.

REFERENCES

Eldem, Vedat. 1970. *Osmanli Imparatorlugunun Iktisadi Sartlari Hakkinda bir Tetkik.* Istanbul: Is Bankasi Yayinlari.

Great Britain, "Commercial Reports," *Parliamentary Papers, Accounts and Papers* (published annually).

Great Britain, "The Statistical Abstract of Foreign Countries," *Parliamentary Papers, Accounts and Papers* (published annually).

Great Britain, "The Statistical Abstract of the Colonies," *Parliamentary Papers, Accounts and Papers* (published annually).

Hanson, John R., II. 1980. *Trade in Transition: Exports from the Third World, 1840–1900.* New York and London: Academic Press.

Imlah, Albert. 1958. *Economic Elements in the Pax Britannica.* Cambridge: Harvard University Press.

Issawi, Charles. 1961. "Egypt Since 1800: A Study in Lopsided Development." *The Journal of Economic History* 21: 1–25.

———. 1966. *The Economic History of the Middle East, 1800–1914.* Chicago: University of Chicago Press.

———. 1968. "Asymmetrical Development and Transport in Egypt, 1800–1914." In *Beginnings of Modernization in the Middle East,* edited by W. Polk and R. Chambers. Chicago: University of Chicago Press.

———. 1970. "Middle East Economic Development, 1815–1914: The General and the Specific." In *Studies in the Economic History of the Middle East*, edited by M. A. Cook. London: Oxford University Press.

———. 1971. *The Economic History of Iran, 1800–1914*. Chicago: University of Chicago Press.

———. 1981a. *The Economic History of Turkey, 1800–1914*. Chicago: University of Chicago Press.

———. 1981b. "Egypt, Iran and Turkey, 1800–1970: Patterns of Growth and Development." In *Disparities in Economic Development Since the Industrial Revolution*, edited by P. Bairoch and M. Levy-Leboyer. New York: St. Martin's Press.

———. 1988. *The Fertile Crescent: A Documentary Economic History*. Oxford: Oxford University Press.

Kravis, Irving B. 1970a. "External Demand and Internal Supply Factors in LDC Export Performance." *Banca Nazionale del Lavoro Quarterly Review* 23: 3–25.

———. 1970b. "Trade as a Handmaiden of Growth: Similarities Between the Nineteenth and Twentieth Centuries." *Economic Journal* 80: 850–72.

Maizels, Alfred. 1968. *Exports and Economic Growth of Developing Countries*. Cambridge: Cambridge University Press.

McEvedy, C., and R. Jones. 1978. *Atlas of World Population History*. Harmondsworth and New York: Penguin Books.

Nurkse, R. 1961. *Equilibrium and Growth in the World Economy*. Cambridge: Harvard University Press.

Owen, E. R. J. 1969. *Cotton and the Egyptian Economy, 1820–1914*. Oxford: Oxford University Press.

Pamuk, Sevket. 1987. *The Ottoman Empire and European Capitalism, 1820–1913: Trade, Investment and Production*. Cambridge: Cambridge University Press.

Rostow, W. W. 1978. *The World Economy: History and Prospect*. Austin and London: University of Texas Press.

XI

ANATOLIA AND EGYPT DURING THE NINETEENTH CENTURY: A COMPARISON OF FOREIGN TRADE AND FOREIGN INVESTMENT

For the economies of the Middle East, the nineteenth century was a period of rapid integration into the world economy. Some of the forces behind this process came from Europe. In the aftermath of the Industrial Revolution, Great Britain and later the Continental economies began to turn towards areas beyond Europe in order to establish markets for their manufactures and also secure inexpensive sources of foodstuffs and raw materials. As a result, European commercial penetration into the Middle East gained new momentum in the 1820s after the end of the Napoleonic Wars. Later, starting around mid-century, commercial penetration began to be accompanied by European investments in the Middle East in the forms of lending to governments and direct investment in railways, ports, banks, trading companies, and even agricultural land. A large part of this investment served to increase the export orientation of the Middle Eastern economies.

The economic history of the Middle East during the nineteenth century, then, can be understood best in terms of the response of the local forces and structures to European penetration and challenge. Two aspects of this interaction might need special emphasis here. First, partly as a response to the growing military and political power of Europe, the central governments in the region undertook a series of reforms to increase their own power. These attempts were facilitated by the availability of new technology in warfare, communications and transport. Secondly, as the economies of the region came into contact with European capitalism, the economic transformation was accompanied by social change and the emergence of new classes.

By the beginning of the twentieth century, patterns of production in the Middle East had shifted considerably. Agriculture had become more commercialized, and a substantially larger part of the agrarian production was being directed towards export markets. Another important long-term trend was towards de-industrialization. In many instances, traditional handicrafts resisted but they were often forced to retreat in the face of competition from European manufactures.[1]

An examination of the patterns of foreign trade and foreign investment in this context will help establish the degree to which different parts of the Middle East were integrated into the world economy. Equally importantly, such a comparison might be helpful in evaluating the nature of the response by local structures. Anatolia and Egypt provide a good pair for comparison. In addition to size and population, the broad contours of foreign trade and foreign investment in the two areas were similar during the nineteenth century. These similarities have already been emphasized in the literature. A closer examination also reveals, however, considerable differences. The present article will examine some of these differences.[2]

Foreign Trade

Tables 1a, 1b and 1c provide a summary of the available estimates on the growth of exports and per capita exports from the Ottoman Empire, Anatolia, and Egypt during the nineteenth century. These tables focus only on exports since the volume of volume of exports. It should also be emphasized that neither the figures for trade nor those for population can be considered very precise due to the quality of the underlying data. Nonetheless, these estimates are sufficiently reliable for a comparison of the broad trends for Anatolia and Egypt, especially when they are used together with other evidence.

Even though estimates for the volume of trade before 1840 are less reliable, there is considerable evidence that the external trade of both Anatolia and Egypt began to expand in the 1820s, after the end of the Napoleonic Wars (Owen, 1981, Chapter 3).[3] The volume of this trade both in absolute terms and in relation to overall production was quite low in the early part of the century. As a result, high rates of export growth were not very difficult to attain. In addition, it appears that per capita export levels of the two areas were fairly close during this early period.

Since the expansion of the trade of both areas with western Europe can be traced back to the 1820s, it would be difficult to argue that the Free Trade Treaty of 1838 was responsible for this trend. Instead, the

1 For the economic history of the Middle East during the nineteenth century, see Issawi (1982) and Owen (1981); also for Egypt, Owen (1969); for Turkey, Issawi (1981a) and Pamuk (1987).

2 For more general comparisons of the economies of Egypt, Turkey, and Iran during the nineteenth century, see Issawi (1970, 1981b).

3 Also for Anatolia, Issawi (1981, Chapter 3) and Pamuk (1984, Chapter 2); for Egypt, Owen (1969, Chapter 6).

Table 1a:
Estimates for Exports from the Ottoman Empire, 1840–1912

Year	Annual exports in millions of British Pounds	Population in millions	Exports per capita in £
1840–42	2.8	12.8	0.22
1880–82	15.2	20.0	0.76
1910–12	26.9	25.4	1.06

SOURCES: In order to maintain geographical unity, the export figures presented here refer to the area within the 1910 borders of the Empire, namely Macedonia, Anatolia, Syria, and Iraq but excluding Arabia. The estimates are based on Pamuk (1987, Appendix 1) and Pamuk (1990, Table 1). Population estimates are taken from Eldem (1970, pp. 52–62) and Issawi (1981, pp. 17–19).

Industrial Revolution in Great Britain and later in Continental Europe should be considered as the primary cause behind the expansion of foreign trade. Nonetheless, the 1838 Treaty proved important in the longer term for both areas. It provided the necessary legal and institutional arrangements such as the abolition of monopolies and temporary restrictions on exports and the reduction in customs duties; and the Treaty made it very difficult for Ottoman governments later in the century to increase tariffs for fiscal or protectionist reasons. In contrast to the earlier period, the foreign trade of the two areas followed rather different paths during the half century following the American Civil War and especially after the 1870s. As shown in Table 1b, exports from Anatolia, measured in current British pounds, barely kept pace with population growth and per capita exports remained roughly unchanged during the three decades before World War I. Measured in volume terms or in constant British pounds, exports per capita from Anatolia show an increase of about 20 percent during the same period. The estimates in Table 1b also suggest that per capita exports measured in current British pounds increased more than threefold between the 1840s and World War I.

Exports from Egypt, on the other hand, continued to increase rapidly until World War I. Approximately speaking, they tripled during the 1860s; and, between the 1870s and World War I, they tripled again. As a result, per capita exports increased approximately tenfold between the 1840s and World War I, as shown in Table 1c. On the eve of the war, per capita exports or per capita foreign trade of Egypt was two-and-a-half times greater than that of Anatolia. It appears that levels of per capita production and income were also higher in Egypt.

Table 1b:
Estimates for Exports from Anatolia, 1840–1912

Year	Annual exports from the six largest ports in British pounds	Estimates for total exports	Population in millions	Exports per capita in £
1840–42	2.2	2.4	8.0	0.30
1880–82	9.5	10.0	11.0	0.91
1910–12	12.8	14.0	14.4	0.97

NOTES: The six largest ports of export are Izmir, Istanbul, Trabzon, Samsun, Mersin, and Iskenderun. Estimates for Istanbul are particularly difficult to obtain. The figures presented here should be treated as no more than crude estimates useful only for establishing the broad trends.
SOURCES: The first column is based on Issawi (1981, p. 82) and Pamuk (1984, p. 35) both of which rely on the Consular Commercial Reports of Great Britain and France. The estimates for total exports are derived from the first column by utilizing Cuinet (1891–94). According to the estimates by Cuinet, the five leading ports excluding Istanbul accounted for 86 percent of all exports from Anatolia in 1890. See Maliye Tetkik Kurulu (1970) based on Cuinet (1891–94). The population estimates are from Eldem (1970, pp. 52–62) and Issawi (1981, pp. 17-19).

Table 1c:
Exports from Egypt

Year	Annual exports in millions of British pounds	Population in millions	Exports per per capita in £
1840–42	1.6	5.0	0.32
1880–82	13.2	8.0	1.67
1910–12	31.5	12.0	2.63

SOURCES: For exports, Owen (1969, pp. 168, 304–7, 376–77) and Crouchley (1936, pp. 173–74). Population estimates are from Owen (1969, p. 35; 1981, p. 217).

However, the differences in per capita incomes were certainly not as large as differences in per capita foreign trade. It would be safe to conclude, therefore, that on the eve of the war, Egypt, in comparison with Anatolia, was distinctly more oriented towards the world markets.

Where do these trends put Anatolia and Egypt in relation to the rest of the world, and more specifically, in relation to what is known today as the Third World ? It appears that rate of growth in commodity exports from Anatolia lagged behind the rate of growth of commodity exports from medium-sized countries in the Third World, especially after the 1870s. On the eve of World War I, per capita exports from Anatolia lagged behind the average for medium-sized countries in Asia,

Africa and Latin America. In contrast, and not surprisingly, both the level and rate of growth of per capita exports from Egypt far exceeded the averages for medium sized countries in these areas.[4]

A partial interpretation of these broad trends might now be attempted. For both Anatolia and Egypt, the expansion of exports starting in the 1820s and continuing until the 1870s can be viewed as the relatively easy first phase of export expansion. Since the share of exports in total agricultural production or the share of export crops in total land under cultivation remained rather low, exports could expand at high rates at this early stage. As the share of export crops in total agricultural production continued to increase, however, one would expect that it became increasingly more difficult to sustain high rates of export expansion without large amounts of infrastructure investment and/or changes in the patterns of land ownership, technology, and a reorganization of production process. Without attempting to provide an explanation until later, we would argue that these far-reaching changes did not occur in Anatolia, whereas such a transformation did take place in Egypt.

An important part of this story and a large part of the contrast between the two areas lie, of course, in the commodity composition of exports. In Anatolia, commodity composition of exports remained diversified and relatively unchanged throughout the century. Tobacco, raisins, figs, mohair, raw silk, cotton, and even wheat and barley were the leading export commodities. Only very rarely did the share of any one of these commodities in any given year exceeded 12 percent of the total.[5]

The Egyptian case stands in sharp contrast. In Egypt the importance of cotton increased steadily throughout the century. Until the 1860s, share of cotton in Egypt's total exports averaged about 30 percent. During the 1860s, the so-called Cotton Famine, caused by the American Civil War, gave a new impetus to cotton production and exports. After the 1860s, share of cotton in Egypt's total exports rose to more than half and ultimately to more than 90 percent after the turn of the century. Egypt's specialization in cotton exports was so extreme that while total exports tripled between the 1870s and World

---

[4] Per capita exports from medium sized countries in Asia, the Middle East, Africa, and Latin America during the years 1860–62 and 1910–12 are compared in Pamuk (1987, pp. 140–41).

[5] Based on Pamuk (1987, Appendix 1 and p. 146); although this figure refers to the commodity composition of export from the Ottoman Empire as a whole, there is considerable evidence suggesting that exports from Anatolia were also quite diversified. See, for example, Issawi (1981, Chapter 3) and Kasaba (1988, Appendix).

War I, exports of commodities other than cotton and cotton seed, such as wheat, beans, and others actually declined after the 1870s. Clearly, the export boom in Egypt was a boom, above all, in the production and exportation of cotton (Issawi, 1961; Owen, 1969).

Foreign Investment in Public Debt

Egypt and the Ottoman Empire attracted considerable amounts of foreign capital during the nineteenth century. In both cases, the state debt absorbed a large part of the inflow. Approximately half of the total foreign investment in Egypt and about two-thirds of all foreign investment in the Ottoman Empire before World War I went to the state debt. In per capita terms, Egypt and the Ottoman Empire were among the most heavily indebted countries in the world between the 1870s and World War I. These two well-known episodes of external debt were also important for their political overtones and consequences. The inability of the Ottoman government to continue payments on the outstanding debt in the 1870s led to the establishment of European financial control over Ottoman finances. In the Egyptian case, a similar moratorium on debt payments triggered a series of events that culminated in the British occupation of the country in 1882.[6]

The Ottoman and Egyptian governments began to seek funds in the European financial markets during the third quarter of the nineteenth century, the Ottoman Empire in the 1850s and Egypt in the following decade. Both governments borrowed large sums under very unfavorable terms in a short period of time. There was an important difference between the two cases, however. The Ottoman government used most of the borrowed funds to finance military expenditures and other current spending. Only a small fraction went into infrastructure investment such as railroads or irrigation schemes. The governments of Britain and France viewed such lending as an important instrument for gaining further influence in the Ottoman domains. They often encouraged their bankers and financial markets to continue lending even when the condition of Ottoman finances made it highly unlikely that the borrowed funds would be paid back.

In the Egyptian case, on the other hand, a large part of the borrowed funds actually entering the Treasury were directed towards large-

[6] There is a large literature on the external borrowing experiences of the two countries before World War I. Most importantly for Egypt, Crouchley (1936), Hamza (1944), Landes (1958), and more recently Owen (1981 Chapter 5); for the Ottoman case, Blaisdell (1929) and Issawi (1966, Part II, Chapter 11) amongst others; also see Ducruet (1964). The following account relies on a recent paper which compares the two cases, Pamuk (1989).

Table 2a:
Public Debt of the Ottoman Empire

Year	Public debt in millions of British pounds	Public debt per capita in British pounds
1876	210.0	7.78
1914	142.2	6.77

SOURCES: Wynne (1951, p. 452) and Pamuk (1987, p. 75).

Table 2b:
Public Debt of Egypt

Year	Public debt in millions of British pounds	Public debt per capita in British pounds
1878	98.7	13.16
1914	96.6	7.87

SOURCES: Crouchley (1936, pp. 18–26).
NOTES: The figures in Tables 2a and 2b refer to total state debt. In 1914 more than 95 percent of the Ottoman debt and more than 90 percent of the Egyptian debt was being held abroad. See Pamuk (1987, p. 75) and Crouchley (1936, p. 128).

scale agricultural and irrigation schemes. These projects failed, however, to provide the expected returns in terms of production and tax revenue. It might also be noted that Egypt began borrowing abroad during the American Civil War when cotton prices were rising sharply. Their subsequent decline made it all the more difficult for the Egyptian economy and Treasury to maintain payments on the rapidly rising debt. The involvement of European governments in the lending process appears more limited in the case of Egypt, at least in the earlier period. After the British government acquired the Egyptian government's shares in the Suez Canal Company in 1875, however, the external debt of Egypt gained considerable political importance (Owen, 1981, pp. 122–30).

In view of the unfavorable terms with which borrowing was undertaken and the difficulties associated with increasing fiscal revenues, it is not surprising that both governments soon found themselves in a position where only additional borrowing could enable them to meet payments on the outstanding debt. When the crisis of 1873 rocked European financial markets and overseas lending stopped, so did the debt payments. The Ottoman government declared a partial moratorium on debt payments in late 1875. It stopped payments altogether in 1876. The government of Egypt followed in early 1876.[7]

The inability to continue payments on the outstanding debt led to European financial control in both countries. In the Ottoman case, the outstanding debt was reduced by about 40 percent but the Ottoman Public Debt Administration (OPDA), as the representative of European creditors, obtained control over major revenue sources of the Ottoman Treasury. Until the turn of the century, new borrowing remained limited and regular payments on the outstanding debt continued thanks to the control exercised by the OPDA. Especially after 1903, however, the Ottoman governments started once again to borrow large sums in the European financial markets as state finances deteriorated in the face of increasing military pressures.[8] In this latter period as well, the governments of France and Germany used lending as a weapon in their ongoing rivalry to gain greater influence over the Ottoman government. New loans to the Ottoman government often were linked to political concessions, and also to the awarding of major economic projects such as large railway projects in Anatolia and Syria to the investors of the lending countries.

In the case of Egypt, the moratorium on the debt payments was the starting point of a series of events that led to the British occupation of the country. With little or no bargaining power left, the terms of the debt resettlement were much more severe for Egypt. Most importantly, the nominal value of the outstanding debt was not reduced. After the occupation, the British colonial administration came to regard the maintenance of regular payments on the external debt, which was owed mostly to British and French creditors, as a matter of the highest priority. Unlike the Ottoman government, the colonial administration of Egypt did not return to the European financial markets for additional borrowing until World War I, with the exception of several bond issues in the late 1880s (Issawi, 1966, Chapter 10; Crouchley, 1936, pp. 22–25).

In the longer term, these external borrowing experiences proved to be important for another reason. The establishment of varying degrees of European control in the two countries—the Ottoman Public Debt Administration and the colonial administration in Egypt—provided considerable security to the European investors. In turn, this

[7] The Ottoman Empire and Egypt were hardly alone in this respect. The financial crises of 1873 led to similar outcomes for many indebted countries. At least eleven countries in Latin America, Africa and Europe defaulted or obtained reschedulings between 1872 and 1875. See Borchard (1951, pp. xx–xxi).

[8] This periodization is based on Pamuk (1987, Chapter 4).

control encouraged the investment of substantial amounts of European capital in the two areas after 1880. As will be discussed below, foreign investment outside the public debt played an important role in increasing the export orientation of both areas until World War I.

Foreign Direct Investment

The other component of European capital inflows into the Middle East took the form of direct investment, or investment in enterprises controlled by European capital. During the nineteenth century and until World War I, a large part of European direct investment in the region was concentrated in infrastructure such as railways, canals, and ports. Additional amounts were invested in trade and finance. In contrast, European investment in agriculture, industry, or mining remained limited. This broad sectoral distribution suggests that until World War I, foreign capital in the two areas did not play a significant role in the transformation of production. Instead it tended to promote trade, especially foreign trade. As such, foreign direct investment in Anatolia and Egypt played an important role in increasing the export orientation of the two areas.

The timing of direct foreign investment was broadly similar in the two areas. It already has been emphasized that until the 1880s most European capital flows into the Ottoman Empire and Egypt went into the state debt, with the important exception of the Suez Canal. The volume of foreign direct investment began to increase in the late 1880s. In Anatolia, the most intensive wave of foreign direct investment before World War I took the form of railroad construction by German and French companies between 1888 and 1896. Foreign direct investment in Anatolia surged again after 1905 lasting until the war (Pamuk, 1987, pp. 62–72).[9] In Egypt, the most important wave of foreign direct investment accompanied the land and cotton boom starting around 1893 and gaining momentum around the turn of the century. The crisis of 1907 brought this period of heavy foreign investment to a close (Crouchley, 1936, Chapters 3 and 4; Owen, 1969, Chapter 10).[10]

Tables 3a and 3b summarize the available estimates on the amounts of foreign direct investment in the two areas. They show that

[9] At the end of 1913, French investors held approximately 50 percent of the directly invested foreign capital in the Ottoman Empire. The shares in the total of German and British investors were 28 and 15 percent, respectively (Pamuk, 1987, p. 66).

[10] In 1914 British and French investors each held approximately 43 percent of all directly invested foreign capital in Egypt. Belgian investors held most of the rest with 13 percent of the total. These figures include The Suez Canal Company (Crouchley, 1936, p. 72-73).

Table 3a:
Foreign Direct Investment in the Ottoman Empire

Year	Foreign direct investment in millions of British pounds	Foreign direct investment per capita in in British pounds
1888	15.8	0.75
1914	74.3	3.52

SOURCE: Pamuk (1987, pp. 65–66).

Table 3b:
Foreign Direct Investment in Egypt

Year	Foreign direct investment in millions of £	Foreign direct investment per capita in £
1888	23.4	2.85
1914	111.0	9.02

SOURCE: Crouchley (1936, pp. 72–73, 145–59). The figures above include the Suez Canal Company whose stocks were held entirely abroad in 1914.
NOTES: The estimates in Tables 3a and 3b refer to the paid-up capital and debentures of joint-stock companies which were controlled by foreign capital. In the case of Egypt, somewhere between 75 and 80 percent of the paid-up capital and debentures of these companies was being held abroad in 1914. Crouchley estimates further that the sum of paid-up capital and debentures of all Egyptian companies including the Suez Canal Company being held abroad was around 90 million British pounds in 1914. Little information is available on similar details in the Ottoman case.

in 1914, per capita foreign direct investment in Egypt was two-and-a-half times higher than in the Ottoman Empire as a whole. Although separate estimates for foreign direct investment in Anatolia are more difficult to obtain, one available estimate provides a figure consistent with the broad picture drawn here. According to Eldem, foreign direct investment within the present borders of Turkey amounted to 51.9 million British pounds around 1909 to 12, or approximately three British pounds per capita; these figures are consistent with the estimates presented in Table 3a for the Ottoman Empire as a whole. They indicate that per capita foreign direct investment in Anatolia and the Istanbul region was close to the average for the empire and lagged substantially behind those for Egypt (Eldem, 1970, pp. 190–91).[11] This comparison of the levels of per capita foreign direct investment in the two areas parallels closely an earlier conclusion of this paper, that on the eve of World War I, per capita exports from Egypt were two-and-a-half times

[11] Eldem's estimate of foreign investment within the present-day borders of Turkey and for the empire as a whole including a sectoral distribution are also presented in Issawi (1981, p. 324).

Table 4a:
Sectoral Distribution of Foreign Direct Investment in the Ottoman Empire in 1914

Sector	Percent Share
Railroads	63.1
Banking	12.0
Commerce	5.8
Industry	5.3
Utilities	5.1
Ports	4.3
Mining	3.7
Insurance	0.7
Total	100.0

SOURCE: Pamuk (1987, p. 66).

Table 4b:
Sectoral Distribution of Foreign Direct Investment in Egypt in 1914

Sector	Percent Share
Mortgage Companies	50.4
Canals and Transport	20.3
Agricultural and Urban Land	11.4
Banks and Other Financial	5.5
Manufacturing, Commerce, and Mining	12.4
Total	100.0

SOURCE: Crouchley (1936, pp. 72–73). These figures include the Suez Canal.
NOTES: Tables 4a and 4b are based on the paid-up capital and debentures of joint-stock companies controlled by foreign capital. See also note to Tables 3a and 3b.

as high as those from Anatolia and the Ottoman Empire in general.

In addition, there were important differences between the Ottoman Empire and Anatolia on the one hand, and Egypt on the other, regarding the sectoral distribution of foreign direct investment. As shown in Table 4a, two-thirds of total foreign direct investment in the Ottoman Empire concentrated in railroads and ports which served to expand agricultural exports. The rest went to mining, trading companies, banking, and insurance. Tokin's estimates for the sectoral distribution of foreign investment in Anatolia and the Istanbul region before World War I provides a similar picture. According to his figures, railroads accounted for 59 percent of all foreign direct investment within the present borders of Turkey; the share of ports in the total was about 5 percent (Eldem, 1970, pp. 190–91).

In Egypt as well, there was a considerable amount of direct foreign investment in infrastructure such as railways and ports. In addition, the Suez Canal Company constituted the largest single enterprise owned by European capital, accounting for almost 18 percent of all directly invested foreign capital in Egypt on the eve of World War I. Nonetheless, Table 4b reveals an important difference in the sectoral distribution of foreign direct investment between the two areas. In Egypt, the largest part of foreign direct investment was closely related to the cotton boom and the spectacular rise in land prices. Mortgage companies, whose primary activity was the financing of investment in agricultural land accounted for one-half of all the stock of directly invested foreign capital in 1914. Since the European investors had taken over the Suez Canal before 1880, these figures imply that mortgage companies accounted for more than 60 percent of all foreign direct investment after 1880. Together with the 11 percent share of agricultural and urban land, they suggest that close to three-fourths of all foreign direct investment in Egypt between 1880 and World War I was related to the boom in agricultural land, primarily cotton land. A large part of these funds was directed at the purchase and reclamation of rural land, irrigation, drainage, and even speculative purchases of agricultural land.[12]

How to Explain the Differences?

These patterns of foreign trade and foreign investment in Anatolia and Egypt demonstrate a number of similarities in the experiences of the two areas. For both areas, the century before World War I was a period of rapid integration to the world economy. The expansion in foreign trade was followed by European financial penetration and finally by waves of European direct investment in enterprises which reinforced the external orientation of the two economies. There were, however, at least two very important differences in the experiences of the two areas. First, the degree of export orientation, as evidenced by the levels of foreign trade and foreign direct investment, were substantially higher for Egypt. Secondly, Egypt exhibited a high degree of specialization in the production and exportation of one crop, whereas agricultural production and exports were quite diversified in Anatolia.

It is not a simple task to attempt to explain these differences.

12 Crouchley (1936) Chapters 3 and 4, and Owen (1969) Chapters 9 and 10.

Clearly, a wide range of factors needs to be taken into account, from geographical conditions and resource endowments to social and political structure and the potential impact of world market conditions. Without going into quantitative detail, we will examine these factors in two groups, as demand side and supply side factors.[13]

On the demand side, a quick review of the available evidence indicates that world market demand for cotton expanded much faster than world market demand for most of the leading commodity exports from Anatolia, such as tobacco, raisins, figs, hazelnuts, and raw silk. In this sense, the different rates of growth of world market demand provide one of the explanations for the different export experiences of the two countries.[14]

It should be immediately emphasized, however, that demand cannot account for the entire difference between the two cases. A comparison of the export experiences of the two countries with world market conditions suggests that factors on the supply side were also responsible for the very divergent outcomes. In the case of Anatolia, until the 1870s, world market demand for the bundle of commodities being exported from Anatolia expanded at relatively high rates, but exports expanded at even higher rates. In other words, in the earlier part of the century, Anatolia increased its share in the world trade of the commodities it exported at the expense of other exporters of the same commodities. After the 1870s, however, these trends were reversed. World market demand for the commodities being exported from Anatolia expanded more slowly. Equally importantly, Anatolia's share in this slowly growing segment of the world market began to decline. Significantly, despite the relatively unfavorable trends in world market demand for its traditional exports, commodity composition of exports from Anatolia did not change appreciably between 1880 and World War I. Agricultural production in Anatolia did not shift towards a different mix of commodities whose demand was growing more rapidly in the world markets.[15] Clearly, the answer to these broad trends needs to be sought on the supply side, in the specific circumstances of Anatolia.

In the case of Egypt, the available evidence suggests that world market demand for cotton expanded more rapidly than the demand for

---

[13] The analytical framework adopted here broadly follows that used by Alfred Maizels (1969) and other in examining the long-term export performance of different countries.

[14] Our calculations based on Hanson (1980), Chapter 2 and Appendices B and D.

[15] Based on the published foreign trade statistics of the United Kingdom and France and the commodity composition of Ottoman exports; for a more detailed discussion, see Pamuk (1987, pp. 36–40 and Appendix I).

most other commodities exported by Third World countries between 1840 and World War I.[16] More strikingly, exports of cotton from Egypt expanded much more rapidly than world market demand during this period. In other words, Egypt steadily raised its share of world cotton exports during the nineteenth century at the expense of other exporters. In fact, after appropriate adjustments are made for the growth of world market demand, Egypt emerges as one of the most striking examples of export orientation of an economy anywhere in the Third World.[17]

It is clear that while world market demand can provide a partial explanation, it cannot account for the entire difference in the rate of growth of exports from the two areas. It is necessary, therefore, to turn to factors specific to the two areas. One obvious candidate here would be geography and resource endowments. It might be argued that the Nile Valley in Lower Egypt, which included a large part of the population and cultivated area of the country, represented a much more compact and homogenous area. It was easier and less costly to link this fertile area to the ports of export and world markets. In Anatolia, on the other hand, labor and cultivable land were more evenly distributed among its agronomically diverse regions. In addition, it was quite costly to build the transportation network to link large parts of Anatolia to the ports of export. For most of the nineteenth century, only western Anatolia, and to a lesser extent the Black Sea coast, was integrated to the world markets. The dry-farming, cereal-growing areas of central Anatolia remained insulated from foreign trade until the construction of the Anatolian Railway late in the nineteenth century. The eastern third of Anatolia where close to a quarter of its population lived remained mostly unaffected by the growing trade with Europe until World War I.

There were important differences in social and political structures as well. One of the more important characteristics of nineteenth-century Ottoman society was the relative strength of the central government vis-à-vis other social classes, such as large landowners and merchants. Starting in the 1810s and continuing with the administrative and institutional reforms of the Tanzimat period, the power of the *ayan* in the provinces was checked. The technological developments of the nineteenth century that enabled the central government to establish a more effective army and improve the transportation and communi-

---

16 Hanson (1980), Table 3.1 on p. 36 and Appendix D.

17 See Hanson (1980), Chapter 6 and especially Table 6.2. Hanson attempts to separate demand and supply side factors by developing "world market" and "own performance" for each of the twelve less developed countries in his sample. His calculations show that Egypt's "own performance" index was higher than all the other countries on the sample.

cations network undoubtedly reinforced the trend towards increasing centralization.

In addition, partly because of this strength of the central government and partly because of the inter-imperialist rivalry in this region of the world, the empire was not colonized until World War I. While balances between Great Britain, France, and Germany changed throughout the century, none of them could eliminate the influence of others. This environment of Great-Power rivalry provided some maneuvering room for the Ottoman governments. In order to resist external pressures, the Ottoman governments often attempted to play one European power against another.

The governments' strength vis-à-vis domestic forces and its maneuvering room against external pressures were perhaps most evident in the attempts to maintain an agrarian structure based mostly on small and medium-sized holdings. The central government had always favored such an agrarian structure since it represented the most favorable conditions for maximizing fiscal revenues and political power. From this perspective, however, increasing commercialization and export orientation of agriculture was viewed with caution. On the one hand, commercialization of agriculture was supported since it would increase production and expand the tax base. At the same time, there was concern that as the economy opened to foreign trade and foreign capital, the government might lose its control over tax revenues. For this reason, the central government supported the small peasantry against the encroachment of large landlords and, also, against foreign investors. For example, the government often issued decrees prohibiting creditors from taking over the land of defaulting peasant owners. In a very telling episode during the 1860s and 1870s, when British investors attempted to establish large-scale farms in western Anatolia, these attempts were resisted by Istanbul which was concerned about losing its traditional fiscal base (Kurmuş, 1974, pp. 95–122).

Under these circumstances, export orientation of Anatolian agriculture proceeded slowly. Small peasant holdings certainly could produce for both the domestic and export markets but they were slow to undertake investments that would improve land productivity. Agricultural technology and organization of production changed very little until World War I. After the relatively easy first round, which lasted until the 1870s, export expansion in Anatolia slowed down. This was particularly evident in western Anatolia where export growth had started earlier than other regions. Exports from Izmir measured in current British pounds remained roughly unchanged between the early 1870s and the early 1910s (Kasaba, 1988, Appendix Table A.1).

In Egypt, on the other hand, export orientation of agriculture took place under a different social matrix. One of the important differences was the more unequal distribution of land and the greater economic and political power of the landlords. Even though a large part of cotton production remained in the hands of small and medium-sized peasant holdings, it appears that large estates, including those of the Royal Family, were instrumental in the inflow of capital into agriculture, including investment in irrigation schemes, thereby raising agricultural productivity in lower Egypt.[18]

In addition, government policy towards development and export orientation of agriculture was quite different in Egypt. The political power of the large landlords and the fact that the Royal Family itself owned large estates was at least partly responsible for this emphasis. Starting with Mohammad Ali and continuing with his successors, government policy actively supported investment in irrigation, distribution of seeds, transport, and other infrastructure designed to promote agricultural development. A large part of these resources went towards the promotion of cotton and the mono-crop model. Such investment in agriculture was in fact one of the primary reasons why the Egyptian government started to borrow in European financial markets during the 1860s. As discussed earlier, only a negligible fraction of the funds borrowed by the Ottoman governments before the 1880s was directed to agricultural development. After the British occupation of Egypt, the contrasts between the two areas became more pronounced. The colonial administration began to emphasize cotton production and exports with large-scale irrigation projects financed not so much by European capital but by domestic funds. From the 1880s until the first decade of the twentieth century, land under cultivation, agricultural productivity, and agricultural incomes rose steadily as the cotton-for-export model assumed new momentum. An important beneficiary of this policy, of course, was the economy of Great Britain which enjoyed increased supplies of an important raw material. In short, it is clear that Egyptian agriculture underwent a more far-reaching transformation than its Anatolian counterpart during the nineteenth century.

Finally, we might entertain another important but difficult question which follows from the basic issues discussed in this paper: Did the growth of foreign trade have an impact on economic growth and on the standards of living? Unfortunately, the evidence regarding changes

[18] For more details, see Owen (1981b, 1986).

in per capita levels of income is limited for both areas. Even more difficult to establish would be the causal links between the growth of foreign trade and economic growth. There is also the important question regarding the distributional impact of the expansion of foreign trade for which little evidence is available. Under the circumstances, we will limit ourselves to one observation which underlines further the differences between the two areas.

In the case of Anatolia, the foreign trade sector remained quite small in relation to the rest of the economy for most of the nineteenth century. There were, of course, substantial regional variations regarding the degree of export orientation. Coastal regions, and most prominently western Anatolia, were more integrated into the world markets than central and eastern Anatolia. For Anatolia as a whole, however, it appears that the share of exports in total production remained below 10 percent at least until the 1880s. Moreover, in this earlier period there was also the long-term trend towards the decline of local manufacturing activities caused by the expansion of imports of textiles (Pamuk, 1987, pp. 12–17). Under the circumstances, it would be inappropriate to link export growth to economic growth until late in the century except for western Anatolia. During the decades before World War I, there was some modest rate of growth in per capita production and income levels in Anatolia and more generally in the Ottoman Empire (Eldem, 1970, pp. 307–9). Because of the limited size of the export sector in relation to the rest of the economy, however, it would be best to conclude that for Anatolia as a whole exports were only one of a number of potential factors contributing to economic growth. In the case of Egypt, however, exports increased more rapidly. Equally importantly, the export sector was distinctly larger in relation to the rest of the economy. As a result, one would expect that foreign trade had a more substantial impact on the rest of the economy and on overall economic growth. Agricultural incomes showed substantial increases after 1880, and levels of per capita production and per capita income in Egypt were rising in the decades preceding World War I (Owen, 1969, Chapter IX). However, there is also considerable evidence that by the first decade of the twentieth century, the cotton boom in Egypt had indeed reached its peak. By the first decade of the century, the large irrigation projects favored by the colonial administration were beginning to face major problems as the area under cultivation reached its limits and cotton yields began to decline. These adverse developments can perhaps be taken as early signs of things to come in the twentieth century, but that is a different story altogether.

REFERENCES

Blaisdell, D. C. 1929. *European Financial Control in the Ottoman Empire*. New York: Columbia University Press.

Borchard, Edwin. 1951. *State Insolvency and Foreign Bondholders, Vol. 1: General Principles*. New Haven: Yale University Press.

Crouchley, A. E. 1936. *The Investment of Foreign Capital in Egyptian Companies and Public Debt*. Technical Paper No. 12, Ministry of Finance of Egypt, Cairo, Government Press, Bulaq. (Reprinted in 1977 by Arno Press, New York.)

Cuinet, Vital. 1891–94. *La Turquie d'Asie*. 4 volumes, Paris.

Ducruet, Jean. 1964. *Les Capitaux Européens au Proche-Orient*. Paris: Presses Universitaires de France.

Eldem, Vedat. 1970. *Osmanlı Imparatorluğunun Iktisadi Şartları Hakkında bir Tetkik*. Istanbul: İş Bankası Yayınları.

Hamza, Abdel-Maksud. 1944. *The Public Debt of Egypt 1854–1876*. Cairo: Government Press.

Hanson, John R. 1980. *Trade in Transition: Exports from the Third World, 1840–1900* New York and London: Academic Press.

Issawi, Charles. 1961. "Egypt since 1800: A Study in Lopsided Development," *The Journal of Economic History*, Vol. 21.

Issawi, Charles. 1966. *The Economic History of the Middle East 1800–1914*. Chicago: University of Chicago Press.

Issawi, Charles. 1970. "Middle East Economic Development 1815–1914: The General and the Specific," in Cook, M. A. (ed.), *Studies in the Economic History of the Middle East*. Oxford: Oxford University Press.

Issawi, Charles. 1981a. *The Economic History of Turkey, 1800–1914*. Chicago: University of Chicago Press.

Issawi, Charles. 1981b. "Egypt, Iran and Turkey, 1800-1970: Patterns of Growth and Development," in Bairoch P. and Levy-Leboyer M. (eds.), *Disparities in Economic Development Since the Industrial Revolution*. New York: St. Martin's Press.

Issawi, Charles. 1982. *An Economic History of the Middle East and North Africa*. New York: Columbia University Press.

Kasaba, Reşat. 1988. *The Ottoman Empire and the World Economy, The Nineteenth Century*. Albany: State University of New York Press.

Kurmuş, Orhan. 1974. *Emperyalizmin Türkiye'ye Girişi*. Istanbul: Bilim Yayınları.

Landes, David S. 1958. *Bankers and Pashas*. Cambridge, Mass.:

Harvard University Press.

Maizels, Alfred. 1969. *Industrial Growth and World Trade*. Cambridge: Cambridge University Press.

Maliye Tetkik Kurulu. 1970. *Osmanlı Imparatorluğu'nda XIX. Yüzyılın Sonunda Üretim ve Dış Ticaret*. Ankara.

Owen, E. R. J. 1969. *Cotton and the Egyptian Economy 1820–1914*. Oxford: Oxford University Press.

Owen, Roger. 1981. *The Middle East in the World Economy 1800–1914*. London and New York: Methuen.

Owen, Roger. 1981b. "The Development of Agricultural Production in Nineteenth Century Egypt: Capitalism of What Type?" in Udovitch, A. L. (ed.), *The Islamic Near East, 700-1900 : Studies in Economic and Social History* . Princeton, New Jersey: Princeton University Press.

Owen, Roger. 1986. "Large Landowners, Agricultural Progress and the State in Egypt, 1800–1970: An Overview with Many Questions" in Richards, Alan (ed.), *Food, States and Peasants, Analyses of the Agrarian Question in the Middle East*. Boulder and London: Westview Press.

Pamuk, Şevket. 1984. *Osmanlı Ekonomisi ve Dünya Kapitalizmi, 1820–1913*. Ankara: Yurt Yayınları.

Pamuk, Şevket. 1987. *The Ottoman Empire and European Capitalism, 1820–1913 : Trade, Investment and Production*. Cambridge and New York: Cambridge University Press.

Pamuk, Şevket. 1989. "Politics and Economics of Nineteenth-Century External Debt: The Cases of Ottoman Empire and Egypt," paper presented to the Colloquium on Foreign Loans, Debt and Economic Development in the Nineteenth and Twentieth Centuries. University of Campinas, Brazil, July.

Pamuk, Şevket. 1990. "The Middle East in Nineteenth-Century World Trade," in Udovitch, A. L. and Esfandiari, Haleh (eds.), *The Economic Dimension of Middle Eastern History: Essays in Honor of Charles Issawi*. Princeton, New Jersey: Darwin Press, pp. 195–208.

Wynne, William H. 1951. *State Insolvency and Foreign Bondholders, Vol. II, Case Histories*. New Haven: Yale University Press.

XII

The Ottoman Empire in the "Great Depression" of 1873–1896

Contrary to the view that the periphery of the world economy benefited from rapidly expanding trade, the Ottoman economy actually faced a distinctly unfavorable world conjuncture during the last quarter of the nineteenth century. Rates of growth of foreign trade dropped, external terms of trade deteriorated, declining wheat prices affected peasant producers, and the establishment of European control over Ottoman finances led to large debt payments abroad. Indirect data indicate that rates of change of agricultural and aggregate production were also lower during the "Great Depression" as compared to the later period.

THERE is considerable evidence, most of it recently compiled, indicating that 1873–1896 was a period distinct from both the mid-century boom lasting until 1873 and the long-term upswing until World War I, for the major industrialized economies and for the world economy as a whole.[1] Our knowledge, however, of how the peripheral countries fared during this period is limited. Reliable statistics on foreign trade, let alone statistics on levels of production, are unavailable for many countries. Equally important, the available data have rarely been arranged with the purpose of examining whether the period of the Great Depression represented a distinct economic conjuncture for one

I would like to thank Hasan Ersel for comments on an earlier version of the paper that was also presented to the Eighth International Economic History Congress in Budapest, 1982.

[1] Whether the Great Depression of 1873–1896 was limited to purely monetary phenomena has been the subject of much debate during the last two decades. See, for example, S. B. Saul, *The Myth of the Great Depression, 1873–1896* (London, 1969); Donald N. McCloskey, "Did Victorian Britain Fail?"*Economic History Review*, 23 (Dec. 1970), 446–59; Jeffrey G. Williamson, "Late Nineteenth-Century American Retardation: A Neoclassical Analysis," this JOURNAL, 33 (Sept. 1973), 581–607; W. W. Rostow, *The World Economy: History and Prospect* (Austin, 1978); and W. Arthur Lewis, *Growth and Fluctuations, 1870–1913* (London, 1978). For the three largest industrial economies—Great Britain, United States, and Germany—this was not a period of absolute decline but of lower rates of increase in the levels of industrial production compared to before and after. See, in addition to the above, Brian R. Mitchell, *European Historical Statistics, 1750–1970* (New York, 1975); Walther G. Hoffmann, *Das Wachtum der Deutschen Wirtschaft seit der Mitte des 19. Jahrhunderts* (Berlin, 1965); Robert E. Gallman, "Commodity Output, 1838–1899" in *Trends in the American Economy in the 19th Century*, Vol. 24 of *Studies in Income and Wealth* (Princeton, 1960); U.S. Bureau of the Census, *Long-Term Economic Growth, 1860–1966* (Washington, D.C., 1970); and Lewis, *Growth and Fluctuations*, Appendices 1 and 2. Moreover, rates of growth of world trade were distinctly lower during this period. See Rostow, *The World Economy*, p. 679; and John R. Hanson II, *Trade in Transition, Exports from the Third World, 1840–1900* (New York and London, 1980), p. 14.

or a group of Third World countries. A major exception is the recent study by Hanson who reaches the conclusion that:

> most countries evidently did not experience an export boom during the late nineteenth century, and retardation seems to have been the normal condition. . . . Perhaps some nations managed to buck the trend, but at a minimum the conventional assertion that world and LDC exports flourished near the end of the nineteenth century requires a good deal of qualification.

As to the causes of this retardation, Hanson appears unwilling to link it to the Great Depression and lower rates of growth of demand in the industrialized countries. While not eliminating that possibility completely, he argues that "some as yet unspecified structural change" might also explain much of the fall in the rate of growth of Third World exports and of world trade.[2]

I shall attempt to show that the quarter of a century following 1873 represented a distinct conjuncture for the Ottoman economy in terms of the impact of the external forces and, as far as can be documented, long-term changes in the levels of domestic production.

LONG-TERM MOVEMENTS IN FOREIGN TRADE

During the nineteenth century, Ottoman foreign trade basically consisted of the exportation of primary products and importation of manufactures. Starting in the last quarter of the century, imports of certain foodstuffs such as grains, rice, and sugar also became important.[3] The rates of growth of Ottoman trade with Europe had remained below 1½ percent per year between 1780 and 1830.[4] In contrast, a reconstruction of nineteenth-century Ottoman foreign trade summarized in Table 1 indicates that average annual compound rates of growth of exports and imports, measured in current and in constant 1880 prices, was at or above 5 percent for 1839/41 to 1852/54 and 1857/59 to 1871/73.[5] It is probable that the rate of growth began to accelerate in the aftermath of the Napoleonic Wars.[6] The free trade treaties signed after 1838

[2] Hanson, *Trade in Transition*, pp. 16, 90–92.

[3] Celal Aybar, *Osmanli İmparatorluğunun Ticaret Muvazenesi, 1878–1913* (Ankara, 1939) for a compilation of the official foreign trade statistics of the Empire; also Charles Issawi, *The Economic History of Turkey, 1800–1914* (Chicago, 1980), pp. 74–145.

[4] Based on Charles Issawi, *The Economic History of the Middle East, 1800–1914* (Chicago, 1966), p. 30; Robert Paris, *Histoire du Commerce de Marseille, Tome V, 1660 à 1789, le Levant* (Paris, 1957), pp. 572–77; and Paul Masson, *Histoire du commerce français dans le Levant au XVIIIe siècle* (Paris, 1911).

[5] As most European foreign trade statistics began to treat present-day Roumania separately after the Crimean War, trade volumes of the 1840s cannot be compared directly with those in the early 1870s. See notes to Table 1.

[6] This was certainly the case for Ottoman trade with Great Britain. See Public Records Office, *Customs 4, Customs 8,* and *Customs 10* series. Also Roger Owen, *The Middle East in the World Economy, 1800–1914* (London and New York, 1981), chap. 3.

TABLE 1
ESTIMATED RATES OF GROWTH OF OTTOMAN FOREIGN TRADE
(average annual compound rates in percent; prices in pounds sterling)

	Exports		*Imports*	
End Years	*In Current Prices*	*In 1880 Prices*	*In Current Prices*	*In 1880 Prices*
1839/41 to 1852/54	5.3	5.3	5.5	6.4
1857/59 to 1871/73	5.0	6.2	4.9	5.2
1879/81 to 1897/99	1.2	2.7	0.6	2.5
1879/80 to 1887/88	−0.9	2.8	−0.8	2.0
1887/88 to 1898/99	2.3	2.2	1.4	2.7
1897/99 to 1905/07	4.3	3.4	6.0	4.3
		Annual Trade Volume in Millions of Current £		
		Exports		*Imports*
1850/52		8.8		9.5
1880/82		15.2		15.4
1910/12		26.9		38.3

Source: The author's calculations based on a reconstruction of nineteenth-century Ottoman foreign trade utilizing the statistics of most of the countries with which the Empire had commercial relations. For details, see Şevket Pamuk, "Foreign Trade, Foreign Capital and the Peripheralization of the Ottoman Empire, 1830–1913" (Ph.D. diss., University of California, Berkeley, 1978), chap. 3, pp. 17–63, and Appendix 1, pp. 163–251.

between the Ottoman Empire and the European countries also played an important role in the increasing world market orientation of the Ottoman economy.[7] Most of the expansion in foreign trade came from the coastal regions of Syria, Anatolia, and Northern Greece, areas that remained part of the Empire in the later periods.[8] The share of Western and Central Europe and the United States in Ottoman foreign trade remained above 70 percent until the early 1870s.[9]

In examining long-term trends one must exclude the years 1874 to 1878 because the War of 1877–1878 with Russia led to the secession of considerable population and land from the Empire. The upturn in Ottoman foreign trade did not come until 1898, and the Ottoman Greek War of 1897 may have been an important reason. The analysis of Ottoman foreign trade during the "Great Depression" will focus, therefore, on the period 1879 to 1898.

Rates of growth of Ottoman trade were distinctly lower during the 1880s and 1890s. As shown in Table 1, the volume of exports and of imports measured in fixed prices of 1880 increased at annual rates below 3 percent during 1879/81 to 1897/99. The break with the long-term trends of the midcentury becomes even more pronounced if we examine annual rates of change in current prices. Exports at current prices

[7] For a study of the economic and political consequences of the Free Trade Treaties, see Vernon J. Puryear, *International Economics and Diplomacy in the Near East* (Stanford, 1935).

[8] Issawi, *The Economic History of Turkey*, p. 82.

[9] Şevket Pamuk, "Foreign Trade, Foreign Capital and the Peripheralization of the Ottoman Empire, 1830–1913" (Ph.D. diss., University of California, Berkeley, 1978), pp. 36–37.

showed a decline at an average rate of 0.9 percent per year between 1879/80 and 1887/88. They recovered somewhat during 1887/88 to 1898/99, thereby averaging 1.2 percent annual growth for 1879/81 to 1897/99. Imports, measured in current prices, also declined during the first subperiod and recovered after 1887/88, averaging an annual rate of growth of 0.6 percent for 1879/81 to 1897/99.[10]

The slowing down in the rate of growth of Ottoman foreign trade was accompanied by little change in its country distribution. The share of the industrialized economies of Central and Western Europe and the United States edged upwards to a little more than 75 percent. In the 1880s Germany began to expand its share in Ottoman foreign trade primarily at the expense of Great Britain, which nonetheless retained until 1913 the largest share in Ottoman exports and imports.[11]

As shown in Table 1, the eve of World War I witnessed, once again, higher rates of growth of Ottoman foreign trade. Because of the Young Turk Revolution of 1908 and the subsequent loss of territory, meaningful comparison of aggregate trade figures can be extended only until 1907. Between 1911 and 1913 the Empire lost about a quarter of its population and over 10 percent of its territory in the commercially and agriculturally more advanced European provinces, where standards of living were above average.[12] But by 1913 the volume of exports had regained the 1907 levels and the volume of imports was more than 25 percent higher than the 1907 levels. In the remaining areas of the Empire the volume of exports and imports continued, therefore, to grow at high rates until World War I.

By 1913 the Empire had a relatively open economy with a large foreign trade sector. According to one estimate, in 1913 over 14 percent of the gross national product was being exported and the value of imports had exceeded 19 percent.[13] Because the rate of growth of foreign trade had remained well above the rate of growth of aggregate production, the share of foreign trade in national product was lower in earlier years. Around the mid-nineteenth century the shares were probably lower than half their levels in 1913.[14] Nonetheless, the foreign trade sector was large enough that the long-term fluctuations in its rate

[10] Annual rates of change for the entire period are somewhat different from the weighted average of the two subperiods, because the years 1881 and 1897 were included in the calculation of the former.

[11] Pamuk, "Foreign Trade, Foreign Capital," chap. 2.

[12] Vedat Eldem, *Osmanli İmparatorluğunun İktisadi Şartlari Hakkinda Bir Tetkik* (Istanbul, 1970), pp. 56–62, 80b, 305–7.

[13] The author's calculation based on Eldem's estimates of the gross national product of the Empire for 1907, 1913, 1914. See ibid, pp. 302–5.

[14] For purposes of comparison, note that for South America as a whole, share of exports in national product is estimated at 10 percent in 1860, 14 percent in 1880, and 18 percent in 1900. The comparable shares were distinctly lower in Asia, averaging 1.0 percent in 1860, 2.1 percent in 1880, and 4.6 percent in 1900. The share of exports in the national product of Jamaica fluctuated around 20 percent during the same period. See Hanson, *Trade in Transition*, pp. 22–23.

TABLE 2
PRICE INDICES FOR OTTOMAN FOREIGN TRADE WITH INDUSTRIALIZED COUNTRIES, 1870–1913
(chain-linked Fisher indices; 1880 = 100)

Years	Export Prices P_x	Import Prices P_m	External Terms of Trade P_x/P_m
1870/72	122.2	115.7	105.6
1887/89	71.1	82.1	86.6
1894/96	66.9	72.8	91.8
1911/13	85.3	80.5	106.0

Source: The author's calculations utilizing the foreign trade statistics of the United Kindgom, France, Germany, Austria, and the United States. Calculations take into account the decline in freight and insurance rates. For the procedure employed and detailed results, see Pamuk, "Foreign Trade, Foreign Capital," chap. 3, pp. 64–90, and Appendix 2, pp. 253–308.

of growth must have had significant repercussions in the rest of the economy. The correlation between long-term fluctuations in levels of industrial production in the larger industrial countries and fluctuations in Ottoman foreign trade strongly suggests that demand conditions were an important determinant of Ottoman exports.

LONG-TERM MOVEMENTS IN EXTERNAL TERMS OF TRADE

The Ottoman Empire can be considered a small country in international trade. The only commodity in which it maintained an important share of world trade was in the exportation of "Turkish" tobacco. Yet, until 1913 the share of this commodity in total Ottoman exports never exceeded 10 percent.[15] The terms of trade can therefore be safely treated as being external to the Ottoman economy.

The analysis of Ottoman terms of trade is limited to trade with the major European countries and the United States. As summarized in Table 2, Ottoman terms of trade with these countries declined rapidly between 1871 and 1889 and recovered somewhat between 1889 and 1896. As the demand of industrial economies for primary products picked up after 1896, Ottoman terms of trade improved, regaining by 1911/13 the levels of the early 1870s.

One dimension of the adverse movements in the external terms of trade during the period of the Great Depression that had a strong impact on the Ottoman economy and finances was the rapid and steady decline in world wheat prices. Between 1865 and 1891 American wheat production increased by 350 percent, making the United States a larger producer of wheat than all of Western Europe and Russia combined.

[15] The value of tobacco exports is taken from Eldem, *Tetkik*, p. 134b.

Mostly as a result of the entry of American wheat into the international markets, world wheat prices declined by more than 60 percent between 1873 and 1894, a rate of decline twice as rapid as the decline in the prices of Ottoman nonwheat exports.[16]

Ottoman exports of wheat declined rapidly. Because the free trade treaties prohibited protection, imports of wheat and flour began to expand.[17] Potentially the most important wheat-growing areas of the Empire, the Konya and Ankara provinces of Central Anatolia, continued to remain outside the reach of Istanbul and other domestic and export markets until after the arrival of the Anatolian Railway in the early 1890s.[18] The results must have been devastating for the small and middle-sized peasant producers.[19] Ottoman government finances were also hurt because the government derived more than a quarter of its revenues from agricultural production in a country where close to 90 percent of all land under cultivation was in cereals.[20]

LONG SWINGS IN FOREIGN INVESTMENT

As summarized in Table 3, direct foreign investment in the Ottoman Empire remained limited during the two decades before 1874. A large part of the foreign funds were invested in railways. By contrast, indirect investment was high and rising. Both inflows of funds due to Ottoman state borrowing in the European financial markets and total debt payments escalated sharply from 1854–1864 to 1865–1874. It is clear in retrospect that there were no realistic prospects that the Ottoman state would be able to pay back the debt. By agreeing to increasingly unfavorable terms, however, the state continued to borrow funds large

[16] See the Appendix "World Supply of Wheat," prepared by M. A. O'Connor in Lewis, *Growth and Fluctuations*. Also, Morton Rothstein, "America in the International Rivalry for the British Wheat Market, 1860–1914," *The Mississippi Valley Historical Review*, 47 (1960), 401–8; W. Malenbaum, *The World Wheat Economy, 1885–1939* (Cambridge, Massachusetts, 1933).

[17] See Aybar, *Ticaret Muvazenesi*.

[18] Donald Quataert, "Limited Revolution: The Impact of the Anatolian Railway on Turkish Transportation and the Provisioning of Istanbul, 1890–1908," *Business History Review* (Summer 1970), 139–60.

[19] Commercial Reports sent from the Ottoman Empire by British consuls are replete with accounts of the unfavorable impact of declining wheat prices on Ottoman producers. See, for example, Great Britain, *Parliamentary Papers, Accounts and Papers*, 1884–1885, Vol. 78, "Report by Consul Dickson on the Trade and Commerce of Damascus for the year 1884"; 1887, Vol. 86, "Report by Consul Dennis on the Trade and Commerce of Smyrna for the years 1882 to 1885"; 1890–1891, Vol. 88, "Report by Consul General Blunt on the Trade and Commerce of Salonica for the year 1889."

[20] Stanford Shaw, "The Nineteenth-Century Ottoman Tax Reforms and Revenue System," *International Journal of Middle East Studies*, 6 (1975), 451–53; Turkey, Orman ve Maadin ve Ziraat Nezareti, İstatistik İdaresi, *1323 Senesi Avrupay-i Osmani Ziraat İstatistiği* (Istanbul, 1326/1910) and *1325 Senesi Asya ve Afrikay-i Osmani Ziraat İstatistiği* (Istanbul, 1327/1911).

TABLE 3
ESTIMATED FUND FLOWS ARISING FROM FOREIGN INVESTMENT IN THE OTTOMAN EMPIRE
(annual averages in millions of British pounds sterling)

	(1)	*(2)*	*(3)*	*(4)*	*(5)*	*(6)*	*(7)*
	State Debt		*Direct Foreign Investment*			*Total Flows*	
Years	*Capital Inflows from New Borrowing*	*Total Debt Payments*	*Net New Investment*	*Profit Transfers*	*Capital Inflows Cols. (1) + (3)*	*Debt Payments and Profit Transfers Cols. (2) + (4)*	*Net Cols. (5) − (6)*
1854–1875	4.7	3.1	0.6	0.2	5.2	3.3	2.0
1880–1898	0.9	2.8	2.3	1.1	3.1	3.9	−0.8
1899–1913	2.7	4.6	1.4	2.7	4.1	7.2	−3.1
1854–1864	2.0	0.8	0.4	0.04	2.4	0.8	1.6
1865–1875	7.3	5.4	0.8	0.3	8.1	5.8	2.3
1876–1879	0.7	0.6	0.04	0.3	0.7	0.9	−0.2
1880–1887	0.8	2.1	0.3	0.7	1.1	2.8	−1.7
1888–1898	0.9	3.4	3.7	1.3	4.6	4.7	−0.1

Note: Some lines do not add up because of rounding-off.

Source: The author's calculations based on information regarding Ottoman bond floatations in the European financial markets, Ottoman Public Debt Administration records, records of the more than 80 joint stock companies, partly or entirely foreign-owned, operating in the Empire; and other sources. For details, see Pamuk, "Foreign Trade, Foreign Capital," chap. 4, pp. 91–132, and Appendix 3, pp. 310–16.

enough to cover the rapidly growing debt payments and its often extravagant expenditures.[21]

The collapse of the Ottoman state finances came with the stock exchange crises of 1873 in Europe and the United States. With the cessation of capital exports from the industrial countries, the default followed quickly. Debt payments were reduced by half in October 1875, and were stopped altogether in 1876.[22] The establishment of the Ottoman Public Debt Administration in 1881 initiated European control over Ottoman finances. The period was characterized by a sharp reversal in the direction of net fund flows. During 1880–1898 new borrowing remained low and debt payments net of new borrowing averaged £1.9 million per year, about 1.5 percent of the gross national product of the Empire within its smaller post-1878 borders and 12 to 15 percent of the total revenues of the Treasury.[23] Moreover, rapidly declining prices until 1896 meant that the real burden on the Ottoman economy and finances of the net payments abroad was rising steadily.

Direct foreign investment in the Empire during the same period presents a somewhat different picture. As shown in Table 3, capital inflows and profit transfers remained limited until 1887. The rivalry between German and French capital to divide the Empire into spheres of influence led to an intense wave of railroad building between 1888 and 1896.[24] The building literally paved the way for the incorporation of new areas of the Empire, especially of Central Anatolia into the world markets and for higher rates of growth of Ottoman foreign trade after the mid-1890s.[25] Direct foreign investment averaged £3.7 million per year during 1888–1898, well in excess of profit transfers. As a result, capital inflows arising from state external borrowing and direct foreign investment roughly equaled debt payments and profit transfers during the decade.

The period after 1898 represented the culmination of the earlier trends in foreign investment. As summarized in Table 3, external borrowing rose rapidly after the turn of the century. Higher levels of borrowing

[21] Donald C. Blaisdell, *European Financial Control in the Ottoman Empire* (New York, 1929), chap. 3; for lists of the Ottoman floatations and their magnitudes, see Issawi, *The Economic History of the Middle East*, pp. 94–106; Owen, *The Middle East in the World Economy*, p. 104.

[22] Blaisdell, *European Financial Control*, pp. 80–84. The Ottoman Empire was hardly alone in this respect. From 1822 to 1825 and the 1870s are regarded as the two periods with widespread defaults on government borrowing during the century preceding World War I. Honduras, Costa Rica, Santo Domingo, Paraguay, Spain, Bolivia, Guatemala, Liberia, Uruguay, Egypt, and Peru also defaulted or obtained rescheduling between 1872 and 1875. See Edwin Borchard, *State Insolvency and Foreign Bondholders, Vol. 1: General Principles* (New Haven, 1951), pp. xx–xxi; Leland H. Jenks, *The Migration of British Capital to 1875* (London, 1938).

[23] For the level of fiscal revenues, see Shaw, "Ottoman Tax Reforms," pp. 451ff.

[24] For an account of the rivalry and this particular wave of railroad building, see Herbert Feis, *Europe, the World's Banker, 1870–1914* (New Haven, 1930), chap. 15; also Edward M. Earle, *Turkey, the Great Powers and Baghdad Railway, A Study in Imperialism* (New York, 1923). After the 1860s, British investment in the Ottoman Empire, in the state debt, in railways, and elsewhere declined.

[25] Quataert, "Limited Revolution"; Owen, *Middle East in the World Economy*, pp. 200–9.

owed as much to the conditions in the European financial markets and the French-German rivalry over the Empire as to the intensification of the fiscal crisis.[26] But debt payments also escalated, so that the direction and magnitude of net fund flows arising from external borrowing remained unchanged after 1898.

Railroad construction and direct foreign investment in other areas continued, but their volume was not comparable to the building of 1888–1896. Foreign capital, mostly in infrastructure, accounted for about 10 percent of the gross domestic investment during 1899–1913.[27] On the other hand, profit transfers rose rapidly, averaging £1.3 million per year in excess of direct foreign investment. As a result, during the period after 1898, debt payments and profit transfers exceeded new capital inflows by £3.1 million per year, a sum equal to about 1½ percent of the GNP of the Empire.[28] As shown in Table 3, net fund flows had been in the other direction during the mid-century boom. Net outflows had not exceeded £0.8 million per year during 1880–1898.

ON RATES OF CHANGE IN THE LEVELS OF PRODUCTION

What can be said about the performance of the Ottoman economy from 1873 to 1896? Should the period be interpreted, as has been argued for the industrial countries, primarily in terms of monetary phenomena, with limited decrease in the rates of growth of aggregate production, or was the Ottoman experience more severe? It should be noted at the outset that no appreciable shift can be observed during the quarter century following 1873 in the composition of aggregate output and in the position the Ottoman Empire occupied in the international division of labor. Unlike the 1930s, when industrialization was underway, the basically agrarian nature of the economy and its increasing specialization in the exportation of primary products continued unchanged. There was no revival in the manufacturing activities based on handicrafts. On the contrary, all evidence points to a stagnation and possible decline in production by urban artisans, primarily due to the stagnation of agricultural and commercial incomes.[29] The emergence of modern industrial establishments such as cotton yarn spinning mills was very slow.[30]

[26] Feis, *Europe, the World's Banker*, chap. 14.

[27] Based on Eldem's estimate of the level of gross domestic investment after the turn of the century. Eldem, *Tetkik*, p. 290.

[28] Based on Eldem's estimates of the gross national product of the Empire for 1907, 1913, 1914; ibid, pp. 302–5.

[29] See, for example, British consular reports from the Syrian and Eastern Anatolian provinces of the Empire during the 1880s and 1890s. *Parliamentary Papers, Accounts and Papers*, "Commercial Reports" from Damascus, Aleppo, Diyarbakir, Erzurum, passim.

[30] For the decline of handicrafts-based manufacturing and the weak beginnings of industrialization, see Issawi, *The Economic History of Turkey*, pp. 272–78, 298–320; Owen, *The Middle East in the World Economy*, pp. 209–13.

Direct statistics are not available for an assessment of the changes in aggregate production levels. But for 1879 and the following years we have data on agricultural tithe revenues and total revenues of the Treasury. If the assumption can be made that rates of change in these revenues reflect, or at least approximate, the underlying rates of change in production levels, it is possible to make some crude estimates regarding trends in production levels.[31]

The results summarized in Table 4 indicate that the rates of change of tax revenues were quite different before and after 1897/98. Measured in constant liras, assessments and actual collections of the tithe and of total revenues of the Treasury increased at rates below 1 percent per year between 1879/80 and 1897/98. By contrast, rates of annual increase of the same ranged from 1.5 percent to 3.7 percent per year after 1897/98. As the rule of Abdulhamid II remained comparatively free of political and military turmoil for more than three decades, there is good reason to believe that the figures until 1908 reflect long-term changes in the levels of agricultural production.[32] On the other hand, some of the increases, especially in actual collections, occurring after 1908 appear to be due to the more efficient methods of collection employed by the new Young Turk administration.[33]

CONCLUSION

An assessment of the period from 1873 to the mid-1890s from the perspective of the world economy needs to take into account changes in the periphery as well as in the core. Our examination of the Ottoman case showed that its economy faced a distinct and unfavorable conjuncture. In addition to slower rates of growth of foreign trade and deteriorating terms of trade, both the rapid decline in world wheat

[31] The agricultural tithe constituted the largest single revenue item in Treasury collections, accounting for more than a quarter of the total revenues. Donald Quataert, who undertook a similar exercise utilizing the tithe revenues of the Anatolian provinces of the Empire, offers the following description and assessment: "during the Hamidian period (1876–1908) . . . the tithe generally was collected by tax farmers who purchased the right at government auction. The amount paid for the tax farm was fixed by the state on the basis of the district's tithe yield for the previous three years. There was, therefore, a lag between increasing production and rising tithe revenues. . . . It is evident that tithe revenue changes only imperfectly registered increases in agricultural production. The conclusions derived from analyzing these revenues should be viewed as only an approximation of shifts in the value of agricultural production." In contrast, for example, "the animal tax, primarily the *agnam vergisi*, was perhaps the best administered (tax falling on the rural producers), but was often paid through an arrangement with the tribal chieftain and related more to the degree of state authority over him than to the number of animals owned by his group." Donald Quataert, "Ottoman Reform and Agriculture in Anatolia, 1876–1908" (Ph.D. diss., University of California, Los Angeles, 1973), pp. 15, 31.

[32] For the 1910s the share of agriculture in the gross national product of the Empire has been estimated at slightly over one-half. Eldem, *Tetkik*, pp. 302–4.

[33] Quataert, "Ottoman Reform and Agriculture," p. 348.

TABLE 4
RATES OF CHANGE IN OTTOMAN TREASURY REVENUES, 1879–1910
(annual average compound rates in percent)

	Agricultural Tithe		*Total Revenues*	
End Years	*In Current Liras*	*In Constant Liras*[b]	*In Current Liras*	*In Constant Liras*[b]
	Assessments or Estimated Revenues			
1879/80–1880/81 to 1897/98–1898/99[a]	−0.6	0.9	See footnote c.	
1887/88–1888/89 to 1897/98–1898/99	0.7	0.4	−0.1	0.1
1897/98–1898/99 to 1906/07–1907/08	2.0	1.5	n.a.[d]	n.a.[d]
1897/98–1898/99 to 1909/10–1910/11[e]	3.6	3.1	2.7	2.2
	Actual Collections			
1887/88–1888/89 to 1897/98–1898/99[d]	0.9	0.6	0.7	0.9
1897/98–1898/99 to 1906/07–1907/08	3.1	2.7	n.a.[d]	n.a.[d]
1897/98–1898/99 to 1909/10–1910/11[e]	3.6	·3.1	4.3	3.7

[a] Ottoman fiscal years ran from March to March. Hence 1879/80–1880/81 in the first line of the table refers to the average of the two-year period starting in March 1879.

[b] To arrive at revenues in constant liras, agricultural tithe revenues were deflated by a composite price index with weights of 50 percent for Ottoman exports, 50 percent for Ottoman cereal exports. Total revenues of the treasury were deflated by a composite index with weights of 75 percent for Ottoman agricultural prices as described and 25 percent for prices of Ottoman imports.

[c] The rates of the agricultural tithe were raised from 10 percent of the gross product in 1880/82 to 11 percent in 1883, to 11.5 percent in 1884, to 12 percent in 1897, to 12.63 percent in 1900. It was lowered to 12.5 percent in 1906, where it stood in 1908. In Ottoman budgets and financial reports, these surcharges appeared under a separate heading. See D. Quataert, "Ottoman Reform and Agriculture in Anatolia, 1876–1908" (Ph.D. diss., University of California, Los Angeles, 1973), pp. 29–30, Appendix A, p. 347. As it is not clear whether such surcharges were applied to other revenue items as well, comparison of the estimated/assessed total revenue figures for the early 1880s with the later period was not included in the table.

[d] Actual and estimated collection figures for total revenues for the fiscal years 1905/06 and 1906/07 and actual collection figures for agricultural tithe for the fiscal years 1879/80 and 1880/81 are not available.

[e] Increases in all forms of revenues, especially in actual collection figures, after 1908 should be treated with caution. See the text. Wars and loss of territory after 1911 make the comparative use of aggregate data after this date rather difficult.

Sources: The assessed agricultural tithe figures for the years 1879/80 and 1880/81 are from E. Akarli, "The Problems of External Pressures, Power Struggles and Budgetary Deficit in Politics under Abdulhamid II, 1876–1909: Origins and Solutions" (Ph.D. diss., Princeton University, 1976), chap. 2. All others are taken from S. Shaw, "The Nineteenth-Century Ottoman Tax Reforms and Revenue System," *International Journal of Middle East Studies*, 6 (1975), 421–39. For price indices of Ottoman exports and imports, see Pamuk, "Foreign Trade, Foreign Capital," Appendix 2, pp. 279–81.

prices and the establishment of European control over Ottoman finances were products of the same conjuncture, the post-1873 Depression. Indirect data indicated that rates of change of agricultural and aggregate production were lower during the 1880s and 1890s as compared to the period after the turn of the century.

At least three considerations strongly suggest that world economic forces were an important determinant of the performance of the Ottoman economy during this period: after the establishment of the Ottoman Public Debt Administration, large net payments on the external debt did have a significant impact on the economy and state finances; the foreign trade sector was not small; and long-term trends in Ottoman foreign trade and domestic production closely paralleled the long-term fluctuations in the levels of economic activity in the major industrialized countries. On the other hand, it is not clear at this stage of the research which internal factors may have also accounted for the relative if not absolute stagnation of the Ottoman economy until the late 1890s. In any case, the findings here do not support the view that the periphery of the world economy benefited from rapidly expanding foreign trade during the last quarter of the nineteenth century. The Ottoman example has relevance at least for those Third World countries that faced slower rates of growth of exports, deteriorating external terms of trade, and large debt payments during the final quarter of the nineteenth century.

XIII

The Ottoman economy in World War I

Introduction: the economy on the eve of the war

On the eve of World War I the population of the Ottoman Empire, comprising present-day Turkey, Syria and Palestine, Iraq, and parts of the Arabian peninsula, was close to 23 million. Of these roughly 17 million lived within the modern borders of Turkey, more than 3 million in Syria and Palestine including Lebanon and Jordan, and about 2.5 million in present-day Iraq. In addition, approximately 5.5 million lived in Yemen and the Hijaz on the Arabian peninsula under nominal Ottoman rule (Eldem, 1970: 49–66; McCarthy, 2002). Despite considerable economic transformation and some economic growth during the nineteenth century and especially after 1880, the Ottoman economy was still mostly agrarian on the eve of World War I. Moreover, the real GDP of the empire in total and per head of the population was substantially below that of the countries of western and central Europe. Perhaps more than anything else, these basic limitations of the Ottoman economy hold the key to understanding the capacity and performance of the Ottoman military during World War I.

For the Ottoman Empire the nineteenth century had been a period of political, social, and economic reforms designed and implemented by the centre in order to keep the empire together in response to external and internal challenges. For the Ottoman economy it had also been a period of rapid integration into the world economy. Between 1820 and 1914 the foreign trade of the empire had expanded more than tenfold. On the eve of World War I, about 12 per cent of Ottoman output was being exported. More than 90 per cent of the exports were a diversified basket of agricultural commodities, foodstuffs, and raw materials, led by tobacco, cotton, barley, raisins, figs, raw silk, and raw wool. Rapid expansion of foreign trade had also turned the empire into an importer of manufactured goods, most importantly of cotton textiles, both cloth and yarn, but also of machinery and intermediate goods. The empire also imported some foodstuffs, most importantly wheat and flour for Istanbul, Beirut, and some other urban centres, as well as sugar, coffee, and tea. Coastal areas were supplied with grains and other foodstuffs from imports because of the shortcomings of the internal transportation network. In many regions the grains from the interior could not compete with imports since the free trade treaties in effect made it impossible to favour domestic producers. More than three-fourths of Ottoman external trade was directed towards industrialised Europe with Germany, France, and Great Britain the most important trading partners.

On the eve of World War I, the Ottoman economy remained predominantly agrarian. In the countryside, small peasant holdings co-existed with larger enterprises. Family enterprises with a pair of oxen and a plot of land large enough to be cultivated by them remained the basic unit of production. Peasant households that did not own a pair of oxen or land of reasonable quality offered their services as sharecropping tenants to larger landowners. While the coastal plains were densely cultivated, scarcity of labour and lack of availability of land prevailed in the interior regions. The commercialisation of agriculture during the nineteenth century was accompanied by a shift from cereals and other subsistence crops towards cash crops and industrial raw materials.

Manufacturing activity was still largely based on artisanal forms. Modern factories such as tanneries, textile mills, flour mills, glass works, and brick factories under private ownership began to emerge only towards the end of the nineteenth century. The Ottoman Industrial Census of 1913 indicates that within the present-day borders of Turkey there existed only about 600 manufacturing establishments employing ten or more workers. Total manufacturing employment in these establishments remained around 35,000 or about 0.2 per cent of the population. Most of this industrial employment was in textiles, food processing, paper and printing, and construction materials. The numbers of enterprises employing at least 100 workers remained fewer than sixty. The Ottoman government had agreed, through a series of international treaties in the 1830s, to fix ad valorem tariffs on imports at 5 per cent. While these low tariffs met with considerable criticism from guilds and manufacturers, they were raised only slightly and remained at 15 per cent on the eve of World War I. Low tariffs on imports made it especially difficult for new manufacturing enterprises to take root in the empire.

Another important dimension of nineteenth-century globalisation for the Ottoman economy was the large amount of direct foreign investment by European capital. On the eve of World War I, total direct foreign or European investment in the Ottoman Empire had reached £75 million. Close to 60 per cent of this amount had been invested in various railways, especially in Anatolia and Syria. By linking the fertile agricultural regions to major ports, these railways facilitated the commercialisation of agriculture and integration of the Ottoman economy into world markets. European direct investment also went into other forms of infrastructure such as ports, utility companies, insurance, and shipping. In contrast, foreign investment in agriculture, mining and manufacturing remained limited (Pamuk, 1987: 55–81).

Another aspect of foreign investment and a source of long-term vulnerability for the empire was the external debt outstanding. Ever since the Crimean War, the government had attempted to finance the budget deficits that often arose from the need to increase military expenditures by borrowing in the European financial markets. The Ottoman state had declared a moratorium on its debt payments in 1876 and the subsequent negotiations had led, in 1881, to the establishment of the Ottoman Public Debt Administration, an organisation of European bondholders. This institution was given the right to develop and collect taxes from some of the leading revenue sources of the empire and direct them towards debt payments. Even though the Ottoman state managed to generate a budget surplus and maintain orderly payments on its outstanding debt during the last two decades of the nineteenth century, rising military expenditure after the turn of the century and especially after 1908 began to create serious fiscal problems once again. Budget deficits began to be financed by further borrowing and the need to secure additional loans created important complications for Ottoman foreign policy. By 1914, the outstanding debt of the government had reached £140 million or close to 60 per cent of the GDP of the empire. French investors held more than half and the German investors held more than 20 per cent of this debt. The share of the British was less than 15 per cent.

Even though the external debt burden was rising and the empire's industry was in poor condition, the Ottoman economy was not in a bad state on the eve of World War I. Except for the loss of territories due to the Balkan Wars of 1912–13, the population of the empire had been growing at 1 per cent annually during the decades leading up to World War I. Standards of living and incomes per head were also rising slowly at a little less than 1 per cent annually from 1880 to 1914. Some figures for Ottoman GDP in 1913 are shown in table 4.1. GDP per head in 1913 has been estimated at about £10 at the prevailing exchange rate (Eldem, 1970: 302–9). In US dollars at purchasing power parity of 1990, this was equal to about $1,200. At such levels, average real incomes in the Ottoman Empire on the eve of World War I were above those of its southern and eastern neighbours, Egypt and Iran. They were, however, below those of eastern and south-eastern European countries such as Serbia, Bulgaria, and Greece. Moreover, Ottoman GDP per head in

Table 4.1. *Ottoman Empire: estimates of the GDP in 1913*

GDP at current prices:	
Ottoman liras, million	240
£ sterling, million	220
GDP per head, approximately:	
£ sterling and current prices	10
US dollars at PPP and 1990 prices	1,200
GDP by sector of origin, per cent	
Agriculture and mining	48
Industry	12
Trade	10
Government services	8
Other services	22
GDP total	100

Note: PPP = purchasing power parity.

Sources: Eldem (1970: 303–5) and Pamuk (2001).

1913 stood at approximately one-third of income levels in France and Germany and one-fourth those of the United Kingdom. Similarly, the total GDP of the Ottoman Empire on the eve of World War I at purchasing power parity was less than one-fourth of the French and less than one-sixth of that of Germany or the United Kingdom (Pamuk, 2001, which provides the basis for the figures for the GDP of the Ottoman Empire before World War I presented by Maddison, 2003: 156–7).

Military preparedness

The Ottoman Empire was less prepared than most of the other combatants to face the economic consequences of a general war of long duration. Excluding territories on the Arabian peninsula, the empire covered a large territory with borders of over 12,000 kilometres and a coastline in excess of 8,000 kilometres, exceeding 1.7 million square kilometres in area. Until the outbreak of the war, most of the external trade of the empire and a large part of its internal trade had been seaborne. After the Allied powers intercepted sea transport in the Mediterranean, the war effort had to rely almost entirely on land transport. In the years leading up to the Great War, government infrastructure programmes had gained momentum. The deposed sultan Abdulhamid II had been a builder of railways, roads, and telegraph lines and the Young Turk government continued this tradition. Nonetheless, the Ottoman transportation network over this sprawling geography remained poor. The total length of railways over this large territory was less than 6,000 kilometres. Railways were lacking completely in eastern Anatolia, an important theatre of the war, because the Ottoman government had agreed not to build them in this region without the consent of the Russian government. Moreover, the railways did not yet link Anatolia to Syria and Mesopotamia when the war broke out. Until tunnels in the Taurus mountains in southern Anatolia were completed in January 1917, materials and men still had to be unloaded, transported by road and reloaded back on the trains in this region. The existing roads were poor and much of the transport was undertaken by draught animals. The empire was also poor in modern means of communication. The network of telegraph lines was very limited (McCarthy, 2001: 95–8; Erickson, 2001: 51–73).

Just as important is the fact that Ottoman manufacturing of war materials remained very limited. On the eve of the war, production of pig iron and steel was insignificant. There was very little chemical production and petroleum refining. There were one cannon and small arms foundry, one shell and cartridge factory, and only one gunpowder factory. All of these facilities were located just outside Istanbul. One of the key shortages to emerge during the war was energy. Although the empire had been self-sufficient in coal before the war, coal had to be imported from Germany after the Russian bombardment of the Eregli coal mines on the Black Sea coast and the sinking of transport ships. As a result, wood was used on the railways in southern Anatolia and Syria for most of the war (Eldem, 1994: 78–9).

Despite these shortcomings, the Ottomans were forced to fight on several fronts: against the British and French at Gallipoli; against Russia in the southern Caucausus and eastern Anatolia; against the British in Iraq, in the Suez Canal area and later in Syria and Palestine; against the Arab insurgents in the Hijaz and Yemen in the Arabian peninsula; and on various European fronts, against Russia in Galicia, Hungary, and Romania; and against the British in Macedonia.

The Ottomans had made use of military advisers from western European countries since late in the eighteenth century. German military missions to the Ottoman Empire had begun in the 1880s during the reign of Abdulhamid II. By the early twentieth century, the Ottoman army was modelled mainly on the German army. Nonetheless, its disastrous performance against an alliance of other Balkan countries during 1912 and 1913 had made clear that radical changes were urgently needed. The military budget was immediately doubled and steps were taken to modernise the Ottoman military. New battleships were ordered from British shipyards, and an air force was established. In 1914 a new contingent of German officers led by General Liman von Sanders was invited to reform and reorganise the Ottoman army. There were important changes in the short period of time leading up to the war. Ancillary corps such as the quartermaster corps, military intelligence, and communications advanced rapidly towards twentieth-century standards. Older officers were retired to make way for better-educated younger men. While the organisational chart of the army showed few changes, Ottoman military power increased considerably.

Nonetheless, in 1914 the military was still exhausted from its involvement in the Balkan Wars. It did not have mobilisation plans designed to manoeuvre an armed mass to a decisive point for early offensive operations (Erickson, 2001: 19, 51, 73). The Ottomans needed many years to develop an army up to European standards, not just one or two years of intensive effort. There also existed serious obstacles in the capacity of the government to mobilise the male population of the empire into the armed forces. Most of the non-Muslims, which made up 20 per cent of the population of the empire, could pay a tax and avoid the draft. The government also had difficulties in drafting and keeping the Muslim population under arms. The maximum size of the Ottoman army during the war was below 800,000. The government was thus able to mobilise less than 4 per cent of the population into the armed forces, a ratio well below that of most other belligerents. The Ottoman army also remained dependent on imported arms and military equipment until the end of the war. Until the restoration of railways lines and other overland communication lines with central Europe after the defeat of Serbia in late 1915, the empire suffered crippling shortages of war supplies and raw materials. Despite all these shortcomings, however, it is remarkable that the Ottoman military managed to stay in the war right until the end in October 1918 while many others were forced to abandon their effort, (Zürcher, 1996).

When the war broke out in 1914, German military assistance was primarily in the form of high-level advisers. Financial and material support was very small. These resources began to increase towards the end of 1914, however, and continued to rise in later years. Nonetheless, German fighting forces inside the Ottoman Empire remained small. In August 1916 there were 640 German officers and 5,900 German soldiers stationed within the Ottoman Empire. By the end of the war, German material assistance to the empire included as many as 20,000 men, 650,000 rifles, 600 guns, and other materials. In contrast, the total of Ottoman men mobilised during the war reached 2.8 million. The sterling value of materials given to the Ottoman side by Germany during the war has been estimated at about £29 million and those from Austria-Hungary at £5.5 million. Additionally, loans from Germany were used to finance imports of various non-military goods from that country. While the importance of German logistical support is debatable, especially in view of the large distance between the two countries, German technical assistance and advisory support played an important role in enabling the Ottomans to make the most of their existing resources and keeping the Ottoman military in the war for as long as possible (Erickson, 2001: 51–73; McCarthy, 2001: 95–8; see also Swanson, 1975; Erickson, 2003; Trumpener, 1968).

To date various estimates have been offered for the total numbers of Ottoman soldiers that died during World War I; these range from over 400,000 to more than 1 million. The most recent figures fall roughly in the middle of these two extremes. In his latest work on the Ottoman army during World War I, Edward Erickson (2003) estimates 2.9 million as the total number of soldiers mobilised into the Ottoman army during the war and 770,000 as the total numbers of soldiers that died or were missing afterwards. To this number should be added the possibly even larger number of civilians who lost their lives due to armed conflict, disease, and malnutrition during the war (Erickson, 2001: chapter 8). Leading causes of civilian casualties are discussed further later in this chapter; the last section of the chapter also deals with demographic changes within Turkey's modern frontiers.

The disruption of external trade and production

It has been pointed out that the Ottoman economy relied on imports not only for its manufactures and war materials but also for meeting the food needs of some of the coastal areas, most importantly the capital city. The earliest and most immediate impact of the war was thus the disruption in external trade which was compounded by the commercial embargo of the Allies around the Mediterranean. As a result, external Ottoman trade was quickly reduced to the movement of goods obtained by rail from Bulgaria alone. Direct trade with Germany and Austria resumed overland only after the German occupation of Serbia at the end of 1915. By 1916, the volume of Ottoman external trade had declined to approximately one-fifth of its prewar levels and more than 90 per cent of this trade was being conducted with Germany and Austria-Hungary (Eldem, 1994: 66). As a result, shortages quickly appeared in both foodstuffs, such as grains and sugar, and various kinds of manufactures.

The shortages provided an opportunity to the supporters of policies of economic nationalism. Even before the war, in the aftermath of the Young Turk Revolution of 1908, an interesting debate regarding economic strategy had emerged between the two wings of these urban intellectuals, activist bureaucrats, and military officers. On one side were the defenders of the western type of decentralisation and economic liberalism who emphasised an open economy model promoting trade and agricultural development. Arguing against them were the proponents of Listian protectionism and a more self-reliant strategy based on industrialisation. Of equal interest was the growing recognition by both sides that the traditional and overriding concern of the Ottoman state for fiscal revenue needed to be abandoned in favour of state policies that promoted economic development. The Ottoman government, however, had already committed itself to the free trade treaties and a concessionary regime that gave extraterritorial privileges to foreign companies and citizens in economic and legal affairs. As a result, these debates had had little impact on policy until the war. One notable exception was legislation passed in 1913 to encourage domestic industry (Toprak, 1982: 166–78).

After its entry into the war, the Young Turk government moved unilaterally to redefine the empire's external economic relations in three key areas. First, it eliminated the low rate ad valorem tariff structure in favour of higher specific tariffs on selected goods. In order to support domestic industry, the government also revised and extended the existing legislation that encouraged and supported domestic industry. Secondly, the government declared a moratorium on payments on the external debt, most of which was held by the citizens of France, Germany, and Great Britain. Thirdly, it abrogated the concessions and thus subjected foreign companies and individuals to Ottoman laws.

The first impact of the war on domestic industry was positive, as some import substitution occurred. Soon afterwards, however, raw material shortages began to emerge. In addition, the decline in coal production after the Russian bombing of the Eregli coal mines on the Black Sea coast unfavourably affected the industrial production that was being carried on. Equally importantly, the urban areas had faced moderate labour shortages, especially of skilled workers, even before the war. The mobilisation of large numbers of males thus exacerbated labour shortages in industry. The mobilisation and employment of large numbers of women in urban areas did not resolve these shortages until the end of the war. Compared with the 1913–14 average, coal production was down by 40 per cent in 1916 and by 75 per cent by 1918. Production of various minerals also fell by between 50 and 80 per cent compared to prewar levels. Even cotton textiles production was down by 50 per cent in 1918 compared to its 1913 level. There is no estimate of the overall decline in industrial output during the war, but this was most probably between 30 and 50 per cent (Eldem, 1994: 75–82).

Wartime conditions also created difficulties for Ottoman agricultural production. Since mechanisation had remained limited, agricultural production

Table 4.2. *Ottoman Empire: wheat production, 1915 to 1918 (percentage of 1913–1914 average)*

	Area under cultivation	Yield per unit of land	Total production
1913–14, average	100	100	100
1915	93	86	80
1916	87	82	73
1917	79	80	64
1918	75	78	62

Note: Parts of eastern Anatolia, Syria, Iraq, and Arabia are excluded.

Source: Eldem (1994: 33–9), based on official statistics or official estimates.

did not depend on imported inputs or machinery. Nonetheless, it was unfavourably affected by the special requirements of the military during wartime. In an economy that experienced labour scarcities in both the rural and the urban sectors even during peacetime, the conscription of males and the requisitioning of draught animals created serious difficulties. As many as 2.8 million males were drafted for military service during the four years of the war. In addition, requisitioning of draught animals by the military reached crippling levels in many parts of the country. The agricultural sector experienced a sharp decline in herds of draught and dairy livestock during the war. By 1918 numbers of draught animals had fallen by more than one-half, and numbers of sheep and goats by about 40 per cent. Even though women assumed a greater burden in agriculture, the acreage under cultivation and levels of output declined sharply. The official statistics (table 4.2) suggest that, as a result of these pressures, both land under cultivation and yields began to decline from the first year of the war. By 1916, total wheat production had declined by nearly 30 per cent. Declines in the output of most of the exportable cash crops were even greater. By 1918, the decline in production in comparison to the 1913–14 levels was close to 40 per cent in wheat, more than 50 per cent in tobacco, raisins, hazelnuts, olive oil, raw silk and cotton. It is possible, however, that these official estimates overstate the extent of decreases in production because the peasant producers hid or understated their production levels in order to avoid wartime taxes or forced deliveries to the military.

Estimates for Ottoman GDP have not been constructed for the war period. On the basis of the available sectoral evidence, some of which has been presented here, it appears that by 1918 the GDP of the empire had declined by at least 30 per cent, and perhaps 40 per cent or more, from its prewar level.

Food supply policies

Wartime conditions were often likely to create significant imbalances between the supply and demand for food. In this respect, however, there was a qualitative difference between the wartime experiences of developed economies and those of the underdeveloped or poorer economies. Typically, the more developed economies showed greater flexibility and a greater ability to maintain levels of food production close to peacetime levels. Since their agriculture used a variety of inputs, the reduction in the availability of one or more of them did not need to affect severely the levels of output. Other inputs could be substituted for the scarce input. If labour became scarcer, for example, it was easier to substitute machinery or fertilisers to maintain the earlier levels of production.

This flexibility was usually not available to the less-developed economies. Their structures of production were much more rigid. Since agricultural techniques of production were rather primitive, machinery could not be easily substituted for labour or draught animals. In addition, the less-developed economies had less-developed transportation networks which were so essential for linking the areas with food surpluses to the areas of food deficit during wartime. In short, less-developed economies were less flexible and much more vulnerable to the disruptions of wartime (Prest, 1948; Millward, 1977).

It is not very surprising, therefore, that wartime conditions created major difficulties for the Ottoman food supply. While imports and production declined sharply, demand for food did not decline during wartime. If anything, demand for food actually increased because of the need to feed a larger army to a better standard. In addition, the Ottoman transportation network could not respond satisfactorily to wartime pressures.

The shortages of food and hunger experienced in the Ottoman empire during World War I were not always due to a decline in food availability, however. As Amartya Sen (1981) has argued in an insightful study of poverty and famines, even though total availability of food may remain unchanged or decline only slightly, hunger and famine will result if some groups in society lose the ability to command food, or what he calls food entitlements. For example, wartime conditions may drive food prices beyond the reach of some segments of the population such as the urban poor or landless agricultural workers. Food shortages and hunger depended, then, not only on the total food availability but also on the distribution of the available food amongst different groups (see also Tilly, 1983).

In short, with or without a decline in total food availability, there was the potential for severe inequities in the distribution and consumption of food among different groups in society to emerge, which would seriously affect morale and hamper the war effort For this reason, securing the food supply of the urban population and the military, and distributing the available food in an equitable manner, were considered to be some of the most important economic policy issues facing the Ottoman government during World War I.

Governments' wartime food supply policies covered many areas, ranging from intervention in agricultural production to transportation and distribution and finally consumption. At one end, the government attempted to reduce consumption of the limited food supplies and ensure a more equitable distribution of the available supplies by implementing a more or less comprehensive system of rationing in the capital city. At the other end, the government attempted to intervene in food production and increase it directly. The Ottoman parliament passed an Agricultural Obligations Law in September 1916 which made large corporations in the urban areas responsible for securing the necessary equipment and labour and cultivating specified amounts of land. Moreover, all farmers were required to cultivate a minimum area for each pair of oxen that they had. The law also gave the government the power to require all men and women not under arms to engage in agriculture. The government could ask families or individuals to work on farms experiencing labour shortages due to wartime mobilisation. In extreme cases, battalions of women were organised by the army and were sent to the fields to help with the cotton harvest in southern Anatolia. In short, a system of war agriculture was apparently in place by the end of 1916. However, the real effectiveness of this dramatic legislation and the related measures was rather limited (Yalman, 1934: 119–34; Toprak, 2003: 81–98; Okçün, 1983).

Another area of intervention was the transportation of cereal supplies from Anatolia to Istanbul. The capital city relied heavily on grains and flour imported by sea until 1914 despite the availability of the Anatolian railway. With the outbreak of the war these imports were disrupted and Istanbul was forced to turn, for the first time, to the grain-producing plains of central Anatolia. Under more normal conditions Anatolian agriculture was capable of producing enough for Istanbul. The wartime decline in production combined with the transportation difficulties, however, to create severe problems for Istanbul.

For most of World War I, the bottleneck in provisioning Istanbul was lack of space on the railway connecting central Anatolia to Istanbul and in ships arriving from the Black Sea. There was an intense struggle regarding their allocation. The environment of shortages created by the provisioning needs of Istanbul gave the Union and Progress Party leadership the opportunity to select a small group of merchants close to the party and allow them to supply the city. Railway truck space and shipping permits were allocated to Muslim merchants linked to the Union and Progress Party in power. This system enabled the Union and Progress Party to share in the wartime profits, as some of them were ploughed back into the party. Equally importantly, it provided an opportunity to create a new group of Muslim-Turkish entrepreneurs with close links to the party. Monopolies were created for importing and distributing many scarce commodities and these were then awarded to the Turkish supporters of the party in Istanbul and the provinces. This strategy, of course, was well in line with the embrace of Turkish nationalism during World War I, if not earlier, as the leading ideology of the Union and Progress Party (Toprak, 1982: 22–35; Yalman, 1934: 135–43; Tekeli and Ilkin, 2004: 1–26).

Another important aspect of food supply policies during the war involved the direct procurement of cereals from rural producers. This was where the government came face to face with the farmers, large and small. Three distinct stages can be observed in the evolution of government procurement policy and the farmers' response. In the first stage, early in the war, the government relied on the market mechanism to provide the cereal supply to the urban areas. The producers were left free to sell their produce at market prices to whomever they liked. The merchants were then expected to transport the cereals to the urban areas and sell it there. The basis for this non-interventionist attitude was the belief early in the war that the conflict would not last long (Ahmad, 1983, 1988; Eldem, 1994: 33–47; Toprak, 1982: 267–312; Ogün, 1999).

Shortages soon began to emerge, however, leading to sharp increases in food prices in some urban areas. The shortages were due to a combination of factors. They were, in part, due to a decline in production. There was also the poor transportation network. In addition, the expectation of shortages by merchants, shopkeepers, and even consumers led them to start hoarding. The second stage began with the emergence of shortages. At that point, it became clear to the government that the food supply problem could not be resolved by market forces alone and that intervention was necessary. This stage was reached in the autumn of 1916. The first response of the government was maximum intervention in the procurement process. It was announced that the government would allow all cereal producers to retain only enough for seed and the maintenance of their households and they were required to surrender the rest to designated government agents at fixed prices that were substantially below those prevailing in the market at the time. The government did not have the administrative capacity to implement this new and ambitious system, however.

All producers were affected adversely by this policy, but those who stood to lose most were the larger landowners who had greater market surpluses. The response of all cereal producers was to resist. Small and large producers alike hid their crops, bribed government officials, and did all they could to minimise the amount they surrendered to the government. Although they were not allowed to move the harvest from the field until the government agent arrived, for example, the producers often attempted to smuggle the harvest from the field and hide it. They tried to bribe the local officials to underestimate their obligations and to deliver grains of lower quality. What they did not surrender, they either consumed themselves or sold to private merchants on the black market. In other words, resistance to wartime state demands often occurred covertly, on a local scale, employing the 'weapons of the weak' as James Scott (1984) has described them: foot dragging, concealment, and evasion. As a result of all of these, the amount of cereals reaching the urban areas declined after this government measure was put into effect. As the food supply problem in the urban areas became more acute, it was further complicated by the hoarding of cereals by others, especially merchants and shopkeepers. In short, not all of the difficulties in the urban areas were due to a decline in production. It is clear that the urban shortages were also due to government policies and the responses of agricultural producers, merchants, and shopkeepers (Yalman, 1934: 119–35; Toprak, 1982: 267–312; Tekeli and Ilkin, 2004: 1–26).

There was a good deal of regional variation within this general picture. Typically, rural areas fared better during the war since most of the rural population cultivated some land and had direct access to food unless the harvest collapsed altogether. It also made a big difference whether a region was a net food exporter or importer. Most of the difficulties occurred in large urban areas located in food deficit regions. Military operations or the presence of large numbers of troops in a region added to the difficulties. The prohibition of internal trade in grains and confiscation of the surplus grain by some local commanders exacerbated the shortages.

The most severe food shortages occurred in eastern Anatolia, northern Syria, and Lebanon. In eastern Anatolia, the forced deportation of Armenians to the Syrian desert by the government in 1915, as well as attacks on them by civilians and government-linked forces, and the subsequent flight of Muslim peasants when the region was occupied by the Russian army in 1916, resulted in the deaths of as many as 1 million civilians, both Armenian and Muslim. Most of these people died of disease and starvation. The policy of forced deliveries certainly also contributed to the difficulties in Lebanon and Syria after 1916. When shortages began to emerge in Syria, because of locusts and poor harvests, the government demanded deliveries from the producers at fixed prices and the producers resisted. As the government intensified the pressure on the villages close to the urban centres, peasants began to flee to the interior where they were given seed and land to cultivate by the Druze shaiks. This only made things worse in the urban areas. But the wartime food problems in Syria and Lebanon were not only due to poor harvests and government policy. Tribal chiefs refused to sell grain to government agents or private merchants for political reasons, or they demanded payment in gold rather than paper currency. There was also a good deal of hoarding by the merchants. Moreover, the British and French governments refused to lift the blockade of Beirut despite widespread starvation. The shortages assumed catastrophic dimensions towards the end of 1916, resulting in hundreds of thousands of deaths, perhaps as many as half a million in Lebanon and Syria (Schatkowski Schilcher, 1992).

With the deteriorating situation in the urban areas, the government recognised that the policy of coercion was not working and it was necessary to provide better incentives to the producers. As a result, a third set of policies was adopted in 1917. In this third stage all cereal producers were asked to surrender some proportion of their produce to the government, either as tax in kind or at some fixed price below the market. They were then left free to sell the rest to anybody they wished. This was, in effect, a mixture of intervention and a free market. Moreover, the responsibility for provisioning both the army and the civilian population was given to the Ministry of War. This change in policy improved the food supply situation in the urban areas as producers responded to higher food prices by selling more. These policies remained in effect until the end of the war.

The freedom to sell at market prices did not mean that all cereal producers benefited from the new policy. The government continued to take away some of the output from the smaller producers, which left them very little or nothing for sale at the market. Since they were still required to surrender part of their crop to the government, they continued to carry the burden of wartime difficulties. The beneficiaries of the new policy were the larger landowners who still had cereal surpluses after delivering part of their crop to the government. They were able to take advantage of high market prices until the end of the war (Yalman, 1934: 132–5).

To sum up, Ottoman agriculture was less flexible and much more vulnerable to the disruptions of wartime than its counterparts in the more developed economies. Wartime conditions thus created major difficulties for the Ottoman food supply. While food production and imports declined, the provisioning and political stability of the urban areas and the army quickly became a matter of political and military survival for the government. There was much less regard for the welfare of the peasant producers. The Ottoman government also lacked the capacity to adopt and implement controls over the food surpluses. In response to the various forms of coercion employed by the government, agricultural producers managed to avoid taxes and other demands and keep a large part of the food for themselves.

Financing the war

In the years leading up to World War I, the Ottoman government had used external borrowing as the basic method of financing its budget deficits, which arose mainly from increased military expenditure. As a result, the total debt outstanding had begun to increase after the turn of the century, and at a more rapid pace after 1908. On the eve of the war, annual payments on the external debt approached 40 per cent of government revenues. In addition, roughly 20 per cent of government revenues had been under the control of the Ottoman Public Debt Administration since 1881. While the outbreak of World War I sharply increased the need for military expenditure, it also eliminated the possibility of external borrowing.

One method of financing the war was to increase taxes. Before the war, the government's tax revenues equalled approximately 12 per cent of the GDP of the empire (Eldem, 1970: 243, 303). More than two-thirds of these revenues were collected from the agricultural sector. Most important amongst the taxes on the rural economy was the 10 per cent tithe collected in kind from agricultural producers by private tax-farmers. With the outbreak of the war, the government increased a variety of direct and indirect taxes that were collected from consumers as well as businesses. Taxes on consumer goods such as sugar, petroleum, matches, coffee, tea, alcoholic beverages, and cigarettes were put in place in 1915. These taxes were increased in 1916. The government also legislated new income and war profits taxes to be collected from individuals and businesses (Yalman, 1934: 157–8; Eldem, 1994: 83–94). In addition, the government and the local administrators, mostly civilian but also military in some cases, increased the tithe demanded from the agricultural producers to 12.5 per cent and even higher in some regions.

These efforts did not succeed in increasing tax revenues, however. One important reason for the decline in revenues was the decline in agricultural and industrial production that began after the outbreak of the war. With the sharp decline in foreign trade after 1914, tariff revenues, which had accounted for close to one-fifth of government revenues before the war, also declined despite the sharp increases in tariffs on some imported items after 1915. Secondly, many taxes, including payments to the government by the tax-farmers, who collected taxes in kind from the agricultural producers, were fixed in nominal terms. With the acceleration of

Table 4.3. *Ottoman Empire: estimated tax revenues and state expenditure, 1913/14 to 1918/19 (fiscal years and million liras at current prices)*

	Revenue	Expenditure	Deficit
1913/14	29.4	35.3	5.9
1914/15	24.9	57.8	22.9
1915/16	22.3	65.6	43.3
1916/17	25.2	83.0	57.8
1917/18	27.7	109.0	81.3
1918/19	34.0	122.5	88.5

Note: 1.1 Ottoman lira = £1 sterling in 1914.

Sources: Yalman (1934: 157–60) and Eldem (1994: 84).

inflation after 1915, nominal revenues lagged far behind prices. Government attempts to adjust the nominal rates of some taxes, such as income tax or the tax on sheep and cattle, with greater frequency were not very effective. Thirdly, and perhaps most importantly, with the emergence of hardships and falling production and incomes, the tendency to evade taxes increased and the government's capacity to collect them actually declined, both in the urban areas and amongst the rural producers. As a result, revenues from the tithe which accounted for more than one-fourth of all government revenues before the war, for example, fluctuated around their prewar levels in current Ottoman liras during the war years, despite the sharp increases in the price level. While the quality of the available data is not very good, they nonetheless indicate very clearly that state revenues in current Ottoman liras actually remained below their prewar levels until the last year of the war, while prices increased about twenty-fold until the end of 1918. As will be shown, most of the inflation occurred in the last two years of the war.

Since budget revenues in current Ottoman liras remained below or close to their prewar levels, rapid increases in expenditure led to increasingly large deficits which can be followed from the estimates of the Ottoman war budgets made after the war (table 4.3). The government tried hard to keep these deficits in check. One obvious target was official salary payments, which had accounted for at least 40 per cent of prewar outlays. During the early years of the war, the government levied minor taxes on official salaries. As inflation accelerated after 1915, the state provided only minimal increases in the salaries it paid. By 1918, therefore, the share of salary payments was reduced to less than 18 per cent of all state expenditure despite an increase in the number of state employees during the war of more than 20 per cent. Reducing the salaries of state employees thus emerged as an important method of financing the war. In addition, many services and requisitions obtained by the government during the war remained unpaid. These have been estimated at 50 million Ottoman liras for the war as a whole (Yalman, 1934: 165; Eldem, 1994: 99).

The government also borrowed modest sums from its allies during the war, a total of 56 million Ottoman liras from Germany and 8.5 million Ottoman liras from Austria-Hungary in addition to the war materials obtained from these countries. In prewar terms, the value of these loans can be estimated at about £20 million. These debts were later cancelled by the treaties of Versailles and St Germain. In addition, in 1917 the Ottoman government attempted to sell German government bonds to the Ottoman public and use the proceeds for war finance, but this bond issue failed. The government also tried to sell its own bonds to the Ottoman public. However, it could manage to sell only 18 million liras (less than £4 million) worth of war bonds towards the end of the war in 1918 (Yalman, 1934: 161–5; Eldem, 1994: 83–93).

When all other methods fell short, especially in the later stages of the war, the government obtained additional revenue by issuing *kaimes* or paper bills. Printing paper money thus emerged as by far the most important instrument of war finance for the Ottoman government. In the prewar period, the only paper currency circulating in Ottoman markets was the gold-backed paper notes that the French-controlled Imperial Ottoman Bank issued in limited amounts. The government issued wartime paper bills with the promise that the state would buy them back in gold within a specified period after the end of the war. This period ranged from six months to seven years depending on the issue. For the first series of paper bills the government deposited their equivalent in gold with the Ottoman Public Debt Administration. For subsequent series, until the last year of the war, German treasury bonds borrowed from the German government were set aside as guarantees.

Paper bills started circulating in 1915. Their volume reached 46 million liras at the end of that year, 124 million liras at the end of 1917, and 161 million liras by the end of the war. They started exchanging at par against the silver and gold coins in circulation in 1915. As the volume of paper bills began to expand and their denominations began to get smaller, however, their exchange rates against gold-backed currency began to decline and the silver coinage soon disappeared from circulation. Most of the daily transactions during the later years of the war were thus undertaken with paper currency whose denominations began as low as 1 piaster. During this later period the Ottoman monetary system thus

Table 4.4. *Ottoman Empire: money and prices, 1915–1918 (end of year)*

	1915	1916	1917	1918
Paper bills in circulation (million Ottoman liras)	8	46	124	161
Exchange rate of gold lira against paper bills (par = 100)	105	188	470	438
Consumer price index in Istanbul, percentage of 1914	130	212	1,465	2,205

Note: 1.1 Ottoman lira = £1 sterling in 1914.

Sources: Yalman (1934: 144–54), Eldem (1994: 47–56), Toprak (2003: 169–8).

consisted of gold plus inconvertible paper with the gold circulating at the market rate against a paper currency which had become the unit of account. The exchange rates of the *kaime* in Istanbul rose from 120 piasters per gold lira early in 1916 to 400 in mid-1917 and 500 at the end of the war. Their rates were even lower in the provinces. In August 1917, for example, while 1 gold lira exchanged for 430 piasters of paper currency in Istanbul, it exchanged for 450 piasters in Bursa and Izmir, 540 in Aleppo, 555 in Beirut, and 766 in Mosul (Toprak, 1982: 232–63; Pamuk, 2000a: 222–4).

Partly because of this monetary expansion and partly because of the difficulties in provisioning the capital city, prices spiralled, especially during the last two years of the war. The cost of living index prepared by the Ottoman Public Debt Administration for Istanbul increased more than twenty-fold from July 1914 to the end of 1918 and more than eighteen-fold by the last quarter of 1918 (Toprak, 1982: 331–3) (see table 4.4). Since Istanbul experienced greater difficulties in its food supply during the war than most other regions, it is likely that the increases in consumer prices in the capital city were greater than the average. Nonetheless, even correcting for such regional differences, it is clear that Ottoman price increases during the war were unprecedented for this part of the world. The annual inflation rate of 600 per cent for 1917 remained unmatched in Turkey for the rest of the twentieth century. Moreover, the overall increase in Ottoman prices was much higher than that experienced not only in western Europe but also in Austria-Hungary and Bulgaria during the war. Ottoman price increases are comparable with the inflation in Russia before the Revolution of 1917.

While consumer prices in the capital city increased more than twenty-fold until the end of the war, increases in wages and salaries lagged far behind. Even though detailed statistics are not easily available, it is clear that real wages and salaries declined, on the average, by at least 80 per cent, in many cases by even more from late 1914 until the end of the war. The decline in the purchasing power of salaries and wages paid by the state was greater than the decline in real wages paid by the private sector (Eldem, 1994: 55). Because of the acceleration in rates of inflation after 1916, most of the decline in real wages and salaries occurred during the last two years of the war (Eldem, 1994: 113).

It is very difficult to calculate the total financial cost of the war to the Ottoman government. Nonetheless, some calculations were made after the war during the period of Allied occupation. These studies have estimated the total cost of the war to the Ottoman government including debts incurred at 400 million current Ottoman liras. A similar estimate was provided in a postwar British study (Yalman, 1934: 144–51; Eldem, 1994: 83–117; Great Britain, Parliamentary Papers, Accounts and Papers, 1920). It is not easy to assess the reliability of these figures. Nonetheless, in the absence of better figures, we will use these estimates as the basis of a discussion of the Ottoman methods of war finance. These estimates suggest that cutting back civilian expenditure, and reducing state salaries, payment arrears, and borrowing abroad and domestically can explain how the Ottoman government met more than 50 and up to 60 per cent of the total financial cost of the war. The remaining 40 per cent was financed by printing inconvertible paper currency after 1915 in ever growing sums.

In the absence of annual series it is also not easy to calculate what percentage of the economy's resources the government was able to direct into the war effort. Nonetheless, the available figures suggest that the Ottoman government mobilised close to but still less than 10 per cent of the GDP of the empire during the four years of the war. In addition, the materials and loans obtained from Germany and Austria-Hungary for military purposes during this period amounted to a little over 1 per cent of the empire's GDP.

These rough estimates allow us to compare the total resources commanded by the government before and during the war. For the prewar period, the government's share in the GDP of the empire has been estimated at 12 per cent. Total resources commanded by the government as a percentage of GDP thus clearly increased during the war, perhaps to somewhere between 16 and 20 per cent. However, because of the considerable decline in the GDP during the war, which may have reached 40 per cent by 1918, the absolute increase in the real total of resources commanded by the government was quite limited.

The substantial decline in GDP and the rise of the government's share in GDP both point to a dramatic decline in private consumption during the war. The available evidence may not be sufficiently detailed for good estimates in this respect, but it would not be an exaggeration to suggest that aggregate private consumption in 1918 must have been 35 to

45 per cent lower in 1918 than prewar levels. In other words, the wartime decline in private consumption was not much greater than the decline in GDP. This is consistent with our earlier point that the government had only limited ability to squeeze private consumption and direct these resources to military purposes. Both the urban and the rural populations were in large part able to evade government demands. While the share of consumption in GDP may not have declined by much, there is no question that there occurred a sharp decline in both the level and the share in GDP of investment expenditure during the war.

The Ottoman case during World War I thus offers the example of an underdeveloped economy and a government with limited administrative capacity which were unable to function effectively under the extraordinary pressures created by war. The Ottoman economy was not prepared militarily or otherwise for a war of long duration. Production, both agricultural and industrial, declined substantially when faced with the pressures created by the war. The government was not able to increase substantially the resources it could direct towards the war effort. As the government's ability to collect taxes declined, reduced salaries and the printing of paper currency emerged as the most important forms of war finance. The government oscillated between coercion and markets as mechanisms for the mobilisation of resources during these four years. Both alternatives provided limited possibilities, however, because of the limitations of the underlying technology and production structure. Despite all these shortcomings, and the fact that they were forced to fight on many fronts, it is remarkable that the Ottoman war effort did not experience a total collapse. The Ottoman side managed to stay in the war and continue to hold its own on most fronts until the end in 1918.

The legacy of the war

To discuss the long-term consequences of the war in the Ottoman case, we need a wider focus than on these four years alone. From 1912 the Ottoman Empire and its principal successor state of Turkey were engaged in a series of wars that continued for a decade. The Balkan Wars of 1912–13 were followed by the World War and then the War of Independence from 1920 to 1922. Demographic changes were one important and long-lasting legacy of this decade. The population of the areas that were later included in Turkey was close to 17 million in 1913. Total casualties among Muslim Turks and Kurds during this decade, military and otherwise, are estimated at close to 2 million. Moreover, the Armenian population of Anatolia declined from close to 1.5 million to less than 100,000 as a result of the deportation of most Armenians to the Syrian desert by the Young Turk government in 1915. Many Armenians as well as Muslims were massacred during this process, even more died of hunger and disease, and the rest of the Armenians fled Anatolia. Finally, in the largest agreement of population exchange signed between two governments, approximately 1.2 million Greeks left Anatolia, and in return approximately half a million Muslims arrived from Greece and the Balkans after 1923. These figures include the large numbers of Greeks who left western Anatolia after the defeat of the Greek occupation army in 1922.

As a result of these massive changes, the population of Turkey stood at around 13 million at the end of 1924; of the decrease of about 20 per cent on a decade previously more than half had died and the rest had fled or emigrated. Ethnically speaking, the population of Turkey emerged as much more homogeneous than the Ottoman population in the same areas, with Muslim Turks and Kurds making up close to 98 per cent of the total. Most of the remaining minorities, Greeks, Armenians, and Jews, now lived in the Istanbul area. The dramatic decline in the Greek and Armenian populations had long-term economic as well as political, social, and cultural consequences. Many of the commercialised, export-oriented farmers of western Anatolia, as well as the artisans, leading merchants, and moneylenders, who linked the rural areas with the port cities and the European trading houses in the long century before the war, had gone. In addition, agriculture, industry, and mining were affected adversely by the deterioration and destruction of equipment, draught animals, and vegetation during this decade. The private sector of modern Turkey would be led by a Muslim bourgeoisie that had benefited from the wartime nationalist policies of the Young Turk government and had also acquired the land and other assets of the departing Greeks and Armenians. Nonetheless, their power remained limited and their strength was confined to small and medium-sized enterprises until the second half of the twentieth century (Owen and Pamuk, 1998: 10–12).

Another important and related legacy of this decade of wars was nationalism, and specifically economic nationalism, both of which were strongly supported by the international environment of the interwar period. The leaders of the new Turkish republic, military officers, bureaucrats, and intellectuals were strongly influenced by the wartime experience. They had strong political and social ties to the Young Turk movement that governed the Ottoman Empire until 1918. The new leadership viewed the building of a new nation state and modernisation through westernisation as two closely related goals. They embraced the nineteenth-century westernising reforms of the Ottomans and, under the determined leadership of Mustafa Kemal, were to carry them further in the interwar period.

Their economic goals followed directly from this outlook. From the outset they strove to create a national economy within the new borders. The construction of new railways and the nationalisation of existing companies were also seen as important steps towards the political and economic unification of the new state. Even more importantly, industrialisation and the creation of a Muslim Turkish bourgeoisie were viewed as the key ingredients of national economic development. The Kemalist leadership was also keenly aware that Ottoman financial and economic dependence on European powers had created serious political problems. The economic policies of the war years, devised in large part out of necessity, would provide the new leadership with an important precedent for departure from the open-economy model and interventionist and protectionist economic policies during the interwar period.

In economic affairs, the first challenge to the new regime occurred at the Lausanne Peace Conference (1922–3) which was to define, among other things, the international economic framework for the new state. After protracted negotiations, agreement was reached in three key areas representing the beginning of a new era in relations with the European powers. First, the regime of privilege for foreign holders of concessions was abolished, and this restored greater freedom of action to the Turkish authorities. This shift also paved the way for the gradual nationalisation of many foreign-owned enterprises, most notably the railways. Secondly, the Ottoman external debt was renegotiated and apportioned to all successor states. The Turkish government assumed 67 per cent of the total to be paid in gold sterling beginning in 1929. Thirdly, the free trade treaties, which had been renewed periodically during the nineteenth century, were discontinued. It was also agreed, however, that the existing structure of low tariff rates and restrictions on the use of quotas would continue until 1929 when the new republic would be free to pursue its own commercial policies.

Beginning in 1930, the economic policies of the Turkish government turned increasingly protectionist, and this sharply reduced the share of foreign trade in the economy. In 1932 the government explicitly adopted *étatisme*, or state-led industrialisation, as the basic strategy of economic development. The acceptance of *étatisme* without much resistance from the private sector was due partly to the wartime experience of state interventionism and perhaps more importantly to the destruction and expulsion of the non-Muslim bourgeoisie during and following the decade of wars. By the 1930s the Muslim-dominated private sector was too weak and too dependent on the state to oppose this important shift. *Etatisme* remained influential in Turkey after World War II right up to 1980. A strong case can thus be made here for path dependence – the importance of history and historical legacies in understanding long-term change. This model also influenced the thinking of many Arab governments after World War II, beginning with Nasser in Egypt in the 1950s.

Another important and interesting legacy of the war years, especially for the 1930s, was the long-lasting memory of wartime inflation. This traumatic experience, combined with the bitter and lingering memories of Ottoman external debt, convinced the leadership of the Turkish republic that it should avoid public borrowing and deficit finance during the interwar period, even during the Great Depression. As a result, the macroeconomic policy mix in Turkey during the 1930s was unusual compared with activist government initiatives in other developing countries in Latin America and Asia. Government interventionism in Turkey was not designed, in the Keynesian sense, to increase aggregate demand through devaluations and expansionary fiscal and monetary policies. The preference of the government was for balanced budgets and a strong currency. Instead of expansionary macroeconomic policies, the emphasis was placed on creating a more closed, autarkic economy through protectionism and increasing central control through the expansion of the public sector. Such preferences were, in turn, directly related to the bureaucratic nature of the regime. These cautious policies still led to reasonably strong economic performance in the 1930s because of the performance of urban import-substituting sectors and the recovery of agriculture (Pamuk, 2000b).

The experiences accumulated during the decade of wars from 1912 to 1922 thus contributed strongly to the rise of Turkish nationalism and shaped the inward-looking economic policies of the new nation state. Self-sufficiency and preparedness for another war remained leading priorities for its economic policies during the interwar period.

References

Ahmad, F. (1983), 'The Agrarian Policy of Young Turks, 1908–1918', in Jean-Louis Bacque-Grammont and Paul Dumont (eds.), *Economie et société dans l'Empire Ottoman*, Paris: CNRS, pp. 275–88.

(1988), 'War and Society under the Young Turks, 1908–18', *Review of the Fernand Braudel Center*, 9(2): 265–86.

Eldem, V. (1970), *Osmanli Imparatorlugu'nun Iktisadi Sartlari Hakkinda Bir Tetkik*, Istanbul: Is Bankasi Yayinlari.

(1994), *Harp ve Mütareke Yıllarında Osmanlı İmparatorluğu'nun Ekonomisi*, Ankara: Türk Tarih Kurumu.

Erickson, E. J. (2001), *Ordered to Die: A History of the Ottoman Empire in the First World War*, Westport, CT: Praeger.

(2003), *Defeat in Detail: The Ottoman Army in the Balkans, 1912–1913*, Westport, CT: Praeger.

Great Britain, Parliamentary Papers, Accounts and Papers (1920), *General Report on the Trade and Economic Conditions of Turkey for the year 1919.*

McCarthy, J. (2001), *The Ottoman Peoples and the End of Empire*, London: Arnold.

(2002), *Population History of the Middle East and the Balkans*, Istanbul: ISIS Press.

Maddison, A. (2003), *The World Economy: Historical Statistics*, Paris: OECD.

Milward, A. (1977), *War, Economy and Society, 1939–1945*, Berkeley, CA: University of California Press.

Ogün, T. (1999), *Kafkas Cephesinin I. Dunya Savasindaki Lojistik Destegi*, Ankara: Ataturk Arastirma Merkezi.

Okçün, G. (1983), *Tarimda Calisma ve Ekme Yukumlulugu, 1914–1922*, Ankara: University of Ankara Publications.

Owen, R. and Pamuk, Ş. (1998), *A History of the Middle East Economies in the Twentieth Century*, London: Tauris.

Pamuk, Ş. (1987), *The Ottoman Empire and European Capitalism, 1820–1913: Trade, Investment and Production*, Cambridge and New York: Cambridge University Press.

(2000a), *A Monetary History of the Ottoman Empire*, Cambridge and New York: Cambridge University Press.

(2000b), 'Intervention during the Great Depression, Another Look at Turkish Experience,' in Şevket Pamuk and Jeffrey Williamson (eds.), *The Mediterranean Response to Globalization before 1850*, London and New York: Routledge, pp. 321–39.

(2001), 'Modern Economic Growth in Southeastern Europe and the Middle East, 1850–2000,' paper presented at the Fifth Congress of the European Historical Economics Society, Oxford.

Prest, A. R. (1948), *War Economics of Primary Producing Countries*, Cambridge: Cambridge University Press.

Schatkowski Schilcher, L. (1992), 'The Famine of 1915–18 in Greater Syria', in John P. Spagnola (ed.), *Problems of the Modern Middle East in Historical Perspective: Essays in Honor of Albert Hourani*, Reading, UK: Ithaca Press, pp. 229–58.

Scott, J. C. (1984), *Weapons of the Weak: Everyday Forms of Resistance*, New Haven, CT: Yale University Press.

Sen, A. (1981), *Poverty and Famines*, Oxford: Oxford University Press.

Swanson, G. W. (1975), 'War, Technology and Society in the Ottoman Empire from the Reign of Abdulhamid II to 1913', in V. J. Parry and M. E. Yapp (eds.), *War, Technology and Society in the Middle East*, Oxford: Oxford University Press, pp. 367–85.

Tekeli, I. and Ilkin, S. (2004), 'Osmanli Imparatorlugu'nun Birinci Dunya Savasindaki Ekonomik Duzenlemeleri icinde Iase Nezareti ve Kara Kemal Beyin Yeri', in I. Tekeli and S. Ilkin, *Cumhuriyetin Harci, Cilt 2: Koktenci Modernitenin Ekonomik Politikasinin Gelisimi*, Istanbul: Bilgi Universitesi Yayinlari, pp. 1–44.

Tilly, L. (1983), 'Food Entitlement, Famine and Conflict', in Robert I. Rotberg and Theodore K. Rabb (eds.), *Hunger and History*, Cambridge and New York: Cambridge University Press, pp. 35–151.

Toprak, Z. (1982), *Türkiye'de Milli İktisat 1908–18*, Ankara: Yurt Yayinlari.
(2003), *Ittihad-Terakki ve Cihan Harbi, Savaş Ekonomisi ve Türkiye'de Devletçilik, 1914–1918*, Istanbul: Homer Kitapevi.
Trumpener, U. (1968), *Germany and the Ottoman Empire, 1914–1918*, Princeton, NJ: Princeton University Press, 1968.
Yalman, A. E. (1934), *Turkey in the World War*, New Haven, CT: Yale University Press.
Zürcher, E. J. (1996), 'Between Death and Desertion: The Experience of the Ottoman Soldier with World War I', *Turcica* 28: 235–58.

XIV

Real Wages and Standards of Living in the Ottoman Empire, 1489–1914

SÜLEYMAN ÖZMUCUR AND ŞEVKET PAMUK

Utilizing a large volume of archival documents, this study establishes for the first time the long-term trends in real wages of skilled and unskilled construction workers in Istanbul and other Ottoman cities in southeastern Europe and the Middle East, from the second half of the fifteenth century until World War I. A detailed consumer price index and nominal wage indices are constructed for the city of Istanbul for this purpose. These price and wage series are then inserted into a larger framework of price and wage trends in European cities during the same period.

During the last two decades economists and economic historians have devoted much effort to estimating the per capita real product of different countries, and to analyzing trends in the gap between "leaders" and "followers."[1] We know that the gap is large today, and we can infer from the growth record of both groups of countries that it was smaller—or did not exist at all—prior to the onset of modern economic growth. Recent research by Angus Maddison and others has confirmed the existence of a gap as of 1820. We have also learned that the gap between developed and developing countries as a whole widened not only in the era of the Industrial Revolution from 1820 to 1914, but also from 1914 to 1950.[2] There is little information, however, about the period before 1820. How large was this gap in 1750, in 1600, or in 1500? These inquiries inevitably give rise to questions about the prevailing trends in per capita incomes, productivity, and institutions during the early modern era, not only in Western Europe but also in today's developing regions.

This research project was supported by the State Institute of Statistics of Turkey, the Academy of Sciences of Turkey, and the Bogaziçi University Research Fund through Projects 99HZ02 and 01Z101. In addition to these institutions, the authors would like to thank Figen Taşkın, Nadir Özbek, and Bağış Erten for valuable research assistance. Thanks are also due to Robert Allen for sharing his data and insights. Earlier versions of this article were presented at the London School of Economics and at the Third Conference of the European Historical Economics Society held in Lisbon, October 1999. The authors are pleased to acknowledge the helpful comments made by the participants of those meetings, especially those by Jeffrey Williamson and Jan Luiten van Zanden. They would also like to thank Jan de Vries and two anonymous referees for valuable comments and suggestions.

[1] Abramowitz, "Catching Up"; Barro, *Determinants*; and Maddison, *World Economy*. See also Hanson, "Third World Incomes"; and Crafts, "Gross National Product."

[2] Maddison, "Comparison" and *World Economy*.

With the possible exception of a handful of countries, estimates of per capita GDP for the period before 1820 are difficult to construct and unreliable. Moreover, it has not been possible to construct detailed estimates for any of the developing countries for any period before 1870. An alternative approach for studying the gap in levels of per capita income or standards of living has been to compare real wages in specific occupations, most often in skilled and unskilled construction work in urban areas. Real wage data are of far better quality than per capita GDP estimates especially for the period before World War I, and they are available for a wider range of countries. In fact, real wage series are virtually the only solid information we have on standards of living in the developing countries for the period before 1870, if not 1914. In short, real wages continue to be the most reliable source of information about living standards before the very recent past.

Although they cannot be described as "national" in any sense, urban real wage series exist for many regions, and large interregional differences within the same country are not apparent in these series. Nonetheless, real wage series are open to valid objections. Even if we accept the representative wage as an adequate proxy for the per capita *earnings* of labor, this does not make it a good proxy for per capita *income*, which includes the returns to capital and land; longitudinal and comparative studies are further complicated by the fact that factor shares have varied greatly over time and across societies. Moreover, households incomes were often determined by changes in employment levels, and in the participation rates of men, women, and children, and, above all, by nonmarket incomes.

Despite these qualifications, the historical link between wages and the standard of living remains. A decline in real wages did result in a decline in household welfare, because each unit of labor commanded fewer consumption goods—or, alternatively, because more labor had to be supplied to command the accustomed basket of goods. Either way, the household suffered by sacrificing consumption, nonmarket income, leisure, or some combination of the three.[3]

A large part of our knowledge about long-term trends in real wages during the late medieval and early modern periods goes back to the vast research effort undertaken by members of the International Scientific Committee on Price History (ISCPH), established in 1929. Most studies to date, including those of the ISCPH, have focused on western and central Europe.[4] Arguably, the most influential project in this respect has been that of E. H. Phelps Brown and Sheila Hopkins, who constructed price and wage series for southern England over seven centuries beginning in 1264. The Phelps Brown–Hopkins findings were notable for their pessimism. They confirmed

[3] Van Zanden, "Wages"; and de Vries, "Between Purchasing Power."

[4] Amongst the classic studies were those by Beveridge ("Wages"), Hamilton (*American Treasure*), and Phelps Brown and Hopkins ("Seven Centuries" and *Perspective*). For an overview of the main results, see Allen, "Great Divergence."

long-term fluctuations, but did not reveal any secular improvement in urban real wages from the fifteenth to the mid-nineteenth century.[5] In recent decades, however, evidence has been accumulating that productivity, standards of living, and per capita GDP were rising in many parts of western Europe before the Industrial Revolution.[6] For this reason, researchers in recent years have been reviewing the old series and constructing new ones in order to reassess the history of real wages. They have also been debating how well the real wage of urban construction workers can serve as a proxy for the living standard of the population at large, and whether more representative indices can be constructed with the available data. Changes in occupational structure and income distribution may have been two important and related reasons behind the divergence of GDP per capita and real wages in western Europe. In other words, it is possible that the wages of construction workers declined relative to other incomes during this period. In addition, households may have increased their labor supply during this period.[7]

In contrast to our advancing state of understanding of Western Europe, only a few real wage series have been constructed to date for cities on the European periphery and in other continents. The Ottoman Empire stood at the crossroads of intercontinental trade, stretching from the Balkans and the Black Sea through Anatolia, Syria, Mesopotamia, the Gulf, Egypt, and most of North Africa from the early sixteenth century up to World War I. At its peak in the seventeenth and eighteenth centuries, its population exceeded 30 million. One might have expected that the economic institutions that sustained this large, multiethnic entity for so long would be of interest to economic historians. Unfortunately, mainstream economic historians have long neglected the land regime, manufactures, economic policies, and the daily existence of ordinary men and women. As a result, the longevity of the Ottoman Empire remains an anomaly and even a mystery for many.

For most of its six-century existence, the Ottoman Empire is best characterized as a bureaucratic, agrarian empire. Its economic institutions and policies were shaped to a large degree by the priorities and interests of a central bureaucracy. Recent literature has emphasized that the Ottoman empire did not simply and irreversibly decline after the sixteenth century. On the contrary, the Ottoman state and society showed considerable ability to adapt to changing circumstances in Eurasia from the seventeenth through the nineteenth centuries. The central bureaucracy managed to contain the many challenges it faced with pragmatism, flexibility, and a tradition of negotiation to co-opt and incorporate into the state the social groups that rebelled against it. The Ottoman state also showed considerable flexibility

[5] Phelps Brown and Hopkins, "Seven Centuries" and *Perspective*.

[6] Maddison, *World Economy*; Persson, *Pre-Industrial Economic Growth*; and de Vries and van der Woude, *First Modern Economy*.

[7] Van Zanden, "Great Convergence," p. 12; and de Vries, "Industrious Revolution."

not only in military technology, but also in its fiscal, financial, and monetary institutions. Despite wars and internal conflict from the 1770s through the 1830s, the Ottomans managed to regroup and survive into the modern era with a strong central state and many of their central institutions intact, while many of their contemporaries in both Europe and Asia collapsed.

Even before the nineteenth century, the Ottoman economy was well linked to Europe via trade across the Mediterranean and the Balkans. Thanks to research in recent decades, we now have a reasonably good picture of the long-term trends in economic activity in the Ottoman Empire. Most economic historians agree that the sixteenth century was a period of demographic and economic expansion, at least in the core regions of the empire. In contrast, the seventeenth century has been characterized as a period of "crisis and partial recovery" when population and economic activity stagnated (or worse) in many parts of the empire. Contrary to earlier assumptions, it has been shown that the eighteenth century was a period of relative peace, stability, and economic expansion that came to an end with the decades of war, fiscal difficulty, and inflation after 1770. Between 1850 and 1914, the overall trend was once again towards limited increases in average incomes. Despite the accumulation of valuable evidence for different time periods, we are still unable to compare levels of per capita income in 1914 with those in 1750 (or 1600 or 1500), for different regions of the Ottoman Empire or for the empire as a whole.[8]

Utilizing a large volume of archival documents, this study will establish the long-term trends in wages of skilled and unskilled construction workers in Istanbul and other Ottoman cities (including Belgrade, Salonika, Edirne, Bursa, Damascus, and Jerusalem) from the late fifteenth century up to World War I. These trends will offer important insights into the long-term performance of the Ottoman economy. The price and wage series will then be inserted into a larger framework of price and wage trends in European cities during the same period. This comparison will provide new and important evidence regarding standards of living and growth in the early modern era. It will also shed light on the origins and evolution of a gap in real wages between developed and developing countries.

PRICES

Sources and Methods

We begin with a summary presentation of the results of a study of prices in Istanbul and other leading cities of the Ottoman Empire from the fifteenth to the twentieth centuries. Additional details about the indices are presented in Appen-

[8] Inalcik and Quataert, *Economic and Social History*; for a recent overview see Pamuk, *Monetary History*, pp. 228–29.

dix 1. Our study utilized data on the prices of standard commodities (food and nonfood items) collected from more than 6,000 account books and price lists located in the Ottoman archives in Istanbul. The first step was to construct three separate food-price indices. One of these was based on the account books and prices paid by the many pious foundations (*vakıf*), both large and small, and their soup kitchens (*imaret*); another index was based on the account books of the Topkapı Palace kitchen; a third utilized the officially established price ceilings (*narh*) for the basic items of consumption in the capital city.[9]

To the extent possible, standard commodities were used in constructing the indices in order to minimize the effects of quality changes. The food indices included the prices of ten leading items of consumption: flour (mostly wheaten), rice, honey, cooking oil, mutton, chickpeas, lentils, onions, eggs, and fuel-grade olive oil. Among these, flour, rice, cooking oil, mutton, olive oil, and honey provided the most reliable long-term series and carried the highest weights in our food budget. In cases where the prices of one or more of these items were not available for a given year, missing values were estimated by an algorithm that applied regression techniques to the available values.

The medium- and long-term trends exhibited by the three food-price indices are quite similar. In addition, account books showing the private purchases by the households of high-ranking bureaucrats also point to similar long-term trends in food prices at the retail level.[10] The fact that *narh* prices closely approximated prices paid by the palace, pious foundations, and private individuals suggests that government intervention did not alter prices, especially in the medium and long term. It also points to a high degree of government pragmatism in economic affairs. Historians have long argued that the permanent application and enforcement of *narh* in urban areas was a typical example of Ottoman interventionism and rigidity in defense of a traditional order. There is, however, a good deal of evidence that the Ottomans became increasingly conscious, after 1600, of the limitations of interventionism in economic affairs. They learned that price ceilings

[9] Most of the account books of the pious foundations used in this study are available from the Maliyeden Müdevver (MM), Bab-ı Defteri, Başmuhasebe Kalemi (BŞM), Evkaf Defterleri (EV), and Evkaf Nezareti, Haremeyn Muhasebeciliği (EV.HMH) Collections at the Prime Ministry Ottoman Archives (Başbakanlık Osmanlı Arşivleri [BOA]) in Istanbul. The account books of the Topkapı Palace kitchen are available from the Bab-ı Defteri, Matbah Emini (D.BŞM.MTE), Bab-ı Defteri, Başmuhasebe Kalemi (D.BŞM) Maliyeden Müdevver (MM), Kamil Kepeci (KK), Cevdet Saray (CS), Maliye Nezareti, Mesarifat Muhasebesi (ML.MSF), Bab-ı Defteri, Odun Emini (D.BŞM.ODE) and Bab-ı Defteri, İstanbul Ağası (D.BŞM.ISA) Collections also at the BOA, and the Dosya (D) Collection at the Topkapı Palace Archives. The *narh* lists were approved by the local judges (*kadi*) and were taken from the Istanbul, Üsküdar and Galata Islamic court archives in Istanbul. A complete list of all archival documents used in this study is presented on year-to-year basis in the appendices of Pamuk, *Istanbul*.

[10] Annual values of these four food-price indices are not provided here due to limitations of space. For further details see Pamuk, *Istanbul*, figures 2.2 and 2.3.

that diverged substantially from the underlying market realities could not be enforced over long periods of time. For this reason, interventionism became increasingly selective. It was used primarily for the provisioning of the capital city and the army, and for selected commodities. Perhaps more importantly, after 1650 the *narh* came to be considered not as permanent policy but an instrument reserved for extraordinary conditions such as wars, exceptional difficulties in the provisioning of the capital city, or periods of monetary instability. With increasing fiscal and monetary difficulties and growing price instability, the price ceilings once again became a regular feature of Ottoman urban life from 1789 to 1850.[11] Because the palace and *narh* prices might be considered official or state-controlled prices, this study gives greater weight to the prices paid by the soup kitchens and the pious foundations. The *narh* prices and the retail prices paid by the households of high-level bureaucrats were not included in the final index.

Since the availability and quality of price observations varied over time for most of the foodstuffs in our list, the period 1460–1860 was divided into five subperiods and indices were calculated separately for each. In each subperiod some commodities had to be excluded from the index due to the unavailability of price observations.

Based on the available evidence regarding the budget of an average urban consumer, the weighting of food items in the overall indices was fixed between 75 and 80 percent. The weighting of each commodity in the overall index was then based on the shares of each in total expenditures of the respective institutions. To cite two prominent examples, the weighting of flour varied generally between 32 and 40 percent of food expenditures and 24 to 32 percent of overall expenditures, depending on the fluctuations in prices. Similarly, the weight of mutton varied between 5 and 8 percent of the overall budget. Diets of private households in the capital city probably differed from those offered by the soup kitchens. At this stage, however, it is not possible to approximate the private diets more closely.

The following commodity basket was used most frequently in the food price index:

11 *kile* of flour (288.6 kg)
4 *kile* of rice (51.2 kg)
9 *okka* of animal-based cooking oil (11.5 kg)
13 *okka* of honey (16.6 kg)
40 *okka* of mutton (51.2 kg)
0.2 *kile* of chickpeas (2.56 kg)
5 *okka* of olive oil (6.4 kg).

[11] Pamuk, *Monetary History*, pp. 9–19.

One important reason why the weightings of the individual commodities was kept constant over time was the unavailability of consumer budgets for different points in time. It is likely, however, that changes in the commodity composition of the consumer budget were small, in part because increases in average incomes were limited during these centuries. On the other hand, some substitution must have occurred over time, away from commodities whose prices rose faster towards those whose prices declined in relative terms. It is thus reasonable to expect that our fixed-weights index overstates the long-term price increases somewhat, as will be further discussed below.

In the second step, various nonfood prices (of soap, wood, coal, and nails) obtained from a variety of sources, most importantly the palace account books, were added to the price indices. From the various account books of the imperial palace it was possible to obtain long-term price series on two types of woolen cloth: the locally produced *çuha*, and the *çuha Londrine* imported from England. However, because the woolen cloth described in palace sources belonged to more expensive varieties, cloth prices were not included in the overall index until 1860.[12] Price data for many other types of cloth have also been collected, but none of these are available for long periods of time. A cost-of-living index should also include the rental cost of housing, but an adequate series for standard housing is not available.

It is well known that premodern prices exhibited wide short-term fluctuations due to harvest conditions, difficulties in transportation, wars, and other causes. In the case of our indices, however, a number of factors worked to reduce such fluctuations. First, the capital city was subject to a higher degree of government involvement in price formation. Secondly, it is likely that soup kitchens and the imperial palace were subject to a lesser degree of price variation than were private households. Thirdly, in processing price observations from archival documents we excluded prices more than 100 percent higher or more than 50 percent lower than the value of the previous year, unless the new price level was observed again in later years. Although most of the excluded observations reflected errors in the original document, some of them must have represented actual prices. As a result we do not have a high degree of confidence in the year-to-year fluctuations of our indices, but we are quite confident about the level of prices in the medium and longer term.

For the period 1860–1914, data from the palace, *vakıf*, and *narh* sources are very limited. For this reason we used the detailed quarterly wholesale prices of the Commodity Exchange of Istanbul, covering about two dozen commodities, and a separate series for imported cotton textiles. Indices based on these prices were then linked to those for the earlier period, with

[12] We compared the woolen cloth prices paid by the palace with the prices of more ordinary varieties worn by the janissaries, as given in Sahillioğlu, "Yeniçeri Çuhasi."

the help of detailed data for both retail prices of individual commodities and prices at the Commodity Exchange for 1860–1862 and 1913–1914.

Results

We have thus obtained, for the first time for southeastern Europe and the Near East, detailed and reliable price series for these four-and-a-half centuries (Table 1). The indices show that consumer prices in Istanbul increased by a total of about 300-fold from 1469 until World War I. This overall increase corresponds to an average increase of 1.3 percent per year, endpoint-to-endpoint, and 1.1 percent per year for the fitted line. They also indicate that Istanbul experienced a significant wave of inflation from the early sixteenth to the late seventeenth century, when prices increased sevenfold. This is the period usually associated with the Price Revolution. The indices also show, however, that there occurred a much stronger wave of inflation beginning in the 1770s and lasting into the 1860s, when prices rose as much as 25-fold. Most of the latter increases were associated with the debasements that began in the 1780s and accelerated during the reign of the reformist sultan Mahmud II (1808–1839). In contrast, prices were relatively stable from the 1690s to the 1760s, and from the 1860s to 1914. (For a period-by-period review of the price trends, see Appendix 1.)

Obviously there were many causes of inflation during the early modern period, as evidenced by the large literature and the extensive debates on the subject. From the *long-term* perspective offered by these price indices and by Şevket Pamuk's recent study of the Ottoman currency, however, it is clear that debasements or the reduction of the silver content of the unit of account by the monetary authorities were the most important cause of Ottoman price increases.[13] In fact, even though nominal prices increased about 300-fold over these four-and-a half centuries, prices expressed in grams of silver rose less than threefold (Table 1). There were medium-term movements in the latter series: it increased from 1500 until 1640 during the period of the Price Revolution, declined until the early decades of the eighteenth century, and increased again until the middle of the nineteenth century. These fluctuations occurred, however, around a secular trend that was rising only modestly. The so-called silver inflation thus contributed to the changes in the overall price level, but its impact paled in relation to that of debasements.

Istanbul was chosen primarily because price data are most detailed for the capital city.[14] However, price data from the account books of pious foundations

[13] Pamuk, *Monetary History*.

[14] Detailed indices on the prices of basic foodstuffs expressed in grams of silver, and the terms of trade between foodstuffs and manufactured goods, have also been calculated from the Istanbul data (Pamuk, *Istanbul*, ch. 2).

TABLE 1
PRICES AND WAGES IN ISTANBUL, 1469–1911
(decennial averages)

	Consumer Price Index (1469 = 1.0)		Nominal Daily Wages				Real Daily Wages (1489/90 = 1.0)	
			Unskilled Worker		Skilled Worker			
Period	In *Akçe*	In Silver[a]	In *Akçe*	In Silver[a]	In *Akçe*	In Silver[a]	Unskilled	Skilled
1469–1479	1.20	1.17	n.a.	n.a.	n.a.	n.a.	n.a.	n.a.
1480–1489	1.30	1.02	4.9	3.3	9.8	6.6	0.93	1.04
1490–1499	1.09	0.85	4.7	3.1	7.7	5.2	1.06	0.96
1540–1549	1.60	1.00	5.3	3.5	9.6	6.3	0.86	0.92
1550–1559	1.64	1.25	5.0	3.3	9.7	6.4	0.78	0.86
1560–1569	1.86	1.32	5.9	3.8	9.3	6.0	0.83	0.73
1570–1579	1.99	1.41	5.6	3.4	9.9	6.0	0.68	0.66
1580–1589	3.35	1.47	8.1	3.5	12.4	5.4	0.65	0.53
1590–1599	4.45	1.46	11.7	2.6	20.7	4.6	0.51	0.50
1600–1609	5.43	1.81	13.9	4.0	22.5	6.5	0.62	0.56
1610–1619	4.44	1.47	14.2	4.1	22.8	6.6	0.76	0.67
1620–1629	5.56	1.54	15.0	3.4	18.3	4.1	0.84	0.57
1640–1649	4.37	1.34	15.2	4.2	29.5	8.2	0.79	0.84
1660–1669	5.82	1.56	19.5	4.4	29.9	6.8	0.81	0.69
1670–1679	7.06	1.69	18.0	3.7	23.0	4.8	0.71	0.50
1680–1689	7.46	1.79	21.8	4.5	33.4	6.9	0.73	0.62
1690–1699	7.96	1.21	26.2	3.4	36.9	4.8	0.78	0.61
1700–1709	6.05	0.92	23.8	3.1	38.0	5.0	1.02	0.90
1710–1719	6.87	1.03	25.2	3.3	38.2	5.0	0.92	0.77
1720–1729	6.98	1.06	26.4	3.5	42.3	5.6	0.97	0.85
1730–1739	7.62	1.10	30.6	3.8	44.8	5.6	0.94	0.76
1740–1749	9.93	1.39	32.5	3.9	51.1	6.2	0.91	0.79
1750–1759	10.1	1.30	32.4	3.6	58.6	6.6	0.76	0.75
1760–1769	11.1	1.23	30.3	2.9	50.8	4.8	0.70	0.64
1770–1779	17.8	1.93	38.7	3.6	71.2	6.7	0.52	0.51
1780–1789	17.2	1.58	56.9	4.7	113.4	9.4	0.86	0.94
1790–1799	24.5	1.50	80.2	4.1	148.4	7.7	0.84	0.84
1800–1809	34.7	1.91	114.4	5.3	217.7	10.0	0.84	0.88
1810–1819	49.5	1.86	202.6	6.9	401.2	13.7	0.95	1.04
1820–1829	62.8	1.26	275.9	5.0	475.4	8.9	1.13	1.10
1830–1839	130.1	1.12	608.8	4.5	1,054	7.8	1.11	1.05
1840–1849	181.0	1.70	717.2	5.9	1,238	10.1	0.99	0.95
1850–1859	240.5	2.32	935.3	7.8	1,599	13.3	1.38	1.30
1860–1869	285.7	2.76	964.7	8.0	1,716	14.3	0.81	0.80
1870–1879	265.6	2.56	941.4	7.8	1,989	16.6	0.86	0.99
1880–1889	238.1	2.30	944.0	7.9	2,061	17.2	0.91	1.04
1890–1899	235.6	2.27	1,063	8.9	2,308	19.2	1.12	1.35
1900–1909	220.9	2.13	993.5	8.3	2,150	17.9	1.10	1.31
1910–1914	294.2	2.84	1,861	12.6	3,450	26.6	1.30	1.51

[a] Grams.
Sources: See the text.

(similarly obtained from the account books of pious foundations in the Ottoman archives in Istanbul) are available for other cities of the empire as well. Observations for a shorter list of commodities were used to construct separate series for the cities of Edirne, Bursa, Konya, Trabzon, Damascus, and Jerusalem. In these cities, both the overall change in the price level from 1490 to 1860 and the two major jumps in the price level that occurred in the late sixteenth and early nineteenth centuries were comparable to the price trends in Istanbul.[15] Price data gathered by Ljuben Berov indicate that the Balkans experienced similar increases in prices during the sixteenth and seventeenth centuries.[16] The evidence thus points to similar price trends for the *akçe* zone as a whole, stretching from the Balkans through Anatolia to Syria. In Egypt the local currency was the *para* or *medin*, whose silver content and rate of debasement differed from those of the *akçe*. Nonetheless, it is possible to construct real price indices for Cairo on the basis of data supplied by Andre Raymond from the court records of that city.[17] These indices indicate that Cairene prices (expressed in grams of silver) moved in line with prices in the *akçe* region from 1624 to 1800, the period for which comparable data is available.[18] The well-developed maritime transportation and commerce networks around the eastern Mediterranean must have ensured the broad convergence of the price levels and trends in different Ottoman cities.

Alternative Specifications

As pointed out earlier, some commodities were excluded from our index because of the unavailability or poor quality of data. It would be useful to see how sensitive our long-term results are to the insertion of these commodities into our consumer price index. Cloth prices were excluded from the index for the period before 1860 due to their poor quality. Nonetheless, since long-term trends in the available Istanbul cloth price series broadly paralleled those in western Europe, these latter can be added to the index.[19] Prices of woolen cloth decreased by about 80 percent relative to our overall consumer price index from 1700 to 1860. The inclusion of cloth prices thus decreases the overall index by a total of 5 percent between these two dates.

Another relatively important item excluded from our index is rents on residential housing. In view of this item's importance in urban consumer budgets, some allowance can perhaps be made for this item by studying

[15] For details see Pamuk, *Istanbul*, figure 3.1 and appendix tables 5.1–5.6.

[16] Berov, *Prices in the Balkans*; a summary is available in Berov, "Changes."

[17] Pamuk, *Istanbul*, appendix table 5.7; Raymond, *Artisans et Commerçants*, pp. 17–80; for these calculations the silver content of the *para* of Cairo is taken from Pamuk, *Monetary History*, pp. 95–101, 172–78.

[18] Pamuk, *Istanbul*, figure 3.2.

[19] As a measure of cloth prices in western Europe in the early modern era, we have used here the textile price index for Netherlands constructed by Jan Luiten van Zanden. This index is available in both nominal and silver terms from the International Institute of Social History website, www.iisg.nl/hwp/.

long-term trends in rental prices of residential housing elsewhere in European cities for which data are available. In view of Istanbul's growth as an urban center, one should expect rents on residential housing to have risen over time. Taking into account patterns in housing ownership, we assumed as a first approximation that rent payments on urban housing doubled in relation to the overall index, and that the share of rents in the average urban budget rose from about 5 percent to about 10 percent, between the sixteenth and early twentieth centuries. The inclusion of rents in our index under such an assumption would increase the overall index by 5 percent, thereby offsetting the inclusion of cloth prices. In the absence of any meaningful time series data on rents, it is difficult to be more specific on this issue.

Finally, we consider the inclusion of sugar and coffee in our price index. Istanbul sugar prices declined by about 50 percent relative to the overall index during the sixteenth century, and by an additional 50 percent during the period 1820–1860. The available price series for coffee in Istanbul tracked the overall index until the nineteenth century, but declined by about 60 percent relative to the index during the period 1820–1860.[20] Since the share of these two items in the average consumer budget was limited until 1860, however, our overall results would not change significantly. We estimate that the inclusion of these two items in the consumer budget would reduce the terminal value of the index in 1914 by no more than 1 percent.[21]

Relative Costs of Living

Thus the cumulative impact of including cloth, sugar, coffee, and rents in the consumer budget would be quite small. The impact would be much greater on the relative costs of living of lower- and higher-income consumers, however. Since cloth, sugar, and coffee had larger shares in the budgets of higher-income consumers, the decline in their prices reduced their cost of living in particular. On the other hand, the inclusion of rent payments would tend to raise the costs of living of lower-income groups more than those faced by higher income groups, since the latter were likelier to own their dwellings. We thus estimate that the inclusion of these four items would shift relative prices in favor of higher-income consumers. With respect to the two groups whose incomes will be examined in the next section, for example, we expect that the expanded price index would widen the

[20] Before the eighteenth century, sugar and coffee were brought to Istanbul from Egypt. It was the arrival of imports from Atlantic sources that led to the sharp decline in the prices of both commodities during the nineteenth century.

[21] For the period 1860–1914 our index includes prices of imported cotton cloth, sugar, and coffee. All price observations used in this study, as well as the indices constructed with them, are presented in Pamuk, *Istanbul*.

difference between the purchasing power of skilled and unskilled workers by about 10 percent for the entire period.

One important and related characteristic of the Istanbul price series is the important divergence in relative prices over the course of these four-and-a-half centuries. Prices of some foodstuffs (meat, flour, milk, eggs) rose 400- to 600-fold in nominal terms (and four- to sixfold in silver terms) during this period, while prices of other foodstuffs (olive oil, honey, coffee, onions) and all manufactured items for which price series are available rose less than 200-fold. Since the commodities with higher rates of price increases were essentials, they had a higher share in the budgets of lower-income consumers. Even after allowing for some substitution away from commodities with more rapid price increases, we estimate that as a result of these relative price movements the overall rate of inflation faced by lower-income consumers was higher, and the overall inflation faced by higher-income consumers was lower, than the averages provided by our index. If we had adopted separate consumer budgets for skilled and unskilled workers, for example, these movements in relative prices would have led, roughly, to cumulative price increases that were 5 percent higher for unskilled workers and 5 percent lower for skilled workers.

When we combine these different effects, we arrive at a cumulative difference of about 20 percent between the prices faced by skilled and unskilled workers during these four-and-a-half centuries. In other words, we estimate that the overall rate of inflation faced by unskilled workers was 10 percent higher, and by skilled workers 10 percent lower, than the averages reported in our consumer price index in Table 1.[22]

WAGES

For the second part of this study, daily wage data were gathered from more than 5,000 account books for construction and repair projects in Istanbul and other cities. These account books contain daily wages for both unskilled and a variety of skilled construction workers. Urban construction work was a relatively homogeneous category of labor over time and space. Moreover, in contrast to the payments made to other employees, urban construction workers received much of their pay in cash rather than in shelter, food, and clothing. As a result, their wages permit comparisons with other preindustrial societies.

The construction account books prepared by the state or by pious foundations usually consisted of a series of attendance records listing the work-

[22] A recent study of prices and inequality in Europe since 1500 (Hoffman et al., "Real Inequality") similarly argues that relative price movements favored higher-income groups and increased income inequality in Western Europe from 1500 to 1800.

man's name, his craft, his rank (master, common laborer, etc.) and his wages. Sometimes the accounts provide a separate record for each day; sometimes several days or weeks are covered by a single attendance sheet.[23] Information about the length of the workday is rare in these records, as is information on the provision of meals. For that reason, we have chosen to ignore those aspects of the daily wage. We have also decided to ignore the seasonal variations in daily wages. In any case, the overwhelming majority of the available observations belong to the construction season (April through October in Istanbul).

The wages for unskilled workers referred mostly to one type of worker, called *ırgad* in the early period and *rençber* after about 1700. In contrast, the account books reveal daily wage rates for more than a half-dozen categories of skilled construction workers. In order to utilize additional information, an index was constructed including the wages of carpenters, cabinetmakers, masons, stonecutters, ditch-diggers, plasterers, and others. Based on its predominance in the account books, the share of carpenters (*neccar*) in the index fluctuated between 50 and 60 percent.

Figure 1 and Table 1 present real daily wage series for skilled and unskilled construction workers in Istanbul, obtained by deflating the nominal daily wage series by the consumer price index. It is not easy to judge to what extent daily wages were influenced by institutional factors, and to what extent by market forces. However, the fact that during periods of rapid debasement real wages initially declined, but soon were adjusted upwards, suggests that the process of wage formation was open to market forces.

Our indices indicate that real wages of unskilled construction workers declined by 30 to 40 percent during the sixteenth century. They then remained roughly unchanged until the mid-eighteenth century, after which they increased by about 30 percent up to the mid-nineteenth century, and then by another 40 percent during the late nineteenth and early twentieth centuries. On the eve of World War I, real wages of unskilled construction workers were about 20 percent above their levels in 1500. But because relative prices had shifted in favor of goods consumed by higher-income consumers during these centuries, and because the skill premium had begun to rise late in the nineteenth century, by 1914 the real wages of skilled workers stood at more than 50 percent above their levels in 1500.

[23] Most of the account books of the pious foundations and the state used in this study are available from the Maliyeden Müdevver (MM), Evkaf Nezareti, Haremeyn Muhasebeciliği (EV.HMH), Evkaf Defterleri (EV), Bab-ı Defteri, Başmuhasebe Kalemi (D.BŞM), Bab-ı Defteri, Bina Emini (D.BŞM.BNE) and Maliye Nezareti, and Mesarifat Muhasebesi (ML.MSF) collections in the BOA archives in Istanbul. Pamuk (*Istanbul*, appendices 7–10) provides a full list of the archival sources on an annual basis, as well as the nominal daily wages for each wage category in the form of annual averages for Istanbul and other cities. Many of the account books also included lists and prices of materials purchased, such as iron, lime, and nails, the last of which was utilized in the construction of the price indices.

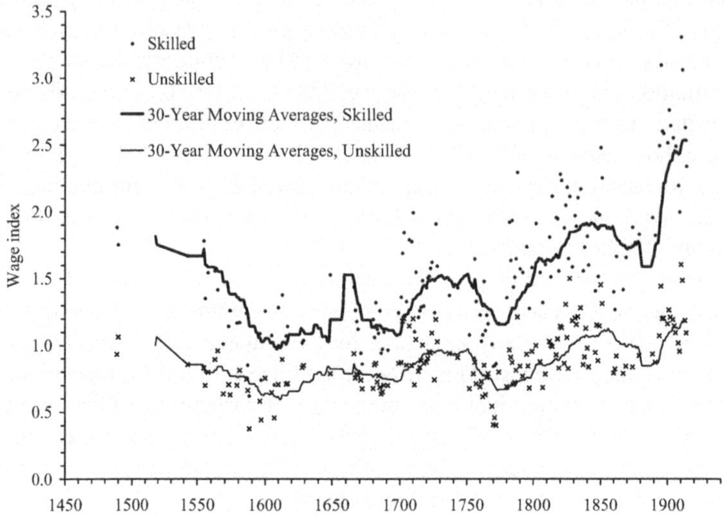

FIGURE 1
REAL DAILY WAGE OF CONSTRUCTION WORKERS: ISTANBUL, 1489–1914
(1489/90 [unskilled] = 1.0)

Sources: See the text.

When we take into account the differential impact of the items excluded from our price indices, as well as the differential impact of the more rapid rise in the prices of essentials, we must adjust the cumulative costs-of-living increases of skilled and unskilled workers by a further –10 and +10 percent, respectively. (See Appendix 1 for a period-by-period analysis of the trends in real wages.) These adjustments to the series in Figure 1 and Table 1 give a better view of trends in the wage premium for skilled labor. After declining during the sixteenth and seventeenth centuries, the wage differential began to increase in the second half of the eighteenth century, reaching its peak on the eve of World War I. Not only changing demand but also decline in supply (due to the emigration of skilled construction artisans) must have contributed to this trend.

The purchasing power of the daily wages of both classes of worker were reasonably high during these four-and-a-half centuries. During the sixteenth century an unskilled construction worker could purchase with his daily wage 8 kg of bread, or 2.5 kg of rice, or more than 2 kg of mutton. The daily wages of skilled workers were 1.5 to 2 times higher. At these levels of pay, skilled construction workers must have enjoyed standards of living well above the average for the population as a whole, and also above the average of the urban areas, even if they worked fewer than 200 days per year. For purposes of international comparisons, it is also possible to express daily wages in Istanbul and other Ottoman cities in grams of silver simply by multiplying the nominal wages by the silver content of the Ottoman *akçe*. Around 1500, for example, daily wages of unskilled construction workers in the capital city equaled 3.4 grams of silver; those of skilled construction workers equaled 6.6 grams of silver (Table 1).

Data were also collected on the daily wages of construction workers, both skilled and unskilled, in other Ottoman cities around the eastern Mediterranean and the Balkans for the same period 1490–1914. These observations were obtained from the account books of pious foundations operating in these cities, and are available from the Ottoman archives in Istanbul. They show clearly that nominal wages in other Ottoman cities also increased by more than 300-fold during this period.[24]

In order to establish whether there was any relationship between daily wages in the capital city and those in second-tier urban centers of the empire (Bursa, Edirne, Belgrade, Salonika, Damascus, Jerusalem, and a few others), we regressed w_I / w_O (the ratio of nominal wages in Istanbul to nominal wages in other cities) on the time trend, using data for each year in which observations were recorded for both Istanbul and any other city. Our separate regressions for the wages of skilled and unskilled workers, as well as a composite wage defined as a weighted combination of the two, indicate that the null hypothesis of an intercept of 1.0 for w_I / w_O cannot be rejected. Moreover, the slope coefficient is not significantly different from zero, indicating no discernible time trend in this ratio.

SHORT- AND LONG-TERM DETERMINANTS OF REAL WAGES

In the short and medium term, the most important determinants of Ottoman real wages were changes in prices and the speed with which nominal wages adjusted to them. Because this adjustment was slow, price shocks led to fluctuations in real wages. Consumer prices exhibited large short-term fluctuations due to harvest conditions, difficulties in transportation, wars, and other causes. The most important cause of changes in the price level, however, was debasement. Even if prices did not rise quickly, because of a specie shortage or some other reason, long-distance trade acted as the ultimate equalizer. Price adjustments after a debasement tended to be more rapid the more open the economy, and the more frequently debasement was resorted to.

Recent research has shown that the urban population and some segments of the countryside were already part of the money economy by the end of the fifteenth century. Even more significantly, there occurred a substantial in-

[24] Pamuk, *Istanbul*, figures 5.1–5.4 and appendix table 9.

crease in the use of money during the sixteenth century, because of both the increased availability of specie and the commercialization of the rural economy. The evidence for this important development comes from a number of sources. First, recent research has pointed out that population growth and urbanization during the sixteenth century were accompanied by the growth of economic linkages between urban and rural areas. As a result, there emerged in the Balkans and in Anatolia an intensive pattern of periodic markets and market fairs, where peasants and larger landholders sold part of their produce to urban residents. These markets also provided an important opportunity for nomads to come into contact with peasants and townspeople. Large sectors of the rural population came to use coinage, especially the small denominations of silver *akçe* and the copper *mangır*, through their participation in these markets.[25]

Secondly, small-scale but intensive networks of credit relations developed in and around the urban centers of the Balkans, Anatolia, and probably elsewhere during the same period. Evidence from thousands of court cases in these towns and cities involving lenders and borrowers leave no doubt that the use of credit, small and large, was widespread among all segments of urban society and parts of the countryside. It is clear that neither the Islamic prohibitions on usury nor the absence of formal banking institutions prevented the expansion of credit in Ottoman society during the sixteenth and seventeenth centuries. Thirdly, the provincial law codes, most of which were issued between the mid-fifteenth and the mid-sixteenth centuries, show very clearly that for every province the Ottoman state issued a long list of activities that were subject to taxation, and the rate to be assessed on each of them. These codes point to an economy with strong urban and rural linkages, considerable market orientation, and frequent collection of small amounts of cash taxes from artisans, merchants, nomads, and peasants. The availability and use of coinage declined during the second half of the seventeenth century, but increased again during the eighteenth.[26]

As a result, debasement had an impact on virtually all groups in Ottoman society; and each group, in turn, adapted to it. Court records make clear that most men and women, both urban and rural, were clear about the distributional consequences of different ways of dealing with the coinage. In general, all persons facing future obligations expressed in the unit of account—most importantly, borrowers and tenants paying fixed rents in cash—stood to gain from debasement. Conversely, those who expected to be paid fixed sums—notably bureaucrats, janissaries, and wage earners—stood to lose from debasement.[27]

[25] Faroqhi, "Early History," "Sixteenth Century Periodic Markets," and "Rural Society."

[26] Pamuk, *Monetary History*, pp. 74–82.

[27] There existed a large overlap between the guild members who were wage earners and the janissaries, after the latter began to moonlight as artisans and shopkeepers in the seventeenth century (ibid., pp. 55–58, 193–200).

We examined the short- and long-term changes in real wages through a time-series analysis of our price and wage indices. For the purposes of this analysis (the more technical aspects of which are presented in Appendix 2), we utilized a composite wage defined as

$$C = \frac{1S + 2U}{3} \tag{1}$$

where S is the daily wage of a skilled construction worker and U is the daily wage of an unskilled construction worker. Our results indicate that in response to debasements, both prices and nominal wages adjusted with a lag. However, because the adjustment of nominal wages was slower than that of prices, debasements led to declines in real wages in the short and even the medium term. These results help explain the unpopularity of—and the often strong political opposition to—debasements among the urban population, especially in the capital city.

For the longer term, it would be best to investigate the determinants of real wages within the framework of supply and demand for labor and a real wage equation. One would expect that changes in the size of the labor force would be an important determinant of the long-term changes in the real wage rate, especially in the early modern period.[28] Specifically, one would expect that strong population growth during the sixteenth century would tend to depress real wages, whereas the depopulation of the seventeenth century would have the opposite effect. Yet none of the dummy variables we employed to reflect these demographic trends were statistically significant when inserted into the real-wage equation. It is of course possible that our knowledge of the prevailing population trends in different subperiods is faulty.[29] It is likelier, however, that the population variables were overwhelmed by the powerful price and inflation variable.[30] It is also possible that our regression model is misspecified in some way, or that changes in population did not have any impact on Ottoman real wages; but we do not attach high degrees of probability to these explanations. (Further details of the real-wage equation are presented in Appendix 2).

The only other variable that is statistically significant in our real-wage equation is the time trend (t). Its coefficient indicates a long-term upward

[28] We are inspired here by a similar study of the long-term trends in English real wages undertaken in Lindert, "English Population."

[29] Annual population series are not available for the Ottoman Empire, or for any part of it, for the period before 1850. Instead, we have some estimates of questionable quality for different points in time. On the basis of the latter, we are certain that the sixteenth century was a period of relatively high population growth. In contrast, 1580–1700 was a period of stagnation or, more probably, decline in population. Trends for 1700 to 1840 are also not entirely clear. They may have varied from region to region; a modest upward trend is our best guess at the moment.

[30] In his study of long-term trends in English wages, Lindert ("English Population") similarly found that short-term price movements overwhelmed the population variable in the real-wage equation.

trend of 0.3 percent per annum, suggesting a modest but steady rise in the demand for labor. We tried to separate the time trend into two subperiods at 1770, hypothesizing that growth in labor demand may have accelerated after the Industrial Revolution. However, *t* in two subperiods did not perform differently than a single *t* for the entire period. It is not easy to interpret the performance of *t*, because even though there is considerable evidence for increases in per capita income after 1880, the existing literature does not suggest a long-term growth trend for the Ottoman economy for the period before 1850. Nonetheless, one now has to consider the possibility that some modest trend for productivity increases did exist in the eastern Mediterranean before the Industrial Revolution. Learning by doing, or the diffusion of new technology from Western Europe, may help explain this trend.[31]

COMPARISONS ACROSS EUROPE

In a recent study of prices and wages in European cities from the Middle Ages to World War I, Robert Allen has utilized a large body of data most of which was compiled under the aegis of the International Scientific Committee on Price History.[32] In order to facilitate comparisons, he converted all price and wage series into grams of silver, and chose as a base the index of average consumer prices prevailing in Strasbourg during the period 1700–1749.[33]

Allen has argued that even though wages in a single city may be accepted as a barometer of wages in the whole economy, international comparisons must be made between cities at similar levels in the urban hierarchy. Since his study uses data from cities at the top of their respective urban hierarchies—such as London, Antwerp, Amsterdam, Milan, Vienna, Leipzig, and Warsaw—it would make sense to insert Istanbul, another city at the top of the urban hierarchy of its region, into this framework. It is not very difficult to do so, since we have already expressed prices and wages in grams of silver. It remains now to express Istanbul prices in terms of the Allen base (i.e., Strasbourg, 1700–1749). For this purpose, Ottoman commodity prices for the interval 1700–1749 were applied to Allen's consumer basket with fixed weights. A second and equally useful method of linking Istanbul's price level to those of other European cities in the Allen set was to employ the detailed annual commodity-price series gathered by Earl Hamilton for Valencia and Madrid over the period 1500–1800 and compare them with the Istanbul prices for the same commodities.[34] Since Valencia and Madrid prices were already calibrated into the Allen set, it was then possible to

[31] Persson, *Pre-Industrial Economic Growth.*

[32] Cole and Crandall, "International Scientific Committee."

[33] Allen, "Great Divergence."

[34] Hamilton, *American Treasure* and *War and Prices.*

determine the Istanbul price level vis-à-vis European cities for each interval. The price series for flour, mutton, olive oil, cooking oil, onions, chickpeas, pepper, sugar, and wood were used in these calculations. The two procedures produced very similar results.

One revision in the Allen series concerns price levels during the 1850–1899 and 1900–1913 intervals. In order to remain consistent throughout, Allen continued to express all prices and wages in grams of silver even after 1870, when silver prices declined sharply and most European countries abandoned bimetallic standards in favor of gold. While technically correct, this procedure gives the impression that most European cities experienced high rates of inflation during this period, when in fact nominal prices and wages remained quite stable. We chose to express all price and wage levels in gold after 1870 by deflating the Allen series by 1.3 and 2.1 for 1850–1899 and 1900–1913, respectively.

One of Allen's major findings is that real (i.e., purchasing-power-parity [PPP] adjusted) wages in these European cities diverged strongly between 1500 and 1914. He shows that the dispersion of real wages was lowest in the early part of the sixteenth century. This picture changed after 1600 as real wages in northwestern Europe (London, Antwerp, and Amsterdam) remained steady, while Italian and Spanish as well as central and eastern European real wages declined until 1850. Allen's study thus suggests that the emergence of a North–South gap within Europe was not the product of developments after the Industrial Revolution, but resulted from long-term trends during the seventeenth and eighteenth centuries.

Our indices show that daily wages in Istanbul and other eastern Mediterranean cities expressed in grams of silver were comparable to those in many other locations in northern and southern Europe in the early part of the sixteenth century. However, because Istanbul prices were higher than those of all other cities in Allen's sample, real wages in Istanbul varied between 60 and 90 percent of real wages in other cities during that period (Figures 2 and 3). It is interesting that while real wages continued to decline after 1600 in many parts of Europe, they remained little changed in Istanbul until late in the eighteenth century. While Istanbul wages approached those elsewhere in Europe, a wage gap of one-third to one-half between Istanbul and the leading cities in northwestern Europe continued until the Industrial Revolution.

Wage and price indices for the western Netherlands recently constructed by Jan Luiten van Zanden present another opportunity to investigate the real wage gap between the eastern Mediterranean and northwestern Europe before the Industrial Revolution.[35] Measured in grams of silver, the nominal

[35] The van Zanden indices are available from www.iisg.nl/hwp/; for prices and real wages in Netherlands during the early modern era, see also de Vries and van der Woude, *First Modern Economy*, pp. 607–54.

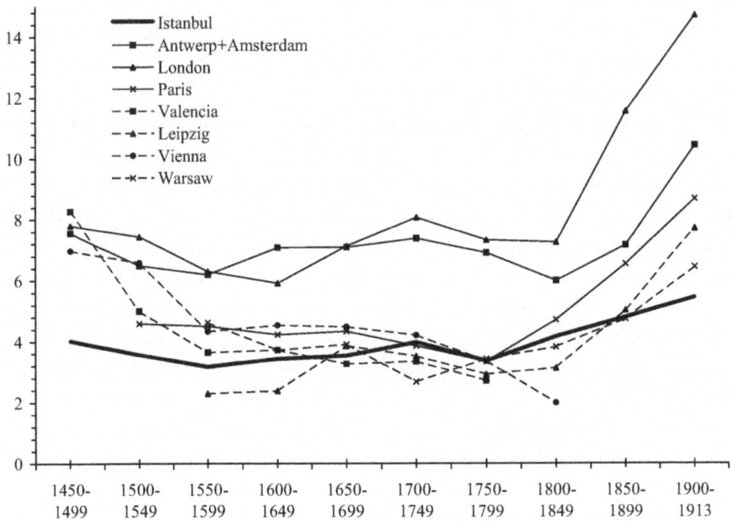

FIGURE 2

REAL WAGE OF UNSKILLED CONSTRUCTION WORKERS IN EUROPEAN CITIES, 1450–1913

(wages [in grams silver] divided by CPI [in grams silver])

Sources: Istanbul: see the text. Other cities: Allen, "Great Divergence."

wages of skilled and unskilled construction workers were quite comparable in the two regions during the first half of the sixteenth century. However, our direct comparison of consumer price levels (based on the prices of more than half a dozen commodities which are available for both regions) indicate that in silver terms Istanbul prices were about 60 to 80 percent higher during the same period. During the next two centuries, or until about 1750, prices and nominal wages in the western Netherlands measured in grams of silver rose by about 250 percent, with the latter lagging somewhat behind the former. In Istanbul, on the other hand, prices in grams of silver remained roughly unchanged while real wages declined slightly. Our preliminary comparison of the two series thus suggests that real wages in Istanbul remained one-third to one-half below real wages in the western Netherlands until the era of the Industrial Revolution. Finally, comparing our Istanbul data to Hamilton's wage and price series for Madrid and Seville reveals real wage trends over the periods 1500–1550 and 1700–1750 that are also similar to those outlined in Figures 2 and 3.[36]

[36] Commodity-price and nominal wage series for Spain are available from Hamilton, *American Treasure* and *War and Prices*, appendices.

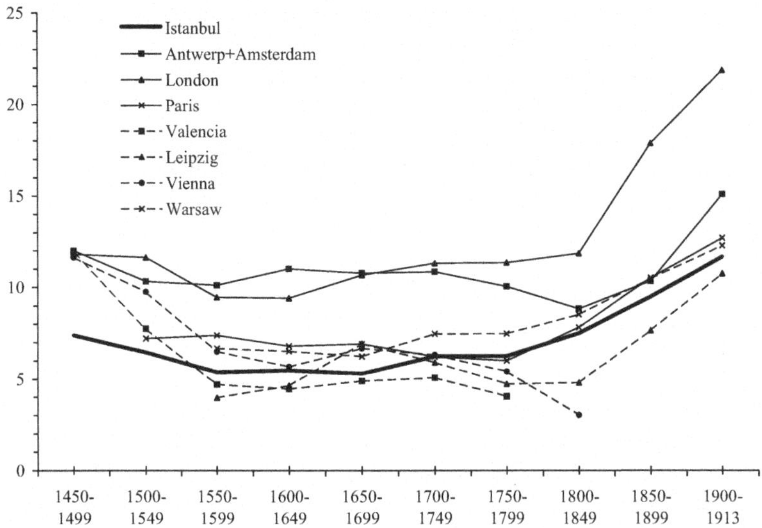

FIGURE 3
REAL WAGE OF SKILLED CONSTRUCTION WORKERS IN EUROPEAN CITIES, 1450–1913
(wages [in grams silver] divided by CPI)

Sources: Istanbul: see the text. Other cities: Allen, "Great Divergence."

WAGES AS AN INDICATOR OF THE STANDARD OF LIVING

Istanbul real wages increased by about two-thirds from the last quarter of the eighteenth century until World War I (Figure 1). As a result, while the gap in real wages between Istanbul and cities in northwestern Europe (London, Antwerp, Amsterdam, and Paris) widened after the Industrial Revolution, that gap was lesser than one might have expected. On the eve of World War I, real wages of unskilled workers in London were 2.7 times as high as in Istanbul; the corresponding ratio for Amsterdam and Antwerp was 1.9, and for Paris 1.6 (Figure 2).

While these results are broadly in line with our expectations, a comparison with the PPP-adjusted per capita GDP series recently constructed by Maddison reveals differences that are not insignificant. The Maddison series show that per capita GDP differences between Turkey and each of four western European countries (the United Kingdom, France, the Netherlands, and Italy) were wider than the differentials in the real wages of unskilled construction workers in the leading cities of each pair of countries.[37]

[37] Maddison, *World Economy*.

Maddison's PPP-adjusted per capita GDP estimates for 1913 point to a 1:5 gap between Turkey and the United Kingdom, a 1:3.8 gap between Turkey and the Netherlands, a 1:3 gap between Turkey and France, and a 1:2.3 gap between Turkey and Italy. In short, the gap in PPP-adjusted per capita GDP between Turkey and these European countries on the eve of World War I appears, on the average, to be twice the real wage gap between Istanbul and the leading cities in these countries. (Indeed, Istanbul real wages were slightly higher than those of Florence and Milan.) This is an interesting and potentially important divergence that needs to be examined further.

Part of this divergence may be due to errors of measurement in the available series. For example, there may be errors in our real wage series for Istanbul. We are aware that most of our knowledge about the wages of construction workers has been based upon state records and records of the middling and larger pious foundations. These larger institutions could seek out the best craftsmen and pay higher wages than smaller employers. Clearly, this bias exists in most wage series but it might be greater the in the case of Istanbul than for other European cities. Otherwise, we believe that our wage series are quite reliable, especially since they are based on large numbers of observations. In fact, the London–Istanbul real wage gap implied by our series is actually larger than the wage gap estimated by earlier studies by Korkut Boratav, Gündüz Ökçün, and Pamuk on Turkish urban wages, and by Berov on Balkan wages. These studies pointed to a gap in nominal wages converted at the prevailing rate of exchange of about 1:2.5.[38]

Secondly, there may be errors in the way our Istanbul prices have been inserted into the Allen framework. We doubt, however, that these can be significant, since our price series was linked to the Allen base by comparing a number of independent price series. In addition, since our real wage series for Istanbul show a 20 to 30 percent overall increase over the four centuries to 1914, raising the nominal price level and lowering real wages for 1900–1913 would not only bring Istanbul prices uncomfortably close to those of London at the endpoint, but it would also raise Istanbul prices across time and thus widen the Istanbul–London real wage gap to more than 1:2 for the early part of the sixteenth century.

Thirdly, there may be room for improvement in the way the Maddison series measure the differences in per capita GDP between high- and low-income countries. In a recent study, Leandro Prados de la Escosura has provided an alternative set of GDP series for the United States and Europe since 1820. While the Maddison series were derived by working backwards from a recent benchmark year on the basis of growth rates, Prados de la Escosura used a short-cut method to obtain current price estimates, also adjusted for PPP. His estimates indicate that the use of current prices reduces considerably

[38] Boratav, Ökçün, and Pamuk, "Ottoman Wages"; and Berov, "Wages in the Balkans."

the gap in per capita income between the high- and low-income countries: specifically, the gap between Turkey and the United Kingdom in 1913 would be reduced from 1:5 (as estimated by Maddison) to approximately 1:3.[39]

Despite these potential sources of error, we still doubt that improvements in the available series can eliminate altogether the divergence between the urban real wage and per capita GDP series. We think there are a number of other factors which may have also contributed to this divergence. First, there had emerged by the nineteenth century important differences between the nominal wages of construction workers in Istanbul and those of other Ottoman cities. Between 1850 and 1914 nominal wages were, on average, 40 to 50 percent higher in Istanbul than in other cities within the borders of modern Turkey. In contrast, official data indicate that in 1913/14 the prices of essential commodities purchased by consumers appeared to be lower in Istanbul than the average of the 20 leading cities within Turkey.[40]

Secondly, there is evidence for a growing scarcity of labor in urban areas from the mid-nineteenth century until World War I. Anatolia was a labor- and capital-scarce, land-abundant region until the middle of the twentieth century; these factor proportions supported peasant ownership and production. The availability of land and the prevalence of small peasant production may have slowed rural–urban migration and contributed to labor shortages in the urban areas. In a recent study of nineteenth-century Anatolia, Boğaç Ergene has provided evidence for the growing scarcity of labor in the urban areas and the increasing gap between urban and rural wages. He also argues that increases in urban real wages must have exceeded increases in per capita GDP during the nineteenth century.[41]

These urban–rural differences combined with the regional differences mentioned above to create large differences between per capita nominal income levels in the Istanbul region and the rest of the country. Vedat Eldem's estimates indicate that on the eve of World War I, per capita income levels in the Istanbul region, which was mostly urban, were twice as high as the average for the Ottoman Empire as a whole.

All this suggests that thc daily wages of urban construction workers in the Ottoman Empire may have been high in relation to the underlying per capita income. In a recent study, Jaime Reis encountered similar difficulties in his attempt to use urban wages as a proxy for per capita GDP. While comparing two groups of countries in the European periphery during the first half of the nineteenth century, he observed that daily wages of construction workers in the capital cities of Spain and Italy were at the same level as comparable wages in Scandinavia; but all other indicators suggested that per capita

[39] Prados de la Escosura, "International Comparisons."

[40] Turkey, State Institute of Statistics, *İhsai Yıllık*.

[41] Ergene, "Wages."

income levels were considerably higher in the northern countries.[42] At the other end of the spectrum, the real wages of construction workers in Milan and Florence during the nineteenth century appear unusually low in relation to the available series for per capita GDP in Italy during the same period.[43]

CONCLUSIONS

One of the more important questions regarding the world economy in the early modern era concerns the emergence and evolution of the gap in levels of real income between today's developed and developing countries. Utilizing a large volume of archival documents, this study has established for the first time the long-term trends in wages of skilled and unskilled construction workers in Istanbul and other Ottoman cities in southeastern Europe and the Near East from the second half of the fifteenth century until World War I. These price and wage series were then inserted into a larger framework of price and wage trends in European cities during the same period. One needs to be cautious about using the daily wages of urban workers as indicators of the standards of living for an entire country. Nonetheless, in the absence of reliable information about production and income, real wage series still serve as the best indicator available for long-term trends in standards of living.

The Ottoman indices indicate that the real wages of unskilled urban construction workers declined by 30 to 40 percent during the sixteenth century. After remaining roughly unchanged until the middle of the eighteenth century, they increased by about 20 to 30 percent from the late eighteenth until mid-nineteenth centuries, and then by another 40 percent during the late nineteenth and early twentieth centuries. On the eve of World War I, the real wages of unskilled construction workers were about 10 to 20 percent above their levels in 1500. Because the skill premium rose during the nineteenth century, real wages of skilled workers in 1914 were 50 percent or more above their levels in 1500.

Comparing these results with Allen's findings for other European cities reveals three basic results. First, real wages in Istanbul and other Ottoman cities remained close to urban wages in many other parts of Europe until the mid-eighteenth century. Real wages in Ottoman cities were lower in 1750 than in 1500, but the decrease was probably not as large as in many other parts of Europe. Secondly, our comparisons suggest that real wages in northwestern Europe (Amsterdam, Antwerp, and London) were already higher than in Istanbul at the beginning of the sixteenth century, and that this gap remained roughly unchanged up to the Industrial Revolution. It would be

[42] Reis, "How Poor?"

[43] Allen, "Great Divergence."

useful to check this result with additional research. Thirdly, the trend was upwards for real urban wages in most regions of Europe in the wake of the Industrial Revolution, especially after 1850; real wages in western Europe increased more than in the eastern Mediterranean during this period.

Our real wage series also point to the existence of a modest but statistically significant upward trend in Ottoman urban wages dating back to the sixteenth century, suggesting a modest but steady rise in demand for labor. It is not easy to interpret this result, because the existing literature does not point to the existence of long-term growth trend, especially for the period before 1850. In light of the new evidence, we now need to consider the possibility of a slow and modest rise in productivity around the eastern Mediterranean in the era before the Industrial Revolution. Learning by doing or the diffusion of new technology from Western Europe may help explain this trend.

Our overall results thus amount to a guardedly optimistic revisionism regarding Ottoman standards of living, both in the early modern era and in the wake of the Industrial Revolution. This picture is consistent with the recent arguments in Ottoman historiography to the effect that the Ottoman empire did not simply and irreversibly decline after 1600. Recent literature has emphasized that Ottoman state and society showed considerable ability to reorganize as a way of adapting to changing circumstances from the seventeenth through the nineteenth centuries. With pragmatism and flexibility, the Ottoman state adapted not only the military technology but also its fiscal, financial, and monetary institutions during this period. This pragmatism and flexibility may help explain the surprising longevity of the so-called "sick man of Europe."

Appendix 1: Long-Term Trends in Indices

Based on trends in money, prices, population, and real wages, it is best to examine these four-and-a-half centuries in *five* distinct subperiods. Separate regressions are used to estimate trend lines for each one.[44]

The first period, 1469–1585, is characterized by stable money, rising population, and rising prices expressed in grams of silver. The trend lines indicate that the silver content of the *akçe* declined at an annual rate of 0.52 percent, prices rose at an annual rate of 1.13 percent, and real wages declined at an annual rate of 0.64 percent during this period.

During the second period, 1585–1690, there was a high degree of monetary and price instability together with declining population. The silver content of the currency fluctuated wildly around a trend of 1.05 percent per annum, prices rose at an annual rate of 0.67 percent, and real wages rose at annual rate of 0.29 percent.

The third period, 1690–1768, was once again a period of monetary and price stability. The silver content of the currency declined at an annual rate of 0.30 percent, prices rose at an annual rate of 0.44 percent, and real wages declined at an annual rate of 0.15 percent.

[44] Poirier, *Econometrics of Structural Change*; and Greene, *Econometric Analysis*.

The fourth period, 1769–1843, is characterized by the most rapid rates of debasement and inflation in Ottoman history, and by rising real wages. The silver content of the currency declined at an annual rate of 3.49 percent, prices rose at an annual rate of 3.81 percent, and real wages rose at an annual rate of 0.49 percent. Frequent wars may have contributed to the rising trend in real wages.

The fifth period, 1844–1914, witnessed stable money under bimetallism, rapidly expanding international trade, stable prices, and rising real wages. The silver content of the currency remained unchanged, prices increased at an annual rate of 0.67 percent, and real wages rose at 0.21 percent per annum. Most of the price increases occurred early in the period and were the lagged result of debasements in the previous period.

Appendix 2 : Determinants of Real Wages

This appendix presents the details of our time-series analysis regarding the determinants of real wages. In the short and medium terms, the most important determinants of Ottoman real wages were changes in prices and the manner in which nominal wages adjusted to them. Because nominal wages were slow to adjust, price shocks led to fluctuations in real wages. The most important determinant of the price level, in turn, was debasements. Ottoman prices almost always rose in the aftermath of debasements because a debasement typically increased the nominal value of coinage in circulation. In order to study the lag structure with which prices and wages adjusted to debasements, we have developed a distributed lag model that relates nominal wages (*W*) and the consumer price index (*P*) to present and lagged values of silver content of coinage (*S*). All variables included in the equation are expressed in logarithms. Using the general-to-specific methodology,[45] equations are estimated with lags up to 10 years; only lags with significant coefficients are included in the final equation. This approach has the advantage of not placing any restrictions on the lag structure, but it has the disadvantage of possible multicollinearity among explanatory variables. The model is of the following form[46]

$$Y_t = \sum \beta_i S_{t-1} + u_t, \quad i = 1,2,\ldots k \tag{A1}$$

where k is the number of lags.

The mean lag indicates the average number of years needed to see the effect of the independent variable on the dependent variable, while the median lag gives the number of years during which half of the effect has occurred. The mean lag can be calculated as

$$\frac{\sum_{i=0}^{k} i\beta_i}{\sum \beta_i}$$

and the median lag can be calculated with the formula

$$\sum_{i=0}^{k*} \frac{\beta_i}{\sum \beta_i}$$

The median lag is the first $k*$ value that gives the sum 0.5.

[45] Hendry, *Dynamic Econometrics*.

[46] Greene, *Econometric Analysis*.

Regression results indicate that the impact of a change in the silver content of the currency was quicker on prices than on wages. When prices are used as the dependent variable, the lags that are significantly different from zero are: zero, one, four, six, and eight. The total effect is –1.088 (sum of coefficients). At equilibrium, a 1-percent decrease in the silver content of coinage causes a 1.088-percent increase in the consumer price index. Furthermore, almost half of the total effect is felt in that year and the year following. *Ceteris paribus*, a 1-percent decrease in the silver content of coinage thus causes a 0.236-percent increase in the price level in that year, and a 0.261-percent increase the following year. The mean lag is 3.59 years, and the median lag is 4 years.

$$P_t = 0.113 - 0.236\, S_t - 0.261\, S_{t-1} - 0.207\, S_{t-4} - 0.129\, S_{t-6} - 0.255\, S_{t-8}$$
$$(0.86)\ (-3.60)\quad (-4.03)\quad (-3.33)\quad (-1.87)\quad (-3.92)$$

$R^2 = 0.993$, SEE = 0.1327, $F = 6814.8$, Durbin–Watson = 2.30, AR(1) = 0.874

The impact on wages of a change in the silver content of the currency occurred more slowly. When nominal wages are used as the dependent variable, zero-, one-, two-, and three-period lags are not significantly different from zero. However, coefficients associated with four-, six-, seven-, and eight-period lags are significantly different from zero. The total effect is –1.323 (sum of coefficients). At equilibrium, a 1-percent decrease in the silver content of coinage causes a 1.323-percent increase in wages. A 1-percent decrease in silver content of coinage causes a 0.232 percent increase in wages after four years, and 0.402 percent after six years. The mean lag is 6.43, and median lag is seven years.

$$W_t = 0.973 - 0.232\, S_{t-4} - 0.402\, S_{t-6} - 0.339\, S_{t-7} - 0.350\, S_{t-8}$$
$$(4.19)\ (-2.43)\quad (-2.99)\quad (-2.57)\quad (-2.47)$$

$R^2 = 0.995$, SEE = 0.1378, $F = 3630.3$, Durbin–Watson = 2.73, AR(1) = 0.871

Our distributed-lag model thus indicates that in response to debasements, both prices and nominal wages adjusted. However, because the adjustment of nominal wages was slower than that of prices, debasements led to declines in real wages in the short and even medium term.

This interaction between prices and real wages can be examined further within the broader framework of a real-wage equation. We have employed two models, one with adaptive expectations in prices, and another one with partial adjustment in real wages.[47] In both models real wages are expressed as a function of inflation and real wages in the previous year. By appropriate substitution, it is not difficult to see that real wages are determined by the present and past inflation rates. In this respect our model is similar to that used by Peter Lindert.[48]

In our regressions, however, only the inflation of the present and past four years appear to be statistically significant. The estimated equation's regression coefficients and determination coefficient are statistically significant; the Durbin–Watson statistic indicates that there is no serial correlation. This was achieved by using generalized least squares, which is indicated by the AR(1) coefficient. It is noteworthy that the time-trend variable t, used to capture the effect of other variables such as population and technological change, is statistically significant. Other things being constant, real wages increased at 0.34 percent per year in this equation:

$$RW_t = -4.496 - 0.900\, P_t - 0.773\, P_{t-1} - 0.649\, P_{t-2} - 0.513\, P_{t-3} - 0.451\, P_{t-4} + 0.0034\, t$$
$$(-2.51)\ (-6.45)\quad (-4.42)\quad (-3.20)\quad (-2.41)\quad (-2.65)\quad (8.23)$$

$R^2 = 0.808$, SEE = 0.140, $F = 40.95$, Durbin–Watson = 2.31, AR(1) = 0.777

[47] Greene, *Econometric Analysis*.

[48] Lindert, "English Population."

REFERENCES

Abramowitz, Moses. "Catching Up, Forging Ahead, and Falling Behind." This JOURNAL 46, no. 2 (1986): 385–406.

Allen, Robert. "The Great Divergence in European Wages and Prices from the Middle Ages to the First World War." *Explorations in Economic History* 38, no. 4 (2001): 411–47.

Barro, R. J. *Determinants of Growth: A Cross Country Empirical Study*. Cambridge, MA: MIT Press, 1997.

Berov, Ljuben. *Prices in the Balkans during the 16th–19th Centuries and the European Revolution of Prices* [in Bulgarian]. Sofia: Publishing House of the Bulgarian Academy of Sciences, 1976.

______. "Changes in Price Conditions in Trade between Turkey and Europe in the 16th–19th Century." *Etudes Balkaniques* 3 (1974): 168–78.

______. "Wages in the Balkans During the Period of Manufacturing Capitalism and the Industrial Revolution." *Bulgarian Historical Review* 1 (1979): 91–115.

Beveridge, W. H. "Wages in the Winchester Manors." *Economic History Review* 7 (1936): 22–43.

Boratav, Korkut, Gündüz A. Ökçün, and Şevket Pamuk. "Ottoman Wages and the World Economy, 1839–1913." *Review, Fernand Braudel Center* 9, no. 3 (1985): 379–406.

Cole, Arthur, and Ruth Crandall. "The International Scientific Committee on Price History." This JOURNAL 24, no. 3 (1964): 381–88.

Crafts, N. F. R. "Gross National Product in Europe, 1870–1910: Some New Estimates." *Explorations in Economic History* 20, no. 4 (1983): 387–401.

De Vries, Jan. "Between Purchasing Power and the World of Goods: Understanding the Household Economy in Early Modern Europe." In *Consumption and the World of Goods*, edited by John Brewer and Roy Porter, 85–132. London and New York: Routledge, 1993.

______. "The Industrial Revolution and the Industrious Revolution." This JOURNAL 54, no. 2 (1994): 249–70.

De Vries, Jan, and Ad van der Woude. *The First Modern Economy*. Cambridge: Cambridge University Press, 1997.

Ergene, Boğaç A. "Wages in Nineteenth Century Anatolia: A Comparison of Urban and Agricultural Trends." *New Perspectives on Turkey*, no. 19 (1998): 125–45.

Faroqhi, Soraiya. "The Early History of Balkan Fairs." *Südost-Forschungen* 37 (1978): 50–68.

______. "Sixteenth Century Periodic Markets in Various Anatolian Sancaks." *Journal of the Economic and Social History of the Orient* 22, no. 1 (1979): 32–80.

______. "Rural Society in Anatolia and the Balkans During the Sixteenth Century." *Turcica* 9 (1977): 161–96, and 11 (1979): 103–53.

Greene, William H. *Econometric Analysis*. 4th ed. Upper Saddle River, NJ: Prentice-Hall, 2000.

Hamilton, Earl J. *American Treasure and the Price Revolution in Spain, 1501–1650*. Cambridge, MA: Harvard University Press, 1934.

______. *War and Prices in Spain, 1650–1800*. Cambridge, MA: Harvard University Press, 1947.

Hanson, John R., II. "Third World Incomes before World War I: Some Comparisons." *Explorations in Economic History* 25, no. 3 (1988): 323–36.

Hendry, David F. *Dynamic Econometrics*. New York: Oxford University Press, 1995.

Hoffman, Philip, David Jacks, Patricia A. Levin, and Peter H. Lindert. "Real Inequality in

Europe since 1500." This JOURNAL 62, no. 2 (2002): 322–55.
Inalcik, Halil, and Donald Quataert, eds. *An Economic and Social History of the Ottoman Empire*. Cambridge: Cambridge University Press, 1994.
Lindert, Peter. "English Population, Wages and Prices, 1541–1913." *Journal of Interdisciplinary History* 15 (Winter 1985): 609–34.
Maddison, Angus. "A Comparison of Levels of GDP Per Capita in Developed and Developing Countries, 1700–1980." This JOURNAL 43, no. 1 (1983): 27–41.
______. *Monitoring the World Economy, 1820–1992*. Paris: OECD Development Centre Studies, 1995.
______. *The World Economy, A Millennial Perspective*. Paris: OECD Development Centre Studies, 2001.
Mokyr, Joel. *The Lever of Riches: Technological Creativity and Economic Progress*. Oxford: Oxford University Press, 1990.
Pamuk, Şevket. *A Monetary History of the Ottoman Empire*. Cambridge: Cambridge University Press, 2000.
______. *Istanbul ve Diğer Kentlerde 500 Yıllık Fiyatlar ve Ücretler, 1469–1914* [500 Years of Prices and Wages in Istanbul and Other Cities]. Ankara: State Institute of Statistics of Turkey, 2000.
______. "The Price Revolution in the Ottoman Empire Reconsidered." *International Journal of Middle East Studies* 33, no. 1 (2001): 69–89.
Persson, K. G. *Pre-Industrial Economic Growth, Social Organization and Technological Progress in Europe*. Oxford: Basil Blackwell, 1988.
Phelps Brown, E. H., and Sheila V. Hopkins. "Seven Centuries of the Prices of Consumables Compared with Builders' Wage Rates." *Economica* 23, nos. 89–92 (1956): 296–314.
______. *A Perspective of Wages and Prices*. London: Methuen, 1981.
Poirier, Dale J. *The Econometrics of Structural Change*. Amsterdam: North-Holland, 1974.
Prados de la Escosura, Leandro. "International Comparisons of Real Product, 1820–1990: An Alternative Data Set." *Explorations in Economic History* 37, no. 1 (2000): 1–41.
Raymond, Andre. *Artisans et commerçants au Caire au XVIIIe siècle*. 2 vols. Damascus: Institut Français de Damas, 1973–74.
Reis, Jaime. "How Poor Was the European Periphery before 1850? The Mediterranean vs. Scandinavia." In *The Mediterranean Response to Globalization before 1850*, edited by Ş. Pamuk and J. Williamson, 17–44. London: Routledge, 2000.
Sahillioğlu, Halil. "Yeniçeri Çuhası ve II. Bayezid'in Son Yıllarında Yeniçeri Çuha Muhasebesi." *Güney-Doğu Avrupa Araştırmaları Dergisi* 2–3 (1973–74): 415–65.
Turkey. State Institute of Statistics. Merkezi İstatistik Müdüriyeti Umumiyesi. *İhsai Yıllık*. Ankara: n.p., 1928.
Van Zanden, Jan Luiten. "Wages and the Standards of Living in Europe, 1500–1800." *European Review of Economic History* 3, no. 2 (1999): 175–98.
______. "The Great Convergence from a European Perspective." Itinerario, *European Journal of Overseas History* 24, no. 3/4 (2000): 9–28.
Williamson, Jeffrey. "Real Wages and Relative Factor Prices Around the Mediterranean 1500–1940." In *The Mediterranean Response to Globalization before 1850*, edited by Ş. Pamuk and J. Williamson, 45–75. London: Routledge, 2000.

XV

Estimating Economic Growth in the Middle East since 1820

This study provides, for the first time, an overview of the growth record of the Middle East since 1820 and inserts it into a comparative framework. GDP per capita estimates are offered for individual countries in the region for the benchmark years of 1913, 1870, and 1820. The Middle East began to participate in modern economic growth during the nineteenth century. Yet, per capita income differences with the high-income regions of the world widened considerably until World War I. In the twentieth century, the most important single factor contributing to increases in per capita incomes was oil.

This is a subject about which we know little and where, in all likelihood, our knowledge will not grow greatly.

Charles Issawi[1]

During the last two decades economic historians have paid a good deal of attention to the estimation of the per capita real product of different countries and the analysis of what happened to the gap between the leaders and followers since the Industrial Revolution. With the exception perhaps of a small number of countries, however, estimates for per capita GDP for the period before 1870 are difficult to construct and not sufficiently reliable. Moreover, it has not been possible to construct detailed estimates for most of the developing countries for the period before 1913 or even 1950.

This article focuses on a region, the study of whose modern economic growth performance has been conspicuously lagging behind. I bring together and analyze data from a variety of sources to provide, for the first time, an overview of the growth record of the Middle East since 1820 and then insert these estimates into a comparative framework. I offer GDP per capita estimates for individual countries in the region for the benchmark years of 1913, 1870, and 1820.

An earlier and longer version of this article was presented at the 12th Annual Meeting of the Economic Research Forum at Cairo in December 2005. The author would like to thank the Forum for support, Subidey Togan and other participants for helpful comments. The author also acknowledges the comments and suggestions by Alexander Apostolides, Roger Owen, Peter Temin, the editor of this journal, and anonymous referees. This study was also supported by the Academy of Sciences of Turkey and Boğaziçi University Research Projects Fund through project number 101Z05.

[1] Issawi, *Economic History of the Middle East*, p. 103.

The estimates indicate that although there were significant differences in the subperiods, the cumulative growth experience of the Middle East during the last two centuries was not very different from that of other regions of the periphery. The Middle East began to participate in modern economic growth during the nineteenth century. Yet, differences in per capita incomes between it and the high income regions of the world (United States and western Europe) widened considerably until World War I. In the twentieth century, the most important single factor contributing to increases in per capita incomes in the region was oil. Despite the sharp rise in oil production and revenues, however, the gap between the Middle East and the high income regions of the world is roughly the same today as it was in 1913 (Figures 1 and 2). In fact, the contribution of oil to economic growth in the region is rather ambiguous. In the half century since 1950, non-oil countries of the region actually experienced greater increases in per capita incomes than the oil exporters, as I will show.

METHODOLOGY AND DATA

In principle, a country's per capita is estimated by adopting a Kuznetsian approach and constructing sector by sector accounts from the available data. GDP per capita thus obtained in individual currencies are then converted into a common denominator. The construction of Kuznetsian national income accounts is not always possible for the earlier periods, however, due to the limitations of data. Moreover, as the International Comparison Project has shown, there are serious problems in converting per capita GDPs by utilizing the current exchange rates. For this reason I will begin with per capita GDPs calculated in purchasing power parity terms for the most recent benchmark year. I will then move backwards on the basis of the annual changes in the per capita real product of individual countries.[2] Angus Maddison presented his estimates in 1990 Geary-Khamis purchasing power parity adjusted international dollars. I present my estimates in the same units and for the same benchmark years in order to facilitate comparisons with his and other estimates.[3]

No country in the Middle East (Turkey, Syria, Lebanon, Jordan, Palestine-Israel, Egypt, Saudi Arabia, Gulf states, Iraq, and Iran) had an official income accounting system in place before World War I. Agricultural production series began for Egypt in the 1880s and for the Ottoman Empire in 1897. Output series for other sectors are not available

[2] Summers and Heston, "Penn World Table"; and Heston, Summers, and Aten, "Penn World Tables."

[3] Maddison, *World Economy: Historical.*

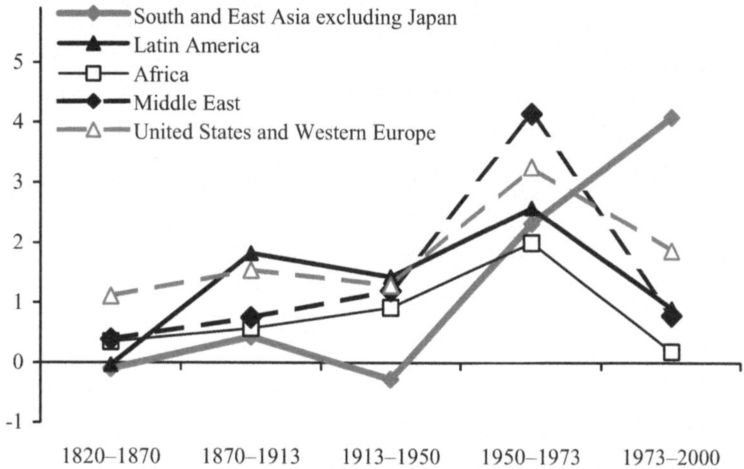

FIGURE 1
ANNUAL RATES OF GROWTH OF PER CAPITA GDP, 1820–2000

Sources: Table 1; and Maddison, *World Economy*.

until after World War I. For the earlier period, only tax assessment and collection series and foreign trade statistics are available. National income accounting systems were established either during the Interwar period or mostly after 1950. For some countries such as Turkey, Egypt, and Palestine-Israel, researchers have pieced together evidence from a variety of sources to construct national income accounts for the years before World War I or some years of the interwar period. In some other cases, there are estimates of the rate of change in per capita national income for different time intervals. Some attempts have also been made to compare the per capita income of two or more of the countries in these regions at different points in time. Because most of this region was part of the Ottoman Empire until 1918, fiscal, production, and trade data from Ottoman sources including per capita GDP estimates for the years immediately before World War I can be employed for making cross sectional and intertemporal comparisons.

DERIVING THE ESTIMATES

I begin with the Maddison per capita GDP estimates for the individual countries of the Middle East for the benchmark year 1950 except those for Egypt and Syria. These estimates have been obtained by working

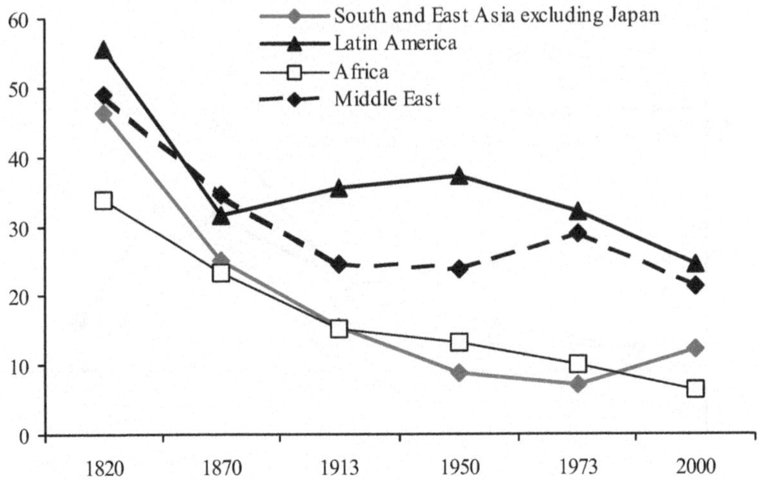

FIGURE 2
GDP PER CAPITA AS A PERCENTAGE OF UNITED STATES AND WESTERN EUROPE, 1820–2000

Sources: Table 1; and Maddison, *World Economy*.

backwards from the most recent estimates of per capita GDP.[4] I then work backwards step by step towards the earlier benchmark years for each of the countries in the region. I proceed in three stages.

In the first stage of the reconstruction procedure, I work backwards to 1913 using the available evidence on rates of change in per capita GDP as well as other estimates on per capita GDP levels for those countries of the region for which estimates or income series are available, most importantly Turkey and Egypt. The first stage enables me to carry the GDP per capita estimates expressed in 1990 international dollars back to 1913 at least for parts of the region.

For Turkey, national income accounts now go back to 1923. We have linked these series to the Ottoman period making use of a de-

[4] The Maddison GDP per capita series for Syria for 1950–2000 provides rates of growth which are consistent with the ICP series but their level is unacceptably high throughout the period (Maddison, *World Economy: Historical*). I have adjusted them downwards by 45 percent to bring them in line with the ICP series, World Bank estimates and other evidence considered in this study. For the ICP series for Syria see, Heston et al., "Penn World Tables"; and for evidence on the Syrian economy during the interwar years, see Himadeh, *Economic Organization.* Similarly, for Egypt, the Maddison rates of growth for 1950–2000 are consistent with the ICP series but the GDP per capita levels were rather low. As explained in footnote 9, the estimate for 1950 was adjusted upwards by 15 percent.

tailed study on this issue with comparisons of agricultural output, manufacturing, and foreign trade on a per capita basis for those areas of the Ottoman Empire that were included in Turkey after 1923. That study reached the conclusion that per capita GDP in Turkey declined by as much as 50 percent or more during World War I and returned to its 1913 levels only in 1929.[5] We are thus able to express GDP per capita for the period before World War I in 1990 purchasing power parity adjusted international dollars for one of the largest countries of the region. This benchmark estimate for 1913 has proved highly useful not only for extrapolating per capita estimates for Turkey towards 1870 and the earlier period but also for comparing and checking our estimates of per capita GDP in 1913 for other countries of the region.

In the absence of national income accounts for Egypt, the most important piece of evidence we have regarding changes in per capita production and income levels in the period before 1950 are the two related studies by Bent Hansen and Michael Wattleworth on per capita agricultural output and consumption of foodstuffs based on production and trade statistics. Most importantly for our present purposes, these studies indicate that per capita income levels in 1950 were about the same as those in 1913. A more recent study by Tarik Yousef that makes use of changes in monetary variables to derive estimates of per capita income reaches the same conclusion that per capita income in Egypt was at the same level in 1950 as it was in 1913.[6] Another source of evidence linking per capita incomes for 1950 to those in 1913 comes from Palestine, where the arrival of large numbers of Jewish immigrants and substantial inflows of capital supported high rates of increases in per capita GDP during the interwar period, as examined in detail by Jacob Metzer.[7]

In the second stage, I make use of detailed data to develop per capita GDP estimates for different parts of the region in 1913. Vedat Eldem had constructed per capita GDP estimates for the Ottoman Empire for the years before World War I utilizing fiscal data and a series of censuses on population, agriculture, and industry as well as statistics on foreign trade. These estimates, given in current Ottoman gold liras, included a regional breakdown for the European and Asian prov-

[5] Ozel, "Economy"; Ozel and Pamuk, "Osmanlidan Cumhuriyete"; for the GDP series for Turkey for 1923–1948, Bulutay, Tezel and Yildirim, *Turkiye Milli Geliri*.

[6] Hansen and Wattleworth, "Agricultural Output"; Hansen, "Income"; and Yousef, "Egypt's Growth."

[7] Metzer, *Divided Economy*. The Metzer series are for 1922–1947, for Arabs and Jews separately. After correpondence with the author, I have assumed that there was a slight decline in GDP per capita from 1913 to 1922 and a larger decline from 1947 to 1950.

inces of the empire.[8] The years before World War I are thus of critical importance in my reconstruction as I use a large body of evidence to check my estimates both longitudinally and cross sectionally. I then compare the existing sector-based estimates for different parts of the Middle East with available estimates on per capita GDP in the Balkan countries, which provides another channel for checking these estimates. Even though I treat the estimates for each country separately, these cross sectional comparisons, not only around the benchmark year 1913 but also at each of the other benchmark years, are very important for checking the reliability and robustness of the estimates.

There were considerable regional differences in per capita income levels within the Ottoman Empire and, in all likelihood, these differences were growing in the decades before World War I. In terms of the later nation-state boundaries, the area of the Ottoman Empire with highest per capita incomes on the eve of World War I was Lebanon followed by Syria and Palestine. While the Istanbul region and European areas of the Ottoman Empire had per capita incomes higher than those of Syria and Lebanon, the area comprising modern Turkey had per capita income levels 10 to 15 percent below those of Lebanon and Syria. Per capita GDP estimates for the Balkan countries, Greece, Romania and Bulgaria in 1913 presented in Table 1 with levels higher than those for Turkey and Syria but close to those for Lebanon are thus consistent with the regional distribution of per capita income inside the Ottoman Empire as reflected in the Ottoman fiscal and production data. At the other end of the spectrum in terms of per capita income in 1913, were regions of the Middle East located around the Gulf. Iraq, Iran, the Arabian peninsula, and the Gulf economies lagged considerably behind regions around the eastern Mediterranean. Both Ottoman data and existing estimates leave no doubt about this divide on the eve of World War I.

One important question in this reconstruction procedure is to determine how per capita income levels in Egypt, one of the largest countries in the region during the twentieth century, compared with those of the other countries or areas in 1913. Available evidence leads me to conclude that on the eve of World War I per capita income levels in Egypt were distinctly lower than those of Syria and Lebanon and also below those of Turkey but above those of Iraq, Iran, and Arabia. We know that on the eve of World War I, many of the wealthiest individuals in the Middle East including many Europeans lived in Egypt. At the same time, however, there is strong evidence that incomes in Egypt were

[8] Eldem, *Osmanli*, pp. 277–309.

TABLE 1
ECONOMIC GROWTH IN THE MIDDLE EAST SINCE 1820

	GDP Per Capita (1990 PPP dollars)						Annual Change in GDP Per Capita (percentage)				
	1820	1870	1913	1950	1973	2000	1820–1870	1870–1913	1913–1950	1950–1973	1973–2000
Turkey	680	880	1,200	1,600	3,477	6,597	0.5	0.7	0.8	3.4	2.4
Syria	680	880	1,300	1,400	2,345	4,364	0.5	0.9	0.2	2.2	2.3
Lebanon	680	950	1,450	2,429	3,155	3,409	0.7	1.0	1.4	1.1	0.3
Jordan	550	700	1,000	1,663	2,389	4,059	0.5	0.8	1.4	1.6	2.0
Palestine-Israel	650	850	1,200	1,992	7,704	12,292	0.5	0.8	1.4	6.1	1.7
Israel				2,817	9,645	16,159				5.5	1.9
West Bank and Gaza				949	2,184	5,124				3.7	3.2
Egypt	600	750	1,050	1,050	1,294	2,920	0.4	0.8	0.0	0.9	3.1
Saudi Arabia	500	520	600	2,231	11,040	8,002	0.1	0.3	3.6	7.2	–1.2
Gulf	600	700	900	17,730	24,533	11,974	0.3	0.6	8.4	1.4	–2.6
Iraq	550	600	800	1,364	3,753	1,221	0.2	0.7	1.5	4.5	–4.1
Iran	550	600	800	1,720	5,445	4,742	0.2	0.7	2.1	5.1	–0.5
Middle East	611	744	1,023	1,592	4,057	5,023	0.4	0.7	1.2	4.2	0.8
United States	1,257	2,445	5,301	9,561	16,689	28,129	1.3	1.8	1.6	2.5	2.0
Western Europe	1,245	2,086	3,688	5,013	12,159	19,806	1.0	1.3	0.8	3.9	1.8
U.S. and W. Europe	1,246	2,159	4,172	6,711	14,029	23,680	1.1	1.5	1.3	3.3	2.0

TABLE 1 — continued

	GDP Per Capita as a Percentage of United States and Western Europe						Population (millions)					
	1820	1870	1913	1950	1973	2000	1820	1870	1913	1950	1973	2000
Turkey	54.6	40.8	28.8	23.8	24.8	27.9	9.4	11.5	16.6	21.1	38.5	65.7
Syria	54.6	40.8	31.2	20.9	16.7	18.4	1.3	1.5	2.0	3.5	6.9	16.3
Lebanon	54.6	44.0	34.8	36.2	22.5	14.4	0.3	0.4	0.7	1.4	3.0	3.6
Jordan	44.1	32.4	24.0	24.8	17.0	17.1	0.2	0.3	0.4	0.6	1.7	4.5
Palestine-Israel	52.2	39.4	28.8	29.7	54.9	51.9	0.3	0.4	0.7	2.3	4.3	9.0
Israel				42.0	68.8	68.2				1.3	3.2	5.8
West Bank and Gaza				14.1	15.6	21.6				1.0	1.1	3.2
Egypt	48.2	34.7	25.2	15.6	9.2	12.3	4.5	6.4	12.1	21.2	35.5	70.5
Saudi Arabia	40.1	24.1	14.4	33.2	78.7	33.8	2.1	2.4	2.8	3.9	6.7	22.0
Gulf	48.2	32.4	21.6	264.2	174.9	50.6	0.2	0.2	0.3	0.4	1.7	5.7
Iraq	44.1	27.8	19.2	20.3	26.8	5.2	1.1	1.6	2.8	5.2	10.4	22.7
Iran	44.1	27.8	19.2	25.6	38.8	20.0	6.6	8.0	10.8	16.4	31.5	66.0
Middle East	49.0	34.4	24.5	23.7	28.9	21.2	26	33	49	76	140	286

Notes: Western Europe includes 12 countries; Austria, Belgium, Denmark, Finland, France, Germany, Italy, The Netherlands, Norway, Sweden, Switzerland, and the United Kingdom. Palestine-Israel roughly refers to the area of the British Palestine Mandate.

Sources: For GDP estimates for the Middle East, see the text. For Middle East population, see Issawi, *Economic History of the Middle East and North Africa*; McEvedy and Jones, *Atlas*; Maddison, *World Economy, Historical*; Behar, *Population*; and the text. For Western Europe and the United States, Maddison, *World Economy, Historical*.

TABLE 2
ESTIMATES OF GDP PER CAPITA FOR 1913–1914 FOR COUNTRIES IN THE MIDDLE EAST AND THE BALKANS
(based on sectoral studies, in current prices)
(converted to British pounds at the prevailing rates of exchange)

Country	GDP Per Capita in British Pounds	Sources
Ottoman Empire	10	Eldem
Turkey	10	Eldem
Syria	11	Eldem
Lebanon	12	Eldem
Iraq	7	Eldem
Egypt	8.5	Hansen, Yousef
Greece	11	Kostelenos-Petmezas et al.
Bulgaria	10.6	Palairet
Serbia	8	Palairet

Note: The estimates for Bulgaria and Serbia are for the year 1910. The estimate for Greece represents the average for 1910–1914. Per capita GDP in the Balkan countries declined after 1912 due to the Balkan Wars.

more unequally distributed than in other parts of the Middle East due primarily to the unequal distribution of landownership.[9]

Table 2 presents the existing estimates of per capita GDP for different countries of the Middle East in 1913 based on sectoral studies including those by Eldem. These estimates were all originally expressed in the current monetary unit of the country they belonged to, and I have converted them to British pounds sterling at the prevailing rates of exchange. Because the countries represented in Table 2 had per capita GDP levels close to each other, we should expect their aggregate price levels to be close as well. As a result, we should expect the purchasing power parity adjusted per capita GDP levels of these countries to be ranked in the same order as their per capita GDP expressed in current domestic prices. The ordering of the countries in the region in terms of per capita GDP given in Table 2 and those given in Table 1 are very similar, if not identical. This comparison should increase our confidence

[9] In earlier volumes Maddison had projected much lower per capita income levels for Egypt for the year 1950, and by implication for 1913. He has since raised the 1913 per capita GDP estimates for 1950 from 500 constant 1990 purchasing power parity dollars in the 1995 edition to 700 dollars in the 2001 volume and most recently to 900 dollars. Compare Maddison, *Monitoring*, p. 206, *World Economy, A Millennial*, p. 323, and *World Economy: Historical*, p. 219. The earlier estimates would have made Egypt the poorest country in the region in 1913, which is not tenable. Maddison's recent revisions point towards more realistic estimates and they fit much better the comparative picture I have outlined for the region on the eve of World War I. In view of the per capita GDP estimates by Hansen, Yousef, and others given in constant 1913 Egyptian pounds for the years 1913 and 1950, I find it more realistic to raise the estimates for per capita GDP for Egypt in 1950 and in 1913 even further to 1,050 dollars. This evidence is summarized in Table 2. Also see United Nations, *Economic Developments*.

in the purchasing power parity adjusted estimates provided in Table 1 for the year 1913.

In the third and last stage, I utilize the Ottoman evidence from fiscal sources and all other evidence on tax revenues, output, and trade to derive long-term rates of change in per capita GDP for the periods 1870–1913 and 1820–1870. However, whereas Eldem and later Osman Okyar accepted increases in per capita tax collections of the central government as a proxy for increases in per capita income, I am reluctant to do so.[10] Increases in tax revenues tend to overstate the underlying expansion of the Ottoman economy during the nineteenth century because part of the increases in tax revenues were due to the increased tax collection capability of the central government. Evidence summarized in Table 3 indicates that tax revenues of the central government increased much faster than the underlying economy during the nineteenth century. The ratio of tax revenues to total GDP was rising fastest during the mid-nineteenth century. This was a result of the centralization drive that began in the 1820s and continued with the *Tanzimat* (re-ordering) reforms proclaimed in 1839. The Ottoman government did not raise tax rates during this period but it was able to reduce progressively the share of revenues held by the private tax-farmers in the countryside. With increasing centralization, the tax collectors and the government were also able to reach a higher percentage of the agricultural producers. This conclusion of slow but positive growth for the Ottoman economy during the decades before World War I is supported by the evidence provided in the Ottoman agricultural censuses and output data that are available for 1897, 1909, 1913, and 1914. These statistics contain a number of problems but they point to increases in both the yields and total production in the leading crops during this period in both Anatolia and the European provinces.[11] Evidence from foreign trade and other scattered evidence on output suggest that the ratio of tax revenues to total GDP continued to rise after 1880, albeit more slowly. This lower rate of growth for the Ottoman economy is also consistent with the recent regional studies on the Ottoman economy.[12]

A variety of evidence including production, foreign trade, and urban wages point to slightly higher rates of growth for Syria, Lebanon, and Palestine from 1880 until World War I. These rates were comparable to those experienced by Greece for this period, the only Balkan country for which sector-based GDP series are available for the period before 1913.

[10] Eldem, *Osmanli*, p. 308; and Okyar, "New Look."

[11] Guran, *Agricultural Statistics* and *First Statistical Yearbook*.

[12] For example, Akarli, "Agriculture."

TABLE 3
TOTAL GDP AND TOTAL TAX REVENUES OF THE OTTOMAN CENTRAL GOVERNMENT, 1840–1913

	1840–1842	1880–1882	1913–1914
Population of the empire in millions	26	20	22
Total tax revenues of the central government in millions of current Ottoman liras	5.6	16	31
Tax revenues per capita in current Ottoman liras	0.22	0.8	1.41
Tax revenues per capita in 1913 Ottoman liras	0.38	0.96	1.41
GDP per capita (approx.) in current Ottoman liras	5	8	12
Total GDP in millions of current Ottoman liras	130	160	260
Tax Revenues/Total GDP	4.3	10.0	11.7

Notes: The Ottoman Empire as defined here excludes Romania, Egypt, and the Arabian peninsula but includes areas in the Balkans as well as Anatolia, Syria, and Iraq. The decline of the total population is due to the loss of territory in the Balkans.

1.10 Ottoman liras equaled 1 British pound sterling throughout this period.

Revenues falling under the jurisdiction of the Ottoman Public Debt Administration after 1881 are not included in the tax revenues for the last two periods.

Sources: For population, Behar, *Population.* For Ottoman budgets, Güran, *Ottoman Financial*; and Shaw "Ottoman Tax." For the aggregate price level, Pamuk, *500 Years*.

In comparison, rates of growth were distinctly lower in Iraq, the Arabian peninsula and Iran (Table 1).[13]

For Egypt, supported by inflows of capital and rapid expansion of cotton cultivation and exports, the decades before World War I were also a period of economic growth. The recent study by Yousef reaches the conclusion that per capita GDP increased by a total of more than 80 percent between 1886/87 and 1913, implying an average annual rate of about 2 percent. This is a rather high estimate not supported by the Hansen and Wattleworth per capita output, consumption, and income indices. The latter point to a total increase of 40 percent in per capita food consumption and income for the same period. Moreover, higher rates of growth for the decades before World War I imply unusually low per capita GDP levels for the 1880s and earlier. I prefer to follow the Hansen and Wattleworth estimates for income growth in Egypt during the decades before World War I.[14]

[13] The most recent study on per capita GDP for Greece since 1830 reaches the conclusion that there were significant increases in per capita growth in Greece during the nineteenth century but that the gap between Greece and the high income countries continued to widen. This study estimates that per capita GDP in Greece increased at close to 0.5 percent per annum before 1870, and at rates below 1.0 percent per annum during 1870–1913. Kostelenos et al., *Gross Domestic Product.* In a recent study Lains, "Southern European," reaches a similar conclusion for the Balkans during 1870–1913. In contrast, Palairet, *Balkan Economies* has argued that the period of early independence in the Balkans was characterized not by sustained increases in per capita income but by economic stagnation due to urban decline and increasing self sufficiency of agriculture in the aftermath of land reforms.

[14] Hansen and Wattleworth, "Agricultural Output"; Hansen, "Income"; and Yousef, "Egypt's Growth."

The 1870s was an unusually difficult decade, with political, fiscal, and economic crises for most of the Middle East and the Balkans. There was a severe famine in central Anatolia during 1873/74. The Ottoman Empire entered a war with Russia during 1877/78, which involved the Balkans. After the spread of the financial crisis of 1873 in the European financial markets, the Ottoman and Egyptian governments were forced to declare a moratorium on their outstanding debt during 1875/76. Incomes were rising in the early part of the decade and there was recovery at the end. For the decade as a whole, I estimate that per capita GDP declined by 4 percent for Turkey and Egypt. In other parts of the region, the impact of these events was more limited and I estimate that income levels had recovered by the end of the decade to their levels at the beginning.

As the last step of the reconstruction attempt, I extrapolate the benchmark year estimates for 1870 towards 1820 employing different rates of growth of per capita GDP for different parts of the region with the help of the insights offered by the available fiscal data, foreign trade data, and studies by various scholars, most notably those by Issawi.[15] Due to larger gaps in available evidence, the estimates for this early period carry greater degree of uncertainty.

An alternative approach for studying levels of per capita income or the standards of living where reliable estimates of per capita GDP are lacking has been to compare real wages of specific occupations, most often of skilled and unskilled construction workers in urban areas. Real wage data are of far better quality than per capita GDP estimates, especially for the period before World War I for all of the developing countries. At the same time, however, real wage series are open to valid objections. In most of the Middle East urban wages was a small category during the nineteenth century. The linkage between urban wages and agricultural productivity was not always strong. Even if we accept wages as an adequate proxy for the annual per capita earnings of labor, this does not mean that it should be a good proxy for income per capita.

With these qualifications, I present in Table 4 evidence compiled from many sources on nominal daily wage rates for urban construction workers in the Middle East and the Balkan countries during the half century before World War I. Although price levels may vary to some extent between countries, it is clear there is a close correlation between my per capita estimates for 1913 and the nominal wage rates in different parts of the region on the eve of World War I. There is a close correlation between nominal daily wages and the available per capita

[15] Issawi, *Economic History of the Middle East and North Africa*, pp. 103–07, and "Egypt."

TABLE 4
DAILY WAGES OF CONSTRUCTION WORKERS IN CITIES OF THE MIDDLE EAST AND SOUTHEASTERN EUROPE, 1860–1913
(in British pounds sterling converted at the prevailing exchange rate)

	Unskilled Workers		Skilled Workers	
	1860–1869	1900–1909	1860–1869	1900–1909
Istanbul, Turkey	0.07	0.075	0.155	0.195
Damascus and Aleppo, Syria	0.05	0.10	0.10	0.22
Beirut, Lebanon	0.05	NA	0.11	NA
Cairo, Egypt	0.05	0.06	0.14	0.17
Iran	0.02	0.03	0.08	0.10
Mousul, Iraq	0.04	NA	0.09	NA
Bulgaria	0.05	0.08	NA	0.12
Romania	0.06	0.09	0.09	0.11
Greece	0.08	0.12	0.12	0.16
Southern England	0.14	0.23	0.23	0.33

Sources: Pamuk, *500 Years*; Özmucur and Pamuk, "Real Wages"; Boratav, Okcun, and Pamuk, "Ottoman Wages"; Issawi, *Economic History of Iran* and *Fertile Crescent*; Egypt, *Annuaire Statistique*; Berov, "Wages," "Le salarie" and "Trends"; Phelps Brown and Hopkins, "Seven Centuries." The author would like to thank John Chalcraft for wage data for Cairo for mid-nineteenth century.

For evidence on consumer prices in urban areas during this period, see in addition, Issawi, *Economic History of the Middle East*, pp. 449–51, for Egypt and *Economic History of Iran*, pp. 339–42, for Iran.

income estimates for the three Balkan countries as well. When the evidence for nominal wage rates is examined together with evidence on prices, one can conclude that urban wages rose faster than prices around the Middle East during the half century before World War I. On the whole, the urban wage evidence supports the per capita GDP pattern within the Middle East region as outlined in Table 1 for 1913. This evidence for total increases in the nominal and real wages for the half century until World War I is also consistent with rates of increase in per capita incomes for different parts of the region as presented in Table 1. I believe that changes in the wages of unskilled workers should be considered a better measure of changes in per capita GDP because the numbers of urban skilled construction workers was a very small category during this period.

CHECKING THE ESTIMATES

A number of economic historians have used input and output prices to measure long-term changes in productivity. It has been shown that this dual approach to growth accounting is equivalent to the one using quantities. Peter Temin employed this approach and used trade data to assess the rate and breadth of productivity increases during the British industrial revolution. More recently, Pol Antras and Hans-Joachim Voth have used changes in factor prices to develop an alternative measure of British total factor productivity growth for the same period.[16] Unfortunately, whereas wage data may be employed for this purpose, data on prices of capital and land rents are not adequate for undertaking a similar study for the Middle East for the period before 1950. On the other hand, trade price data may be of some use for our purposes. The Middle East exported almost entirely agricultural goods and imported mostly manufactured goods and to some extent foodstuffs during the century before World War I. Ottoman exports to Great Britain, for example, consisted almost entirely of agricultural goods, and imports from Great Britain almost entirely of manufactures, with cotton manufactures accounting for the largest share. The only study on the subject shows that Ottoman net barter terms of trade in trade with the United Kingdom improved by about 30 percent from 1854 to 1913. Improvements in the same Ottoman terms of trade were much greater in the first half of the nineteenth century. Even after taking into account declines in transportation costs, and under the assumption of some inelasticity of demand for Ottoman exports, this pattern suggests that productivity increases in export-oriented Ottoman agriculture lagged behind productivity increases in export-oriented British manufacturing during the nineteenth century.[17]

Another method for assessing my results would be to conduct simple sensitivity tests for the growth rate estimates. Because it is possible to go back to GDP per capita levels for 1913 mostly on the basis of existing series and because my estimates for GDP per capita for different countries of the region are consistent with a large body of other evidence, I will focus here on the period before 1913. I will consider growth rates below and above the rates I have estimated for the region for the period 1820–1913. I will then calculate what these alternative growth rates imply for levels of GDP per capita in 1820. This exercise should help assess the fragility of my estimates and establish a range within which growth rates need to fall.

I have estimated the long-term rate of increase of per capita GDP for 1820–1913 for the region as a whole at 0.56 percent per annum (Table 1). If we adopt a significantly higher rate of increase, such as 1 percent per year for this period, we arrive at a GDP per capita level of 405 dollars for 1820. This level is simply too low because 400 dollars (1990 and PPP adjusted) represents the subsistence minimum in the Maddison framework. Conversely, if we adopt an average rate of increase of

[16] Temin, "Two Views"; and Antras and Voth, "Factor Prices."
[17] Pamuk, *Ottoman Empire*, pp. 172–75.

0 percent for 1820–1913, we arrive at a GDP per capita level of 1,023 dollars for the region in 1820. This level appears too high, as it is equal or above the existing estimates for GDP per capita levels for Southern Europe as a whole and well above those for Eastern Europe at this date.[18]

This simple exercise has established that the rate of growth of per capita GDP for the Middle East was between 0 and 1 percent per annum during century before World War I. It can easily be extended to the individual countries to show that the growth rate of most if not all countries of the region for this period need to fall in the same range especially because intercountry differences within the region were limited until 1913.

INTERPRETING THE RESULTS

The estimates indicate that the Middle East began to participate in the global process of modern economic growth during the nineteenth century. Long-term rates of per capita income growth for the region as a whole increased as the century progressed but remained below 1 percent per annum. During the nineteenth century there also emerged inside the Middle East an important divergence between those parts of the region that were linked to world trade through ports around the eastern Mediterranean and those linked to trade through the Gulf and Red Sea. Those parts of the Middle East that were connected to world trade through the eastern Mediterranean enjoyed faster growth in trade and attracted more foreign direct investment. In the Ottoman Empire and to some extent in Egypt there were significant institutional changes during this period, in law and property rights as well as trade policy. These institutional changes called the *Tanzimat* reforms in the Ottoman Empire combined with the expansion of trade and direct foreign investment to lead to considerable differences in per capita income levels between the two parts of the region by 1913.

This pattern of rising long-term rates of growth of per capita GDP for the nineteenth century is consistent with the experience of many other regions of the world, most notably Europe, North and South America, and to a lesser extent Africa. Per capita GDP was also rising in South and East Asia during the period 1870–1913.[19] Despite the arrival of modern economic growth, however, rates of growth experienced in the Middle East remained distinctly below those being experienced in industrializing Western Europe and the United States. Differences in per capita incomes

[18] Estimates for other regions are based on Maddison, *World Economy: Historical.*
[19] Maddison, *World Economy: Historical.*

between the Middle East and these high income regions widened during both 1820–1870 and 1870–1913 (Table 1 and Figures 1 and 2).[20]

The Middle East experienced major political changes after 1914. The end of the Ottoman Empire, incorporation of large parts of the region into the British and French colonial empires, and the subsequent creation of new nation-states led to the erection of tariff barriers and a variety of other obstacles to the largely free movement of goods and labor within the region. In addition, the two world wars, especially the first, and the world depression caused serious dislocations.[21]

On the other hand, parts of the region benefited from a new development during this period. Production of oil in the region began, with the exception of very small amounts in Iran, after 1914. By 1950 Iran, Saudi Arabia, Iraq, the Gulf countries, and Iraq, in that order, were producing and exporting significant quantities of oil. Even though the multinational oil companies kept a large share of the profits during this early period, per capita GDP almost doubled in Iraq, more than doubled in Iran, and increased almost threefold in Saudi Arabia during 1913–1950. The largest increases in per capita GDP occurred, however, in Kuwait and the other Gulf states where large amounts of oil revenue accrued to a very small population (Table 1).

Some of the non-oil countries of the region also enjoyed significant increases in per capita GDP during this period. The fastest increases were experienced in Mandate Palestine largely due to the arrival of Jewish immigrants and significant inflows of capital. Turkey was the only country in the region to experience a significant degree of industrialization during the interwar period. The shift to protectionism and the adoption of a strategy of state-led industrialization after 1929 provided a model that would be influential elsewhere in the region after World War II. In Egypt, on the other hand, the exhaustion of new land and the decline in yields combined with the great depression to end the long boom based on cotton. It is estimated that per capita GDP in Egypt did not change between 1913 and 1950.

The pace of economic growth picked up during the second half of the twentieth century. GDP per capita for the region as a whole increased at an annual rate of 2.3 percent per annum or by more than twofold from around 1,600 dollars in 1950 to more than 5,000 dollars in 2000, both in 1990 PPP adjusted dollars. These aggregate figures actually hide a good

[20] In Figures 1 and 2 I use the estimates provided in Maddison, *World Economy, A Millennial* and *World Economy: Historical* for per capita GDP levels of other regions. The Maddison estimates may tend to understate the levels of per capita income for the regions of the periphery in 1820.

[21] Owen and Pamuk, *History*, pp. 3–90.

deal of intertemporal and intraregional differentiation. The Middle East economies did much better until 1973 or 1980. Per capita GDP for the region as a whole increased at above 4 percent per annum in this earlier period. The rate of increase of per capita GDP for the region as a whole was less than 1 percent per annum after 1973 or 1980.

Dividing the countries of the region into two groups, oil exporters and non-oil exporters provides additional insights into the differing performances of the Middle East economies during the second half of the twentieth century. For the oil-exporting countries of the region (Saudi Arabia, the Gulf states, Iraq, and Iran), the contrasts between the period before and after 1973 or 1980 is dramatic. GDP per capita in these countries increased at an annual rate of 5.3 percent during 1950–1973. As a result, differences within the region between higher income oil exporters and the lower income non-exporters widened until 1973 or 1980. In sharp contrast, due to the decline in the relative price of oil as well as the wars that some of these countries were engaged in, GDP per capita for the oil exporters as a whole actually fell by one-fourth between 1973 or 1980 and 2000. We may thus conclude that the important contribution of oil to increases in per capita incomes in the region occurred early, in the interwar period and until the 1970s.

The growth performance of the non-oil countries of the region (Turkey, Syria, Lebanon, Jordan, Palestine-Israel, and Egypt) was more stable. GDP per capita increased at 2.9 percent per annum during 1950–1973 and at 2.4 percent per annum during 1973–2000 for these countries as a whole. Import-substituting industrialization became the leading strategy of economic development during the 1960s especially amongst the larger non-oil countries of the region such as Turkey, Egypt, and Syria. The decline in the rate of growth after 1973 and especially after 1980 was due both to the slowdown of the world economy and the decline in the per capita incomes of the oil exporters of the region because there existed strong economic linkages between these two groups of countries in the form of trade, capital flows, and more importantly, labor and remittance flows. It is also striking that non-oil countries actually experienced higher average rates of growth during the half century after 1950 (2.6 percent per annum) then the oil exporters of the region (1.9 percent per annum). This pattern also holds if the economies of North Africa (Libya, Algeria, Tunis, and Morocco) are included in the comparison.[22] Even if we take into account the contribution of oil to the incomes of non-oil countries, this long-term outcome confirms, for this region at least, that oil is, at best, a mixed blessing.

[22] Based on the GDP per capita series in Maddison, *World Economy: Historical*.

Despite large oil revenues, increases in per capita GDP for the Middle East as a whole since 1913 have been roughly comparable to increases in the two other regions of the periphery, Latin America and South and East Asia. As emphasized earlier, the Middle East did better than these regions until the 1970s but has lagged behind since. The gap in per capita incomes between the Middle East as a whole and high income economies of the United States and Western Europe was roughly the same in 2000 as it was in 1913. In other words, after experiencing significant divergence in the nineteenth century, the Middle East did not exhibit any tendency for convergence in the twentieth century. (Figures 1 and 2)

Growth accounting studies, which are available only for recent decades, indicate that increases in per capita GDP in the region have been mostly due to the accumulation of physical capital. By contrast, increases in human capital formation and total factor productivity have been rather slow. These results underline that the region has been better at mobilizing resources and acquiring new technology than utilizing the existing resources efficiently.[23] For the Middle East to improve its economic growth performance in the future, in both absolute and relative terms, it will be necessary to deal more effectively with the negative effects of oil revenues, not only through Dutch Disease, but more generally on economic institutions and politics. It will also be necessary to reconsider more forcefully the long tradition and persistent legacy of interventionism in the region.

[23] Yousef, "Development," pp. 96–97.

REFERENCES

Akarli, Ahmet. "Agriculture in Ottoman Macedonia, 1870–1910." In *Mediterranean Responses to Globalization before 1950*, edited by Ş. Pamuk and J. Williamson, 109–33. London and New York: Routledge Press, 2000.

Antras, Pol, and Hans-Joachim Voth. "Factor Prices and Productivity Growth During the British Industrial Revolution." *Explorations in Economic History* 40 (2003): 52–77.

Behar, Cem. *The Population of the Ottoman Empire and Turkey, 1500–1927*, State Institute of Statistics, Ankara, 1996.

Berov, Ljuben. "Le salaire des Ouvriers Qualifies dans les Pays Balkaniques au cours de la période du Capitalisme Manufacturier et de la Révolution Industrielle." *Etudes Balkaniques* 14, no. 1 (1976): 30–54.

______. "Wages in the Balkan Lands During the Period of Manufacturing Capitalism and the Industrial Revolution." *Bulgarian Historical Review* 7, no. 1 (1979): 91–115.

______. "Trends in the Level and Structure of the Incomes of the Working People in the Balkan Countries in the Eighteenth and Nineteenth Centuries up to 1912."

Bulgarian Historical Review 15, no. 4 (1987): 65–83.

Boratav, Korkut, Gündüz A. Ökçün, and Şevket Pamuk. "Ottoman Wages and the World Economy, 1839–1913." *Review, Fernand Braudel Center* 8, no. 3 (1985): 379–406.

Bulutay, Tuncer, Nuri Yildirim, and Yahya S. Tezel. *Turkiye Milli Geliri, 1923–1948*. Ankara: University of Ankara Publications, 1974.

Egypt, Ministere des Finances. *Annuaire Statistique de L'Egypte, 1914*. Cairo, 1915.

Eldem, Vedat. *Osmanli Imparatorlugunun Iktisadi Sartlari Hakkinda Bir Tetkik*. Istanbul: Is Bankasi Yayinlari, 1970.

Guran, Tevfik, ed. *Agricultural Statistics of Turkey during the Ottoman Period*. Ankara: State Institute of Statistics, 1997.

______. *The First Statistical Yearbook of the Ottoman Empire, 1897*. Ankara: State Institute of Statistics, 1997.

______. *Ottoman Financial Statistics, Budgets, 1841–1918*. Ankara: State Institute of Statistics, 2003.

Hansen, Bent. "Income and Consumption in Egypt, 1886/1887 to 1937." *International Journal of Middle East Studies* 10, no. 1 (1979): 27–47.

Hansen, Bent, and Michael Wattleworth. "Agricultural Output and Consumption of Basic Foods in Egypt, 1886/7–1967/8." *International Journal of Middle East Studies* 9, no. 3 (1978): 449–69.

Heston, Alan, Robert Summers, and Bettina Aten. "Penn World Tables, Version 6.1, Center for International Comparisons at the University of Pennsylvania", 2002; http://pwt.econ.upenn.edu.

Himadeh, Said. *Economic Organization of Syria and Lebanon*. Beirut: American Press, 1936.

Issawi, Charles, ed. *The Economic History of the Middle East, 1800–1914*. Chicago: University of Chicago Press, 1966.

______. *The Economic History of Iran, 1800–1914*. Chicago: University of Chicago Press, 1971.

______. "Egypt, Iran and Turkey, 1800–1970." In *Disparities in Economic Development since the Industrial Revolution*, edited by Paul Bairoch and Maurice Levy Leboyer, 227–52. New York: St. Martin's Press, 1981.

______. *An Economic History of the Middle East and North Africa*. Columbia University Press, 1982.

______. *The Fertile Crescent, A Documentary Economic History*. Oxford: Oxford University Press, 1988.

Kostelenos G., S. Petmezas, D. Vasiliou, E. Kounaris, and M. Sfakianakis. *Gross Domestic Product 1830–1939, Sources of Economic History of Modern Greece. Quantitative Data and Statistical Series, 1830–1939*. Athens: Historical Archives of the National Bank of Greece, (forthcoming).

Lains, Pedro. "Southern European Economic Backwardness Revisited: The Role of Open Economy Forces in Portugal and the Balkans, 1870–1913." *Scandinavian Economic History Review* 50, no. 1 (2002): 24–43.

Mc Evedy, Colin, and Richard Jones. *Atlas of World Population History*. Harmondsworth, New York: Penguin Books, 1978.

Maddison, Angus. *Monitoring the World Economy, 1820–1992*. Paris: OECD Publications, 1995.

Maddison, Angus. *The World Economy, A Millennial Perspective*. Paris: OECD Development Studies Centre, 2001.

Maddison, Angus. *The World Economy: Historical Statistics*. Paris: OECD Develop-

ment Studies Centre, 2003.
Metzer, Jacob. *The Divided Economy of Palestine*. Cambridge and New York: Cambridge University Press, 1998.
Okyar, Osman. "A New Look at the Problem of Economic Growth in the Ottoman Empire, 1800–1914." *The Journal of European Economic History* 16, no. 1 (1987): 7–49.
Owen, Roger, and Şevket Pamuk. *A History of the Middle East Economies in the Twentieth Century*. London and Cambridge, MA: Tauris Publishers and Harvard University Press, 1998.
Ozel, Isik. "The Economy of Turkey in the Late Ottoman and Republican Periods: A Quantitative Analysis." unpublished M.A. thesis, Ataturk Institute for Modern Turkish History, Bogazici University, 1997.
Ozel, Isik, and Şevket Pamuk. "Osmanlidan Cumhuriyete Kisi basina Uretim ve Milli Gelir." In *Yetmis Bes Yilda Paranin Seruveni*, edited by Mustafa Sonmez, 83–90. Istanbul: Tarih Vakfi, 1998 .
Özmucur, Süleyman, and Şevket Pamuk. "Real Wages and Standards of Living in the Ottoman Empire, 1469–1914." This JOURNAL 62, no. 2 (2002): 293–321.
Palairet, Michael. *The Balkan Economies, c. 1800–1914, Evolution without Development*. Cambridge and New York: Cambridge University Press, 1997.
Pamuk, Şevket. *The Ottoman Empire and European Capitalism,1820–1913*. Cambridge and New York: Cambridge University Press. 1987
______. *500 Years of Prices and Wages in Istanbul and Other Cities*. Ankara: State Institute of Statistics, 2000.
Phelps Brown, Henry, and Sheila V. Hopkins. "Seven Centuries of Building Wages." In *Essays in Economic History*, edited by E. M. Carus-Wilson, 168–78. London: St Martins Press, 1962 .
Shaw, J. Stanford. "The Nineteenth Century Ottoman Tax Reforms and Revenue System." *International Journal of Middle East Studies* 6, no. 3 (1975): 421–59.
Summers, Robert, and Alan Heston. "The Penn World Table (Mark5): An Expanded Set of International Comparisons, 1950–1988." *Quarterly Journal of Economics* 106 (1991): 327–68.
Peter Temin, "Two Views of the Industrial Revolution." This JOURNAL 57, no. 1 (1997): 63–82.
United Nations. *Economic Developments in the Middle East, 1945 to 1954*. New York, 1955.
Yousef, Tarik. "Egypt's Growth Performance under Economic Liberalism: A Reassessment with New GDP Estimates, 1886–1945." *Review of Income and Wealth* 48, no. 4 (2002): 561–79.
______. "Development, Growth and Policy Reform in the Middle East and North Africa since 1950." *Journal of Economic Perspectives* 18, no. 3 (2004): 91–116.

INDEX

For Product Safety Concerns and Information please contact our EU representative GPSR@taylorandfrancis.com Taylor & Francis Verlag GmbH, Kaufingerstraße 24, 80331 München, Germany

Printed and bound by CPI Group (UK) Ltd, Croydon, CR0 4YY

14/10/2025

01975744-0002

Also in the Variorum Collected Studies Series:

PASCHALIS M. KITROMILIDES
An Orthodox Commonwealth
Symbolic Legacies and Cultural Encounters in Southeastern Europe

ELIZABETH ZACHARIADOU
Studies in Pre-Ottoman Turkey and the Ottomans

MIROSLAV HROCH
Comparative Studies in Modern European History
Nation, Nationalism, Social Change

RHOADS MURPHEY
Studies on Ottoman Society and Culture, 16th–18th Centuries

NEHEMIA LEVTZION (Ed. Michel Abitbol and Amos Nadan)
Islam in Africa and the Middle East
Studies on Conversion and Renewal

EKMELEDDIN IHSANOGLU
Science, Technology and Learning in the Ottoman Empire
Western Influence, Local Institutions, and the Transfer of Knowledge

ANDRÉ RAYMOND
Arab Cities in the Ottoman Period
Cairo, Syria and the Maghreb

COLIN HEYWOOD
Writing Ottoman History
Documents and Interpretations

NIKOLAI TODOROV
Society, the City and Industry in the Balkans, 15th–19th Centuries

R.B. SERJEANT and G. REX SMITH
Society and Trade in South Arabia

GILLES VEINSTEIN
Etat et société dans l'Empire Ottoman, XVIe–XVIIIe siècles
La terre, la Guerre, les Communautés